D0215602

Electronic
Bill
Presentment
and
Payment

Advanced and Emerging Communications Technologies Series

Series Editor-in-Chief: Saba Zamir

ADVANCED AND EMERGING COMMUNICATIONS TECHNOLOGIES SERIES

Series Editor-in-Chief: Saba Zamir

Electronic Bill Presentment *and* Payment

Kornel Terplan

CRC PRESS

Boca Raton   London   New York   Washington, D.C.

Library of Congress Cataloging-in-Publication Data

Terplan, Kornel.
    Electronic bill presentment and payment / Kornel Terplan.
      p. cm.
    Includes bibliographical references and index.
    ISBN 0-8493-1452-6 (alk. paper)
     1. Electronic funds transfers. 2. Payment. 3. Invoices—Data processing. I. Title.

HG1710 .T47 2003
658.15'2—dc21

2002191166
CIP

This book contains information obtained from authentic and highly regarded sources. Reprinted material is quoted with permission, and sources are indicated. A wide variety of references are listed. Reasonable efforts have been made to publish reliable data and information, but the author and the publisher cannot assume responsibility for the validity of all materials or for the consequences of their use.

Neither this book nor any part may be reproduced or transmitted in any form or by any means, electronic or mechanical, including photocopying, microfilming, and recording, or by any information storage or retrieval system, without prior permission in writing from the publisher.

The consent of CRC Press LLC does not extend to copying for general distribution, for promotion, for creating new works, or for resale. Specific permission must be obtained in writing from CRC Press LLC for such copying.

Direct all inquiries to CRC Press LLC, 2000 N.W. Corporate Blvd., Boca Raton, Florida 33431.

Trademark Notice: Product or corporate names may be trademarks or registered trademarks, and are used only for identification and explanation, without intent to infringe.

Visit the CRC Press Web site at www.crcpress.com

© 2003 by CRC Press LLC

No claim to original U.S. Government works
International Standard Book Number 0-8493-1452-6
Library of Congress Card Number 2002191166
Printed in the United States of America 1 2 3 4 5 6 7 8 9 0
Printed on acid-free paper

Preface

EBPP (electronic bill presentment and payment) is revolutionizing the entire billing process by offering online and real-time presentment of bill content and payment choices. Taking full advantage of the EBPP potentials, B2C (business to consumer) and B2B (business to business) interaction processes can be simplified and unified. In addition, value-added capabilities significantly improve customer care and customer relationship management (CRM) on behalf of issuers of statements, bills, and invoices.

Chapter 1 offers introductory observations about EBPP, characterizing its present status and adoption depth, and outlining the challenges that hinder its wider implementation. In the current market, EBPP is positioned between the first and second evolutionary phases by offering value-added services in addition to presenting bills on the Web. In the near future, revenue generation will follow as the ultimate evolutionary step. EBPP offers benefits to all of the entities who use it, including consumers, billers, biller service providers, consolidators, aggregators, portals, exchanges, and distributors.

Chapter 2 is devoted to the billing process. Typical components of the paper-based and electronic billing processes are explained first, followed by an in-depth analysis of each process step. The process stages include bill creation (data collection, mediation, rating, content creation, and bill design), bill presentment (conversion into electronic formats, content creation and deployment, notification, and presentment), and bill payment (electronic payment, collection, remittance, and revenue assurance). Similarities and differences between paper-based and electronic solutions are highlighted, and cost components are identified and quantified.

Chapter 3 identifies, defines, and evaluates a variety of EBPP business models: biller direct, e-mail-based, thin consolidator, thick consolidator, consumer-centric, portal, application service provider, service bureau, and pull. The discussion focuses on the functionality and applicability of all EBPP business models. The benefits and disadvantages of each business model are evaluated.

Chapter 4 is devoted to an in-depth discussion of value-added features and attributes of EBPP solutions. The tangible benefits include savings on paper and postage costs and greater efficiency in delivering customer care. The opportunity to improve the quality of customer care while cutting costs is another important benefit. This chapter focuses on the possibility of improving cash management; insertion of cross-sale and up-sale personalized marketing messages in electronic bills; online settlement of billing disputes; bill chunking; and unifying and connecting workflows at accounts-receivable and -payable integration points between billers and payers. Examples of best-of-breed EBPP solutions are identified and described. This chapter also addresses the tight relationship of EBPP to document management as the basis of document conversion into digital formats. Guidelines and recommendations are included for Web-site design and deployment based on converted digital documents. Special emphasis is placed on the use of EBPP solutions for B2B, B2C, and SME/SOHO (small and medium enterprises/small office home office) applications. Improved CRM is seen to be a key element in avoiding customer churn and fraud. The discussion also touches on the different adoption rates in the various EBPP solution domains.

Chapter 5 addresses risk and security-management issues. The risk areas with EBPP include transaction errors, repudiation of contracts, privacy and confidentiality violations, hacking, denial of service, fraud and illegal acts, continuity, and viruses. A variety of solutions and tools are offered for improving security and protection. Legal and regulatory impacts are also addressed.

Chapter 6 deals with various document and payment standards related to EBPP. Documentation standards are covered first, including HTML (hypertext markup language), XML (extended markup language), WML (wireless markup language), and WAP (wireless application protocol), followed by payment standards, such as bank transfers (OFX [open financial exchange], GOLD, IFX [interactive financial exchange]), online credit card payments, and smart cards. Alliances among EBPP entities, such as Spectrum, Transpoint, and MasterCard, are briefly addressed.

Chapter 7 focuses on EBPP service providers, products, and services. The discussion centers on solutions offered by software vendors, application service providers, financial service providers, billing service providers, consolidators, portals and exchanges, document and postal service outsourcers, and service bureaus. Products and services are evaluated using various criteria, and the discussion suggests a recommended process for evaluating and selecting an EBPP solution for issuers of statements, bills, and invoices. The final selection depends on the chosen business model, the estimated volumes and growth rates, and the financial stability and reputation of suppliers. In many cases, the optimal choice for both billers and payers might involve a combination of multiple products and services.

When an EBPP solution is implemented, the entire transaction process between the biller and payer must be designed, tested, deployed, and supervised. Chapter 8 describes the fault, performance, and security metrics that can be applied to achieve these objectives. Data management is particularly important because of the legal requirements to archive billing and invoicing data, and this chapter offers alternatives for storage management. The discussion also touches on service-level agreements and service support desks, which play an important role in increasing payer satisfaction and avoiding customer churn. Best-of-breed products are identified and reviewed at the end of Chapter 8.

Chapter 9 presents three case studies of successful EBPP implementations. The first case study involves an EBPP solution for an incumbent service provider that decided to extend its legacy billing software by offering electronic presentment for both residential and business customers. The solution was developed and deployed without any vendor products or service-bureau assistance. The second case study demonstrates how a billing-software vendor and an EBPP solution provider collaborated to achieve a paperless electronic presentment and payment solution for a startup telecommunications service provider. The results have been encouraging, with payers enthusiastically supporting this innovative solution. The third case study presents financial results for a successful EBPP implementation. Computation of several metrics — return on investment (ROI), payback periods, breakeven points — demonstrate very favorable financial results for EBPP deployments.

Finally, Chapter 10 summarizes the benefits of developing and operating an EBPP solution. The discussion also presents reasonable assumptions about the adoption speed of EBPP in various geographical regions, such as the Americas, Europe, and Asia/Pacific. The impact of demographics on the choice of a given EBPP model is also evaluated. The outlook for EBPP emphasizes the importance of properly positioning EBPP into a practical OSS/BSS/MSS (operations support system/business support system/marketing support system) environment.

Kornel Terplan
Hackensack, New Jersey
January 2003

Acknowledgments

Four principal information sources helped me to write this book. I have learned the basics about electronic bill presentment and payment (EBPP) from the outstanding EBPP market assessment study prepared and distributed by the Philips Group. I have used this research, in particular, as input for the EBPP business models, security, and standardization. Most of the leading suppliers of EBPP solutions have contributed to some extent, and special thanks are due to Avolent, BillingZone, CheckFree, docSense, Doculabs, and Xenos. Altogether, I expected more support from the EBPP vendor side in reviewing, evaluating, and comparing products and services.

Service providers and consulting companies provided the concrete information used to prepare the three case studies presented in Chapter 9. Particular thanks are due to Béla Mitnyik (MetaGroup Hungary) for case study 1; Debbie Brown, Joe Oesterling, Minaz Vastani (Cbeyond Communications), Frank Dickinson (Daleen), and Jeff Wood (CheckFree) for case study 2; and Karl Schumacher and Scott Gerschwer (Pitney Bowes docSense) for case study 3. Finally, I have utilized my consulting experience in the billing sectors of telecommunications service providers in both Europe and the U.S. as well as my teaching experience in the Telecommunications Management Program at Stevens Institute of Technology in Hoboken, NJ.

I would like to thank Adam Szabo for preparing the artwork, Marie Dama and Arthur Travis for reviewing products and suppliers, and Tamas Szabo for editing the text and the graphics.

Special thanks are due to Rich O'Hanley, Jamie Sigal, and Gail Renard of CRC Press, all of whom were extremely helpful in every phase of this production.

The Author

Kornel Terplan is a telecommunications expert with more than 30 years of highly successful multinational consulting experience. He has provided consulting, training, and product development services to over 75 national and international corporations on four continents following a scholarly career that combined some 140 articles, 22 books, and 115 peer-reviewed papers.

During the last 30 years, he has designed five network-management-related courses and presented more than 80 seminars in 15 countries. He received his doctoral degree from the University of Dresden and has completed advanced studies, researched, and lectured at Berkeley, Stanford University, University of California at Los Angeles, and Rensselaer Polytechnic Institute.

His consulting work concentrates on network management products and services, operations support systems, traffic management, service management, outsourcing, central administration of LANs, network management centers, strategy of network management integration, implementation of network design and planning guidelines, products comparisons, and benchmarking network management solutions.

His clients include AT&T, BMW, Boole & Babbage, Coca Cola, Creditanstalt Austria, Commerzbank (Germany), Hewlett Packard, Ford Europe, France Telecom, Georgia Pacific Corporation, German Telekom, Groupe Bull, GTE, Hungarian Telecommunication Company, Kaiser Permanente, Objective Systems Integrators, Salomon Brothers, Siemens Corporation, State of Washington, Swiss Credit, Telcel, Union Bank of Switzerland, Unisource, and Walt Disney World.

Terplan is an industry professor at Brooklyn Polytechnic University in New York and at Stevens Institute of Technology in Hoboken, NJ.

Contents

Chapter 1

Introduction to EBPP

The following chapters examine electronic bill presentment and payment (EBPP) models, technologies, and solutions in greater detail. In some cases, it may be difficult to differentiate whether statements, bills, or invoices are presented. As far as possible, the following definitions are followed:

- Statement: an itemized listing of purchases, sales, and other activities for a specific account and a specific time period; differs from an invoice or bill in that it does not constitute a request for payment, although it typically specifies an amount due
- Bill: an itemized account of the separate cost of goods sold, services performed, or work done; an amount expended or owed; a request for payment
- Invoice: an itemized account of goods shipped, usually specifying the price and the terms of sale; a consignment of merchandise; a request for payment

Statistics for expected savings and additional predicted revenues are invaluable in justifying investments into EBPP processes and tools. Unfortunately, the numbers differ greatly by geographical area and by industry. Instead of offering hard numbers to the reader, the following important metrics are presented and recommended:

- Volume of Internet commerce in targeted areas
- Number of Internet users in targeted areas
- Number of households in targeted areas
- Number of online households in targeted areas
- Number of issuers of statements, bills, and invoices by industry and by geographical area
- Number of recurring bills in targeted areas

- Price of issuing and distributing paper-based statements, bills, and invoices by industries in targeted areas
- Percentage of issuers offering electronic presentment, electronic payment, or both
- Number of direct billers, consolidators, aggregators, and billing service providers in targeted areas
- Market share of B2B (business to business) and B2C (business to consumer) by industries in targeted areas
- Number of statements, bills, and invoices received monthly by average households and businesses

Market research can identify the right investment targets on behalf of issuers of statements, bills, and invoices.

1.1 Definition of Electronic Bill Presentment and Payment

EBPP is the term used to describe the capability of presenting bills to customers and supporting their payment by electronic means. EBPP helps to eliminate the costs associated with printing paper bills, reduces delivery delays, saves time for customer-service representatives, and provides a channel for bidirectional communication between service suppliers and their customers on a one-to-one basis. Customers (payers) benefit by simplifying management of bill payment.

Figure 1.1 shows the basics of EBPP, including bill preparation, presentment, and payment. The potential impact of EBPP is significant when we consider that 20 billion bills are generated annually just in the U.S. at a cost of $2 to $5 in processing fees for each bill. The market opportunity for EBPP is particularly significant for solution providers.

While the term EBPP is used widely in the billing industry, there are also related terms frequently used by billers, consolidators, aggregators, distributors, and payers:

- IBPP (Internet bill presentment and payment)
- EBP (electronic bill presentment)
- OBPP (online bill presentment and payment)

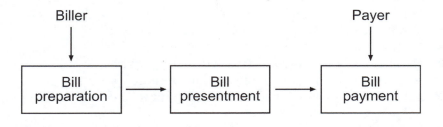

Figure 1.1   EBPP basic process.

- ED&EP (electronic delivery and electronic payment); electronic delivery is the Internet-based distribution and presentment of documents, which may or may not be payment related
- BIPS (bill and invoice presentment and settlement)

The billing, invoicing, presentment, and settlement process is one of many direct interfaces between billers and payers. Other interfaces are call centers with customer service representatives (CSR), customer self-care solutions, and the sales force. In state-of-the-art applications, all can be considered as part of an integrated customer relationship management (CRM) package.

Independently from the targeted industry, EBPP or BIPS are part of a larger process from the perspective of suppliers, consisting of (Patel, 2002)

- Acceptance of an order
- Fulfillment of an order
- Settlement of an order

Automation has already been implemented for the first two process areas, leaving room for automation of the settlement process.

1.2 EBPP Service Types and Basic Business Models

Several service types can be considered as the basis for EBPP business models. The main types are:

- Biller-direct model, in which billers provide their bills on their personalized Web sites; electronic payment is assumed
- Consolidator model, in which billing service providers use one of several models allowing customers to access and process bills from multiple original billers:
  Thin client model
  Thick client model
  Customer consolidation model
  Financial institution model
- Consumer-centric aggregator model, in which billing service providers send their invoices to the aggregator site, rather than to the consumer, and are paid directly from the site; similar to direct-debit payments
- E-mail-based model, in which invoices containing rich-text graphics are sent to the consumer and then linked back to sites for online payment or detailed bill viewing
- Service-bureau model, which facilitates connections to large-scale consolidators, in particular for small and medium enterprises (SME)
- Portal model, which benefits from the portal's established relationship with the user; the portal streamlines invoices from billers toward customers

■ Alternative service provider (ASP) model, in which applications supplied by another provider may help to initiate a business relationship with minimal financial investment

Figure 1.2 summarizes these service types and business models, indicating also the payments side via banks and financial service providers.

EBPP vendors can be categorized in one or more service types or allocated into general areas based on their business origins. These broad categories are:

■ Special EBPP providers — companies that are completely focused on EBPP, e.g., CheckFree i-Solutions and Edocs
■ Document and postal service outsourcers — companies that originally undertook bill and document processing in paper format and have now moved to EBP and EBPP, e.g., Pitney Bowes and DST Output
■ Significant billing vendors — large billing vendors that offer various rating, billing, and related services and are interested in incorporating EBPP as part of their services, e.g., Daleen and Telesens
■ Personal financial applications — consumer services related to the Internet for individual users, e.g., Yahoo, Quicken, and banking service providers, such as Corrilion, Digital Insight, MasterCard, and Visa
■ Specialist telecom and utility providers — companies that offer a complete package bundled on a single site and that may expand into other services when EBPP makes further inroads, e.g., Servista and Essential.com

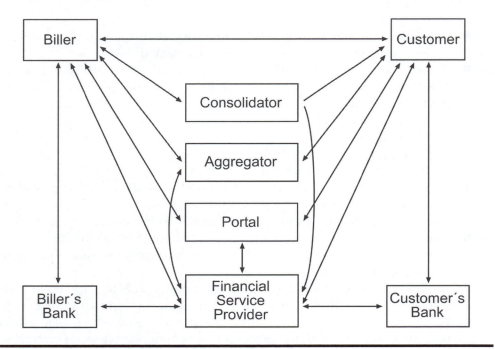

Figure 1.2   EBPP service types and business models.

1.3 EBPP Evolution Phases

EBPP is expected to be implemented in multiple phases. These phases are (Patel, 2002):

- Phase I: Print-to-Web, indicating the migration of existing printing structures to a Web presentation format
- Phase II: Adding value to EBPP by offering analysis, data mining, money savings, workflow support, and customer care
- Phase III: Revenue generation for the EBPP user — billers, consolidators, aggregators — by the maturing of previously implemented value-added services

Figure 1.3 shows an estimated timeline for the increasing value of these three EBPP phases as each is implemented. Phase II currently dominates the majority of solutions. Figure 1.4 shows a timeline for the adoption cycle of the three EBPP phases (Patel, 2002):

- Phase I: Innovation
- Phase II: Maintain competitive advantage
- Phase III: Cost of business

As in Figure 1.3, Phase II in Figure 1.4 is the typical adoption average.

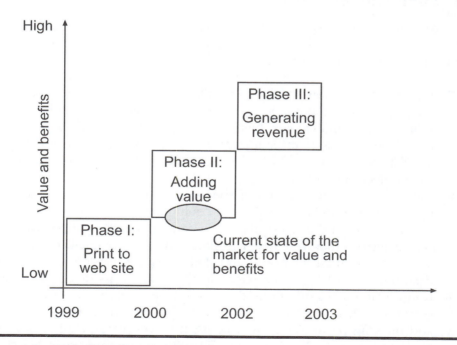

Figure 1.3   Evolution phases of EBPP.

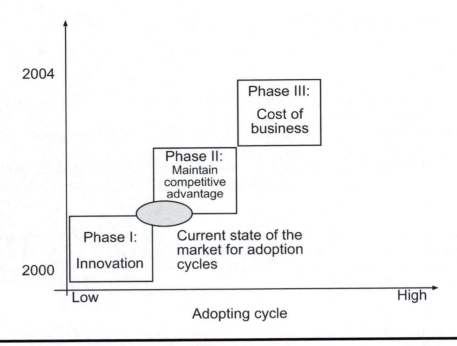

Figure 1.4   Adoption cycles in the EBPP evolution.

1.4   EBPP Entities and Players

EBPP represents a complex relationship between participating entities. Inter-related workflows are the best tools to control this relationship. The following entities play a key role in EBPP:

- Billers: organizations that present bills directly to their customers. This entity provides goods and services that customers want to purchase. Billers can be individuals, businesses (e.g., telcos, utilities), or government agencies (e.g., tax authorities). Billers assemble the invoice and send it to the payers. EBPP replaces the traditional paper document by an electronic format.
- Biller service providers (BSP): special organizations that billers use to outsource their billing functions. It could be a vendor or service bureau that generates and delivers bills, statements, and orders of confirmations on behalf of other vendors. The BSP may also complete the cycle by accepting payment response and delivering corresponding automated clearinghouse (ACH) transactions to the biller or its designated bank.
- Consolidators: organizations that consolidate bills from various types of billers. This entity is responsible for invoice preparation, delivery, and tracking of invoice-related items. It serves as the central point for these functions and charges the biller for supporting these functions. Consolidation is usually consumer-centric. This entity is usually different from banks and billing service providers.

- Portals/distributors and exchanges: organizations that are responsible for distributing bills to customers. This entity is actually an aggregator that performs the function of aggregating invoices for a set of customers that frequently access a network where all their billers would like to present their invoices. Examples are the Web sites of Internet service providers (ISP) that could serve as the home site for invoices for certain consumer clusters.

- Payers: customers who are expected to view the presented bill and pay it electronically. This entity makes the final payment for goods and services. It could be an individual (e.g., consumer, household), another business, or a government organization. This entity receives the invoices for purchases in electronic format (EBP). Electronic bill payment takes this process further by enabling the payer to make the payment electronically, thereby eliminating the need for paper used for checks, money orders, and envelopes.

- Banks: financial organizations that offer electronic access to their customers' accounts. Most noncash payment methods require this entity to play a principal role. With EBPP, banks are representing payers and billers. They complete the payment and posting functions, making sure that the billers receive the compensation for their goods and services by the payers once payments have been authorized. All processing takes place in back-offices by entities like clearinghouses and lockboxes, where payments are physically processed in financial institutions.

- Vendors: organizations that offer software and hardware to enable EBPP. This entity provides the necessary EBPP applications to all other entities. They are specialist providers, outsourcers, billing vendors, and special EBPP providers.

- Communications service providers: organizations that offer their infrastructure to the transaction processing service. This entity is responsible for the network, servers, server farms, and efficient storage management.

The relationships among these entities are complex, since a number of companies provide overlapping services, with some offering full coverage of EBPP phases, presenting different payment methods, and supporting dynamic alliances. Figure 1.5 shows the value chain with participating entities. It is a generic chain, and not all chain components are implemented in every case. Chapter 4 extends this chain by a control umbrella that collects and computes process-specific data.

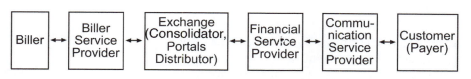

Figure 1.5   Value-chain of the EBPP process.

Even within the same company, multiple stakeholders are responsible for various issues. Examples are (Schumacher, 2002):

- Operations for seamless functioning of hardware, software, and applications
- Treasury for supervising payments and payment metrics
- Market research to evaluate customer behavior
- Customer service to help customers and avoid customer churn
- Auditing to continuously evaluate the accuracy of bills and invoices
- Management to guide investment directions by evaluating the return on investment (ROI)

1.5 Who Is Using Electronic Bill Presentment and Payment?

The greatest interest to implement EBPP solutions within the billing environment is expected from telecoms, utilities, insurance companies, and from the banking sector. These businesses would benefit the most from the functions, qualities, and features of EBPP. Particular interest is predicted due to the overlapping nature of these four industry branches. Other industries might be interested in the future, including health care, government administration, manufacturing, wholesale, and retail. The adoption rate, however, is not yet too deep in these industry sectors.

In the case of telecom service providers and utilities, EBPP is attractive because of the level of detailed data that can be included in an online bill, e.g., call detail records and gas/electricity/water usage details, as well as the analytical and data-mining tools that EBPP can deliver. In the case of the banking industry, the driving force for EBPP is its proximity to the core business model of the financial industry. Most importantly, all of these businesses benefit by placing their recurring statement and billing cycles online because it reduces the need to print and deliver paper documents, a costly and resource-intensive activity.

1.5.1 Telecommunications Service Providers

EBPP can be positioned in the operational service model of telecommunications service providers. Figure 1.6 shows the two principal dimensions of this service model: customer interaction and life cycle. As seen in Figure 1.6, the EBPP targets include all phases of billing that are assigned to the four principal processes:

1. Customer relationship management
2. Service management and operations
3. Resource management and operations
4. Supplier/partner relationship management

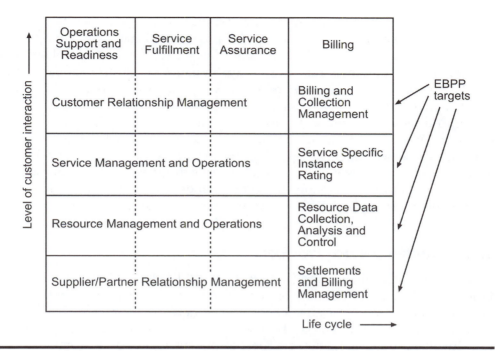

Operations Support and Readiness	Service Fulfillment	Service Assurance	Billing
Customer Relationship Management			Billing and Collection Management
Service Management and Operations			Service Specific Instance Rating
Resource Management and Operations			Resource Data Collection, Analysis and Control
Supplier/Partner Relationship Management			Settlements and Billing Management

Level of customer interaction

EBPP targets

Life cycle

Figure 1.6 Operational service model of telecommunications service providers.

The relative importance of the telecom market in the EBPP business process is demonstrated by the fact that up to 80% (Phillips Group) of all recurring bills are produced by this market in the U.S. With as many as 50,000 recurring billers worldwide annually generating up to 20 billion bills in the U.S. marketplace and around 60 billion bills worldwide, the resource demand for this back-office function is considerable. If we add the degree of competition and the shake-up of legacy business models (e.g., price of bandwidth, licenses for third-generation wireless, usage-based rating models, etc.), any cost savings on the part of the telecommunications providers are relevant.

At this time, telecommunications service providers are one of the prime movers in the EBPP market, with most hoping to implement an online EBPP solution of some sort. Little planning and homogeneity is evident in these solutions, while the dilemma of which type of EBPP solution to implement is particularly marked. No particular business model is favored. Many providers are developing their own billing solutions for the future. In the meantime, they combine various EBPP models to bridge the time gap.

Originally, most service providers attempted to build their own EBPP solutions due to the fact that a midsize company would utilize up to 30 different internal legacy billing systems. Under these circumstances, the billing-direct business model was too complex. This is one of the main reasons that service providers outsource to specialist EBPP companies. EBPP vendors have recognized this trend and are aggressively marketing solutions. A particular issue arising from this development is the degree to which functionality can be extracted from legacy data delivered by mediation devices to the EBPP vendor. The more data that can be extracted from the legacy data, the greater is the front-end functionality that can be provided to the customer (payer). This demand has led to the development of powerful parsing capabilities and transparent open systems that can accept numerous industry standards and translation applications. The importance of XML and Java in this process should be reemphasized.

One problem is common to both telecommunications and utility service providers. Where is the demarcation line between those who receive paper bills and those who are willing to accept electronic bills? It is unlikely that these service providers will be allowed to switch off paper bills completely, and they will have to continue supporting paper bills. Unlike new providers, incumbents must support legacy customers for a considerably long term.

1.5.2 Utilities Service Providers

It is obvious that utilities are moving into EBPP. Much of the demand for EBPP has come about because of deregulation in the utility marketplace and the subsequent growth of new start-ups. The deregulated market faces some complex problems brought on by the increase in the number of providers now involved in service delivery. These problems relate to the complexity of the bill, since the biller must be able to break the bill up into its constituent parts to accommodate potential disputes over charges; for instance, a consumer might dispute the amount of electricity used. In such an event, the biller would still have to pay the network owner or the company that owns the cable for distributing electricity. This causes severe problems in presenting a consolidated bill for services. However, EBPP offers the capabilities to allow for "chunking" with other words for partial payments and other complex bill dissection capabilities. Paper-based bills cannot offer these features.

In a deregulated market, competition for and access to customers becomes very important. While marketing addresses this issue to some extent, it is expensive and meets with only limited success. The excess of advertising and hype surrounding deregulation, with every provider seeking to acquire a certain number of consumers, can result in customer (consumer) confusion. In this scenario, customers look to the one communication that they regularly have with the utility industry, their bill. The bill is the best basis for the customer relationship and is the most effective means of retaining customers and reducing the churn that competing companies are likely to create. This relationship can be strengthened and built upon through the CRM capabilities that EBPP offers, e.g., information, one-to-one communication requests, etc. In this way, the customer relationship is the "stickiness" and is the primary reason to stay with one provider over another, particularly in an environment where switching suppliers has become very easy. These statements are valid for all service providers that are serving a deregulated marketplace.

Figure 1.7 shows the structure of a simplified energy model with multiple entities. The top is the power generation entity consisting of multiple energy generation technologies. It could also represent an energy exchange. Then,

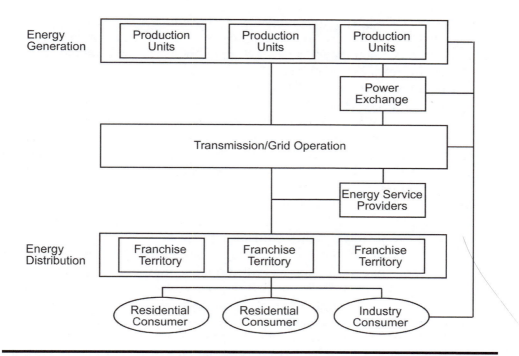

Figure 1.7 Energy model with multiple entities.

the energy goes through an independent transmission/grid system operated by other service providers. An energy service provider (ESP) will be selling and marketing energy to customers directly. Next are the franchise territories of the distribution company. Finally, there are the end users, the customer. This is a logical diagram and does not imply that the ESP takes physical possession of energy. The industrial customer, as shown on the right side of Figure 1.7, might have direct connections to the production units or to the power exchange. This figure illustrates that there are a number of B2B and B2C relationships, making the bill presentation and payment process very complicated.

Billing alternatives differ, depending on the state and the legislation in effect, but there are some common aspects that billers and payers should be prepared for. In the case of an ESP, it can bill the customer directly as well as manage the usage acquisition (e.g., the customer's energy consumption). All ESPs understand the absolute necessity of predicting the load requirements. The major impact of EBPP will be on the utility distribution company. In some cases, it has been proposed that the distributors will become the exclusive billing company — at least initially, until the customer-choice environment has matured. They will have to be in the position to support the billing for the ESP and the billing to the ESP while also providing billing services for the customer. This means, in effect, that the distributor will have to obtain the billing information from the ESPs and other providers regarding transmission charges, supply charges, and any other products and services that may be involved in the billing equation.

The current billing systems of most utilities cannot handle this. Many billing systems that are currently on the market are rapidly making changes and extensions to accommodate this new environment. One major issue that billers should be aware of is remittance. Remittance seems like a routine process, but in the new environment, there are multiple parties involved with the billing process, each with its own particular set of products, services, billing, and accounts receivable. The various parties also have different rules governing what can be collected and how payments should be distributed for partial payments. Making adjustments is very difficult, and once adjustments have been made, it is necessary to go back and resettle with all the participants in the billing process.

Additional challenges, such as offering bundled or unbundled products, avoiding customer churn, and supporting data acquisition, are comparable with those encountered in other industries.

Commonly cited reasons for low EBPP adoption rates include the lack of a single site to pay all bills, the lack of a total solution (some percentage of the bills must still be paid by check), the perception of the cost and effort involved in the setup, and the high number of retailers who permit the regulated utility to bill on their behalf. Regulated energy companies have additional barriers to realizing the full EBPP potential. Regulations may require energy companies to charge customers a premium to recover the costs of alternative payment methods (e.g., credit or debit cards, electronic checks), to disallow incentives (e.g., discounts, miles, car rentals, flexible due date), and to require the mailing of paper bills to all customers. Finally, customers who are using alternative payment methods, such as automatic bank drafts or prepayments, reduce the pool of potential new EBPP users.

Business customers have the following needs:

- Bill consolidation
- Guaranteed security of business-related information
- Collaboration with internal approval processes
- Availability of detailed energy data for business analysis

Energy utilities and energy retail companies should aggressively pursue the implementation of bill presentment technologies as an opportunity to improve customer relations, obtain valuable customer information, and provide value-added services to business customers. The value of an energy company's size and regular customer contact should be leveraged in negotiating contracts with EBPP entities (e.g., billers, aggregators, portals, consolidators, and service bureaus) to ensure that the company maintains continued direct or indirect relationships with its customers for energy services.

1.5.3 Banks and Financial Institutions

The financial industry is fully involved in quantifying the potential of EBPP. Indeed, they are well positioned to become synonymous with EBPP in the consolidator or aggregator role. The interest is great, as evidenced by the creation of organizations, such as BITS and numerous other groups, working to standardize and bring electronic transactions to the bank. Nevertheless, the financial industry regards EBPP as both an opportunity and a threat.

The process of EBPP is very close to what the banking industry does now. Thus, EBPP transaction processors — specifically consolidation EBPP services — are a real threat. A bank's relationship with its customers is weakened by visits outside its own site, e.g., at a site of an EBPP vendor. This complexity is compounded when one moves from national to international markets. For example, in the U.S. there is a large check-based industry with a financial infrastructure of billions of dollars. In contrast, payers in Europe rely on direct debit as their principal payment vehicle. Consequently, a vendor that was perceived as a threat in the U.S. industry would not be seen as much of a threat in Europe.

The lack of initial support for EBPP in the U.S. was a significant barrier to its development. The financial industry was afraid of EBPP because of its potential to weaken the industry's influence and unique relationship with its customers. But that attitude is changing. Banks are now identified as one of the strongest entities for consolidated EBPP, at least in the area of B2C. The market now sees banks utilizing third-party vendors to support their EBPP services. Similarly, there is good collaboration between banks and vendors. The dramatic turnaround in this acceptance process, moving from extreme reaction to consolidation, appears common in the industry, as witnessed recently by the financial industry's reaction to screen scraping, which passed through fear and threats of lawsuits to acceptance and utilization.

The financial industry has been criticized for its reluctance to embrace new technology for fear of jeopardizing its favored position with customers, who generally trust the financial institutions with whom they bank. Given the nature of this relationship with its customers, the industry is well placed to start driving the development of EBPP, but so far, it has taken the position of watching the market and waiting for the right entry time. The financial industry needs to be more proactive to increase the speed of development. EBPP will become the most important aspect of future online banking offerings. If one considers the bank site as a consolidated entity of insurance policies, mortgages, Internet payments, savings accounts, brokerage accounts, and financial consulting, EBPP may well be the glue that binds these services together. EBPP can accomplish this due to its "stickiness" and its ability to continuously draw the customer back to the bank site that offers these services.

The B2B market is potentially the greatest market on the Internet, and it is one that the banking industry is strategically placed to exploit. Banks are already billers in the area, billing for products and services such as corporate financing and lending. Banks are also bill publishers for both internal billers and on behalf of business customers. Moreover, banks act as business customers (payers) when dealing with its customer's vendors. The strengths of the B2B market in relation to the banking industry promise potentially great financial savings as well as customer retention and the ability to attract new customers through implementation of EBPP business models and solutions.

1.5.4 Insurance Companies

Insurance companies are interested in fulfilling the promise of customer centricity in their products and services. They must provide common statements and billing to their customers. In an ideal case, all insurance products are presented to the client for payment in one bill. Progressive property, casualty, health, and disability insurance carriers currently have the technology to integrate different product lines on a single consolidated bill for presentation to their customers. Carriers, such as Liberty Life and The Hartford, are using an integrated, Internet-based platform to provide this convenience to their customers. Cotton State Insurance has outsourced this function to a service bureau, using an application service provider. Farmer's Insurance is using an outsourcer for supporting EBPP, forwarding its billing information to Metavante via the Internet. The information is then parsed and presented to customers via a Web site, and if desired, customers can download the bill to an internal back-office program and pay online via electronic funds transfer, credit card via the Web, or debit from a checking account. Maryland Casualty has installed a special billing system that runs on a mainframe and generates consolidated bills that are e-mailed to the customers. These insurance companies are not only providing a service to their customers, they are also reducing paper and postage, streamlining workflow processes, and providing easier reconciliation of the customer accounts within their own organization.

There is significant interest within the insurance industry for driving EBPP to cut costs, improve collections, and better engage customers. When EBPP dominates the entire customer relationship, many insurance companies hope to realize a competitive industry advantage in customer retention and cost reductions. Benefits can accrue from creating exit barriers by information aggregation and personalization, increasing revenues through online marketing, generating branding opportunities, creating an insurer- or broker-centric portal, providing faster account maintenance and reconciliation with the accounts receivable or enterprise resource planning (ERP) systems, and consolidating other online financial management packages.

There are, however, a few barriers to the initiation of common billing in the life insurance industry, and these may delay the implementation of EBPP solutions (Pfeiffer, 2001):

- The current life insurance regulatory environment. Life insurance has different cancellation and premium payment requirements than products offered by the property, casualty, and health sectors.
- The complexity of processing changes to life insurance policies. Addition or deletion of riders to existing policies, and subsequent required billing of these riders, could become a time-consuming activity due to adjustments to policy premiums and the determination of effective dates of riders.
- The tax environment involved in the selling and processing of life insurance products.

Life insurance companies, using EBPP, can achieve measurable savings on postage, printing of envelopes and paper bills, better reporting, slight staff reduction, and automated billing and accounts receivable processes. Coupling presentment and payment is very important. Keeping them separated equates to a time-consuming step in the bill receipt process and increases the number of exception items, which results in higher processing costs.

The present adoption rate is low due to many factors, including consumers' reluctance to lose interest on checking accounts; loss of float time in making payments; the difficulties of canceling electronic billing, which requires a signed request; and trust issues with electronic payments. This reluctance can be reduced or eliminated by providing:

- Multiple payment options (credit card, debit card, electronic checks, automatic balance transfers)
- Reduction in annual premium or credits toward future products
- Sign-on bonuses, gifts, or frequent-flyer miles in states that allow such incentives
- A focus on privacy and security concerns

In summary, the benefits and adoption rates in the insurance industry are comparable with other industries.

1.5.5 Postal Industry

The various paper-based and postal service companies of the world could lose out significantly in the EBPP world. The loss of billing postage is not just the loss of the posted bill, it is also the loss of business connected to the billing process, including envelope stuffing and complete outsourced billing services that some postal service companies offer. To put this into perspective, nearly two-thirds of all recurring bill payments are delivered by the postal service in North America. Analysts have speculated (Phillips Group) that if all bills migrate to electronic payment following one of the business models, the postal service in North America might lose between $15 billion and $18 billion annually. Many national postal organizations have recognized the threat of EBPP, but they prefer to see the coming electronic bill as an evolution of their own industry. The argument follows that e-mail is merely an extension of the postal services' paper-based mail system and that there may be an EBPP model that postal services can adopt. Postal companies have also been involved in EBPP business models.

In many countries, postal services try to extend their reach to their customers by offering new value-added electronic services. A convincing argument in favor of electronic postal services is its existing relationship with customers as part of the billing process. Supporting arguments are:

- People's expectations are a powerful force. Consumers expect bills to be delivered by their postal service.

- The postal service is a brand in its own right and is a relatively trusted brand for delivery of documents.
- Customers do not necessarily take the initiative to look for and pay their bills. Instead, the bills come to them. The postal service delivery of bills is a customer-pursuing process.

The electronic post office offers the ability to reach out to customers via e-mail and offer an enhanced version of the existing postal service, including hosting, secure mailboxes, and electronic storage capabilities. Partnerships with other EBPP users may even deepen the relationship with customers (payers).

1.6 Requirements for EBPP

To be successful, EBPP must meet a number of requirements. These may vary by major EBPP entities, such as billers, biller service providers, consolidators, distributors, payers, vendors, service providers, geographical areas (e.g., the Americas, Europe, Africa, and Asia/Pacific), and finally by the users (e.g., telcos, utilities, banks). The principal requirements for successful implementation of EBPP include the following:

- Offer benefits to both billers and payers. Mutual benefits are the basis for expedited implementation. Depending on the business model in use, joint ventures of multiple players are highly recommended.
- Save money and time — the two highest-priority benefits — while providing better customer service, competitive advantages, and greater customer loyalty and retention.
- Support the standards, such as OFX, IFX, XML, and others, used by the vendors of EBPP solutions. Multiple standards are under consideration, e.g., for documentation and for payments. Certain alliances will continue working with their own standards.
- Guarantee high accuracy of bills through high-quality back-office processes supported by data-collection and mediation solutions.
- Offer value-added capabilities for analysis, fraud discovery, dispute management, and remittance clarification.
- Provide integration into the workflow of billers and payers (e.g., ERP systems, accounts payable and accounts receivable packages).
- Provide integration with both billers' and payers' back-end accounting systems.
- Support multiple business models. This is difficult because these systems are usually customized to the biller and payer. Special integration efforts are more likely with B2B than with B2C.
- Guarantee high security for presentation and payments. State-of-the-art authorization and authentication technologies are required. All participating entities are expected to collaborate.

- Support multiple business relationships, such as B2B, B2C, and P2P (person to person), that enable both billers and payers to agree on a mutually preferred solution. The quality of customer relationships depends on the business model chosen.
- Support businesses of various sizes, ranging from SME to large enterprises, on behalf of the vendor while recognizing that different business relationships need different solution platforms.
- Manage very large data volumes on behalf of the vendor. Scalability of the EBPP tool is required to serve various business sizes. For this type of management, the same entity is in charge as for bill presentment. All previous steps, such as data collection and mediation, are dealing with the generation of new data. Presentment may be offered with various details to customers. Details should be maintained in storage areas with real-time access. Records of paid bills must be kept for an adequate duration for use in supporting dispute management and auditing.
- Automatically feed legacy accounts receivable systems, which can vary widely. Open APIs (application programming interface) are required to connect them with EBPP solutions.
- Support self-care and e-care and offer electronic presentment, the essential prerequisites. Payers must obtain additional tools to access and download additional detailed data.
- Objectivate help-desk and hot-line services. It is a clear operational aspect of EBPP. Given adequate and accurate data, customer service representatives can answer frequently asked questions and solve problems more easily and quickly.
- Consolidate invoices; consolidator and aggregator business models support this at the cost of losing direct relationships between billers and payers.
- Profile customers by their spending and consumption patterns. This guarantees that customers receive valuable information in addition to their presented bills.
- Maintain excellent site performance where the bills are presented for any types of businesses.

1.7 Driving Forces for EBPP

A number of drivers are helping EBPP solutions to emerge. The most important drivers are summarized below (Kumar, 2001):

- Improved customer service: By presenting the bills in an electronic format and providing access to varied levels of detail about the bill, the billers make it easier for their customers to manage their own accounts and troubleshoot any problems. At the same time, billers can provide customers with the ability to interact with a customer service representative online and resolve their queries. This service can be made available on a 24 × 7 × 365 basis. Customers can access their account details any time they want.

- Greater customer loyalty: Once a customer signs up for EBPP services, it is hard for them to change and leave, as it would mean changing many billing accounts. At the same time, with the control of the bills in their hands, the billers can track the customer movement across their Web site and use this information to learn more about the customer. With this additional source of information, the billers can further enhance the customer satisfaction level by providing them with relevant services and offers and cross- or up-sell in the process. Given that the bill may be the only medium through which some billers contact their customers, an enhanced customer experience in viewing the bill would help in retaining their loyalty.
- Competitive necessity: Some billers are under great pressure to move to EBPP solutions to remain competitive with other billers. In the race to capture and keep customers, EBPP may play the role of a differentiator. Providing a good customer experience with an EBPP solution provides a competitive advantage for billers and biller service providers.
- Cost reduction: The implementation of EBPP can save money for both the billers and payers. The areas in which these savings can be realized are billing costs, processing costs, paper costs, lockbox costs, and customer service costs owing to reduced call volumes to the call centers. With EBPP, the cost of producing a single bill can be reduced 25 to 40% compared with paper-based bills. This range of potential savings is lucrative enough for many providers to intensify the competition.
- Customer demand: The convenience of being able to access the bills anywhere, at anytime; the ability to access the minute details; and the comfort of paying the bills with the mere click of a button are incentive enough for many customers to replace the traditional method of paper transactions. With technology advancing at high speed, customers have already started demanding access to these capabilities through their cellular phones, PDAs (personal digital assistant), and other mobile devices.

Customer demand for EBPP has not been great. There are various reasons for this state of affairs:

- Mutual waiting for each other: billers for customer's demand and customers for biller's service offers. Neither wants to make the first step of investing into an EBPP solution.
- Lack of a killer application that encapsulates and delivers all of the promised advantages and improvements of EBPP in one cohesive package. Billers and payers must put single benefits together to prove profitability. Given the numerous process steps, this is not an obvious task.
- The initially offered value-added services did not convince the EBPP entities that the technology represented a real breakthrough. These

value-adds are interpreted and quantified very differently by the participating entities, and their value depends to a great extent on the business model selected.

■ Customers of EBPP — practically all entities — considered implementation of EBPP to be too much effort. With accurate ROI data, customers might reconsider their perception that implementation efforts are too high.

■ Some EBPP vendor solutions have charged for this service, scaring payers away. That was a big mistake; billers and consolidators should concentrate on other income sources and savings potentials.

■ There is no clear understanding of which markets are the primary targets for EBPP. The first target was the B2C market, but that is now shifting toward B2B. In this case, the number of implementations may be less, but the value of the relationships is much higher.

■ Lack of education promoting EBPP as a habit. Consumer education needs continuous improvement. The new Internet generation is adapting to electronic presentment and payment more quickly than the previous generation. If combined with convenience and small savings, the "electronic" habit will catch on and spread.

Billers, large and small, are worried about multiple items that may convince their management to move more aggressively towards EBPP. These pain points are:

■ Fear about the safety of postal mail
■ Obsolete and complex accounts receivable processes
■ Long DSOs (days of outstanding sale)
■ Increasing bank fees for payment receipts and payment processing
■ Unsatisfactory customer care combined with high human resource expenses
■ Too much paper involved in the billing/invoicing process

All of these points help to justify EBPP investments.

1.8 Challenges to EBPP

EBPP is not yet a winner. Proposed EBPP solutions must meet tough requirements before being accepted by EBPP entities. EBPP must face challenges and open issues from several directions. The most important challenges are summarized as follows:

■ Anticipate that the main selling point may change from saving money and time on bill production and distribution to one-to-one and P2P services.
■ Set priorities for implementation by focusing on B2B or B2C or both. Determine which application represents the driving force.

- Recognize that wireless transactions and mobile-commerce demand real-time bill presentment and access details.
- Identify the critical mass driving EBPP implementations. Which entity is the primary driving force promoting a significant takeoff?
- Implement EBPP as part of a wide Web-enabled customer-relations management by offering direct dialogs with customers about bill details, churn, fraud, and other service details.
- Understand that references need to be from high-value customers with tradition; this is related to B2B EBPP solutions.
- Develop standards in the areas of document exchange, presentation, law, application design, and business practice.
- Encourage customer acceptance of EBPP service types or business models by comparing insourced and outsourced solutions.
- Identify how high-security standards for authorization, authentication, integrity, privacy, and nonrepudiation can be selected and implemented for EBPP solutions.
- Develop tools to facilitate scalability of EBPP vendor products to accommodate large and very large data volumes.
- Identify methods of integrating EBPP solutions into the workflow of billers and payers.
- Develop tools that can guarantee adequate service levels to customers while offering EBPP services.

1.9 Summary

Potential markets for EBPP include the following market segments:

- P2P: Good basis due to the Internet culture (P2P was born out of the Internet); good potential with billing portals and ASP models.
- B2C: Good numbers, but the profit margin is very limited; B2C will be driven by B2B; penetration goes from workplace to private customers. EBPP has the technological potential to reach out to the widest customer base. Reductions in the expenses of bill preparation, presentment, and payment are present but not significant. Reducing the "average days sales outstanding" by a few days and reducing the magnitude of bill disputes may have some beneficial effects.
- B2B: Represents quality instead of quantity; good profit margins; shorter "average day's sales outstanding." The profit margins are much greater than with B2C. When the "average day's sales outstanding" and the number of disputes are reduced simultaneously, the savings are significant. This market will drive the B2C market, similar to the evolution of e-mail, which started in the business workplace and gradually gained acceptance until it became an everyday tool. Solutions need to address scalability and risks for fraud and competition, such as EDI (electronic data interchange).

- SME: a very promising market for EBPP; the use of ASPs is likely because of their lower operating costs; service quality problems in certain countries; security may impact operations. Risk management would be important. SMEs cannot undertake activities they perceive as a risk, because any mistake that impacts them financially could have very severe consequences. Expenses are critical and should be kept low. In many countries, there is a compromise between available infrastructure to guarantee performance and security.

EBPP is part of a wider scope of various products and services. It includes business relationships (B2C and B2B), customer relationship management (CRM), financial and trust services (identity and wallet management, account aggregation and management), supplier relationship management (SRM), and enterprise resource planning (ERP).

For vendors of solutions designed to facilitate communication with trading partners and customers (e.g., document automation, document engineering, document exchange), EBPP presents an ideal opportunity to develop an electronic business basis to their otherwise highly specific supply-chain solutions through integration of bill presentment capabilities. The increasing integration of electronic bill presentment capabilities into other formerly isolated customer/partner communication channels presents an ideal sales/product extension opportunity. Alternatively, these vendors could add an e-business service component to their offerings through the aggregation, dissemination, or presentation of bills.

For users, EBPP will become a critical component of customer and e-commerce solutions, supporting e-procurement, sell-side commerce, logistics management, etc. EBPP can significantly improve business processes (e.g., eliminating data reentry, adding enhanced financial process management, integrating collaborative workflows), and future EBPP adoption outlooks are positive given the current cost-cutting mood of both billers and payers.

Successful EBPP implementations are expected to meet the needs of both billers and payers.

Biller needs include the following:

- Creation of invoices
- Elimination of printing and equipment costs
- Shortened time to deliver invoices
- Receipt for delivery of invoices
- Ability to approve and reject line-item disputes and receive partial payment
- Reduction of employee/call-center time by handling disputes electronically
- Improved receivables
- Compatibility with existing accounts receivable (AR) systems

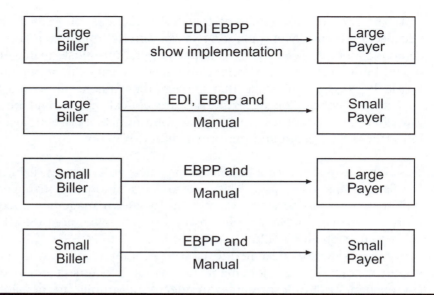

Figure 1.8   Target markets for EBPP.

Payer needs include the following:

- Notification of invoice preparation
- Receipt of invoice in usable format
- Administrative and workflow management
- Ability to make line-item disputes online
- Use of multiple payment systems
- Reduction in bank costs through fewer remittance transactions
- Ability to track payables and avoid late fees
- Compatibility with existing accounts payable (AP) systems

In many cases, the biller/payer relationship and size determine the applicability of EBPP solutions. EDI, EBPP, and manual processes are competing against each other, as shown in Figure 1.8. In the case of large billers and large payers, EDI has been implemented for some time. The costs of replacing these operating EDI processes are estimated to be very high. In the other three cases, EBPP may become very successful and replace EDI and all manual processes.

EBPP has great potential over the next few years, but all entities involved should proceed with great care. Scalable technology is important, but so is education of the payer. Critical success factors include the following:

- The process supported by various business models
- The tools used in each process step
- The people in charge of process steps and the tools implemented into those process steps

The following chapters will focus on all of these issues in greater depth.

Chapter 2

The Billing Process

Before an electronic statement or bill reaches a customer, the data for the bill or statement must pass through numerous stages in the complex EBPP process. Statements and bills are not the same. The statement is an itemized listing of purchases, sales, and other activities for a specific account over a specific period of time. While a statement typically specifies an amount due, the statement is differentiated from an invoice or bill in that it does not constitute a request for payment.

In both paper-based and electronic cases, the billing process has three principal stages:

1. Creation of the bill
2. Presentment of the bill
3. Payment

Figure 2.1 shows the three billing stages in a very simple display. These stages are described in some detail in this chapter. Practical examples of the three stages are presented from the telecommunications industry.

Participating entities will very carefully evaluate the pros and cons of EBPP. The following questions are frequently asked by billers, consolidators, and aggregators (Hurley, 2000):

- Bill fidelity: Is it important that the electronic bill look exactly the same as the printed bill? Can the bill be redesigned to take advantage of the capabilities of the Web interface?
- Presentment format: Do bills need to be presented in HTML (hypertext markup language), XML (extended markup language), or in other formats to meet support requirements of various browsers? Can universal browsers of customers support Java server pages (JSP) and active server pages (ASP)? Is PDF (portable document format) needed for print fidelity?

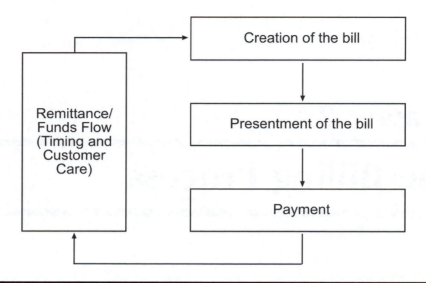

Figure 2.1   Billing process stages.

- Conditional inserts: Does the solution of the vendors allow the use of conditional inserts? Can rules be driven by customer data? Are they going to be driven by billing data? Can conditional inserts be easily pulled from outside data stores such as databases, file servers, or legacy systems?

- Overall complexity: Does the solution provide a GUI (graphical user interface) to simplify bill creation and design? Are special technical skills required for development? Can less-technical individuals play a role in bill creation and design?

- Notification: How is the notification to the customer handled? Is the biller to select the optimal option for notification messages? Can the biller direct and restrict the consumer options for messages received?

- Traffic considerations: What type of traffic is expected from customers wanting to see their bills online? Does the infrastructure of the biller provide the scalability to accommodate peak usage? Can the existing hardware and software be reused? Can existing hardware and software systems provide the expected level of reliability and fault-tolerance?

- Security and audits: How sensitive are the billing data? What level of security will the online site provide? What types of audit functionality will be needed? Can existing security infrastructures be reused for EBPP, or is a new security infrastructure is needed? Can outsourced solutions be trusted?

- Advanced functionality: Do billers want to provide the consumers with the ability to re-sort billing data or categorize bill line items? Can bills enter internal-approval workflows? Are reporting and analysis on billing data supported? Can customer service requests be submitted via e-mail or over the Web?

Customer adoption rates will depend on the answers to these questions. EBPP penetration will not be rapid, but the market remains very attractive.

2.1 Creation of the Bill

The steps in creating an electronic bill are similar to those taken in creating a paper bill. The principal functions are data collection, mediation, rating, and bill design.

2.1.1 Data Collection

The data required for billing the customer must be extracted from the biller's systems before it can be sent to the customer or consolidator for presentment and payment. This may not always be easy because of the different formats in which data are stored in the legacy systems. Multiple systems that house these data also complicate the extraction and affect the integrity of the data. At the same time, from the perspective of customer care, these data and bills also need to be stored in-house in order to assist the customer care representative in answering queries from customers. They need to look at the data in the same manner as they are presented to the customers.

Data sources are very different, depending on the industry, such as utilities, telecommunications, or others. In order to support the billing process, data should be collected on consumption by utilities. This is supported by metering consumption. Figure 2.2 shows the basic consumption acquisition process.

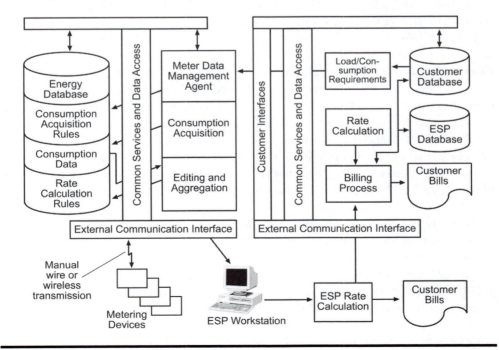

Figure 2.2 Metering consumption.

Load consumption requirements are forwarded to the meter data-management agent. This would indicate that consumption information is needed. It will go through the composition acquisition first, followed by editing and aggregating consumption data in the energy database. The energy database becomes key because it contains all the information for rate calculation. Everything is prepared so far, and the rating process can be executed. Rating can be done by the ESP (energy service provider), or data can be sent back to the distribution company if it is in charge of rating and billing. Billing data are extended by entries from the customer database. When complete, the data are sent to the customer.

In collecting consumption data, there are three principal components. First are the meters. The usual ruling is that they have to be read every month and collect hourly data (for customers who choose hourly billing), and they have to meet industry standards for accuracy and other requirements. Meter certification is done by the manufacturer of the metering device. Second is the meter service provider, an organization that does the physical work of installing, maintaining, and testing the meters. Meter service providers are certified by the public utilities commission. They must demonstrate that they can provide safety and other training, and they must have an electrical contractor license. Third is the meter data-management agent, an organization that reads the meters, communicates the data, performs validation, edits and estimates data, and posts that data to a server for retrieval by utilities or ESPs. Their approval is by the utilities, and they are certified by the utility distribution companies. Depending on the state or country, these functions may be slightly different. On the gas side of the business, similar processes can be identified.

In the case of telecommunications service providers, fully converged networks are not yet operational. Consequently, usage data must be collected individually for voice, data, and video services. In voice environments, the switches are the key data sources; in data environments, it is the routers. Practically, all networking elements in addition to switches and routers are able to collect data on resource usage. In order to avoid unnecessary overhead, collection and extraction should be well organized. For streamlining the collection process, mediation solutions are very helpful.

There is a standardized way to keep track of the internal activities of switches. Switches, regardless of their size, generate logs that are known as call detail records (CDRs) and assemble these CDRs into automated message accounting (AMA) files. This standard has been proposed by Bellcore (now Telcordia).

New network services and comprehensive measurement strategies are creating a need for enhanced tools to manage these data. In addition to new data-generating network elements, new applications that require access to these data are also being developed, e.g., for marketing and customer care. The value given to these data also varies widely, requiring the capability to treat different AMA data in different ways.

The increasing complexity of network services and the sophistication of customer needs are multiplying the degree of flexibility required of accounting management. The concept of "billing data" is changing as the infrastructures

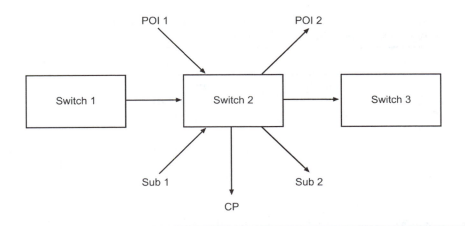

POI 1   POI 2

Switch 1   Switch 2   Switch 3

Sub 1   Sub 2

CP

Figure 2.3   Generation of call-detail records.

of the network and operations systems are enhanced to support increasingly complex products and services.

There is a definite need to streamline the CDR collection process. Switches have a limited number of ports where data can be exchanged with external devices. Both vendors and operators are careful about access rights to these ports. In other words, everybody wants to limit the number of access entries. Element managers, maintenance personnel, vendors, and CDR collectors are all competing for access to these ports. The best way to facilitate access is to use mediation systems that fully control input and output data streams to and from switches.

Figure 2.3 illustrates a very unsophisticated switching environment, and Table 2.1 lists the CDRs that would be generated in that environment. Table 2.1 shows four different types of CDRs: outgoing, incoming, billing, and intelligent networks (IN).

CDRs and the AMA standard together are capable of covering the voice and the circuit-switching environment, but the Internet protocol (IP) and packet-switching environment need standardization of IP detail records (IPDR). In this respect, the IPDR initiative may help. The IPDR initiative has made progress on creating a standard record format for IP service usage. The group has already addressed a number of topics, including terminology, syntax, and transport procedures. Member companies are now working on prototype experiments, which they hope to demonstrate to several service providers.

Each phone connection generates a CDR that contains important information about the transmission, such as start and end times, duration of call, and originating and terminating number. CDRs for circuit-switched voice are nothing new, and the service providers have their own method of storage and maintenance. And while the use of traditional CDRs is growing rapidly, many providers are experiencing a need for IP-based services in the form of IPDRs. Currently, IP services are generally billed at a flat rate rather than by usage. IP services such as voice and video could be billed on a whole set of parameters other than simply duration and distance of the call. Moreover, the real-time nature of billing for IP-based services introduces a number of new

Table 2.1 Example of CDRs Generated in the Switching Environment Illustrated in Figure 2.3

From	To	Description	CDRs[a]
Sub1	Sub2	Local (on-switch)	12
Sub1	POI2	Outgoing (external)	5, 12
Sub1	Switch3	Outgoing (internal)	(5), 12
Sub1	CP	IN (on-switch)	15*
POI1	Sub2	Incoming (external)	6
POI1	POI2	Transmit (off-net/off-net)	5, 6
POI1	Switch3	Transmit (off-net/on-net)	(5), 6
POI1	CP	IN (external)	(6), 15
Switch1	Sub2	Incoming (internal)	(6)
Switch1	POI2	Transit (on-net/off-net)	5, (6)
Switch1	Switch3	Transit (on-net)	(5), (6)
Switch1	CP	IN (internal)	(6), 15

Note: Sub = subscriber; POI = point of interconnect; CP = central provider; IN = intelligent network; RT = record type; (*n*) = removed from billing stream; * = missing record type generated.

[a] 5 = outgoing; 6 = incoming; 12 = billing; 15 = intelligent network (IN).

challenges besides collecting usage data. One of these challenges is forwarding raw data for mediation (Karvé, 1999).

During the process of collecting data from switches, moving it through operations support systems, and ultimately storing it, a number of issues and concerns often come up as volumes increase. These include problems with redundancy of data. Because a number of back-end support systems rely on CDR information, there is a tendency to create multiple copies of these networks. Not only does this add to the data bottleneck, but it can also be confusing when it comes time to figure out which customer used what types of services.

Another issue is scalability (Karvé, 1999). Some larger service providers are handling millions of call records daily and need to develop storage solutions to accommodate this amount of data, whose volume in many cases is reaching the terabyte level. For other service providers, the concern regarding IP services is not so much how to extract the CDRs from a switch or router, but how to do it quickly and without losing data along the way to the mediation device. In the case of regular, public switched telephone network (PSTN)-based phone calls, CDRs might accumulate on a carrier's switch before being moved in batches at predefined intervals to a database and then to the rating and billing applications. Traditional switches usually have a lot of random access memory (RAM) as well as local storage space. Therefore, they can record all relevant metrics and then dump the data into storage. Once the switch reaches a predefined threshold, it either pushes the data out in batch to the mediation device or billing application, or it holds onto the information until a mediation application pulls it out.

The batch method is not so effective in an Internet or intranet model, mostly because CDRs for IP services stay on a switch or router for only a few seconds and therefore need to be captured quickly. Instead of operating in a batch mode, service providers need to continually collect the raw data from a router and bring it into their system without dropping it during the process. In most cases, the data are pushed from the router when a session ends and goes to some kind of local data store. Not much processing is required in this phase; the emphasis is on not losing data. After raw IPDRs are captured by the local data-storing application, they usually go immediately to the mediation platform. Typically, the data are only rudimentary, containing detailed metrics such as duration, byte count, number of packets, etc. But since most customers use dynamically allocated IP addresses, the raw CDR may not contain information about the user. To find out which user had access to a particular IP address and at what time, the mediation application would have to communicate with the authentication server or other databases. It could then link up that information to the metrics about the session. The result of this processing is a set of billable data records that can be sent to the billing system.

After CDRs are collected, rated, and billed, the archived data can be used to reconcile accounts, and this record is indispensable to many of a carrier's customer relationship management strategies. In addition, regulations may require the carrier to keep these records for several years. The challenge of making these data useful for many purposes lies in setting up an application to not only store the CDRs, but also to make them easily accessible in a format that is meaningful. While they are extracting and processing CDRs, service providers also have to think about managing them as efficiently as possible. Network attached storage (NAS) and storage area networks (SAN) may be helpful to connect with and maintain data storage.

Another method of archive management for CDRs is to use a data warehouse. Larger service providers are completing millions of phone calls each day, resulting in multiple terabytes of data that need to be stored. After CDRs have been processed, the task of managing these records is very complex. Many service providers use relational databases to handle the task of storing CDRs, since they can provide access to large amounts of data with the intelligence to sort data according to the user's preference. However, they sometimes fall short when applied to a very specific task, such as managing millions of such CDRs. Databases are helpful in reducing the total storage demand, offering accessibility, analysis, and reporting. Performance is always a problem with relational databases, particularly in cases with complex relationships and large data volumes. Another drawback is that many larger service providers are using multiple relational databases to store CDRs. In such cases, they then need a metadatabase or an excellent data dictionary to find the right database with the data they are looking for.

Service providers need to streamline the process of loading data into the data warehouse. One way to load CDRs, especially those based on IP-services, is directly from a mediation device. Once IPDRs go through the billing application, they are generally in a format that is optimized for billing but not for other uses. Instead, after IP call detail information has been processed by the mediation application to include not just the raw metrics, but also the correlation to the customer, some service providers are pushing those records directly to a data warehouse. The data will be needed by different departments, and not only for billing purposes. By sending information directly from mediation, the billing system is not overloaded because they take data out of the records for billing purposes only. Using the mediation platform for supporting data warehouse entries means that customers are drawing information from as close as possible to the source, instead of waiting until further downstream, when it will become more difficult to reformat or retrieve information.

Using the data warehouse to accommodate CDRs and IPDRs may generate a scalability problem. Even a few months of data can easily add up to multiple terabytes, requiring very powerful processing of data within the data warehouse. For older detail levels of data, external data storage solutions must be considered.

2.1.2 Use of Mediation Solutions

Customers usually do not understand exactly what mediation means and what mediation systems can accomplish. The traditional view of mediation systems is that they are a replacement for magnetic tapes in the billing process. In other words, they are viewed as little more than automated data collectors and transporters. This view only applies to the first generation of mediation systems. While the first generation collected raw data and transported it to specific systems, current systems are able to operate in complex, multivendor network environments, perform postcollection processing, make intelligent routing decisions, and are read-write capable to refine data before transport to downstream systems (Finegold, 1998).

Mediation refers to those systems that collect data from network elements and pass it on to downstream back- and front-office applications, such as billing, customer care, fraud management, and decision support. In addition to data collection and routing, mediation systems perform such functions as usage data verification, network event reconstruction, filtering, and data format translation.

Figure 2.4 shows an unsophisticated example for a generic mediation system. An important aspect of a good mediation system is its ability to reconstruct complex network events out of data delivered from multivendor, multitechnology networks. The barriers between wire-line, wireless, voice, and data networks are falling. It is conceivable that a customer could use a wireless modem on a laptop PC to place a roaming personal communication service (PCS) call to an Internet service provider (ISP) roaming number. The customer could then browse for items that he or she wanted to consider buying. In the case of a purchase, the transaction would include funds transfer or a charge to a debit or credit card. This mix of services might be billed through a single provider but actually delivered by multiple carriers with interconnect agreement. The transaction in this example needs to be accounted and billed for, but just as important is the service provider's ability

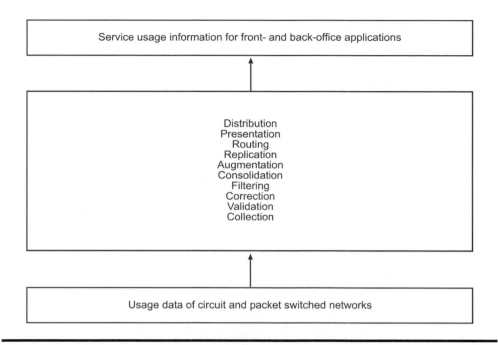

Figure 2.4   Architecture of a generic mediation system.

to reconstruct the events of this transaction to develop a customer profile for marketing (and perhaps also for fraud protection). Modern mediation systems are designed to provide event reconstruction by correlating various CDRs, partial CDRs, or other bits of usage data and then translating the multiple data formats into data appropriate to a carrier's specific downstream applications, as well as performing data verification to avoid duplicates and to support revenue assurance. Because data will come from multiple carriers that supply the underlying network services, a mediation system must be able to support carrier interconnection, both for intercarrier settlement purposes and for event reconstruction.

In voice environments, it is straightforward to walk through the procedure indicated in Figure 2.3.

Telecommunications service providers have been collecting experiences with CDRs for many years. Mediation needs customization in terms of switch vendors, geography, real-time processing, optimal use of bandwidth, and minimizing inquiries toward switches on behalf of mediation systems. Figure 2.5 (Terplan, 2001) shows a practical example with three different kinds of switches. Service providers typically work with different vendors. In this case, concentration is by switch vendor, not by geography. It is assumed that there is a data communication network (DCN) carrying internal data only. These data include CDRs, mediation output, inquiries toward switches, commands, and returns. Error management as part of mediation is extremely important. Many service providers have registered considerable business losses due to corrupt CDRs that cannot be processed and billed.

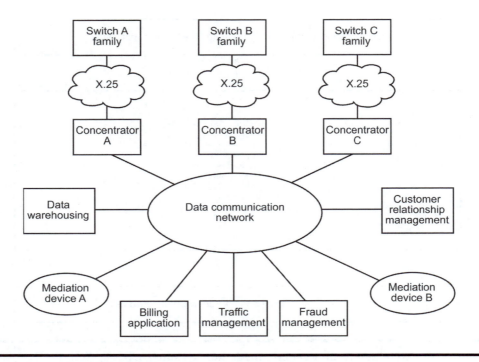

Figure 2.5   Mediation solution for various switches.

Vendors of mediation systems often stress the real-time capabilities of their solutions. The problem is, there is no true definition for the term, and there is some question as to the usefulness of real-time capabilities, especially in billing. The most practical applications for real-time functionality seem to come in prepaid billing and fraud detection and management for fraud, the reasons are simple. The faster they can be detected, the faster they can be stopped. A common function of a mediation system is data delivery to fraud-management applications. Prepaid billing is dependent on real-time information to debit customer accounts.

Although mediation systems have grown in functionality and versatility, most of the products on the market are not yet designed to work in a packet world. Some systems do support automated teller machine (ATM) and frame relay equipment, but most only include interfaces to major circuit and wireless switches. Some are designed with an open architecture and can be customized to accommodate virtually any type of network equipment that produces usage data, but this is rarely a simple task. Similarly, there are products designed specifically for IP networks, but these generally do not support circuit-switched or wireless environments. Because the market probably cannot wait for an all-encompassing solution, it is important to select vendors that will provide continuing support and upgrades for their implemented systems and who have the experience and resources to deliver integrated solutions.

IP provides a means for service providers and enterprise operations to provision service at the network layer of the open system interconnection (OSI) model of computing. The great potential for new IP-based services has resulted in the rapid development and deployment of diverse new services by carriers, ISPs, ASPs, and enterprises. In delivering these services, there is a fundamental need to automate the process of service provisioning, account for network costs, and generate revenue accordingly by billing customers on the basis of service usage. To meet these business requirements, IP operations increasingly rely on hardware and software that have been specially developed to support real-time provisioning and billing processes unique to IP infrastructures.

These front- and back-office innovations challenge service providers to create the IP equivalent of call detail records (CDRs) using a manageable framework to rate and bill for services. Without such CDRs, successful emerging revenue models for IP network services cannot be implemented. Mediation provides a process for integrating and efficiently managing real-time data streams between network elements and back-office applications. Therefore, as ISPs, carriers, ASPs, and enterprises decide on service expansions, there is a growing need for an IP-related mediation solution to be implemented with IP-related provisioning and billing applications.

IP mediation software helps to glue together the network usage data collected from heterogeneous network elements, such as servers, probes, routers, etc., in a manageable fashion that facilitates the support of rating and billing processes defined according to business policy requirements. With mediation software made specifically for the IP service marketplace, carriers, ISPs, ASPs, and enterprises can efficiently coordinate CDR data between the heterogeneous hardware and software elements used to create and deploy new services. Figure 2.6 shows an example of IP mediation.

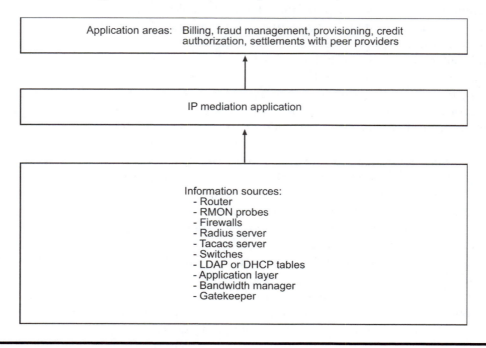

Figure 2.6   Example of IP mediation.

The largest obstacle is that the IP protocol suites were not originally designed to provide feedback concerning network or application usage or about service-level performance. Instead, the intelligence and management operations were handled by end systems (e.g., transmission control protocol [TCP]). The result is that usage information is collected by the various network and service elements and stored in log files. One mediation design approach is to read and analyze log files for particular usage data and then forward them to the business support systems, such as billing applications. For example, when the user dials into an IP network, the access server collects a user ID and password. The log-in information is then authenticated at a RADIUS server, which logs the event. At the end of the billing period, the amount of time the user spends on the network can be determined by evaluating the log files. The same approach is used to account for e-mail or for Web page visits (Lucas, 1999).

The new generation of mediation systems will have to handle a large number — over 100 types — of different network elements. Service providers will see the level of complexity increasing with multiple elements, like gateways, routers, switches, log files, counters, database information, and complicated IP flows. Mediation systems will need to collect information from several sources in the IP network, filter large amounts of data, correlate information, and aggregate information; and everything must happen in real time. In this new world of mediation, performance, flexibility, and fault tolerance are key success factors for suppliers of mediation solutions.

In the area of EBPP, the term *profiling* is used to deal with adding, changing, or deleting customer data to or from the customer database. To perform activities, information in multiple files and databases needs to be managed. One of the important considerations in profiling is the decision on who performs the additions, deletions, or changes to the files. It could be either the biller or the consolidator/processor, depending on the type of EBPP business model being used. In the case of the direct-biller model, the biller is responsible for profiling, whereas in the case of the consolidator model, the processor has this responsibility. However, in all cases, the processor needs to authenticate the existence of the customer with the biller.

Error management will create cases based upon parameters defined by users. Gap identification can be defined by both time points and sequence numbers. Duplicate call and duplicate batch identification can also be carried out in accordance with client-defined criteria. According to client-defined parameters at the validation, guiding, and rating stages, detail records in error can be dropped or put into a warning file. After a set number of recycle days, uncorrected detail records enter special procedures, with an allocated error code for investigation and action that can invoke manual adjustments or resubmittal of the detail record. A fraud file is also contained in the error management module. Should a match be detected on any of the numbers involved or specified, the CDRs are automatically routed for special investigation. Figure 2.7 shows this process in some detail.

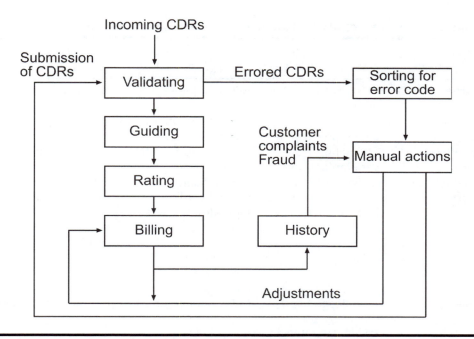

Figure 2.7 Process of error management.

2.1.3 Rating

In the rating step, events, duration, usage, and services at large are extended by monetary units agreed upon previously by the service provider and consumer of the services. In particular, in the telecom industry, real-time rating is gaining serious consideration.

2.1.3.1 Apply Service Rates to Usage

Once the customer record has been populated and the service activated, calls and events (or, in general terms, usage) must be collected and billed. An event can be a usage-sensitive call or any customer-generated activity that must have a charge to it. A processing module with or without a mediation device is used to collect, format, and apply an initial rate to each activity. The rated event is then guided to the correct service offering within the customer record.

Calls that are collected by the call-processing module are rated according to the type of call. Usage calls are rated according to a user-defined initial-charge table. They are later rerated at the time of billing according to the customer's rate plan. Event calls such as access to online services or custom calling events are rated according to a user-defined table and can be rated at time of billing according to a service-offering rate table.

The network operator can establish unique rating plans based on conditions within the CDRs. For example, plans can be created to target geographic areas,

Table 2.2   Example of Master Rate Table for a Telecommunications Carrier

Call Plan Attributes	Description	Example of Variables	Required Data Element on the Call Record
Carrier	The network operator	ABC company	Carrier ID
Serving area	Originating geographical area	Country number ID code	Originating number
Destination	Terminating geographical area	Country number ID code	Terminating number
Products and services	The types of calls that should be included into the plan	Direct dialing Charge card Operator assisted	Call type (a unique identifier within the call record that can link the call to the product type)
Charge period	The time periods the plan is in effect	Day of week Start time End time	Connect time
Mileage	The mileage bands that are used to assign call rates if the plan is to be distance sensitive	Miles (kilometers)	Terminating numbers
Rates	The charge that should be assessed for the call	Initial increment length Initial increment charge Additional increment length Additional increment charge	Duration
Minimum charge	Criteria for assessing a minimum charge for a minimum duration for a call	Minimum duration Minimum currency amount Round up/down flag Rounding threshold	Duration

specific call types, or specific calling patterns. Optional calling plans can then be developed that specify charges or discounts that may apply to one or many master rate plans. The master rate plan is linked to the applicable optional plans, and the message-processing module uses all the rating criteria to calculate the initial charge for the customer. The following paragraph describes the steps to be taken to create single-call rating plans:

Step one: The network operator assigns a product code (a user-defined description) for the plan that the customer can subscribe to. For example, one plan might be created for domestic calling and another for international.

Step two: The network operator populates the following tables (Tables 2.2 and 2.3) to specify the call types that are to be included in the plan and how

Table 2.3   Example of Optional Rate Tables for a Telecommunications Carrier

Call Plan Attributes	Description	Examples of Variables	Required Data Element on the Call Record
Connect fees	Criteria for assessing a charge for the call connection	Call type Connection amount Connection percent	Call type
Setup fees	Criteria for assessing a charge for setup	Call type Setup charge Setup amount	Call type
Discount	The discount that should be applied to calls made during a specific time period	Day of week Start time End time Discount percent	Connect date Connect time
Holiday	The discount that should be applied to calls made on a specific date. The holiday table overrides any time-of-day discounts that are in effect	Holiday code Date Start time End time Discount percent	Connect date Connect time
Other line set up	The surcharge that should be applied to calls to a specific destination	Holiday code Date Start time End time Discount percent	Terminating number
Surcharge	The surcharge that should be applied to specific call type	Surcharge code Setup amount Setup percent	Call type
International rating	The rate table that should be used to rate overseas calls. The terminating overrides can be used if the overseas calls are to be rated according to a third-party carrier's table(s)	Terminating countries Terminating overrides	Terminating number

those calls should be initially rated. Tables must be created to link all number codes and combinations to the carrier and service-area tables. The following rating alternatives are likely (Terplan, 2001):

- Event rating: Customer-generated activities can be processed by the event-rating module. A client-defined table is utilized to apply a charge to the record. The table is message-type specific; therefore, different record types can be uniquely rated.
- Usage-sensitive rating: Instead of being distance or serving-area sensitive, wireless or data products have traditionally been rated on a

usage-sensitive basis. The usage-rating module is designed to accumulate calls that were generated during a billing period and to rate the calls based on client-defined criteria. This method of rating has been used for:

Cellular
Packet data
Personal communication services (PCS)
Satellite voice usage

The customer structure should enable multiple service offerings for a single service user. Each service offering can be associated with its own set of rate plans, options, and promotions. When the user is populating the customer structure, the user is presented with the product catalogue that is specific to the service offering. The customer's call details are rated according to the rate plan, and the details are stored with the applicable service offering. When billing generates the customer's bill, the call details are presented in order of service offering.

The attributes within the rate-plan presentation specify the charging instructions for the accumulated traffic at time of billing. Usage limits are the conditions that the customer must satisfy in order to qualify for the discount levels. The client can also specify whether the rate should be applied incrementally to the usage levels or whether the rate should be applied retroactively to the usage. In a convergence system, the network operator utilizes the same master-file concept to establish rates for rate plans, billing options, equipment products, or promotions. If the user selects a rate plan as a product type, the user is presented with the usage rating presentation.

- Usage rating: The usage master file stores specifics on how to rerate accumulated usage at time of billing. Usually, applications can support the following actions:

  Rerating of usage for volume-sensitive plans
  Tapered pricing
  Threshold-level pricing
  Application of price overrides
  Calculation of price according to contract terms while monitoring
    for compliance with contract terms
  Term commitment
  Volume commitment
  Combination of term and volume

- Service rating: The service-offering master file stores specifics on how to calculate charges for services. The offering types are rate plans, options (including different kinds of managed objects, such as facilities and equipment), promotions, and service bundles. Rate plans can be single-call rating plans, where a charge is applied to the individual call, or a usage plan, where the accumulated traffic is rated at time of billing. Usually, applications can support the following actions:

  Apply weekly, monthly, quarterly, or annual charges to a service

Apply the charge at time of billing or calculate the prorated charges back to the activation, modification, or deactivation date

Apply nonrecurring charges

Apply discount attributes to the rate plan, e.g., a plan can utilize direct-dialed plan A for direct-dialed calls, packet-data plan B for packet-data usage, and discount plan C to discount the usage based on total spent

Include or exclude certain usage or call types from the discount plan, e.g., a discount plan might exclude calling cards during the discount process

Table 2.2 shows an example of a master-rate table.

Service providers can create optional tables that define additional charging or discounting criteria that should be applied to the call at the time of rating. Any number of variations can be created for an attribute, and a specific rating criterion can be assigned to each variation. Optional labels can then be linked to the master rate plan. This design approach reduces keystrokes for service representatives, since they select the master rate plan from an online catalogue and do not have to select the optional plans. Table 2.3 shows an example of an optional-rate table.

2.1.3.2 Apply Negotiated Discounts

One of the main benefits of a convergent customer-care and billing system is that it allows a cross-service discounting. This can be a useful marketing tool for service providers as they market for new customers and increased usage of individual and bundled services. There are many discounting options, including the following:

- Time-of-day discount: This type of discount permits users to establish discounts based on the time when an event occurs.
- Holiday discounts: This allows special discounts for usage on holidays (e.g., Christmas Day, Easter Sunday, Thanksgiving, etc.).
- Rate plans and promotions: These can be associated with volume-discount attributes that are applied at time of billing.
- Promotions: Customers can receive proportions on their recurring charges, in the form of whole or partial credits.
- Enhanced holiday discounting: A separate holiday discount file can accommodate usage-based rating to complement or take the place of the generic holiday discounts.
- Longevity discount promotion: The network operator can reward long-term customers by offering discounted or free usage during, for example, their "nth" month of service.
- Free or discounted usage promotions: Billing systems handle the application of discounts that provide free or distributed usage to specific areas. This is not a volume-based discount that might be assigned to customers via a promotional service offering. For example, this type

of discount could provide clients with the ability to offer 60 free minutes or 20 calls at a specific discount to a specific area.

■ Frequent-calling discounts: This enables network operators to offer plans that provide discounts to frequently called areas, e.g., by country or city code.

■ Free terminating numbers: This file enables users to establish terminating numbers that can be rated as free.

Enhanced volume discounting permits service providers to offer discounts based on user-defined thresholds. Plans can be established to discount customers based on length of contract term or charge categories (weekly charge, monthly charge, nonrecurring charge, cellular usage, packet data, etc.). In order to take advantage of volume discounts, customers are expected to meet certain criteria:

■ Total spent
■ Total minutes of use
■ Total number of events
■ Length of contract
■ Type of usage (e.g., 30% cellular, 10% fixed wire, etc.)

Tiered volume discounting is also possible with most billing applications. This type of discounting is becoming increasingly popular as service providers look for methods to increase usage. The flexible discounting capabilities of billing applications ensure that operators will have sufficient system flexibility to consider change requests due to market demands and competitive advances.

2.1.3.3   Apply Rebates

Rebates are sometimes granted, even when service-level agreements (SLA) are not met. The trouble-ticketing application provides the actual data on SLA status. It is expected that SLAs include paragraphs on penalties for noncompliance. These paragraphs must be interpreted and quantified by this function. Results are forwarded to the invoicing and collection process.

2.1.4   Content Creation and Bill Design

This is the stage that decides the content that the customer sees on the bill. The content can be developed in-house, or the raw data can be sent directly to the consolidator, who then works on the composition and format of the content. Content development is not merely the formatting of the raw data. It involves much more, since the raw data may be residing in various source systems and mediation devices in multiple formats. The task of formatting involves converting the different formats into an Internet-friendly HTML or XML format. Electronic bills also provide the opportunity of posting marketing messages that help in cross-selling and up-selling the biller's products and services. These events are also managed through the process of content creation and formatting.

Invoice format applications are usually custom-designed to meet customer-specific marketing preferences as well as regulatory requirements. In-country and in-state regulations also must be considered in representing the invoice as a legal document. At a minimum, the invoice should support:

- A system-generated invoice number
- A summary or legal remittance page in the legal language of the country
- A remittance stub to afford account payments at bank or by check
- Numbers to call for customer service
- Invoice messages at the summary level and at the current account detail level, which provides the customer with supplementary information
- A breakdown of taxes
- A listing of account payments
- A listing of account and service-location adjustments
- A summary of charges for each service location, detailing the usage, whether recurring or nonrecurring, and adjustments for each service (packet data, switched data, frame relay, others)
- A statement of charges if the customer's preferred method of payment is credit card or bank debit; statement stamped "do not pay, the amount due will be transferred to your credit card or bank account"
- Page-N-of-N numbering to aid in customer contracts
- Item numbers assigned to each call detail

Printed call details, if required and paid for, should include:

- Date and time
- Called number
- Calling number
- Call type (direct dialed, calling card, etc.)
- IP address if VoIP (voice-over IP)
- Duration
- Method of rating (minutes, distance, number of pulses, etc.)
- Discounted amount
- Net charge for the call
- Call detail subtotals for each telephone or IP number that is linked to a service offering
- Optional call details for packet data, frame relay, ISDN, xDSL, and other services

A facility to tailor printed call details as governed by data-protection requirements also should be considered and implemented. Support for billing verification is usually expected. Such an application has built-in edits and checks to assure the accuracy of the invoice. This includes autobalancing routines as well as online data control and bill images that can be verified prior to the printing step of the billing process. There are separate balancing routines to ensure that the billing inquiry screens, the account balance screens, and the printed bills are in balance. This application also ensures that the general-ledger reports are in balance with the charge fee.

Billing packages are expected to collect CDRs from multiple switch formats. Data modeling can be performed specific to switches. The collection method and frequency is negotiated on a per-client basis. Usually, the following options are under consideration:

- Real-time data transport
- Tape/cartridge transport
- Client-defined transport frequency
- Transmission-type identification
- Immediate notification to verify receipt of transmission
- Gap identification (time points, sequence numbers)
- Duplicate call identification within batch
- Duplicate batch identification
- Data-element editing and error identification

During mediation, original CDRs are converted into the format of the billing application. After editing, the original record and the converted record are stored in special processing files. User-defined data elements can be extracted and stored in special files to assist service representatives in responding to customer queries. The raw data also can be used to generate traffic analysis reports.

Billing data may be useful for many areas besides billing. For instance, billing reports can summarize:

- Accounts receivable
- Revenue by rate plan
- Taxes by jurisdiction
- Trend analysis
- Account activity
- Activity by service
- In/out collect
- Cycle comparison

Not only batch, but also ad hoc reports can be extremely useful. These reports might include:

- Account status
- Equipment inventory
- Network performance analysis
- Payments overview
- Staff productivity
- Sales activity
- Prepaid summaries
- Aged unbilled call detail records

- Number of adjustments made
- Pending orders due to lack of provisioning completion
- Marketing analysis

Technically oriented reports are also useful for trunk and route analysis, including traffic volume summaries, volume by directions, blocked routes, and identification of underutilized facilities and equipment.

For service providers that cover large geographical areas and multiple tax jurisdictions, assigning correct tax jurisdictions is very important to determining the right rates and correctly reporting and disbursing tax revenues. Postal code identification is a good start, but up-to-date tax rates by jurisdiction are essential. The customer database is the right place to maintain this information. Taxation may become an area with great savings potentials for both service providers and customers, especially in the U.S. and Europe.

2.2 Presentment of the Bill

The following sections show the basic differences between paper versus electronic bills. The first section shows alternatives for converting paper formats into electronic forms; the second section provides guidelines for site design and management; the third section deals with notification; and the fourth section covers bill presentment.

2.2.1 Transitioning from Paper-Based to Electronic Formats

EBPP solutions are as good as the data they get from the principal billing procedures. Billing data can be provided in three different ways (McCalpin, 2001):

1. Raw data or data in XML directly from a billing database or from transaction files
2. Raw data or data in XML from composition systems, which generate data of the XML in parallel with print streams
3. Raw data or data in XML that might be extracted from existing print streams

In the simple case of a database and an EBPP product, the methodology of billing presentment on the Web is straightforward. The Web site has a number of home pages that can be utilized to generate a billing Web site. The system then builds HTML or XML pages or frames dynamically to present the highly variable billing data.

Using the print stream might not be the most elegant technique, but it is working in most application cases. Arguments for its use include the following:

- In many merged organizations, print streams may be the only common denominator to exchange and review data.

- Most print streams are extended by business logic to meet payer's requirements that cannot easily be reproduced.
- In many organizations, bills have to be printed, independently from the use of EBPP.

The print stream represents one of the input alternatives for billing data. There are five different methods of porting printed documents and their information content to an online form that can be utilized by EBPP (McCalpin, 2001):

1. Conversion to PDF format
2. Rasterization to GIF, JPG, or PNG formats
3. Recomposition into HTML or XML
4. Conversion to normal HTML or XML
5. Translation to highly formatted HTML or XML

These methods may preserve some, all, or even none of the print formatting information contained in the original print stream that is the basis of paper bills. Each method has benefits and disadvantages to its use, depending on the enterprises that are going to use them. Most likely, organizations will choose different technologies for different applications, even within a single enterprise. This is one of the reasons for the wide use of electronic statement presentment in addition to EBPP. There are cases when a static statement really deserves different treatment than an electronic bill.

2.2.1.1 Conversion to PDF Format

This process is the straightforward conversion of a print stream to a PDF document that has the same look and feel as the original paper bill. Since this is a print-stream-to-print-stream conversion, the output in PDF usually looks identical or very similar to the original printed document. In addition, many tools that create the PDF can also add value, such as including hypertext links, bookmarks, and so on to the new PDF document.

The benefits are:

- High similarity to the original document
- Wide availability of the PDF reader software
- Reasonable transportability
- Widely used in certain industries

The disadvantages are:

- PDF files tend to be large
- PDF documents are paper-size-centric
- Browsers require additional software to read PDF files
- PDF files are difficult to modify once created

2.2.1.2 *Rasterization to GIF, JPG, or PNG*

The print stream is converted into a bit stream. This is the electronic equivalent of printing and scanning existing paper documents. There are three different types:

- Graphical interchange format (GIF), supporting 256 colors or eight bits
- Joint Photographic Experts Group (JPEG), supporting more than 256 colors with better compression capabilities but with some "lossiness" from dropping insignificant pixels to reduce the size of the image file
- Portable network graphics (PNG), a proposed license-free and royalty-free replacement for GIF

The benefits are:

- The image is an exact copy of the original document.
- Images can be viewed on any browser that accepts GIFs and JPGs.
- PNG is license- and royalty-free.

The disadvantages are:

- Resolution is hard-coded at one size.
- There is no text to search.
- Downloads may take longer.
- There is no exact correspondence of printed pages and the images.

2.2.1.3 *Recomposition into HTML or XML*

Data are extracted from one place, while the presentation information comes from somewhere else. The data are extracted from a print stream and then merged either with static HTML templates or integrated into dynamically created HTML pages using active server pages (ASP) or Java server pages (JSP). Both alternatives require programming before presenting billing data on the Web. There are no restrictions on the number of output pages in HTML or XML; conversion can follow optimization rules for browser windows and information content.

The benefits are:

- HTML and XML pages are well suited for the browser windows.
- HTML and XML are considered simpler than PDF.

The disadvantages are:

- HTML and XML pages do not necessarily match the printed pages, causing problems when comparing printed pages with Web pages.
- All pages (templates) must be precomposed, or dynamic HTML pages must be coded.

2.2.1.4 Conversion to Normal HTML or XML

This case is the original method of converting a print format to HTML. In this method, both data and formatting information are extracted from the print file. Some formats easily correspond to an HTML tag. Complex formatting is frequently approximated by the use of table tags, even though there was no table in the original print stream. This is because the original flavors of HTML presentation with cascading style sheets (CSS) do not support absolute addressing in the browser window.

The benefits are:

- HTML and XML pages look similar to printed pages.
- Pages in HTML or XML, as opposed to PDF or raster, are usually smaller.

The disadvantages are:

- Fidelity is approximate, with some dissimilarity.
- Reader can substantially alter the presentation by changing the browser fonts and other attributes.
- Graphics may not be supported.

2.2.1.5 Translation to Highly Formatted HTML or XML

This method uses a particular set of CSS commands to control exact placement of text in the browser window. The ability to do this was substantially complete a couple of years ago. This is as close as XML gets to guaranteeing exact fidelity without rasterization. The user can control part of the browser attributes, e.g., the use of fonts, with the result that the user can change the look and feel of the page. Furthermore, the products that generate the tags necessary to control the exact placement of text normally do not attempt to preserve a meaningful XML tag name; rather, they name the spaces something like "position 1 or 2 or 3," which may destroy the real value of the tagged language.

The benefit is that the author of the Web page maintains a high level of control over the presentation of text. The disadvantages are that:

- Much of the value of the tagged language is lost.
- Portrait print pages still do not fit on landscape browser windows.
- It may not work with all browsers.
- Certain fonts can still be overridden.

2.2.2 Content Creation and Deployment

The principal steps of content authoring and deployment are critical in the bill-presentment stage, which includes the following major steps:

- Creating content
- Reviewing content

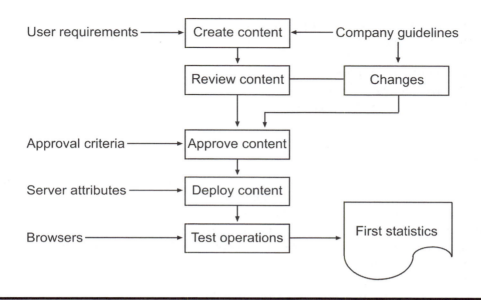

Figure 2.8   Process of content authoring and management.

- Approving content
- Changing content
- Deploying content

Figure 2.8 shows the process of creating, reviewing, changing, enhancing, approving, and deploying home pages. The prerequisites to successfully execute these tasks are:

- Users must be able to easily add and update content on a periodic basis.
- Users must be able to protect their page contents from changes by other users.
- A content approval process should be defined and in place. This process should encompass ways to manage and control document revisions, especially changes to shared documents.

As policies and procedures relating to content management are formulated, it is important to designate responsibilities to specific individuals to ensure that they are properly implemented and followed. An internal style guide should be developed that provides page layout, design elements, and HTML code guidelines. Usually, case tools are also involved. The style guide will help the users to maintain a consistent look and feel throughout the Web pages. Sometimes television-like techniques are helpful in this respect. The style guide should contain information on where to obtain standard icons, buttons, video, and graphics, as well as guidelines on page dimensions and how to link the pages to each other. As part of the style guide, it is helpful to create Web page templates. These templates consist of HTML/XML files and are used to provide a starting point for anyone interested in developing

Web pages or content for the intranet. Although it is very easy to create a working Web page and to publish for mass viewing, the real challenges are to:

- Maintain the page
- Size the Web server
- Configure the access network

2.2.3 Notification

Notification about the invoice can be sent to the customer in many ways. The most common way has been e-mails. However, this method is very much limited in its graphic and dynamic content capabilities. A modified version of this method of notification is to send the customer (payer) the URL (universal resource locator) of the Web site that hosts the invoice. Customers can also access their bills by directly visiting the Web sites of the billers, consolidators, portals, or the aggregators, depending on the business model being used. Today, with the booming wireless business, customers can receive notification about their bills via their mobile phones and wireless-capable personal digital assistants (PDA). The possibilities of m-commerce are immense. Notification in the traditional case is via regular mail that includes the actual bill.

2.2.4 Bill Presentment

Bill presentment is when the payer receives the actual bill with all the necessary details in paper format. With EBPP, it is the stage where the biller or the consolidator/aggregator presents a copy of the bill to the customer (payer) in an electronic format. The billers may choose to present the customers with a summary or complete details of the invoice. This activity also provides an opportunity to the billers and consolidators to interact with the customers, guide them to their areas of interest, capture their preferences and other important information about the customer's habits and expectations, cross-sell and up-sell, and build loyalty by providing the customer with an enhanced or compelling experience. The service providers (billers) include dynamic features alongside the invoice, like informing the customer about the status of pending orders, details of past payments, pending payment status, and cumulative usage of services since the last bill. In particular, telecommunications service providers emphasize convergent bills, putting together the invoices from local and long-distance carriers, ISPs, mobile providers, etc.

Billing applications should guarantee invoice information according to customer-preferred media. As an enhancement, the customer can choose to receive the invoice in a medium other than the traditional paper offering (e.g., diskette, CD-ROM, electronic data interchange (EDI), EDIfact, or e-commerce). The customer always receives at least the summary (remittance) page of the invoice on paper.

The output of the process is customer-defined according to the client's specific requirements. The typical billing options are:

- Generate a paper invoice along with optional telemanagement reports
- Copy billing data to tape, cartridge, or CD-ROM
- Transmit billing data to a fulfillment or clearinghouse
- Transmit billing data to a customer-defined database
- Produce invoices in the language of choice

Billing applications are also expected to support the creation of a customer bill on demand. The client defines the business rules for generating an on-demand bill (e.g., immediately after the service has been finalized, when the customer exceeds a predefined credit limit, or upon user request). The customer is linked to the next available bill cycle, and the invoice generated as part of that bill run.

A special billing cycle is also available to run on a daily basis if the customer does not wish to have these accounts included in "standard" bill runs or if a billing run is not scheduled. This billing cycle processes only those accounts in the on-demand request file. The unbilled call details are available online at the conclusion of the message-processing run. Therefore, the current account balance of the customer, including unbilled calls, can be compared with the credit limit.

2.3 Payment

This final stage concentrates on the actual payment, posting, collection, and revenue assurance.

2.3.1 Collection and Revenue Assurance

Credit-verification applications assign each customer a credit classification when the account is created. Based on the account-receivable amount and the credit-class parameters, bill-collection applications automatically determine whether the account should be assigned to a credit controller. The applications then populate the credit controller/collector work queue with specific account details.

The credit-classification master file stores the client preferences regarding collection action for each risk category. Typical values in the master file are:

- Should this credit class go to collections/credit control?
- What credit limits and credit days should this account be assigned?
- How many days after the account is in the collector queue should the supervisor be notified?
- Should the application automatically upgrade and downgrade the amount based on payment habits?
- What credit-control steps should the system process, and how many days should elapse between steps? The valid steps are phone call, letter, suspend service, deactivate service, apply security deposit, assign to a collection agency, write off account.

Based on the account-receivable amount and the credit-class parameters, the application automatically determines if the amount should be assigned to a collector and, if so, which one. The application then populates the collector work queue with account details. The collector can view:

- Collection history
- Account/service details
- Payment history, including postdated checks
- Current or previous promises to pay
- Current collection/credit-control status
- Future steps that the application would carry out for the account credit control, and the timing of each step

The collector then interacts with the customer and carries out the appropriate actions, including modifying the type of step and timing of steps that the application should action in the future. Supervisors have their own queue that is used to review the work of collectors within their work group. The collection application is entirely user-maintained and provides clients with a valuable work tool to ensure that customer segments are treated correctly, that bad debt is controlled, and that the cost of collections is minimized. The following is a sample list of functions that a collection application should include:

- Automated assignment, credit control, and dialing of accounts based on account profiles
- Automated letter generation for overdue accounts
- Setup of minimum values per credit classification for collection steps to be initiated
- Amendment of a credit limit for an individual account
- Suspension and reset of collections steps and timing
- Ability to enter promises to pay with automatic resumption of collections if payment is not received
- Automated account notation for overdue accounts
- Automated calculation of interest charges
- Automated assignment of accounts to collection agencies
- Automated write-off of account balances based on user-defined criteria
- Automated and manual escalation of exception items
- Reporting of overdue accounts by collector, agency, and managers
- Reporting of days sales outstanding
- Automatic disconnect or suspension, direct connect to collection agency, or automatic reconnection if the service activation module is in use
- Online function to amend text of collections letter
- Online function to alter collections and timing for each credit classification

Usually, invoice formatting, invoice presentment, and collection are supported by the same billing application. The accounts-payable clerk must open the invoice, route the paper invoice, contact the vendor for discrepancies/clarification, resolve disputes, make multiple copies for internal distribution, and enter the data into a back-office system. The approving manager may also receive the bill, route it for approval, and resolve disputes accordingly. At regular periods, finance management must review the payable processes for late payments, lost discounts, and poor negotiations and must audit for keying errors. Electronic presentment and payment processes can be leveraged to automate most of these manual steps and provide a return on investment (ROI) within a few months.

2.3.2 *Electronic Payment and Posting*

The last stage in the EBPP process is payment processing and posting. Billers and consolidators need to provide the customer with multiple payment options that include direct debit from accounts, direct debit to recur monthly automatically, one-time payment, check payment, online payment, electronic funds transfers, bank card payments, or monthly credit card payments, either automatically or at the customer's discretion. Customers have a choice of making multiple payments to individual providers or one consolidated payment, for multiple services, to the consolidator/aggregator, depending on the business model used. Posting refers to the process of documenting information on when, how, and how much the customer paid for the services he/she has used and then updating the accounts-receivable systems. For this, the billers have to build the capability to interact well with financial institutes, remittance processors (lockboxes), and credit card payment processors in order to process payment and remittance information and facilitate reconciliation.

2.4 Comparison of Paper-Based and Electronic Solutions

Figure 2.9 shows the stages addressed throughout this chapter for a traditional paper-based billing cycle. Figure 2.10 shows the same stages, but with electronic bill presentment and payment.

2.5 Operational Aspects

Auditing and tracking are key parts of the EBPP process. They refer to the task of keeping an audit trail of all activities that the data go through until they reach the customer (payer) in the form of an electronic bill. This becomes important in cases where errors in the process need to be identified and tracked. Customer habits and interactions can also be tracked using cookies as they access their invoices on the World Wide Web. However, the decision about who receives these valuable data depends on the business model in

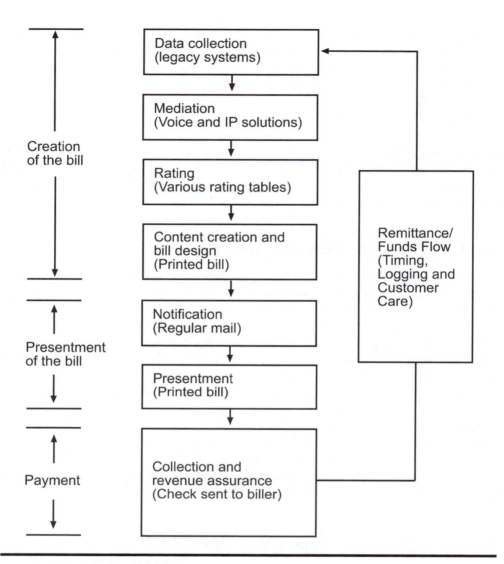

Figure 2.9   Paper-based billing cycle.

use. In the direct-biller model, the biller can use this information to enhance its customer care and marketing approach. In the consolidator model, the consolidator/aggregator benefits from capturing this information. Audit of the events also enables a better customer-care process, as the billers/consolidators can better answer customer queries by knowing exactly what happened during the billing process and when.

More than 70% of the customer queries received by service providers concern invoices. This makes it imperative for billers and consolidators to design resolutions for the most frequently asked questions (FAQs). These can then be incorporated into the presentment system to resolve the issues in an efficient and effective way. Some ways of accomplishing this include providing

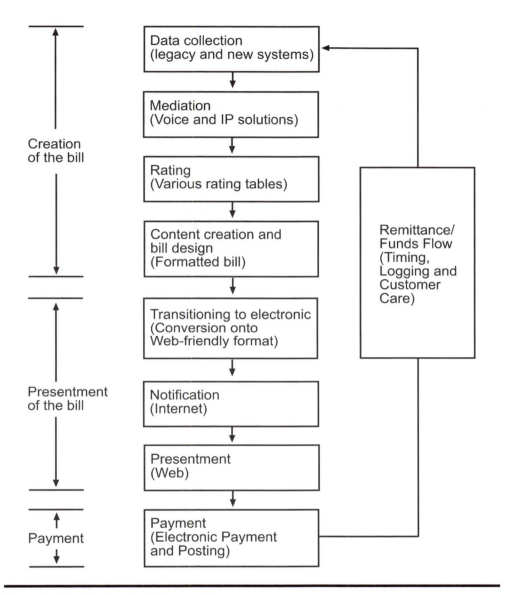

Figure 2.10 Electronic billing cycle.

self-care features like querying present and past invoice data, capability to talk with a customer-care representative, ability to open and send trouble tickets online to dispute charges, and posting quick and easy answers to FAQs that help the customer self-diagnose and troubleshoot the problems. Another important consideration is that both the biller and the consolidator should be able to handle questions from the customers. This means that both parties should have access to all shared information required to completely answer customer questions.

Chapter 8 addresses operational issues in more detail.

2.6 Summary

This chapter addresses the three principal stages of generating invoices: creation, presentment, and payment. The creation stage is almost identical for both paper-based and electronic billing. The presentment stage is completely different. The payment stage may show similarities, depending on the selection of the customer. The payment stage offers a range of options for the customer; the right selection is heavily dependent on the geographical location of the billers and payers.

Most of the practical examples illustrating the technology are from the telecommunications industry, but the basics apply to other industries.

Issuers of statements, bills, and invoices should carefully select their solution providers; experience, references, and customer base are critical selection factors. Solution providers with a history in paper-based bill creation and distribution who are gradually transitioning toward electronic document composition should be seriously considered.

Additional details about suppliers, services, and products can be found in Chapters 4 and 7.

Chapter 3

Business Models for EBPP

This chapter addresses the various business models for EBPP by introducing their functionality, evaluating their benefits, listing their disadvantages, and identifying the most likely service providers for the business model under consideration. Currently, both business and consumer customers can receive bills through the following models.

- Biller direct
- E-mail
- Consolidation alternatives
- Consumer-centric aggregation
- Use of portals
- Service bureaus
- Application service providers
- Invited pull

3.1 Business Model: Biller Direct

One of the first and most widely used EBPP model is the biller-direct solution. In this model, billers or biller service providers (BSP) provide their bills on their respective Web sites. Users log onto the biller's site using a universal browser and receive their billing data. The level of detail in this bill-presentation phase is controlled by the biller, as shown in Figure 3.1.

One of the benefits of this model is the capability to maintain a direct relationship with the customer in a media-enriched environment. Advertising, direct marketing, and bill chunking can easily be incorporated into the Web site while the customer is captive, unlike other more or less aggressive advertising and marketing forms.

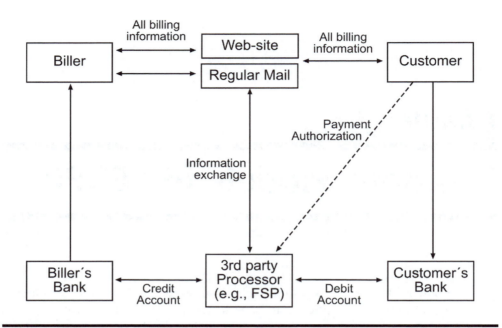

Figure 3.1   Biller-direct business model.

Personalized, profile-led, one-to-one marketing is also easy to implement, and the Internet is helpful in collecting data for profiling customers without violating privacy laws. The downside is that it is inconvenient for the customer to log onto multiple billers' sites separately. Performance issues — long downloads, excessive response time, link breakdowns — can discourage the customer, particularly when confronted with a large number of different bills. Surveys indicate that an average customer (household or small business) deals with 10 to 20 recurring bills each month.

While the biller-direct model provides the highest level of contact between biller and customer, this model is also the most time-, effort-, and cost-intensive for billers and has met with discouragingly low customer response. These factors have hindered the success of this model.

The direct-biller model is useful for billers who provide services that entail generation of a detailed bill. For example, customers making substantial long-distance calls need to verify the details before paying for them. Many of the phone companies host the long-distance-service bills for their customers and make them accessible online, thereby successfully implementing the direct-biller model.

The other area where this model is successful is for corporate customers (biller-to-business relationship) for whom one bill represents a large percentage of their total spending, so that they require the capability to route the bill through multiple departments for reconciliation and charge-back purposes. One of the other drawbacks of this model is that customers need to make multiple payments — one at each of the biller Web sites — to clear their duties. This model would work well for billers who use a direct-debit model of payments.

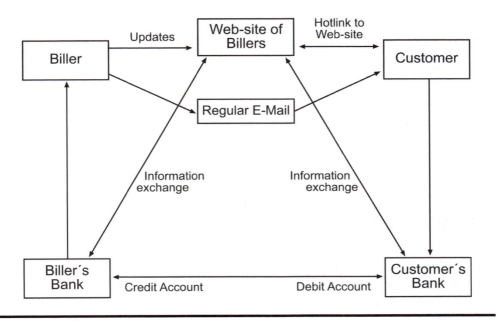

Figure 3.2   E-mail-based business model.

The direct-biller model also represents a huge investment in technology by the biller. Billers need to set up systems that can handle the conversion of raw billing data into an Internet-compatible presentation format, and they must build a system to accept payment online. The huge costs associated with setting up the infrastructure do not always make a strong business case and a targeted return on investment (ROI) for execution of the direct-biller model.

3.2   Business Model: E-Mail

This model also maintains direct contact between the biller and the customer. In this model, the bill details are presented and delivered to a customer-defined e-mail address. It is similar to an electronic post box. Detailed invoices containing rich-text graphics and intrusive direct-marketing messages can be sent to a customer, with links embedded in the e-mail allowing billers to bring users to their site for online payment or, if payment is not supported, a detailed view of the bill. Figure 3.2 shows the structure of this business model.

In comparison with the previous model, the e-mail model is much simpler than media-rich Web-centric billing solutions. Important benefits include pro-file-led, one-to-one marketing while being as intrusive as a paper bill. Customers are familiar with e-mail, and they are comfortable with this solution, which assists transition from legacy to electronic bill payment. The operating costs are much lower than in the case of a Web-centric solution. Legal and contractual issues around data and date and payment deadlines can be solved by a tracked and arrival-confirmed e-mail bill, while the delivery format of the bill can be chosen by the customer.

The downside is the management of the customer base, which requires ever-increasing amounts of server power to organize, categorize, and deliver the e-mail invoices. Address inaccuracies can cause troubles, although multiple addresses may alleviate this shortcoming. The perceived level of security with e-mail systems needs improvements, particularly when financial data are being exchanged.

The e-mail model of bill delivery is evolving to include a category of tools called "desktop consolidation software," which will allow customers to integrate various e-mailed bills into one tool and make payment through a variety of channels.

3.3   Business Model: Consolidator Alternatives

The basic premise of this business model is surrendering the bill data to an external party, to a greater or lesser degree, for presentment to the customer (payer). This model allows various bills from different sources to be presented in one place through an online bill consolidator. Some billers fear that this model drives a wedge between the biller company and the customer. However, customers prefer the convenience of a centralized service.

For customers who have multiple service providers and need the convenience of accessing all their bills from a single source, the direct-biller model is cumbersome. The consolidator model addresses these needs by aggregating multiple bills and presenting them at a single location. In this model, the customers need to log onto just one site to access summaries and details of all their bills. This model transfers control of data from the billers to the consolidators, who consolidate multiple customer bills and present them through an aggregator (e.g., financial institutions). The aggregators use online applications to provide customers an interface to electronic bills. With the consolidators acting as the central link in this model, it is their responsibility to invest in infrastructure and open systems and standards that are needed to communicate with numerous billers as well as financial institutions. Consolidators perform the function of enrolling customers, thereby eliminating the need for customers to enroll with multiple billers. By doing so, the consolidators get access to key customer data, which they can use to drive traffic to their Web site. They also manage the payment processing functionality by providing debit information to consumer banks and sending credit information to the biller banks.

There are two basic alternatives to the consolidator model: thick consolidator and thin consolidator.

3.3.1   Thick Consolidator Model

This model allows the consumer to view all of his/her bills at one site run by the consolidator (Figure 3.3). With this model, the biller delegates all control of the bill data by outsourcing the bill-presentment process to the consolidator. In this arrangement, the biller has the least control over the bill and customer

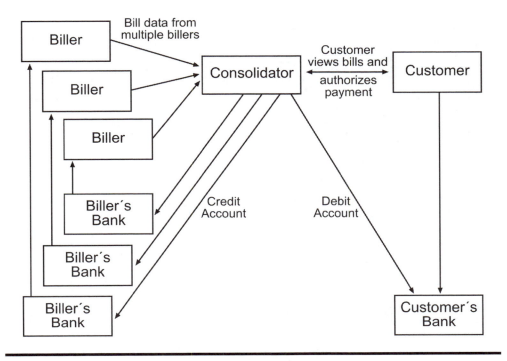

Figure 3.3   Thick consolidator business model.

ownership. Billers send the billing data to the thick consolidator, who is responsible for both presentment and payment. The thick consolidator hosts the bill summary and details, and it presents the bills to the customer through an aggregator-branded Web site.

3.3.2 Thin Consolidator Model

Within this model, a summary of the bill details is presented at the consolidator's site, while detailed data are kept on the biller's site. Payers are encouraged to view the data by visiting the home pages of the billers, thus maintaining a direct relationship between the biller and the consumer. Direct one-to-one marketing is supported, as seen in Figure 3.4. The obvious advantage of this consolidator model is that the consumer has the ability to pay multiple bills simultaneously. By presenting all the bills at one Web site, the supplier empowers the customer to compare respective bills and monitor spending habits. This is especially beneficial in the business-to-business (B2B) sphere, which profits from the add-on analytical tools that can be integrated into an EBPP solution.

There are some problems with this model, however. The level of accountability should be set between the biller, consolidator, and payer when dealing with service-level problems such as systems outages, crashes, lost data, inefficient Web-site response, lost deliveries, etc. The legal issue of bill delivery, payment, and liability compounds this problem. Electronic bills and payments

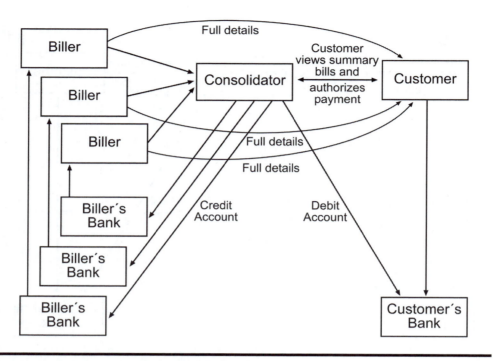

Figure 3.4   Thin consolidator business model.

do not have the official weight of a paper document. Other issues with this model include:

- Who will handle customer complaints? For efficient operation, there must be a sequence starting with the consolidator and continuing with the financial institutions and the biller.
- Who owns the customer? All participating parties may try to claim ownership, since this brings additional benefits, especially in management of the customer relationship.
- How to quantify the payments? Billers are expected to pay at several points: paying for converting the print stream, paying the consolidator, paying the fee processor, and finally paying the consolidator to complete the billing cycle.
- What is a fair profit sharing among the providers? All participants in the supply chain want to be paid. Fair payment is the result of fair negotiations among the providers.
- Who is entitled to person-to-person (P2P) relationships? This is related to the issue of customer ownership; by observing the behavioral patterns of payers, additional marketing messages can be personalized and included into the bill presentment.

Solutions to these issues are addressed in Chapters 4 and 8.

An additional question relates to the degree that the payer comes to rely on the consolidator. It is quite possible that the consolidator could become

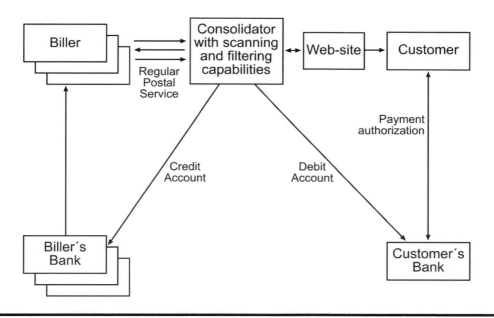

Figure 3.5   Consumer-centric business model.

the single point of contact for the payer. Consolidators might become the primary provider of customers' (payers') purchasing needs because of their bill presentment and payment relationship with the consolidator. The consolidator has the relationship with the customer, not the biller. The consolidator is thus able to negotiate with its clients, the billers, in order to resell their services. The final result is that the biller may become a subcontractor or wholesale service provider company.

3.4   Business Model: Consumer-Centric Aggregation

This model shows deep similarities with the thick consolidator model. Billers without electronic capabilities deliver their bills to a consolidator who scans and filters the bills before presenting them on a Web site, as seen in Figure 3.5. This model provides the widest access to customers by supporting billers who have electronic delivery mechanisms and those who do not. Billing service providers can deliver their billing data electronically or by mail. The customer can view all kinds of bills. The consolidator benefits by offering a wide mixture of bills from very different billers.

Technologically, this solution represents a transitional phase. Given the slow takeoff of EBPP, the aggregator model offers some benefits without the risks of investing heavily in EBPP technology. A further step to this model would entail fully automated consolidation and payment, resembling the European direct-debit service, where the consumer bill is sent to the aggregator rather than the consumer and is paid directly and automatically from the site. This model simplifies bill presentment and payment with minimal investment on behalf of the consumer.

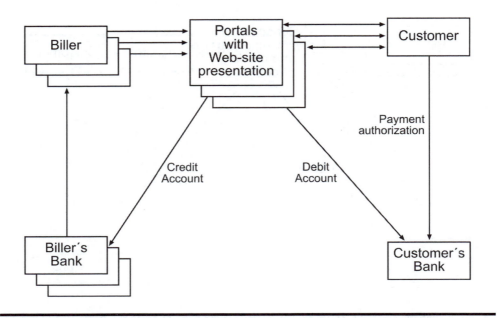

Figure 3.6   Portal-based business model.

3.5   Business Model: Use of Portals

The growth in portals and their relative importance has had a profound effect on the Internet world by providing individual users the benefits of personalized usage and data filtering. Portals can be utilized in the consolidation model serving customer markets at large companies and at small and medium enterprises (SME). Actually, this model is supported by major EBPP vendors, but it relies on portal brand loyalty as the driver for activation.

This model primarily supports the business-to-consumer (B2C) market and the smaller businesses. The largest portals offer wide coverage, but at present, B2B seems to be the better target for EBPP. This model needs significant support by a large number of customers.

Figure 3.6 shows the architecture of the portal-based business model.

3.6   Business Model: Service Bureau

This solution allows smaller billing service providers to gain access to large consolidators and vice versa. The service bureau acts as an intermediary between billers and bill presentment aggregators, collating bills from smaller billers and then delivering them to aggregators. A very strong target for this model is the SME. Figure 3.7 shows the process flow of the service-bureau model.

The service bureau can also act as an application service provider (ASP) by managing its customers' needs and outsourcing a complete EBPP solution

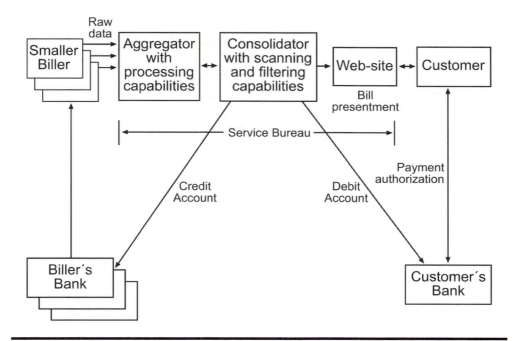

Figure 3.7   Service bureau business model.

hosted on the service-bureau site, which can be branded as the biller's service-bureau site. In particular in the U.S., the offering of portal services via an ASP model by service-bureau companies seems to be gaining momentum. BillServ™ is a good example, with its service bureau and its bills.com portal in partnership with CheckFree™.

It is an interesting business model with a number of benefits. As a remote-site solution, the model removes the problems of constructing the expensive Internet protocol (IP) and support infrastructure needed for the EBPP solution. The service bureau manages the entire presentation and payment process while appearing as an extension of the biller's own services. Speed to market is enhanced, as the biller can go online as soon as it can deliver its bills to the service bureau. This model serves companies who want to enter e-billing but have limited internal resources.

One problem with this business model is the lack of control that billers have over their bills. The outsourcing decision removes the contact between the online customer and the biller. A biller can still decide to present the bill on its own Web site, but this option is not likely in this scenario. Generally, the service bureau sends even the bill details to a larger consolidator. Customer billing relations suffer in this model, as the payer is no longer in direct contact with the biller. The distance between biller and payer may even be greater than with the consolidator business models. Consequently, rectification of payer problems involving the biller is compromised.

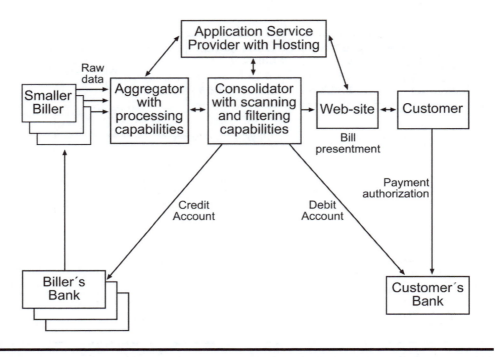

Figure 3.8   ASP business model.

3.7   Business Model: Application Service Provider

The ASP model is a new development in the consolidation of bill presentment and payment for smaller companies who want to utilize EBPP. Without this option, these smaller companies would have to use the services of consolidators because of the high costs of introducing EBPP.

The ASP business model, illustrated in Figure 3.8, removes some of the cost of setting up and running an EBPP site and allows the biller to maintain a personal relationship with its customers. The risks of compromising the customer relationship are thus much lower than with the service-bureau business model. With the ASP business model, the cost and infrastructure investment is significantly reduced. The biller still owns the customer, and the site remains the biller's site, which is merely hosted by an ASP EBPP provider. However, the mission-critical nature of billing creates immense pressures on the network infrastructure providing the ASP service. As a result, a high-performance private network is required. Provisioning or using such a network is expensive, and such networks may not even be available for this purpose in certain regions of the world.

3.8   Business Model: Invited Pull

The biller-direct model requires connection to a number of biller sites by a universal browser. Browser-enabled consolidation helps to aggregate data

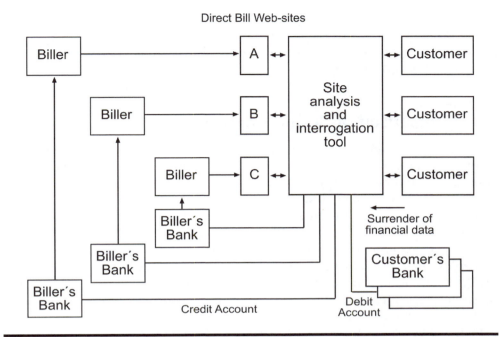

Figure 3.9 **Invited-pull business model.**

from biller-direct Web sites. The invited-pull concept can be used wherever the consumer has bills presented in an electronic format. Figure 3.9 illustrates the invited-pull process. This business model has a strong development potential because of its ability to draw divergent and fragmented models into one place.

One of the problems with this solution is the time demand of downloading data from the various sites, with the speed of the download dependent on the system capacity of the payer rather than that of the biller or consolidator. For the biller, this solution also involves losing its direct relationship with the customer. This direct contact is the main reason for the popularity of the direct-biller business model, which allows a personalized relationship with the payer.

A development of the invited-pull model in the U.S. is so-called screen scraping, also known as account-data aggregation. In this business model, the consumer surrenders financial data, such as account and password access details, to a third-party who then accesses and "scrapes" billing and related data from banking and billing sites. This solution has a couple of problems, the most serious being related to security issues surrounding the surrender of account details and passwords. Legal disputes can be avoided when the payer gives permission to the scraper.

Another area that needs more attention in the future is the P2P market. The content economy is likely to support the transactions that take place within the P2P market, with any individual having the potential to become his own content provider who needs to bill for his services. Likely business models for this type of service will be based on the service-bureau and personalized consolidator models due to the close relationship of these models to the process framework of personal transactions. The use of a consolidator business model would allow the numerous transactions carried out through P2P to be tracked, presented, and billed for in one place.

3.9 Comparison of Business Models

There is a growing trend to compare and eventually combine customized software and ASP alternatives for EBPP implementations. A combined approach gives businesses the ability to start on a small scale using a hosted ASP service with low initial investment and migrate later to a more powerful and sophisticated customized solution.

Implementing a full-blown EBPP application makes sense for companies that want to retain control over their billing data and who have the resources to deploy and maintain the system in-house, including operational support. An EBPP application provides the flexibility to add functionality stepwise and integrate the EBPP application with other front- and back-office applications, such as accounting, enterprise resource planning (ERP), and supply-chain management. Other applications can also be integrated, including customer relationship management (CRM), content management, and portal servers. Indeed, the EBPP application can become an integral part of the internal workflow.

The ASP approach makes sense for companies that do not have the support resources required to implement a new application within their information technology (IT) organization. Using an ASP, businesses can get started in EBPP more rapidly with a minimal capital outlay, and the ASP gives them the ability to spread costs out over longer periods. However, outsourced approaches generally lack the flexibility of an in-house deployment, which can be problematic for companies that are reluctant to give up control of their data or that have specialized application development or integration needs.

Table 3.1 summarizes the benefits and disadvantages for each of the proposed eight business models. Specific service providers and EBPP product vendors are referenced in Chapter 7, which includes matrices showing how the various service providers and products fit into the EBPP business models.

Of the eight listed options, only the latter two — ASP and invited-pull models — provide the convenience currently demanded by customers (both businesses and consumers) who wish to handle their bill reviews and payments through a centralized user interface. Desktop consolidation software may provide a solution in the B2B sector, but consumers thus far seem unlikely to install and use yet another independent piece of software to perform a function that offers much lower savings to them than to the billing companies.

Table 3.2 lists the pros and cons of using in-house software from various EBPP vendors versus the use of ASP services (Patel and Greenfield, 2001).

Table 3.1   Benefits and Disadvantages of Business Models

Business models	Benefits	Disadvantages
Biller direct	Closest relationship with end user Facilitates profile data gathering One-to-one personalization Good for B2B applications	Inconvenience of having to visit multiple sites Dependence on the Internet for each site to download High first-time investments Support of multiple payment methods
E-mail	Optional hotlinks for marketing Shares a close affinity to legacy delivery mechanisms Inexpensive solution Easy combination with other business models	Scaling issues in terms of need for invoice organization, categorization, and delivery mechanisms Administrative overhead with remittance and assign
Consolidator model (general)	Ease of use for customer (payer) Ease of monitoring spending habits	Accountability is an issue, compounded by the fact that a system outage is likely to affect all customer bills Many consolidators charge billers and payers to use the system Issue of who is liable for bill errors, complicated by the number of parties involved
Thick consolidator	Allows all details to be viewed in one place	Loss of contact and relationship with customers (payers)
Thin consolidator	Combines the ease of use of a consolidator and the direct customer relationship of the biller-direct business model	Customer must still make the effort to visit the biller's site if they want to view their bills in detail
Consumer-centric	Allows all details to be viewed in one place Totally automates the bill process Full conversion into electronic formats Support for transitioning from paper to electronic billing	Loss of contact and relationship with customers (payers)
Portal	Ease of use for customer (payer) Ease of monitoring spending habits Ready audience Brand loyalty Less expensive option than ASP because of reduced costs for staff and infrastructure	Accountability (see consolidator model) Complaint reporting and rectification is more complex than with the straight consolidator model, as the hosting portal must contact the hosting company, consolidator company, and the biller

(continued)

Table 3.1 (Continued)   Benefits and Disadvantages of Business Models

Business models	Benefits	Disadvantages
Service bureau	Allows smaller billers to utilize large EBPP companies solutions Allows large-scale consolidator companies access to smaller companies As an outsourced ASP solution, it reduces the cost of running an EBPP solution	Lack of biller control in the outsourced model Difficulty with problem reporting and rectification, similar to the consolidator model
Application service provider	Good for starting with EBPP Less risk of losing customer relationship	High infrastructure investments Settlement disagreements may occur
Invited pull	Consolidates account data by browser Strong development potential to draw divergent and fragmented models into one place	Download time from different sites might be considerable Customer relationship may be lost Security risks

Table 3.2   Comparison between In-House Software and ASP Solutions

	In-house software	ASP solution
Strengths	Development and integration flexibility After initial investment, ongoing software cost is reduced to a standard maintenance cost	Convenient way to offload an application that is outside a company's core competency Less up-front expenditure; most vendors charge based on transaction volumes, with reduced per-transaction charges as volume increases More flexible payment model, such as a monthly subscription fee Faster deployment
Weaknesses	Customization is required IT resources may need specialized expertise and skills or product training Slower deployment	Potential lack of control over data Customization and integration with back-end systems typically requires additional professional services Depth of integration may be limited Usually limited to batch-file updates

3.10 Summary

There are significant differences among the business models described in this chapter, but the market can be characterized by the fact that the boundaries of EBPP business models are disappearing. This blurring is a result of current developments in the EBPP market, with companies trying to service the widest possible customer base by offering several alternatives and combinations of the EBPP solution. Considering this, it seems reasonable to assume that any dominant EBPP business model will either incorporate or offer a secondary model. It is obvious that customers (payers) differ greatly in their needs and demands. Consequently, service providers must offer a range of solutions.

Chapter 4

Value-Added Attributes of EBPP

EBPP has a great potential to save costs and generate revenue. However, two major obstacles must be overcome first: Bill payers will have to change their behavior, and billers will have to make the investment required to bring EBPP services to market. Organizations (billers, aggregators, consolidators) contemplating an EBPP implementation should be aware of the potential benefits.

Savings on paper and postage are obvious: Billers can save as much as $1 per bill by converting a paper-based transaction to an electronic format. For companies with customer bases that range in the hundreds of thousands or even millions, the potential savings are significant. However, these savings are not likely to offset the initial investments for a long time because it will take some time until a substantial level of customers accept this way of bill presentment and payment.

Another benefit of EBPP is improved customer care, which has been confirmed by many entities: Studies indicate that Internet users tend to have higher education levels, higher income, and higher levels of discretionary spending. Consequently, people likely to use EBPP services are profitable customers. With consumers increasingly able to choose providers as a result of deregulation in the utility and telecommunications industries, companies have been looking for ways to improve customer service, to find other revenue-generating activities, and to reduce customer churn. EBPP is very helpful in these areas. For business customers, EBPP can add a great deal of value by providing online analysis results. Bills can be segmented by department for bill-back purposes — a very important function for business-to-business (B2B) applications. An EBPP site can also enhance customer services by providing related functionality such as fraud detection and analysis, provisioning, and dispute resolution.

4.1   Value-Added Features to EBPP Core Solutions

In addition to the core features, outlined in Chapters 1 to 3, value-added attributes promote the development and implementation of EBPP solutions. The most important value-added results are:

- Faster payments and cash management
- Opportunities for cross-selling and up-selling
- Online resolution of disputes
- Use of chunking
- Validation of the availability of credits and funds
- Ability to connect workflow capabilities
- Deployment of advanced security features
- Ability to handle multiple invoices and remittance management
- Support for multiple payment alternatives
- Data-analysis capabilities
- Distribution channels and online account management
- Personalization

These value-added functions are summarized below.

4.1.1   *Faster Payments and Cash Management*

Payers could be encouraged to pay faster. With this goal in mind, many billing systems provide a number of notification and marketing options combined with a reminder about payments due. Early payments can be honored by discounts or other incentives. The result is more predictable receivables, improved cash-flow forecasting, and better liquidity from the perspective of issuers of statements, bills, and invoices. The following value-added attributes can be quantified:

- Better cash management: Many customers think EBPP would negatively impact cash flow because it enables bill payers to hold onto a payment until the very last minute. Actual experience contradicts this point of view. On average, bill payers settle their bills electronically a few days sooner than with paper-based bills. Online billers can also offer customers the option of automatically scheduling payments for a recurring bill. An e-mail can notify customers that a billed amount will be automatically debited from their checking account or credit card on a specific date, which is similar to a direct debit. To make this more acceptable to the customer, the e-mail notification can contain a hyperlink to a Web site where the customer could view bill details, reschedule the payment, or cancel it altogether. Because the customer is never more than a click away from full control over the payment process, it is much more acceptable to the customer than a direct debit. For the biller, cash flow is improved because scheduled payments are almost never changed.

■ Faster and cleaner remittances: Electronic payments replace the error-prone process of inputting, processing, and reconciling paper-based payment transactions. Electronic payment transactions can be aggregated by an EBPP server and processed by the biller's bank at low cost. Many EBPP systems can also generate credit card payments via third-party service providers. It is important to note, however, that third parties charge for initial deployment and for the transactions executed. A biller can also still expect charges from its own bank when credits arrive at its account. Electronic payments are easy to implement, but transaction fees can be as high as 3% of the value of the transaction.

InFlow™ from DST Output brings desktop control to cash management. The InFlow suite of cash management tools helps to reduce float, working cash balances, and short-term financing costs. It improves efficiency in billing and streamlines collection-center activities. When combined with B2B and B2C electronic billing capabilities and sophisticated viewing solutions, these tools can speed remittance and lower costs by reducing the time that customer-care and accounts-receivable representatives spend with each customer.

InFlow solutions allow the biller to optimize its production timetables to meet days of sale outstanding (DSO) goals. This includes establishing optimum logistics for the delivery of mail, applying due dates on invoices, and personalizing remittance and reinvestment stubs. Other InFlow tools bring the advantages of address cleansing and postage savings optimization to billers.

Accelerating receipts provides more cash to apply to internal and external investments and enables organizations to pay their own bills. Improving cash flow means producing more goods and services faster, generating more revenue, and getting paid faster to enhance shareholder value. Bottomline's electronic invoice presentment and payment (EIPP) product, called NetTransact™, is a secure, interactive system for B2B transactions that allows organizations to present invoicing information, provide online dispute resolution, and accept payments over the Internet. With the addition of Bottomline's SmARt Cash™ product, customers can automate receivables matching. When it comes to accepting lockbox payments for open invoices, customers want to match the cash with open invoices as quickly as possible. Bottomline's SmARt Cash enables customers to do that by automating the receivables collection cycle, which replaces manual matching. Using sophisticated algorithms, the SmARt Cash matching engine looks to logically pair payments against open invoices according to predefined business rules of customers and payers.

Chapter 7 provides additional information about other products from Bottomline and DST Output.

4.1.2 Cross-Selling and Up-Selling

Revenue per customer can be increased by EBPP when conditional marketing messages and promotions are inserted into the electronically presented bill. This function also supports personalization and one-to-one marketing. The prerequisites are a powerful business logic and accurate basic data for profiling customers.

Cross-selling and up-selling can generate considerable revenues. EBPP can be a revenue-generating opportunity because it can enable the kind of interactive one-to-one marketing that is not possible with paper bills. The bill itself contains information that can be used for targeted promotions. The bill amount and the customer profile can be matched, and a special advertisement can be included into the attachment of the bill.

Campaign Manager™ from DST Output enables its customers to deliver customization to formerly routine communications. Authorized personnel, authenticated each time through Campaign Manager's secure direct-access Internet portal, can:

- Define an unlimited number of audience targets
- Select or create personalized messages
- Apply or create promotional and educational inserts
- Create personalized letters
- Send targeted e-mail

Some of the important features of Campaign Manager are:

- Scheduling: Customers can define and schedule multiple communication campaigns simultaneously, with different data ranges for personalized messages or synchronized inserts.
- Text formatting: It creates multifont messages utilizing bold, italics, underline, and bullet options with variable font types, sizes, and styles.
- Compatibility: It functions, no matter which back-office data provider is used.
- User-defined component naming: All components (messages, inserts, images, or templates) and target group selections are configured with names and labels familiar to customers.
- Sophisticated rule-building engine: It selects from a wide variety of data elements to create simple or complex rule conditions when applying a message, insert, or other component to the specified target groups within the campaign.
- Filter and sort capabilities: Advanced segmenting is possible by data range, output type, staging level, and status, allowing easy viewing of messages, business rules, and campaigns.
- Message and insert priority control: Personalized messages or synchronized inserts are sequenced by level of importance with priority level control.
- Online help: Context-sensitive help is only a click away, providing guidance and instruction specific to the process that the customer is working on.
- Audit reporting: Audit reports provide detailed information on personalized messages, target groups, or scheduled campaigns.

- User authorization control: Only specific authorized users can release campaigns from development to test mode and, finally, into distribution channels.
- Storage: All campaign-related data are stored and frequently backed up on special secure databases.

The benefits to issuers of statements, bills, and invoices who use this product for supporting cross-selling and up-selling include:

- Performance: Personalization can significantly increase sales on behalf of billers or consolidators.
- Convenience: A single online interface controls multiple campaigns. The customer can create messages, schedule inserts, and select components to promote campaigns.
- Ease of use: The user requires very little training to become proficient. Billers and consolidators can begin to address marketing communications needs immediately.
- Tailored to customer's needs: Customized naming conventions, data ranges, and text-formatting options create a more user-friendly and productive experience.
- No need for additional software: Accessing Campaign Manager requires only a standard browser, eliminating the need to maintain and update software.
- Format controls: Customers cannot select an unavailable format or inadvertently schedule campaigns that will interfere with predetermined and formatted configurations.
- Security: Authorization control at the user level protects against unintentional changes and provides secure oversight. Access to the database is only available through secure servers that utilize 40- or 128-bit encryption technology.
- Reporting: Billers and consolidators have access to detailed campaign information regarding targeted groups, with related messages, inserts, and other included components.

The online statement is the best platform to create recurring one-to-one relationships with customers, as it provides personal, time-sensitive, and financially relevant information. Transactional account data — such as purchase history, investment activity, and service and usage charges — allows the user to gain the most insight into customers' expectations and optimally personalize marketing campaigns.

With eaMarket™ from Edocs, billers and consolidators can deploy targeted marketing and customer service messages based on the customer's dynamic account and transaction data. It integrates with the eaDirect™ platform (see Chapter 7 for more details), enabling companies to place the right message in front of the right payer at the right time. By means of this product, e-serts can replace envelopes full of one-size-fits-all inserts. Acceptance rates can be increased when personalized messages are based on the actual purchase history of payers.

Online marketing demands real actions in real time. The Edocs product allows marketing teams to design, schedule, evaluate, and manage the entire process from any browser-based interface. Personalization drives the process. Historical transaction data are used to create profiles of specific customer target groups. The personalized content is stored in a data library and can be easily associated with customer profiles based on account transaction history. The personalized messages and promotions are then deployed in key areas of the online statement to target groups at the discretion of the marketing team based on user-specified rules.

Scheduling multiple campaigns is simplified by allowing marketing professionals to view all active and pending promotions at a glance using one graphical interface. This ensures that the right message is viewed at the right time. Workflow is streamlined into an online environment, yielding a smoother, more efficient flow from concept to customer. Role-based security and work groups facilitate a smooth transition of information from design to review to deployment. Security is customized to match the roles within the marketing department, from executive levels to Web masters and creative teams. Built-in electronic tools facilitate communications among team members, and content and promotions are automatically deployed upon the completion of the approval process. Reporting and evaluation features allow users to track, compare, and analyze promotion effectiveness while the campaign is active. Billers and consolidators can determine whether campaign objectives are being met and make changes to active campaigns in real time. Graphical tools and charts make it easy to evaluate success and determine critical next steps.

This product allows billers and consolidators to take full advantage of each customer's online transactions, which provide the best opportunity to establish a recurring dialogue with customers (payers). The dialogue drives revenue by offering customers complementary products and services based on established purchasing patterns. The product leverages real-time transactional account data along with traditional click-stream data to create truly customized profiles for targeted marketing. The product is part of a suite of products addressing various parts of EBPP.

Market Direct™ from CheckFree brings companies beyond electronic bills and statements into an interactive connection with their customers. Offering tailored solutions to companies in the telecommunications, banking, brokerage, insurance, credit card, and utility industries, the software builds on the powerful, scalable, XML-based i-Series platform. The result is that all aspects of EBPP and customer-relation management for billers can be integrated on one platform. This product combines targeted message management with customer-care and end-to-end event tracking from bill creation and delivery to the ultimate posting of the payment.

Chapter 7 provides more-detailed information about the products referenced in this section.

4.1.3 Online Resolution of Disputes

If payers are willing to access and pay their bills on the Web, they should also have the ability to initiate a dispute process. Many vendors offer tools to automate this process online, minimizing the need for customer service representatives (CSR) or accounting personnel to get involved in this traditionally cumbersome process. The prerequisites are the automation of routine cases, including adjustments. This can be combined with chunking, where parts of the bill are paid with the exception of parts under dispute.

In theory, more disputes are resolved and paid within the same billing cycle, rather than being pushed into the next cycle, when these issues are dealt with online. Billing systems can set up bills to require payment for items that are not in dispute by a particular due date, while extending the due date for disputed items. Certain companies have developed rules-based logic for dispute resolution. For example, if a company initiates disputes that total less than $100, the system might automatically approve them without human intervention. If the amount is greater than $500, the system might route it to a manager of customer care for review. A biller could also remove a disputed item from the total immediately and then retotal the bill to be reconciled in the next statement. Then the biller can have e-mail notification to alert a business as to accepted or rejected disputes.

4.1.4 Use of Chunking

Summaries of billing information are presented to the payers, who can then drill down deeper into the details when they are online. This avoids the need to transmit large data volumes at the beginning of the transaction and helps prevent scalability problems that can arise when very large data volumes must be handled simultaneously.

This is a classic example of the thin consolidator business model. Within this model, a summary of the bill details are presented at the consolidator's site, while detailed data are kept on the biller's site. Payers are encouraged to view the detailed data by visiting the home pages of the biller, which helps in maintaining a direct relationship between the biller and the consumer and preserves the ability to conduct direct one-to-one marketing. The obvious advantage of this consolidator model is that the consumer can pay multiple bills simultaneously. By presenting all the bills at one Web site, the consolidator model empowers the customer to compare various bills and monitor spending habits better.

4.1.5 Validation of the Availability of Credits and Funds

Billers need this validation information about their customers, and EBPP simplifies the validation process. Assuming electronic payment as part of EBPP, the issuers of statements, bills, and invoices can use the payment-validation procedures for credit and fund checking and validation. Simplifying online credit and funds-availability validation is a key demand of billers. Many billing systems provide integration with online banking systems and networks to ensure the availability of funds before enrolling a consumer or company in the billing system or before formally accepting their payment submissions. Such capabilities minimize bad-debt risks.

Credit-verification applications assign each customer a credit classification when the account is created. The applications then populate the credit controller/collector work queue with specific account details. This function is directly related to the collection function as outlined and explained in Chapter 2.

4.1.6 Connecting Workflow Capabilities

In selecting EBPP solutions, the internal processes and accounts-payable operations of payers must be considered. Some vendors allow payers to create routing schemes and approval workflows that can be customized to fit their existing workflows. The problem with fitting data into an accounts-payable system is that businesses will use systems that vary radically based on their size. Many systems allow the customer (payer) to download payment history and details into an Excel spreadsheet, add different billing codes, and import the file back up to the system. The whole process initiated by the biller must be supervised. The value chain is supervised visually with a workflow analysis tool that uses an open application programming interface (API) for all components of the value chain. This workflow engine is responsible for identifying bills and invoices, calendaring, job profiling, launching the process, visualizing status, and collecting process-specific data. Figure 4.1 shows the architecture.

SiteView™ from docSense is a Web-enabled job-monitoring and management system that provides visibility of the entire document production process. This control system outperforms current job-tracking procedures that are often slow, error-prone, and fragmented. SiteView gathers and delivers real-time, accurate, and relevant production data and reports, detailing every workstep throughout the document production process for hard-copy and electronic documents. It offers a broad range of online and offline production reports and creates electronic job tickets that are updated automatically. Managers gain a total view of their operations as well as accessibility to historical data, ensuring that they are equipped with the information they need to eliminate potential problems, or resolve them quickly, while meeting or exceeding the demands to achieve the required level of productivity.

The principal benefits of deploying SiteView are:

- Quick response to potential production problems, even preventing them from occurring
- Ability to pinpoint and improve specific production processes
- Efficient allocation and management of equipment, labor, and materials
- Increase in profits by ensuring operations run at peak frequency
- Ability to plan and measure successful service-level agreements (SLA)

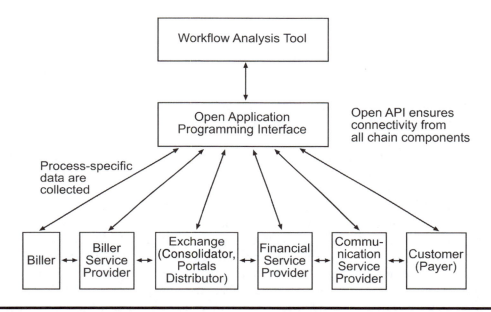

Figure 4.1   Value chain of the EBPP process extended by open APIs.

- Ability to identify which jobs are profitable and those that are not
- Access to real-time status information for every electronic or paper-based job that arrives in production, enabling reduced lead times; higher quality services; and timely, cost-effective completion
- Higher production throughput levels

The Web-enabled capability of SiteView also means that production managers can, via online reports, provide a controlled and real-time view of operations to key employees, customers, and vendors. As a result, specific document production data can be shared across the organization. This capability benefits other departments that must interface with and support print/finish operations, such as customer service, finance, and information technology. It can also easily connect with other enterprise reporting systems and effectively interface with enterprise resource planning (ERP), advanced planning and scheduling, as well as inventory management and other workstep planning tools.

In addition to meeting growing demands for increased productivity and reduced costs, document production managers also face more varied and stringent SLAs. SiteView monitors the entire process, enabling efficient management of a wide and complicated range of work types and levels. It ensures all SLAs are met and accurately documented. The system provides an alert message when operations are running behind or failing to meet specific SLAs. This product also aggregates and reports on actual job performance.

Specific data-collection and processing attributes include:

- Automation and streamlining of the data collection process for print/finish jobs, including Web-directed distribution

- Collection of real-time information without adding tasks to operations personnel
- Collection and organization of data from a wide range of worksteps, including printers, inserters, and other processing and finishing equipment
- Control of records and forms associated with jobs, including instructions, worksteps, and comments

InSite™ from DST Output transcends work management solutions. Near-real-time monitoring and management products and services in this solution suite let customers audit and control the statement process from the time billers or consolidators begin processing the statements until they leave the facilities. By closely predicting statement arrival, customers are better able to forecast revenue and staff their call centers accordingly. Even before payers receive their print or electronic statements, InSite's viewing solutions deliver duplicate statement images that put customer service representatives on the same page as payers, thus speeding calls, increasing customer satisfaction, and providing cross-selling opportunities. Via advanced, encrypted methodologies, InSite's tools also provide access to comprehensive reports that allow customers to track performance. Customizable reports provide production statistics, insert tracking, and postage costs, among others. The combination of multiple tools and reporting features ensures that billers and consolidators receive the information they need to take customer communications to their most efficient, cost-effective level.

Very strong integration capabilities are offered by the i-series™ solutions from CheckFree for leading ERP and customer relationship management (CRM) applications. The company offers the ability to transfer back-office data, at the file level, among other legacy systems.

Metavante Corporation is one of the technology providers to offer solutions and services in each area of the electronic presentment and payment (EPP) delivery chain. The complete end-to-end Metavante EPP solution delivers documents to customers in the format and to the location they specify.

The manual shuffling of paperwork that customers must do to pay their bills can be a time-consuming and cumbersome process. The person who ends up issuing funds for purchases may not be the person who placed the order, who authorized the order, or who authorized the payment. The product suite of Princeton eCom can make it easy for bill and statement issuers to streamline the process with automation. The product is specifically designed to automate the payables process, including the following process steps: invoice receipt, reconcile with receiving records, identify and record discrepancies, approve invoice, initiate payment, authorize payment, schedule pending payments, and maintain history of payments.

Chapter 7 provides additional details about the product suites of docSense, CheckFree, Metavante, Princeton eCOM, and DST Output.

4.1.7 Deploying Advanced Security Features

Payer companies need to be able to apply security to particular line items and ensure that only those people with the appropriate rights can see and review the data that applies to them. This is critical for companies that are pursuing cost-accounting or charge-back procedures in their procurement areas, especially if the approvers are in different locations.

Clients of CheckFree, one of the leading providers of EBPP products and services, can display the CheckFree Guarantee symbol to minimize consumer concern about fraud or late fees. It was developed to educate consumers about the terms and conditions, which include limited liability, that make electronic billing and payment through CheckFree as safe or safer than using credit cards or mailing paper checks.

Paytru$t™ offers the highest level of customer service and ensures that consumer information and transactions are guarded with the utmost security. All Paytru$t transactions are encrypted; all accounts are password-protected; and subscriber information is withheld from all outside parties.

Chapter 7 provides additional information about CheckFree's and Paytru$t's product suites.

4.1.8 Handling Multiple Invoices and Remittance Management

A payer may have multiple invoices coming from one biller; it may even have multiple accounts with a single biller. In such cases, it makes sense for the receiver in the accounts-payable department to be able to view consolidated statements that include data from multiple invoices and to submit a single remittance from which funds can be allocated against different invoices or accounts.

IPlanet, for example, uses XML technology to allow its customers to create their own hierarchy during the registration process. The customer (payer) sends the hierarchy to the biller via an XML template, and it is housed within the application. Once the biller sends out the invoice, it matches the hierarchy and is distributed through the customer side accordingly with accounts payable. Routing the right information to the right manager within the accounting department can be supported by this hierarchy. Within a large business, there may be someone responsible for telecommunications services and someone else for energy, and neither one of them may be interested in seeing an aggregation of the company's entire statement. EBPP products are designed to allocate calls to different cost centers so that all numbers originating from a specific number go to finance, for example, and to remember from bill to bill where to allocate that information. Business rules can be created to determine routing information. A system then knows, based on specific criteria, to route bill details to certain individuals.

Typically, accounts-payable departments receive the bill and break up the authorization and approval of the invoice. A business EBPP product must be able to map a clear, automated path for this process. When a seller receives an electronic payment, the seller also needs to receive the remittance information stating what the payment is for. This would include information that can be integrated back into the accounts-receivable system. This improvement is essential for successful B2B implementations. Unfortunately, existing standards do not yet fully support remittance information in the necessary depth.

4.1.9 Supporting Multiple Payment Alternatives

Payers need the ability to pay by their preferred mechanism, which may include credit cards, banking or debit cards, electronic checks, balance transfers, electronic data interchange (EDI), or automated clearinghouse transactions. Payers also want the ability to schedule their payments, take advantage of rebates or other favorable payment terms, and generally improve management of their cash outlays.

Complete payment flexibility to billers and their customers can be provided by eaPay™ from Edocs. Built upon the eaDirect™ online account management and billing platform, it uses a cartridge-based approach to support a variety of payment methods, such as direct debit and credit card, as well as a variety of payment processors, such as banks, utilizing the automated clearinghouse (ACH) network. It integrates with back-end processes and supports reconciliation with accounts-receivable systems. Accounts-focused corporations, whether they are financial services firms, telecommunications providers, retailers, energy providers, or health-care companies, need to be paid promptly for the goods and services they provide. Incorporating payment functionality into online account management and billing solutions will ensure quicker and more efficient payment. Online payment is cost effective in many ways. Billers maximize their valuable investments in online account management and billing solutions by making it easy to use so that their B2B and B2C customers will change their bill and invoice payment behavior. As online payment becomes the preferred way to pay bills, the large number of customers contacting service centers will decrease, and customer-care expenses will go down. At the same time, payers will gain flexibility and convenience. They can visit the Web-sites of billers and consolidators and easily pay their bills, schedule future payments, track payment status, and access payment histories. Payers will appreciate having more control of and access to their own accounts. This time-saving, complete, and convenient online account management experience increases consumer satisfaction, resulting in greater loyalty to the biller or consolidator's company. By providing anytime, anywhere access to online account information, billers engage their consumers in a recurring, mutually beneficial online relationship. Using eaPay, billers and consolidators can supply their consumers with the valuable tools to effectively self-manage their accounts.

Using e-payment™ solutions from CheckFree, consumers can sign-on at one site and transfer funds among accounts, whether or not they reside at the same financial institution, in the same session that they pay their bills, saving time and adding another layer of convenience and control.

BillingZone's apConnect™ and arConnect™ services empower buyers and their suppliers to streamline the complexity of invoicing and payment transactions. Both parties benefit from cost savings through the elimination of paper and manual practices and from better communications between trading partners.

Chapter 7 provides more information about the product suites of Edocs, BillingZone, and CheckFree.

4.1.10 Data-Analysis Capabilities

Billers can offer additional value to their customers (payers) by providing them with data-analysis capabilities. If payer companies can conduct historical analysis of their billing data to identify spending or consumption patterns, they can use this information to forecast future purchases or to negotiate a modified contract with a supplier. Likewise, analysis capabilities can help payers to identify redundant or unauthorized spending. Analysis and reporting are very important tasks. Process-specific data must be collected and converted into customer information using special-purpose applications. Customer payment behavior can be analyzed, e.g., day-of-week or day-of-month payment habits of the customer. Quantification of payment dates helps to determine the average number of days sales outstanding (DSO). For instance, the docSense company has observed the following results:

- EBPP payers pay 8 to 10 days earlier in a B2C environment.
- EBPP payers pay up to 20 days earlier in a B2B environment in the leasing industry

These and similar numbers are useful in computing realistic returns on investment (ROI) and in justifying EBPP investments on behalf of billers and billing service providers (BSP). Targets of analysis may include:

- Most frequently used day of week or month for payment
- DSO analysis
- Time spent in the value chain

BillDirect™ from Edocs offers role-based access that allows customer-service representatives to locate customer accounts, modify profiles and passwords, and view and analyze the same bill as the customer. This increases customer satisfaction and reduces the costs associated with handling customer account inquiries. This feature also enables system administrators to assign specific access and authorization privileges to customer-service representatives (CSR), resulting in higher security, improved auditing capabilities, and enhanced productivity.

With this product, bill and statement issuers can enable their customers to sort, group, filter, and subtotal transactions by any number of parameters. Customers can also download transaction sets in a variety of formats, including

Excel, comma-separated variables (CSV), or XML, for offline analysis. These advanced analytical tools build on Edocs's existing customer-care functionality, which allows customers to request previous copies of bills and statements, initiate disputes, change address or account information, and perform a number of other self-care services.

BillDirect also supports simulation of the personalization and composition features of this product. This allows billers and consolidators to preview how business rules combine account information with Web content to produce an online customer-account-management experience. These simulation capabilities decrease the amount of time and money needed to deploy an Internet billing and customer-management solution. Rapid simulation of complex data through this platform leads to better decisions about how to personalize and compose XML presentations of bills and statements to customers.

The workflow-based verification component of BillDirect enables the quality-assurance group of bill and statement issuers to verify the accuracy and quality of online bills and statements before delivery. This helps companies to reduce billing errors, which can have significant downstream costs for customer care and liability. The verification component mirrors the audit process that exists in the paper-based world, making it easy to integrate into a payer's existing business processes.

Chapter 7 provides further details about the product suites of Edocs and docSense.

4.1.11 *Distribution Channels and Online Account Management*

The distribution of summary account information to any end point is a complex process. Aggregation sites, such as Fidelity, Citibank, American Express, and other portals, make it easy for customers to view all of their electronic bills and statements in one place. The growing number of user enrollments at aggregation sites proves that customers want to choose where to view their online account information. The more choices that are offered to consumers to access their personal, financially significant account data, the more likely they are to leverage to a standard online account-management solution of the consolidator.

Built on the eaDirect online account management and billing platform, eaPost™ from Edocs uses a cartridge-based approach to distribute summary account information to any end point while driving customers back to the Web sites of consolidators and aggregators to securely manage their online experience. Distribution works the following way: Account information and customer identification data are exchanged between statement providers and portals using different technologies and customized data feeds. The result is a thin consolidation of information at the portals — a display of only summary-level account information — that is used to drive payers back to the biller's Web site to view account details and drive higher adoption rates.

Distribution of account information involves complex data-exchange standards, such as open financial exchange and interactive financial exchange (OFX and IFX, respectively; see Chapter 6 for more details), to facilitate the connection with aggregation networks. EaPost utilizes individual cartridges that encapsulate the data standards, protocols, and security models of each of the individual aggregation sites, allowing consolidators and portals to preserve their initial investments in EBPP. Distribution sometimes involves the use of screen-scraping technology that acts on behalf of the customer, a process where the aggregation site logs in as the actual customer to access online statement information. This process happens outside the biller's or consolidator's control, creating the potential for thousands of unnecessary hits that can put stress on the Web site under consideration. This product optimizes Web-site security and traffic flow by feeding account summary information electronically to the aggregator site, eliminating the need for scraping.

The eaPost product integrates with a variety of platforms, including eaDirect from Edocs, to distribute online account information to a wider audience through aggregation portals. It provides the leverage for one system to securely distribute electronic statement data to multiple delivery channels. Permission-based technology means that billers control the delivery process of data to the portals chosen by the biller. Usage reports allow analysis of which end points are most effective in reaching the customer (payer) base, eliminating the need to speculate on which channels provide the greatest return. The result is an optimal distribution strategy that creates more opportunities for payers to activate or interact with their accounts, thus boosting the number of payers opting for online payment to the biller.

Combinations of products and services also could represent an excellent solution for billers and consolidators. Southern California Edison is using a combination of CheckFree and Edocs products to support an electronic billing and payment service that enables residential and commercial consumers to view and pay their Edison bills over the Internet. The utility biller is using Edocs's BillDirect application to make monthly statements available online at CheckFree's electronic billing and payment distribution sites, such as First Union, Charles Schwab, Bank One, Merrill Lynch, and others. The utility biller has also selected e-Bill™ from CheckFree, which utilizes direct distribution, a valuable business model linking customer data to CheckFree distribution end points, such as online financial institutions, brokerages, portals, and financial software. This product also provides enhanced customer care, event tracking, and Internet security features. BillDirect from Edocs is a complete, off-the-shelf software application enabling bill creation, customer enrollment, and statement delivery to service providers like CheckFree. In addition, the Check-Free Genesis 2000™ platform gives clients the ability to offer consumers an electronic billing and payment service that integrates electronic bills, "pay everyone" capabilities, and an infrastructure that can scale to support millions of households.

Chapter 7 provides further details about the product suites of CheckFree and Edocs.

4.1.12　Personalization

Personalization is extremely important to attract and hold the attention of payers. The surest way to hold their attention is to talk about things that interest them. Those simple, yet powerful, ideas can transform customer communications of billers and consolidators into in-depth customer connections that inspire action, build loyalty, reduce churn, and lead to greater selling opportunities.

The InTouch™ suite of products from DST Output for personalization management allows customers to segment and target the customer database at the most definitive level that maintained data allow. Customers can define audiences, select or create personalized statement messages, design or select promotional and educational inserts, and write personalized letters. The InTouch solution suite also allows the user to schedule campaigns to coincide with other marketing activities.

Chapter 7 provides further details about software products and services.

4.2　Electronic-Component Composition

Document management is a marketing tool. Many technological improvements — automated-teller machines (ATM) for banking, online interacts with call centers, online portfolio management, and others — improve operational efficiencies at the price of distancing billers from customers. Business documents such as statements, letters, notices, bills, and invoices can fill the gap between customers and billers. These documents are often the only communications that customers consistently receive from billers and consolidators, so they need to serve as corporate ambassadors. In addition, documents must persuade, inform, sell, collect receivables, and differentiate a company from its competitors. The monthly statements can be used to carry targeted cross-selling messages. People open and read documents sent from organizations they already do business with, especially statements and bills. These documents can become the ultimate selling medium. Well-designed, individualized statements, especially those that use color effectively, will help differentiate billers from each other.

Using DOC1™ from Group1, various data- and conditional-processing capabilities let billers tailor information to the needs of payers. Output to the Web can be in HTML, XML, and PDF formats. Information technology (IT) professionals are expected to develop document applications quickly and to keep those applications current as the business changes. These challenges tax even the most experienced subject-matter experts. The task is especially difficult for companies using a legacy print application or inflexible billing systems. The script-based and code-intensive programming techniques of the past cannot accommodate today's time-to-market requirements. Applications are often tied to a hardware platform or a specific printing environment. Many do not leverage the capabilities of electronic printing, such as color, data-driven graphics, and conditional messaging. DOC1 addresses the need to

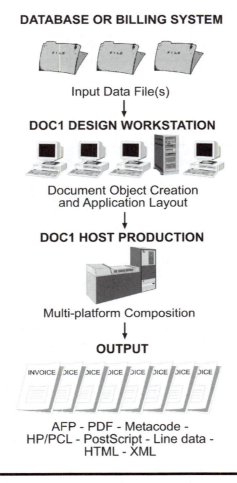

DATABASE OR BILLING SYSTEM

Input Data File(s)

DOC1 DESIGN WORKSTATION

Document Object Creation
and Application Layout

DOC1 HOST PRODUCTION

Multi-platform Composition

OUTPUT

AFP - PDF - Metacode -
HP/PCL - PostScript - Line data -
HTML - XML

Figure 4.2   Document development process using DOC1.

produce high-impact documents quickly and to deliver those documents across the enterprise.

The DOC1 system has two primary components, a design workstation running Windows NT and a multiplatform production engine. Document applications can be easily created on a PC and then hosted in any environment: mainframe, client/server, or PC. Figure 4.2 shows the document development process using DOC1. The DOC1 design workstation simplifies document creation and speeds development and testing. Users develop the application on the PC using intuitive drag-and-drop techniques similar to those found in desktop-publishing packages. This product gives full control over typography, alignment, and graphics, extending these desktop-publishing techniques far beyond page layout. Users also control complex document behavior — pagination, production control, conditional processing, and error reporting — using the same drag-and-drop techniques.

There is no need to build and maintain two applications, one for paper bills and one for e-bills. With DOC1 Digital™ from Group1, billers and consolidators define and access data only once for both print and Web. The

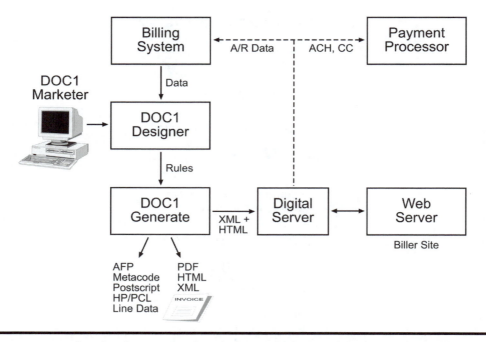

Figure 4.3   Joint development and maintenance of paper-based and electronic documents.

product allows users to design and maintain logic and layout for both printed and online documents, simultaneously. Users can also drive coordinated marketing messages and campaigns down both paper-based and electronic channels with a single communication platform. This integrated EBPP approach saves time and reduces costs throughout the whole process, including maintenance and change management. Figure 4.3 illustrates the entire process.

DOC1 Archive™ from Group1 is a scalable, intelligent software solution that allows for real-time indexing, storage, compression, and retrieval of high-resolution business documents regardless of their age or size. This product increases productivity, reduces costs, and enhances customer service. The principal attributes of this solution are:

- Provides subsecond response time for document retrieval through the interactive Windows-based client
- Provides seamless integration with precision display and high performance into existing Web environments
- Renders documents on-the-fly in the customer's preferred viewing format, eliminating the need for proprietary viewers or software plug-ins
- Provides portable document format (PDF) for local printing
- Accepts line data in addition to IBM AFP (Appletalk filing protocol), Xerox DJDE, and Xerox Metacode natively without the need of conversion tools
- Supports thousands of concurrent users with no degradation in performance

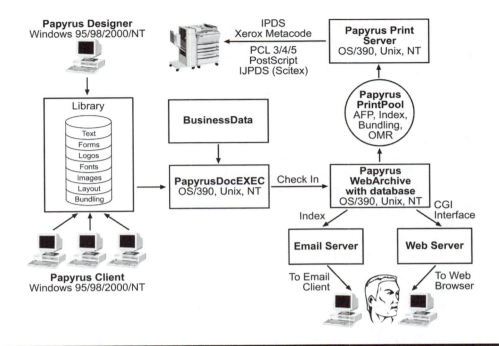

Figure 4.4   Effective customer communication using Papyrus solutions.

- Advanced compression algorithms enable massive quantities of documents to be stored online using industry-standard disk arrays
- Eliminates the need for expensive, high-maintenance storage devices, such as optical disk drives, CD juke boxes, and tape silos
- Provides high-resolution viewing, so even the smallest point sizes are legible
- Minimizes application maintenance, since the DOC1 Archive Server automatically distributes enhancements/updates to client software without requiring dedicated administrative personnel

This product can successfully be integrated with a wide variety of business applications, including customer call centers, customer relationship management, and enterprise resource planning.

The key to EBPP success in the current market is a combination of paper-based and electronic documents. Suppliers with a great deal of experience with composition of paper documents have an excellent chance of succeeding with EBPP. Papyrus™ is another example of a software solution that focuses on this combination of print and electronic billing streams. Figure 4.4 illustrates the Papyrus system for communicating with customers through the creation of highly personalized bills for Web delivery and automated print. The most important process steps are:

- Document development: All document resources are developed centrally with Papyrus Designer on a PC platform including "prompting" requests for the end users, if required. Prompts can be defined to

control the layout, execute dynamic text editing and new text generation, and to call external elements such as text and images.

- Messaging: The Papyrus Client is used to edit text elements in a front-
  end document application. To ensure that only authorized text elements
  go into production, a sign-off based on the "four-eye principle" can be
  implemented. All documents generated by the users are stored in a
  transfer area to be picked up by the application.
- Bill formatting: The input data are selected and transferred to the server.
  The layout/forms and text elements are dynamically loaded by
  DocEXEC to be formatted with the billing data into an AFP file. In case
  of missing elements, an error log file is generated.
- Web delivery: The document file produced in batch is split up according
  to the AFP index information and checked into the Papyrus WebArchive.
- E-mail notification: The customer (payer) is informed by an e-mail
  notification that his/her bills are available on the Web site. These e-
  mail notifications are sent at night and contain a hyperlink to the Web
  site.
- Internet viewing: The payer logs on through the corporate Web site,
  where security and authorization is performed by the transaction server.
  The WebArchive interface generates an HTML page of available bills
  for this payer. Once the user selects bills from WebArchive, the documents are converted immediately to PDF/GIF formats for viewing.
- Output management: In cases where the payer does not pick up his/
  her bills via the Internet, they are checked out from the WebArchive
  after a few days and transferred to the Papyrus PrintPool. Each night
  a bundling and sorting run produces an AFP file with enveloping optical
  mark recognition (OMR) markers, which is transferred to high-speed
  printing and mailing.

DST Output is a company that designs, produces, and delivers bills,
statements, and documents with high-quality marketing impact. Whether billers
deliver their data via a single data feed or multiple data streams, the integrated
network of DST Output is capable of delivering all mission-critical communications across one or multiple channels. It delivers more than 2 billion print
and electronic customer communications annually with near 100% reliability
and accuracy. The company operates through collaborative partnerships with
its clients. Through a process of discovery and knowledge sharing, it helps
companies develop communications programs that address specific, identified
business issues. Selecting from the most comprehensive offering of integrated
communications products and services, the company allows billers to complement or replace in-house communications production capabilities. The
following example shows the benefits of redesign.

Attributes before redesign:

- Plain base-paper stock
- Poor utilization of white space
- Unclear summary date
- Ineffective display of marketing messages

Attributes after redesign:

- Significant paper and postal cost savings with more images per sheet
- Attractive summary and detail pages
- Use of eye-catching icons
- Convergence of multiple products/services on one statement
- Customized and colorful logo and preprint
- More detail lines per image

DST Output is a communications solutions company reaching many homes and business every month with high-impact statements, bills, financial communication products, marketing collateral, and educational materials. By offering an integrated print and electronic network capable of delivering communications across multiple channels, this company strengthens the relationships between its clients and their customers. Because each client is unique, each DST Output communications solution is tailored to the exact needs of the company and its markets.

4.3 Content Authoring and Deployment

Chapter 2 describes the principal steps of EBPP. Content authoring and deployment are key stages of bill presentment. These stages include the following major tasks:

- Creating content
- Reviewing content
- Approving content
- Changing content
- Deploying content

Operational support includes in-depth recommendations for site and page design and implementation. The most important items addressed are as follows (Terplan, 2001):

4.3.1 Site and Page Design and Management

4.3.1.1 Site Design Considerations

4.3.1.1.1 Site Navigation

There are two points to consider when constructing the navigation layout for a Web site: (1) the structure of the information and (2) how to provide access to that information. First, the layout of the site is usually the most difficult part of the site design process, particularly if a lot of information will be accessible from the site. Adequate time must be put into designing the structure of the information to allow easy access for all users. Second, navigation tools must be clear and easy to use as well as functional within all types of browsers that will be used by the target audience. Navigational design must consider all of the same factors as many other graphical user interfaces (GUI). Since movement within a Web site is typically nonlinear, navigational menus should be planned to allow users quick access to any part of the site.

4.3.1.1.2 Content Organization by Menus

A user's ability to move through a Web site and find the information or functions he is searching for plays an important role in determining how successful a site is. Menus and submenus are powerful tools in the design of a Web site. In the same way that menus are used in traditional Windows-based design, HTML menus can be used to subdivide and group relevant content to guide the user to topics of interest. The use of more than four levels of menus forces the users to work too hard to find the information they are looking for. Using too few levels may be equally difficult to navigate, particularly when the information volumes grow. Three to four levels should generally provide appropriate depth and guidance for the user. However, because of the varying content of sites, this is a flexible guideline. The menu structure for the site should be continually evaluated and improved as the site grows.

4.3.1.1.3 Interaction Models

There are many ways to organize information contained within a Web site. The term *interaction model* refers to the structure that is implemented to allow the user access to the various pages within a site. The type of model best suited to a particular page will depend on the content and complexity of the information that the page presents. There are a number of interactions models in use. These models can be used independently or in combination throughout a site. These models are:

- Table of contents: This approach is taken from printed books. Users can easily find the headings they are looking for and then hyperlink directly to that page. This type of access is useful for sites that provide textual or encyclopedic information.
- Image maps: This graphic technique uses an embedded linkage map that relates hot spots on the graphic to URLs (universal resource locators) within the Web site. In this way, the user can view the graphic and point and click to move to different locations on the site.
- Graphic menus: This technique provides the same visual approach to site navigation as image maps without incurring the disadvantages of employing one single large graphic mapped with links. Graphic menus employ smaller, simpler graphics that are strategically placed to provide visual impact.
- Search: Web-site searches provide a useful means of allowing a user to access information contained on a particular Web site. Some form of search facility is usually a requirement for larger sites.

■ Indexing: The Web index provides functionality similar to a book index, allowing a user to rapidly locate information pertaining to a specific key word or topic. It also can be used in combination with search.

4.3.1.2 Page Design Considerations

The actual layout of a Web page is highly dependent on the type of information that is being presented. This section provides some fundamentals of good page design.

4.3.1.2.1 Header

The header provides a user with access to commonly used functions within the company-wide intranet and clearly differentiates intranet content from Internet content. The standard header provides links for navigation to common functions via the following graphics:

■ Company logo: links to the company home page
■ Directory: links to the company's intranet directory Web site
■ Services: links to the company's intranet service page
■ Search: links to the company's search Web site
■ Help: links to the company's intranet help Web site

Pre-imaged mapped versions of the company's header are available on the intranet development and support site.

4.3.1.2.2 Footer

The footer gives the user important information about the page and provides consistency within the company's intranet. The standard footer contains usually the following:

■ A standard horizontal rule as a separator
■ Copyright statement
■ Statement regarding content ownership with an optional e-mail link to the designated page maintainer or webmaster, not the name of an individual
■ Date of the last revision

4.3.1.2.3 Page Size

Page size must be designed with the actual usable space of the browser window in mind. Typically, this would be the lowest amount of useable space for the standard browser configuration in a 640×480 video monitor resolution. When designing a Web page, designers want to limit horizontal scrolling as much as possible. Keeping the width of Web pages to less than 600 pixels (using tables) makes it much easier for users to navigate information. In some cases, horizontal scrolling is normal and acceptable.

An acceptable size for an intranet page is 100,000 bytes or less. This limit includes all of the images that are embedded on the page. This size will keep performance within acceptable limits for both local area networks (LAN) and wide area networks (WAN).

4.3.1.2.4 Home Page

The layout and design of the home page of any Web site is extremely important. Besides being the first thing a user sees upon entering a site, it defines the organizational structure and tone for the entire site. Some essential elements for every home page include:

- Visually appealing design
- Overview of site content
- Links to contents of site
- Company/organization identifying information

4.3.1.2.5 Page Layout

HTML or XML does not provide graphic designers with the flexibility they are accustomed to in existing page-layout and editing programs (e.g., MS Word, Adobe PageMaker, Quark XPress). However, this does not mean that complex and functional applications cannot be created using HTML or XML. Rather, one must realize that, when used inconsistently, the graphic and typographic controls of HTML or XML can result in inconsistent designs.

To avoid a haphazard look in their documents, designers should take care in how graphics are placed and organized. A consistent style will also allow for a consistent conversion from non-HTML documents. It is better to use simple icons and images instead of complex ones. Navigation tools should be kept in a consistent place.

4.3.1.2.6 Text Style

Text needs to be short and to the point. Text should be organized in sections of a paragraph. When browsing, visitors tend to scan rather than read. They are usually searching for information and appreciate when sections are placed in logical order. Similar ideas or facts should be presented in a consistent way, with the same components presented in the same way in the same order. Consistency is a very important consideration in Web design.

4.3.1.2.7 Graphics

Graphics images should be used where appropriate to help the user navigate and find information more quickly. Graphics also provide a "look" to the site that will help users to identify where they are. Graphics should not be overused for internal publishing applications. Whereas external marketing Web sites often are graphically intense to catch attention, use of graphics in internal Web sites should be based on ease of navigation and usage. The type, size, and location of graphics throughout a site should be presented in a consistent manner; items of similar importance should have the same size and type of graphic. If a larger-than-normal graphic is used, the user is likely to assume that there is some additional significance. Often, the visibility and intended use of the site will dictate the level of graphics required for the site.

Graphic images should be designed for a 256-color resolution. A common mistake that professional graphic designers make is designing with higher resolutions and greater color depth than the deployment environment. The color scheme that was designed in 16-bit color may look bad in 256 colors or even worse in 16-color environments. Design should follow the requirements of the target environment.

Most images are between 10 and 30 kilobytes. The exception would be image maps on navigational pages or photographic images, which should be around 50 kilobytes. One of the drawbacks with using images on a network is the time it takes to download very large files. Images must be kept as small as possible and fit within the size of the browser's viewable space. The best formats for image files are GIF and JPG, both compressed formats. The GIF format is better for smaller graphic or line-art images.

4.3.1.2.8 Local Navigation Elements

Each Web site should include a site map showing a detailed layout of the site with links to all possible sections and documents. Each page within a Web site should include a link to the site-map page. Users can link to a Web site or Web page from a number of different places (navigation page, search results page, hyperlinks, etc.). The site-map page gives users a quick and easy way to locate the information they need. On long pages, the user may want to quickly go to the top of the page to view the table of contents or other introductory information. The top-of-the-page icon helps users more quickly navigate to the top of the current page.

4.3.1.2.9 Links

While many Web sites incorporate graphics to support navigation, text links still play an important role in ensuring the usability of a site. Working with text in HTML is easy. In general, because it is easy to create links and change font types, there are several mistakes commonly made. Several guidelines that aid in ensuring a site's readability and usability are listed below:

- Design the page for scanners of information, not for readers.
- Explain the page's benefit above the fold.
- Use bold typeface to draw attention to a particular section.

- Avoid typing in all caps; it is difficult to read.
- Links must be underlined in addition to being colored to assist users who may be color-blind or using black-and-white monitors.
- Avoid blinking text; it is difficult to read and annoying.

A typical Web page provides both informational text and links to more-specific information. Most people are looking for visual clues to whether a page is useful or interesting enough to be worth reading. If they do not find what they want quickly, they will move to another site. One of the difficulties in using text for navigational purposes is the wording of the links. Proper wording of the text allows users to jump to a new topic or continue reading without losing their place.

All links to default pages should be set with a trailing "l." This eliminates the problem of DNS (domain name server) names turning into IP (internet protocol) addresses. By default, the Web browser converts any hyperlink that does not include a Web page (such as a link to a home page) to the default page for the server. However, depending on the browser, this may convert the DNS name into the physical IP address of the hosting server. If the DNS name is converted to an IP address and the user adds the page to his "favorites" folder, the URL will be stored with the IP address. If the IP address of the site changes, the bookmark will no longer work. To eliminate this problem, simply include a trailing "l" on any link that does not include a page file name.

Abstracts and summaries are very helpful for large pages or large graphics. Whenever possible, users should have the opportunity of linking to further information if desired. Very large files or files that are not in a useable browser format (e.g., ZIP files, BMP files, etc.) should have a link that allows the user to download the file to his local PC.

4.3.1.2.10 Other Graphic Elements

Separators are graphic or possibly textual elements that are used to break up or visually divide the contents of a single Web page. Separators can be as simple as a horizontal line to a shadowed line graphic or an actual image file. The use of separators helps in visually varying the subject matter on the page. While separators can be effective, it is important to remember that separators should not distract the user from page content. Rather, their purpose is to divide the information into logical groupings.

HTML and XML provide tags for standard information-gathering controls like radio buttons, drop-down boxes, and exit boxes. In general, guidelines created for traditional GUI-based development apply to Web page design. Web-site designers should keep the following considerations in mind:

- The eye moves from left to right when reading (in most countries), so text should be left-aligned.
- Exit boxes should be similarly sized and left-aligned.
- The tab key should move the user downward through the page.
- Controls should be evenly spaced and aligned when possible.

- A default button should be provided.
- Mixed-case text should always be used; all capitals are annoying and difficult to read.

Bullets are used in HTML and XML in the same manner that they are used in traditional word processing to define a list of items. While textual bullets are fine for use on Web pages, there are also many available graphic bullets that will add just a touch of color to an ordinary Web page.

4.3.1.2.11 Background and Text Colors

The use of appealing backgrounds and text colors can add an artistic look to Web sites, but the way colors are used also affects the usability of the site. Designers must be wary of improperly using color, as colors may have different meanings to different people, and some users may be unable to distinguish some colors clearly. The following guidelines for using color in designing user interfaces on the Web are helpful:

- Color is second only to movement in attracting attention.
- Three colors are sufficient for a color scheme.
- Specific colors should be used carefully.
- Shades of red attract attention, while the retina responds to yellow the fastest.
- Blue is more difficult to focus on, making unsaturated blue a good choice for backgrounds.
- Gaudy, unpleasant colors and combinations of red/green, blue/yellow, green/blue, and red/blue should be avoided.
- If backgrounds are going to be used, they should be either a light-colored pattern or a solid color.

4.3.1.2.12 Printing

When the nature of a site is documentation, users must have the ability to print individual Web pages or an entire site's content. This can easily be accomplished by adding a link to a printable form of the entire document. Documents are provided in multiple formats, such as Microsoft Office formats, to accommodate the maximum number of users.

4.3.1.3 *Summary of Site and Page Design and Management*

The guidelines for design and management of bill pages can be summarized as follows:

- Standardize page layout.
- Standardize links.
- Use one or more interaction models, such as table of contents, image maps, graphic menus, search tool, indexing.

- Provide navigation tools for users.
- Segment long documents into smaller ones.
- Provide a local search utility on sites that contain many pages or a significant amount of data.
- Design pages for rapid and slow search.
- Use text pages for users with narrow bandwidth.
- Test pages and links before practical use.
- Test content on different browsers.
- Use webmaster-recommended templates to create new pages.
- Use abstracts or summaries for large text pages or images, giving users the option of linking to detailed information.
- Create a link to download a concatenated file of a series of Web pages so that a user can print an entire document rather than printing multiple Web pages.
- Use backgrounds carefully, making sure that users can easily read the text of a page when backgrounds are used.
- Use GIFs for small graphics (where there are a limited number of colors) and JPEGs (Joint Photographic Experts Group) for photographic images.
- Manage links: When a user links to another site listed on the biller's Web page, the owners of the linked site must be informed so that they can notify the biller's webmaster if the link changes.

The majority of products supporting content authoring and deployment are capable of creating optimized content. Usually, however, these features do not evaluate the performance of pages under normal and stressed conditions, caused by many payers hitting the site — supported by server farms — simultaneously. Site performance optimization tools address the dynamic aspects. They not only check for incompleteness and errors, but also try to repair problems. It would be optimal to test the performance of Web applications on public and private Web sites before they are deployed. Such testing applications are supposed to help in the following areas:

- Predict how sites will react to numerous hits from end users
- Monitor application interactions
- Measure Web access performance from the end user's perspective
- Correlate events with load profiles
- Analyze impacts of traffic load on selected clients trying to access a Web site
- Predict the performance of Web servers under stress
- Help to optimize Web servers and bandwidth for traffic profiles

4.4 Customer Relationship Management (CRM)

An intensified customer focus can facilitate more effective and efficient customer care, which in turn can reduce churn, acquire new customers, increase revenue per subscriber, and provide growth in high-value segments. Historically, the communications and utilities industries have focused their investments on services, networks, and internal operational efficiency. In a regulated environment, where the goal was universal access and the ability to serve all customers equally well, the industry naturally focused its resources and attention on building efficient infrastructures and systems rather than understanding and forging relationships with various customer segments. Three trends are pushing service providers to focus on customers and to develop deeper customer relationship management (CRM) capabilities that take a more effective and profitable approach to reaching those customers:

1. Continued deregulation is opening previously protected local and global markets, providing new opportunities and new challenges. In truly competitive segments, such as long distance and wireless, market shares for incumbents have dropped 40% or more in a relatively short period.
2. Technology-driven markets provide opportunities for communications companies to expand their offerings, but they also give consumers alternatives. For example, Internet telephony is emerging as a long-term potential competitive threat to service providers' core competency. Many customers are giving up their local phone connections in favor of wireless — a trend that is maturing in many parts of the world.
3. Recent surveys from market research companies show that local, long distance, cable and cellular/PCS (personal communication service) providers are falling below customers' expectations on pricing, simplicity of pricing structures, and customer service.

Compared with customer relationship management, tangible projects such as billing provide instant gratification. But while CRM leads to less churn and increased revenue, its value is difficult to quantify over the short term. CRM helps to focus resources on high-value, high-potential customers while also treating customers that may be of low future value to the provider appropriately by not bombarding them with marketing messages and, perhaps, taking a more passive retention approach. It is important to realize that CRM is not a product; it is a strategy that needs products to become successful. It is not one or a set of application products. It is very important that service providers understand that they cannot buy CRM in a box.

Customers interact with companies in many ways, and CRM depends on a number of specific capabilities within marketing, sales, and service. For top management trying to allocate resources, the broad array of CRM capabilities presents a bewildering range of options. In short, executives of service providers face a basic challenge: They need to invest in CRM capabilities, but they do not know where to invest to get the highest return or how to justify those investments. Many initiatives are undertaken based on experience and intuition rather than on reliable financial data.

Determining the business drivers for CRM implementations is an important first step. The drivers can include churn reduction, geography expansion, and market-share exploitation, among others. Beyond classifying customers, data can also be used for detailed analysis, including:

- Customer profiling:
    - Descriptive segmentation and tracking
    - Residential customers: geographic location, demographics, lifestyles
    - Business customers: industry code, total revenues, head count
- Advanced analysis:
    - Behavioral/predictive
    - Segmentation and tracking
    - Time series, regression, induction trees, and modeling tools
- Guided and *ad hoc* analysis:
    - Dynamic assessment and tracking

Most of these techniques use real-time aggregation, rotation, filtering, ranking, and custom calculation with a graphical, easy-to-use interface.

Service providers who rely solely on their billing systems for CRM are missing an opportunity to use publicly available demographics information. The second area of neglect is credit and risk management. For instance, customers may be high-value from a marketing and up-sell perspective while posing a tremendous credit risk. Service providers are also missing loyalty-program opportunities and the direct customer response that comes with it. Billing data give service providers a purely transactional view of the customer, and customers are not mere transactions. Customers are living, breathing people who might have service problems and questions and preferred buying patterns to whom providers can up-sell or cross-sell or deter from churning, but sellers cannot obtain these objectives by just using billing data. This is why billing-applications vendors are aggressively trying to position themselves upstream of the biller or as an added-value part of the billing stream. Billing is about bits and bytes, time stamps, and receivables. A customer relationship is about listening, understanding, changing, and responding appropriately. Billing data are narrow and capture only a piece of the information needed to understand and appreciate the customer. Timely payments are no guarantee that customers and service providers have an optimal relationship.

One of the biggest challenges for service providers is that their organizations are structured around business and infrastructure rather than customer support. This is especially true of incumbent service providers. The result is that customers end up facing monolithic infrastructure operations and business operations that split their customer-facing responsibilities. If customers are experiencing technical disconnects, they are referred to an infrastructure support desk; if the disconnect is due to nonpayment, customers are referred to business operations. The ultimate result is that customers end up with a fragmented customer experience.

CRM is frequently considered as an additional cost because its benefits cannot be easily quantified. This may change with the arrival of anticipated developments in data warehouses and data-mining capabilities. Data-mining tools will provide the opportunity to conduct *ad hoc* analysis on special subscriber segments. The significance of EBPP for CRM and vice versa is obvious. As a best-case scenario, CRM capabilities in an EBPP solution should be considered when evaluating the overall solution. CRM is undoubtedly an additional benefit and opportunity when deploying EBPP. Independent of the business model selected, the key elements of the solution should include (The Phillips Group, 2001):

- Composition/content formatting: This gives the billing service provider the opportunity to generate personalized bills that contain targeted marketing information. Targeted marketing shares a close relationship with CRM and is included here as a result to provide better customer service.
- Management and tracking capabilities: This gives service providers and billers the option of tracking log-on time, bill retrieval history, and other information for targeted marketing.
- CSR information integration: This prepares the CSRs for the most up-to-date version of the bill combined with the consumer's most-recent retrieval activity, thus speeding up and facilitating dispute management and increasing user satisfaction.
- Extensible application programming interfaces: This facilitates deep integration between customer care, billing engines, and CRM systems.
- Customer-centric workflow capabilities: This facilitates integration with billing applications to allow a single view of a service provider's or biller's customers, products, and back-office and front-office procedures.
- Real-time capabilities: This promotes faster dispute/problem turnaround times and allows Web-based applications to be used in real time.
- Use of rules-based engines: This facilitates creation and implementation of new marketing and sales strategies based on customer information, customer queries, and traffic profiles taken from the site. Rules-based engines are faster than table-driven systems.

Product combinations are very popular in the CRM field. Internet billing and payment based on BillDirect™ from Edocs is integrated with eFrontOffice CRM™ from Clarify Inc. (now an Amdocs company). This integration enables companies across multiple industries, including communications, utilities, and financial services, to improve customer loyalty, create new revenue generation opportunities, and better leverage online customer interactions.

4.5 Use of EBPP for Business-to-Business (B2B) Relationships

4.5.1 Concepts

Current B2B electronic delivery and payment systems focus primarily on the biller side of the invoice-to-pay process. Most lack payer-centric features that allow payers to view their invoices in one place and to provide online management of their accounts-payable workflow (dispute resolution, order

Table 4.1   Comparison of Two Basic B2B Approaches

	Recurring Purchase	*Purchase Order*
Industries	Primarily for services	Primarily for products
Relationships	Supports ongoing relationships with business customers	Must support ongoing and "spot" relationships
Accounting	Balance-forward accounting	Requires integration to handle open-invoice accounting
Dispute resolution	Disputes handled directly off the invoice, and the invoice is compared with the service used or received	Disputes handled by comparing the invoice to receipt of goods/shipping documents and the purchase order/contract terms

reconciliation, payment authorization workflow, reporting and analysis). In addition, most models of EBPP solutions require payers to pull their invoices from the biller rather than having the invoice automatically delivered to them. Despite these hindrances to payer adoption, the B2B invoice-to-pay market has been increasing significantly. In recurring-purchase-based B2B, invoice presentment is driven by the passage of time, i.e., a monthly invoice. In purchase-order-based B2B, invoice presentment is driven by an order or series of orders. Table 4.1 compares the two basic B2B approaches; comparison criteria include industries, relationships, accounting, and dispute resolution.

There is a larger future revenue potential with B2B than with business-to-consumer (B2C) or person-to-person (P2P) payment, even though B2B generates 70% fewer invoices. This is due in part to the larger average amount of each invoice but, more importantly, to the relative complexity of B2B invoices themselves and the correspondingly complex processing workflow. The savings potential for both billers and payers is huge, with payers realizing the majority of direct benefit. However, billers gain the secondary benefit of improving customer relationship ties to the payer, and higher integration may yield even tighter bonds. Vendors who can offer enhanced payer-side features will surely lead the market. If billers and payers are to get the full value from electronic delivery and payment systems, they will have to integrate them with their existing accounts-receivable (A/R) and accounts-payable (A/P) systems, respectively. There is also increasing demand for integration with enterprise resource planning (ERP) systems, banks, and payment service providers. This suggests that the major systems-integration firms will share significantly in the B2B boom.

The coming changes in the B2B EBPP market stand to impact independent software vendors (ISV), BSPs, consolidators, billers, payers, e-procurement vendors, net markets, and banks. Billers and payers prefer a model that does not distinguish between requisition-to-order and invoice-to-pay but instead delivers flexible, dynamic, end-to-end business processes enabled by internal and external integration. Each would prefer that the other bear the cost of implementation. Currently, independent software vendors partnered with systems integrators are in the best position to meet market demands. However, there is no doubt that banks will pursue this market aggressively as well.

With a B2B solution, several factors should be considered. The most important ones are (The Phillips Group, 2001):

- Notification: The B2B system should offer some form of notification that informs both the biller and payer when to take action with regard to a bill, e.g., notifying the payer that a bill is ready for review. Because the B2B EBPP user is likely to receive a great number of bill reminders, user-enabled deactivation should be supported.
- Presentment: The presentment module determines the ease of invoice management, which is extremely important in the B2B arena. Because users are likely to receive invoices across several accounts, have numerous invoices in single accounts, or have stand-alone invoices and line items, a flexible invoice-management system is invaluable. The ability to sort and categorize by line items should also be supported within the presentment module.
- Invoice separation: As bills are likely to be very large, the ability to separate invoices into sub-invoices should be an essential consideration. This allows breakdown by division, department, or individual. These edited invoices can then be directed through the hierarchy of the company's employee organization for approval by respective departments, groups, and individuals.
- Payer-controlled workflow: The bill payer must have control of routing bills from department to group to individual. This requires a flexible user interface that allows user-defined changes to the workflow and simple workflow-management capabilities. Without this provision, information can be lost as it moves along the human chain in the payer's company.
- Electronic payment: Presentment without payment is hardly applicable in the B2B arena, as payment surrounding B2B is extremely complex. Partial automation of the billing process is inefficient if the processes surrounding payment must be made separately. Functionality should include multiple payment options (e.g., full, partial, and scheduled payments) and a selection of payment processing options.
- Online dispute management: This should be linked to the workflow management of the B2B solution. Online dispute management should allow the bill payer to dispute bills with the biller and with parties within the payer's organization. Organizational dispute management allows mistakes within the payer's organization to be rectified while within the workflow process (e.g., misallocation of funds). Standardized dispute codes enable a faster resolution time and allow tracking the progress of any disputes as they pass through the rectification process. This is important when one considers the size of B2B billing events and the number of disputes that may be running concurrently within any one organization. Open-text capabilities on the dispute forms

should be provided to allow detailed description of problems and aid effective communication.

- Reporting and analysis: Analysis capabilities are particularly important within a B2B system due to the increased level of payment and service complexity. Analysis capabilities should include both long- and short-term expense tracking, system usage, and dispute tracking.
- Integration with existing systems: System integration is extremely important in the B2B market due to the degree of legacy investments made by B2B participants into existing applications. B2B companies will also have complex interoperation issues between their ERP, CRM, and accounting applications.

EBPP is new to the B2B world. As expected at this early stage, very few understand the full benefits it affords to both sides of the billing equation. Biller benefits include:

- Significant cost savings through reduced paper and postage
- Streamlined internal processes
- Reduced call-center traffic and customer service costs
- Automated dispute resolution to reduce customer service demands and increase payer control
- Less human intervention, which reduces data errors
- Specific targeting of messaging
- Competitive advantage in the marketplace

The growing B2B market may ultimately embrace EBPP because of the potential for substantial savings on financial and human resources, but adoption of EBPP comes with its own set of complexities and problems. The principal problems are (The Phillips Group, 2001):

- Invoice (bill) complexity: The B2B invoice is usually extremely complex, making online presentment very difficult. Invoices can contain thousands of lines and cross many different products and services. The file size, as a result, is likely to be huge, thus limiting the delivery mechanisms.
- Payer workflow and approval processes: Once the bill is presented, the organizational hierarchy of the customer (payer) and the approval processes must be walked through. Complex hierarchies are not unusual.
- Dispute handling: A number of items may be challenged in large bills. This is particularly true in the B2B arena. Disputes can occur within the payer companies or between the biller and the payer. With such a degree of potential disputes, tracking the progress of the rectification and dispute processes is complex and complicates efficient credit application.
- Automating payments: Payers authorize large, complex payments using a number of different payment systems, including ACH, credit cards,

bank cards, and other similar systems. The B2B solution must support all of these options and be capable of allocating each part of the payment to each respective system. This problem is aggravated when partial payments and ongoing disputes are added to the complexity.

■ Integration: In the B2B market, the EBPP solution must be capable of very close integration with existing billing, accounting, and customer service functions. The cost of changing these back-end infrastructures is prohibitive because of the size, complexity, and cost of these infra-structures.

In terms of competition, nobody should underestimate the impacts of existing electronic data interchange (EDI) infrastructures. They are in place and working well between trading partners. They may not compete in terms of flexibility, but they do in terms of stability and scalability between existing partners. A key advantage for EBPP over EDI is that it can offer other services beyond mere electronic payment and presentation, the most valuable being customer relationship management.

4.5.2 Reasons for Biller Resistance

Keeping the end goal in mind — substantial savings on financial and human resources — is important as business partners begin developing an EBPP solution. It is also important to acknowledge that the concerns of employees of billers and payers are valid. Despite the best intentions, new business processes disrupt business and threaten customer relationships. With a subject like billing, already a delicate issue, the potential for problems is heightened.

Billers express a variety of concerns about B2B electronic billing. Primarily, their concerns revolve around customers' responses to new business processes, the need for cross-functional teams, and a lack of information about electronic billing or a lack of communication about the specific billing initiative being contemplated.

4.5.2.1 Sales Force Concerns

The sales forces of billers, especially those who deal with the largest customers, have a very real fear that the move to electronic billing will upset their customers. At best, they see the change as a disruption that creates work and expenses for their customers. At worst, they fear customers will become upset and leave. By including the sales staff in the development process, management can keep them informed and enthusiastic about the benefits their customers will soon receive. Customers stand to benefit significantly from the move to electronic invoicing, since it will help them eliminate the costs to pay a paper bill, which may include photocopying, routing costs, and physical archiving. In addition, the customer will gain benefits of enhanced integration with their internal accounting processes and considerably streamlined workflows.

4.5.2.2   Incomplete Design

While an unfair stereotype, it is possible that an electronic solution designed and implemented by an IT department will be filled with engineering bells and whistles but lack the attractive, branded, easy-to-use interface necessary for a complete solution. Likewise, an electronic solution driven by the marketing division or the customer service department may be found lacking in the back-end tools that will make it work within the enterprise systems. Employing a cross-functional development team that integrates the perspectives of IT, sales and marketing, accounting, and customer service can prevent unbalanced design.

4.5.2.3   Lack of Internal Communication

An electronic solution that is brought online without adequate involvement and training of all employees, particularly the customer service department, can create resentment and confusion. Including an internal communications plan in the development process is an important ingredient to creating a smooth electronic transition.

4.5.2.4   Additional Drawbacks

One potential drawback is the use of tools that lack scalability. This is true of tools that originate with B2C solutions, which cannot support the very complex structures of B2B organizational structures of accounts receivable. Another issue is liability. As the EBPP transaction is carried out in cyberspace and sometimes between remote sites and remote countries, the issue of payment and fraud is always likely to be a problem. In the B2B application area, this problem is magnified by the size of the transactions likely to be undertaken. Security features such as authentication and encryption will help.

4.5.3 Avoiding the Pitfalls

The easiest way to get around potential problems is to be aware of them and build a plan that addresses each issue before it becomes a concern. The development plan should include a step-by-step process that goes beyond engineering issues and is inclusive of all internal stakeholders. The following five issues should be considered when building the development and implementation plan:

1. Build a team: Begin the project by pulling together a team that includes IT, accounting, marketing, sales, and customer service personnel. This will help in developing a well-rounded solution that takes in ease-of-use, information hierarchy, branding, support issues, existing internal systems, and other key ideas that will affect later adoption. While it is

more complicated to involve many people in the development process, it is far easier than working against opposition or cleaning up a mess later.

2. Test thoroughly: Enlist the help of a few of your best customers to participate in a pilot program. Roll it out and get as many bugs ironed out as possible with these groups first. Use them again later to test new features as they are added to the core solution.

3. Market the solution: Develop marketing and communications plans for internal employees and for customers. Sell the idea and generate excitement before the launch.

4. Reward salespeople: Provide incentives that encourage the sales force to speed adoption with their customers. Since they interact with customers more frequently than do other members of the company, they can be influential supporters of EBPP. On the other hand, if they are not educated and courted, salespeople can become the greatest detractors.

5. Train the teams: Train customer service teams in advance of the pilot programs and use their input in fine-tuning the system. Establish a realistic schedule that allows the service department to train thoroughly so that they can help put customers at ease.

D3™ (Digital Document Delivery) from docSense helps to speed up the payment process with customized electronic approval paths. A typical scenario consists of the following steps:

- D3 notifies the accounts-payable administrator via e-mail that invoice is available in customer's (payer) in-box.
- Administrator examines invoice and determines required review, approval, and routing process (e.g., roles, rules, thresholds, and permissions) and forwards to next reviewer.
- Reviewer analyzes invoice for accuracy and either approves or rejects it. Disputed line items can be identified and notes attached at any stage in workflow.
- D3 continues to forward invoice through routing list until all required approvals are completed and payment is initiated.
- If not approved, system returns invoice back to previous reviewer for corrective action.

BizCast™, the Avolent B2B EIPP solution, is a complete, feature-rich solution that meets the needs of business-to-business billers, service providers, and payers. BizCast includes the functionality required to import invoice data and present, process, and pay invoices. BizCast is designed to provide billers with the capability to reach a wide array of payers.

Chapter 7 provides more information on D3 from docSense and BizCast from Avolent.

4.6   Use of EBPP for Business-to-Consumer (B2C) Relationships

Billing and invoicing requirements are very different, depending on the type of biller-payer relationships. To highlight the differences between B2B and B2C, the drivers for the business relationship can be differentiated as follows:
    The B2B drivers are:

■ Cost reduction for billers and payers: Invoices are usually complex and volumes are high. Accurate and timely settlements, combined with mutual savings, are the principal targets.
■ Supply-chain integration: Both parties are interested in finding acceptable exchange points for their supply chains.
■ Better cash management: More predictable invoice distribution and payment schedules provide better control of liquidity on both sides of the transaction.
■ Workflow and invoice process optimization: Similarly to the supply-chain integration, workflows of both parties can be synchronized. In particular, accounts payable and accounts receivable are the interexchange points of the workflows.
■ Automation of dispute management: Invoices might not be accepted by the payers in their full content. Identification and separation of disputed items help to continue with the invoice processing. Disputed items can be further discussed and resolved by implementing business rules on both sides.

The B2C drivers are:

■ Focus on customer service: Each customer must be served well by using the right tools and procedures. This includes presentment options, payment options, data-mining capabilities, excellent support-desk service, and online dispute management. Consumers are different in terms of their expectations, so issuers of statements and bills should be flexible in their offers. Partnering with a software vendor who offers a core product that might be very easily customized would be an excellent choice.
■ Personalization: Customer profiles must be well known. If sufficient information is available, one-to-one campaign development and execution are successful. Getting the right data is time-consuming, but maintaining these data is easier. The receiver is the consumer, who is the target for all marketing campaigns.
■ Cross-sell/up-sell: Both are extremely important and successful when customer profiles are known. It may take some time to develop basic profiles. This is much different from business environments. The billing clerk of an organization is not impressed by sales and marketing alternatives presented by billers, but an individual consumer might find the right marketing message in a personalized campaign.

- Revenue generation: This is a future potential due to high volumes, but with very narrow profit margins. The right tools must be selected for ease of implementation and maintenance. Simplicity and unification are key. If enrollment is easy, security is guaranteed, and consumers are very likely to join. When applications by third-party vendors are reusable, issuers of statements and bills can still make money by offering EBPP options.
- Focus on recurring bills: Independently from the targeted industries, it is assumed that bills are not too complicated and that they are created, presented, and distributed periodically. Success rates may differ by industries. Telecommunications and mortgage bills might include interesting new offers for new services, service bundles, or new financing alternatives. On the other hand, recurring utility bills might not offer too many surprises for consumers.

E-billing can significantly reduce printing, paper, postage, and handling costs for billers and consolidators. Payers typically pay e-bills faster, which improves cash flow. Even more important, electronic statements are a customer's first point of contact with billers on the Web, making the e-bill a powerful component of an e-commerce strategy and the focus of effective customer relationship management.

D3 (Digital Document Delivery) from docSense is built to install swiftly, upgrade easily, and integrate smoothly with existing systems. Usually, payback periods are very short. D3 is vendor inclusive and channel neutral. It is a payer- and biller-friendly system that acts as a single-point gateway to multiple consolidators and portals. Customers can extract information and present bills via virtually any channel, such as:

- Web site of payers
- Bill consolidators like CheckFree or Spectrum
- Portals and consumer service providers like AOL and Yahoo

Despite the convenience of e-billing, a number of payers may prefer to receive their documents on paper. D3 helps to monitor and control both paper and digital production from one system. By plugging into the document production operation of customers, D3 is a gateway for producing statements in any combination of hard copy or electronic forms. Should electronic delivery fail or if a payer fails to respond online, D3 can easily switch channels and trigger hard-copy document preparation. D3 provides customers of billers and consolidators with more choices and convenience than before. They can go online and set up recurring payments, access account histories, and select from multiple payment options. Billers can use D3 to send out bill status messages, keeping payers informed every step of the way. D3 is also designed to work in conjunction with existing document composition, print-stream engineering, one-to-one marketing software, enterprise resource planning, and customer-relationship-management systems.

BillCast™ from Avolent is the premier enterprise application platform for Internet billing and interactive customer care in the electronic channel. Using BillCast, service companies can deliver superior billing and customer-care conveniences through the Internet, increasing customer satisfaction and reducing churn.

More details about these products from docSense and Avolent can be found in Chapter 7.

4.7 Use of EBPP in Small and Medium Enterprises (SME) and Small-Office and Home-Office (SOHO) Environments

The small business and small office/home office (SOHO) market has, until recently, been largely overlooked by many service organizations. Instead, they have paid more attention to large corporations with their wholesale offerings and individual consumers with their retail offerings. However, the small-business segment has emerged, in particular for financial service providers, as an attractive target. An increasing number of announcements have been aimed at small businesses. For instance, several financial services providers have launched small-business portals that provide electronic billing and payment (EBP) solutions, wrapped around other services such as access to credit, cash management, payroll services, account aggregation, and discounted office products, among others.

For small businesses, EBP provides a strong value proposition by streamlining their accounts-payable processes and enabling these organizations to simply click to approve their bills for payment, significantly reducing the amount of time spent paying their bills each month. In addition, EBP provides capabilities that enable small-business owners to access past bill-payment history online and download this payment information into their small-business accounting software. This is important, since many small businesses do not have accounting and finance departments, forcing owners to play several roles and ultimately taxing these time-pressed owners even further. EBP delivers better, more convenient, overall financial management of their operations. Savings for small businesses will come from two sides: savings through replacement of paper-based bills by electronic bills and, even more significantly, time savings.

Technology advances are also enabling financial services providers to serve small businesses more efficiently. The Web browser will serve as the centerpiece of the small-business electronic access medium, overtaking accounting software, commercial online services, and proprietary PC-based software.

For small businesses, it is important to select an EBP solution from their financial services providers that is tailored to the unique needs of their operating environment. To that end, the ability to be able to pay anyone electronically is a critical feature for small companies that want to maintain flexibility to do business with a variety of suppliers of all sizes. Meanwhile, some EBP solutions are now delivering other key small-business-centric features, such as extended payment information, including invoice number, invoice account, check number, and data regarding discounts and adjustments. It is critical that small businesses be able to capture these key payment fields electronically.

The ability for small businesses and for SOHOs to receive their bills electronically and to be able to export their billing history into small-business accounting packages goes a long way toward better overall record-keeping and operational management. Full integration with these small-business accounting solutions will ensure that their bill-payment activity is completely synchronized.

Increasingly, financial services providers are developing financial services portals aimed at meeting the needs of small businesses by offering a suite of products, including electronic billing and payment services. The bottom line is that EBP through a trusted financial services provider can deliver small businesses greater control over their financial operations by streamlining their accounts-payable processes. In the end, this will help these small businesses better manage their cash flow while saving them time and money that they can use to build better, more stable businesses.

4.8 Real-Time and Convergent Mediation

EBPP will drive real-time or near-real-time mediation. Mediation is the process of collecting raw usage data from a network, transforming it into useful information that describes a transaction, and then delivering that information to operational, business, and decision-support systems. In order to provide up-to-date billing details for payers, detail records for voice, data, and video must be collected and processed in real time. EBPP is the driver, but it is not the only application that needs actual and up-to-date data. Prepaid applications and fraud management require the same level of actuality as EBPP. EBPP is different to a certain extent because the rating process also should be executed in real time.

The information that is to be collected for EBPP depends on the billing model under consideration. One of the most important and fundamental concepts that anyone who wants to get into the business of delivering value-added services and content must understand is that there are many ways of structuring or rating consumption charges.

4.8.1 Models for Telecommunications Service Providers

Generally, rating schemes can be broken down into the following six categories:

1. Flat-rate: This is currently the most common approach for generic Internet access as well as sites offering paid content. Users pay a flat fee on a monthly or annual basis for access to the service or to download as much content as they like. Flat-rate pricing has been used as a market-share-capture strategy, since it can be very attractive to

customers. However, content and service providers realize that, over the long term, such pricing can inhibit profitability. Users have no incentive to restrain their consumption, so the service provider's costs are driven higher and higher. Undifferentiated pricing also makes it easier for customers to compare service providers, leading to high churn rates.

2. Service usage-based: The most common alternative to flat-rate pricing is to bill customers based on usage. Usage can be defined in terms of time (as with a voice service) or traffic volume (as with site-hosting services). Usage billing can also be done on a per-unit basis (i.e., every minute has a certain cost), a combination of flat rate and per unit (as with cellular service), a tiered basis (X cents per MB for the first 500 MB, Y cents per MB thereafter), or any one of several other rating schemes.

3. Service value: Where the value of the service being offered to the customer can be determined, service providers have the option to charge for that value, regardless of the cost to support the service. This works best where new services can be supported on existing infrastructures at little incremental cost. Services offered on this basis include intelligent network services, such as premium rate numbers, ring back, and network voice-mail (in the telephone world) and information and entertainment content services (in the broadband Internet market).

4. Session-based: This approach is more logical for streaming media and/ or special net events. Rather than being charged for a given amount of time or volume, the customer is charged for a single session that may vary in length and volume, depending on the particular content stream. The content provider's business model might also permit customers to buy several sessions for a single price and then purchase additional individual sessions for another price. Depending on the provider's business model, several executions of the same net event might not incur additional charges for a specified duration.

5. Per incident: With this type of billing, the customer is charged based on the occurrence of a specific incident or user action, such as clicking on a particular hyperlink. This approach is particularly applicable to content purchases such as MP3s or e-books. It can also be applied by caching services to their hosting-service-provider clientele (i.e., per-hit pricing). Again, customers may be offered multiple incidents for one flat rate — with additional incidents at an additional charge — or they may be offered discounts on their nth incident. This approach is also used for measuring clicks-per-million for advertisements.

6. Delivered service value: The value of a service is determined by a variety of factors, such as business benefit, novelty, and the availability of alternative options. As the market matures and more players become involved, downward pressure is applied to prices. To counter this, the service provider must find ways to maintain value by differentiating the service. One way to achieve this is to address the quality of the delivered service.

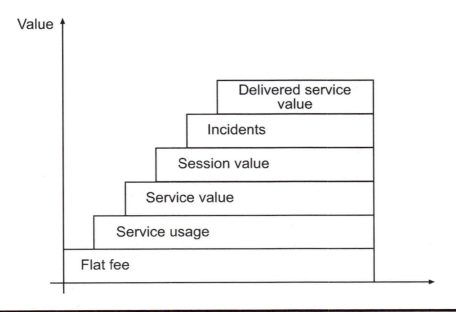

Figure 4.5   Service-charging models.

Figure 4.5 shows the service-charging models as a function of time (Bassa, 2002).

Many other parameters can affect a content- or service-ratings scheme. It may be that a premium level of service is available for a certain price or for users of other linked services. Sometimes, discount pricing may apply to users who sign up by a certain date, while those who sign up later pay a different price. Sometimes, geography may enter into the equation. Sometimes, an individual user's affiliation with a corporation or other organization may affect pricing.

Anyone with a strong marketing background can appreciate how flexible such rating schemes have to be. Marketers often need to develop and offer new value packages to customers for promotional purposes, and they often have to do it very quickly. In other words, to effectively support their business objectives, marketers need a service rating system that is highly dynamic and that allows new rating schemes to be implemented in near real time. The ability to rapidly activate and deactivate rating schemes is a crucial capability for anyone who wants to successfully and aggressively market Web-based content or services.

4.8.2 Data Sources for Usage-Based Billing in the Telecommunications Industry

Since there are no IP call-detail records (CDR) — as there are in the telecommunications industry — all Internet vendors cobble together usage data from a variety of sources, including remote monitoring (RMON) probes, RADIUS servers, Web-server log files, and router software agents. Three data sources that can be used in collecting customer utilization of Web-based services for billing purposes are:

1. URLs and site logs
2. Infrastructure instrumentation
3. Network-level data

4.8.2.1   URLs and Site Logs

Any company that wants to implement pay-to-play content or services will rely heavily on the visitor activity data captured by their Web site. These "clicks" are already used extensively for assessing the effectiveness of site design, as well as for other business purposes such as advertising and referral fees. However, the simple capture of URL data is insufficient for effective Web billing because the different elements of a URL can have very different meanings in a billing/business context. Data sources are:

- Domain names: This first rung in the URL ladder is obviously critical in determining that a user has accessed a given site. For Web hosting services, the domain name indicates which hosted customer's meter is now running. Some e-business sites also create separate domain names for individual services or content areas.
- File names and extensions: In contrast to domain names, file names and extensions allow providers to bill for specific content or types of content, such as video streams, MP3s, PDF files, etc. File types can each carry a different price tag. Individual files of the same type might even be processed differently from each other.
- Variables: Many sites give users the ability to enter some type of variable as part of their service or content request. A site offering information about various geographic areas, for example, may have "city" as one of its variables. Each time a new city is entered, another click on the billing meter may be required. Or a user might be allowed to check several cities for one price. Or users might be allowed to search cities in their own state for free and only be charged for cities outside the state. Regardless of how the charges are specifically structured, such a variable is a distinct element in the utilization and billing formulas.
- URL substrings: When the domain name, the file name and extension, and any variables from a URL are eliminated, the universal resource indicator (URI) is still available. This substring might also help define what type of content or service a user has accessed. Again, this URI might be important to a hosting service that is billing a customer separately for different content/service areas, or it might be used by the site's owner to differentiate a premium server or other value-added features.

4.8.2.2 Infrastructure Instrumentation

Networked infrastructures are built with a variety of devices, such as routers, switches, firewalls, load balancers, etc. In addition to performing operational/transport functions, these devices also generate highly valuable site activity data. Such data sources include:

- NetFlow records network and application resource utilization.
- RADIUS log files provide access information on a continuous basis.
- RMON data adapters provide utilization data for various network layers.
- Proprietary and/or device-specific protocols capture useful information.

These data are extremely useful in determining who accessed what and for how long and/or how much of it they accessed. Many device vendors and third-party developers are introducing powerful application-aware monitoring tools that can help value-added content and service providers more accurately track the consumption of infrastructure resources. An effective rating system must be able to tap into all of these various data types and flexibly translate them into the specific types of utilization parameters that each particular rating formula requires.

4.8.2.3 Network-Level Data

This type of data is most often used by network service providers (NSP) and hosting, although it can also be applied to a variety of Web business models. NSPs determine rating by monitoring network utilization, such as 95th percentile. In addition, a given network service may be running on a specific user datagram protocol (UDP) port number, or a certain protocol may have a specific UDP port number, or a certain protocol may have a specific utilization charge attached to it. In such cases, basic network-level data will also have to be captured and incorporated into the service-rating formula. In order to support a particular business objective, these diverse metrics of activity may have to be aggregated with greater flexibility, precision, and speed.

With so many different information sources available, it is essential to specify where a billing system gets its data. For instance, since RADIUS servers track who accessed a particular Web host and for how long, their log files can be valuable for billing, especially when tallying up charges for Web-server space. But RADIUS servers only disclose a portion of the picture; they can track access to Web servers, but they cannot report on network utilization, i.e., how much bandwidth on a given IP connection was consumed by a particular application or end user. This sort of information is becoming important to providers as they start selling multiple IP services.

Network probes and monitors are another excellent source of utilization data. RMON1 and RMON2 probes can be stand-alone devices, embedded hardware, or software. These probes continuously measure LAN segments and bandwidth utilization by end user and by application. They can report metrics on Layer 2, 3, and even higher. Usually, the large amount of captured data causes problems for processing. Thus the bandwidth requirements to transfer data from probes to the centrally located processing facility are an important consideration.

Web servers maintain logs that can be used to obtain application-related and end-user-related metrics: Who are the visitors; what is the duration of their visits; what is the frequency of their visits; what is the resource demand of those visits. Most of these metrics can be utilized as a basis for IP billing.

Routers and switches are also valuable sources for accounting information. For instance, routers and switches from Cisco Systems run Netflow, a proprietary flow-monitoring utility — a module under internetwork operating system (IOS) — that monitors packet activity. Most billing vendors can tap directly into Netflow data. Vendors of IP billing packages should also consider other vendors. The principle of data gathering will be the same, but API support on behalf of the vendor is necessary.

4.8.3 Convergent Mediation for Efficient Billing in the Telecommunications Industry

Mediation refers to those systems that collect data from network elements and pass it on to downstream back- and front-office applications, such as billing, customer care, fraud management, and decision support. In addition to data collection and routing, mediation systems perform functions such as usage-data verification, network-event reconstruction, filtering, and data-format translation.

Customers usually do not understand exactly what mediation means and what mediation systems can accomplish. The traditional view of mediation systems is that they are a replacement for magnetic tapes in the billing process — in other words, little more than automated data collectors and transporters. This view only applies to the first generation of mediation systems. While first-generation systems collected raw data and transported it to specific systems, current systems are able to operate in complex, multivendor network environments; perform post-collection processing; make intelligent routing decisions; and are read-write capable to refine data before transport to downstream systems.

An important aspect of a good mediation system is its ability to reconstruct complex network events out of data delivered from multivendor, multitechnology networks. The barriers between wire-line, wireless, voice, video, and data networks are falling. It is conceivable that a customer could use a wireless modem on a laptop PC to place a roaming personal communication service (PCS) call to an internet service provider (ISP) roaming number. The customer could then browse for items he or she is considering buying. If a purchase is made, the transaction will include funds transfer or a debit or credit card charge. This mix of services might be billed through a single provider but actually delivered by multiple carriers with interconnect agreement. The transaction in this example needs to be accounted and billed for, but just as important is the service provider's ability to reconstruct the events of this transaction to develop a customer profile for marketing and, perhaps, also for fraud protection. Modern mediation systems are designed to provide event reconstruction by correlating various CDRs, partial CDRs, or other bits of usage data and translating the multiple data formats into data appropriate to a carrier's specific downstream applications, as well as performing data verification to avoid duplicates and support revenue assurance. Because the data come from multiple carriers that supply the underlying network services, a mediation system must be able to support carrier interconnection, both for intercarrier settlement purposes and for event reconstruction.

Mediation is straightforward in circuit-switched voice environments. The switches generate CDRs that are periodically provided by the switches for processing. With packet-switched services, especially with IP applications, mediation is becoming more complex. The mediation application is expected to correlate multiple information sources to generate an IP detail record (IPDR) that may be completely different from the CDRs. In these particular cases, mediation is a great help in offloading both the data-collection and rating functions. Scalability is much better when the right mediation application is deployed.

There are several mediation alternatives:

- The mediation application concentrates on data collection and formatting and — in the case of IP — on correlation of collected data, but it does not offer rating and billing functions.
- The mediation application supports data collection, formatting, correlation, and rating, but it does not support billing features.
- The mediation application offers the full functionality from data collection to correlation, including rating and billing functions.

The ultimate decision may depend on such factors as the number of different voice switches that have been deployed, the number of different IP-related data sources, and whether the service provider owns a customizable billing application.

Quality of Service (QoS) could become a key differentiator as service providers search for ways to extract maximum revenue from existing and new services. Mediation plays a pivotal role in supporting service providers by reducing the cost and time to introduce and differentiate new services that exploit the offered bandwidth. Convergent mediation provides business systems with a clear view of service use, protects them from technology differences and changes, and supports a single point of change for new business models. Figure 4.6 shows a generic architecture for convergent mediation.

Service providers may support other models for content QoS mediation and billing, but mediation will either be an enabler of, or a barrier to, their ambitions. A product capable of supporting the full range of voice, video, data, and content services is required, and the product must be flexible enough to accommodate network changes, creation of new services, and introduction of novel billing models. Operators will then have an open view of new service

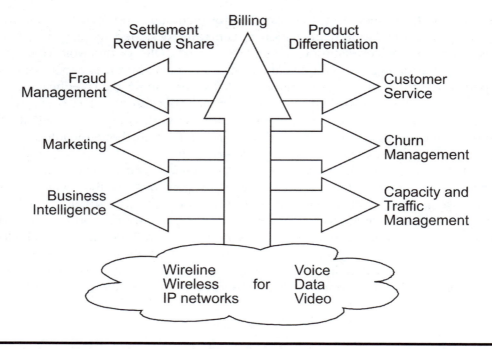

Figure 4.6   Basics of convergent mediation.

opportunities ahead and the facilities available to differentiate and maximize their revenues.

The role of convergent mediation is the following (Bassa, 2002):

- Single-network service-usage data resource
- Protect business systems from network technologies
- Support multiple business function requirements
- Foundation for revenue assurance

Mediation is the key to real-time support for EBPP. Mediation has been implemented for some time for circuit-switched services (first generation) and for packet-switched services (second generation). However, traditional mediation was born out of the fact that participating networking equipment lacked any detailed view of networks, and they were unable to support intelligent processing of raw billing data.

With mobile IP applications such as VoIP, VoD, and videoconferencing, there will be a need for smarter mediation that offers granular billing and revenue information for transaction-oriented IP services involving a very large number of variables for traffic volume, QoS and content value, and complex relationship management. There is no question that conventional billing, rating, and mediation systems struggle to participate in online charging, as they do not have a real-time orientation. Systems built around circuit-switched networks focus on call-duration information derived from CDRs that are issued after events have occurred. Consequently, there is a lot of data going up layers of protocols, whether wireless application protocol (WAP), transmission control protocol/IP (TCP/IP) services, or others. As a result, there are a number of so-called premediation alternatives that mediate among traditional mediation, billing, and intelligent-network platforms. They target the mobile Internet or edge developments for a more data- and consumer-aware network (Schwartz, 2002).

Efforts are under way to create edge devices and routers that are IP- and user-aware, so that operators can have a network-centric approach with business applications in mind. Premediation solutions claim to be able to give operators control and visibility into their networks (Schwartz, 2002). The mission of these suppliers is to build next-generation, intelligent, service-aware systems that integrate with carrier-class switching and routing platforms for CDMA (code division multiple access), GSM (global system for mobile communications), and UMTS (universal mobile telecommunications system) networks. Simply stated, premediation systems sit between the switch and the mediation systems in order to eliminate redundant IP data, thus enabling data service details to be processed in real time for real-time billing. These special boxes and next-generation routers are designed for mobile networks and thus can handle data packets more efficiently than conventional systems. Rather than rely on network element managers to build equipment, premediation companies have developed solutions that sit in the flow of packets, taking a more active role in shaping traffic as well as policy management.

This new term of premediation is very helpful in including early consideration of delivering QoS into the billing process.

4.9 Summary

EBPP should be positioned into the existing business processes of both billers and payers. The integration points are the accounts-receivable (A/R) and accounts-payable (A/P) workflows. Besides actual and tangible benefits — cost savings, better liquidity, improved cash-flow management, and reduced DSOs — issuers of statements, bills, and invoices can offer a number of value-added services to consumers and businesses (payers). These services are tools for strengthening their customer relationships, with the result of reducing churn and generating additional revenue by personalized cross-selling of products and services. Implementation volumes, deployment schedules, and penetration depths differ considerably for the B2B, SME, SOHO, and B2C markets.

Automated Web-based customer service, which requires no employee assistance, lets users navigate to and search for important information. Some Web self-service systems also let customers submit inquiries and converse with customer service representatives through such techniques as Web forms, e-mail, and online chat. Web service modules typically are accessed through standard browsers and let customers personalize the interface to obtain the information they want. These new technologies are useful for fully utilizing value-added features offered by EBPP solutions providers.

Chapter 5

Risks, Security, and Privacy with EBPP Business Models and Solutions

The development of the Internet, intranets, and extranets has enabled a large variety of services and solutions, previously accessible to only a narrow segment of the society, to be accessed by all. Examples include Internet banking, Internet travel, online investment, and the services developing from them, including EBPP. However, with these opportunities have come threats, fears, and risks, both real and imagined.

In essence, the security problem is twofold. On the one hand, there are issues of the security of financial and personal information used against the individual in a criminal or fraudulent manner. On the other hand, there are issues of excessive use of an individual's information for marketing and advertising, with subsequent infringement of the privacy of the individual. The importance of security cannot be underestimated. Companies that conduct online transactions over the Internet cite security as a primary concern.

5.1 The EBPP Security Assurance Process

Security management is in charge of protecting all systems solutions. This process includes a planning and controlling function. Security assurance includes four main functions:

1. Identification of information to be protected
2. Analysis of access options to protected information
3. Selection and implementation of solutions for protection
4. Periodic reassessment of security solutions

5.1.1 Identification of Information to Be Protected

Sensitive information is any data an organization wants to secure, such as that pertaining to customer accounts, price lists, research and development data, payroll, addresses, bill of material processors, acquisition and marketing plans, products announcements schedules. The possibilities are almost limitless.

The identification is positively a team effort, where practically all departments or business units are participating. After agreeing on the sensitive information, the team is expected to determine the most likely location where this information is kept. It could become a relatively long list due to the distributed nature of servers. The most likely locations are the mainframe, which may play the role of a big server, or the database engine and all the servers in interconnected networks. Occasionally, even workstations maintain important information that should be protected.

Identifying sensitive information means the classification of information. Most organizations have well-defined policies regarding what information qualifies as sensitive; often it includes financial, accounting, engineering, and employee information. But there are also environments that can have sensitive information unique to them. The main purpose of intranets is to improve the internal documentation and communication within enterprises. Web servers are the focal point of information maintenance. Clearly, not everyone should have access to everything. Depending on the individual responsibilities, access rights to information sources can be relatively easily structured and implemented.

In summary, sensitive information resides on the home pages, with particular content residing on Web servers. In this case, content is represented by statements, bills, and invoices.

5.1.2 Analysis of Access Options to Protected Information

Once the webmaster and network managers know what information is sensitive and where it is located, their next task is to identify how intruders might access these locations. This often time-consuming process usually requires that webmasters and network managers examine each piece of hardware and software offering a service to users. In this respect, intranets are not different from any other complex network. Generic sensitive access points are illustrated in Figure 5.1:

- End-user devices, such as browsers
- Access and backbone networks
- Web servers maintaining sensitive information

5.1.3 Selection and Implementation of Solutions for Protection

The next step in security management is to apply the necessary security techniques. The sensitive access points dictate how the protection should be

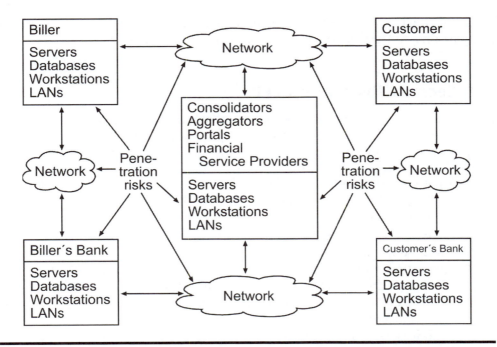

Figure 5.1   Access points with security risks.

deployed using a combination of policies, procedures, and tools. In this respect, the following levels of security techniques must be considered:

- End-user devices, such as universal browsers (use of chip cards or chip keys)
- Access and backbone networks (use of encryption, authentication, and firewalls)
- Web servers (use of server protection, operating systems protection, special tools, and virus protection)

5.1.4   Periodic Reassessment of Security Solutions

The last step in effectively securing access points in the server and networking infrastructure is maintenance. The key to maintenance is locating potential or actual security breaches. It requires an ongoing effort of stress testing the infrastructure, assigning tasks to outside professional security companies, reviewing case studies of security violations, and evaluating new security management techniques and tools.

Network and systems management systems must know the current operating system and application configuration at all times. Attacks will cause changes to one or more of the standard configurations, be it a physical or logical change. In addition, normal operating performance indicators will change, e.g., utilization increases or decreases, source and destination addresses change, service request types and volumes change. The systems must have the ability to know the baseline performance and then, at periodic intervals, perform comparisons and generate alerts for predefined discrepancies.

5.2 Security Risks with EBPP

Each stage of the EBPP process presents a potential security risk. The following is an assessment of the risks for the principal stages of EBPP — bill creation, bill presentment, and bill payment:

- Creation of the bill:
    Data collection (medium)
    Mediation (medium)
    Rating (low)
    Content creation and bill design (low)
- Presentment of the bill:
    Transformation into electronic format (low)
    Site and page design and management (none)
    Notification (high)
    Bill presentment (high)
- Payment of the bill:
    Collection and revenue assurance (high)
    Electronic payment and posting (high)

Other types of security breaches and risks include:

- Viruses: Rogue software penetrates the operating system or applications with the purpose of changing and/or destroying code. Viruses can take many hostile forms: deleting important files, extending files, multiplying files, generating load until systems crash, etc. E-mail attachments are frequently a source for viruses.
- Employee access abuse: Frustrated employees or those with a "gambler" nature may exceed their authority and attempt to access restricted operating systems or applications. Such behavior could place an unacceptable load on resources and affect the morale of other employees.
- Unauthorized access by outsiders: An intruder might trigger a sequence of events that affects network and system performance. Such activities include changing the configuration files, reassigning resources, redefining eligibility and access rights, or simply overloading critical resources with requests for service.
- Theft or destruction of computing resources: This is a severe breach involving the physical removal and/or destruction of resources. As a secondary effect, impacts on users by denying service for certain applications could also have severe business impacts.
- Leak of proprietary information: Trade secrets might be directed to competitors, creating severe competitive disadvantages and financial losses. Such breaches are usually traced to frustrated employees.

■ Theft or destruction of data: This is a combination of the previous two breaches. The theft is intentional, with the purpose of causing losses to the enterprise. The source is usually an external intruder working on assignment for a third party.

■ Access abuses by authorized nonemployees: Trading partners commonly receive authorization to access certain services and resources, but because they are not employees of the enterprise, some rules may not apply. When the rules governing access are less strict for a trading partner, there is a possibility that an unscrupulous partner might exploit this to penetrate systems and obtain valuable information.

Given these potential breaches, billers, consolidators, and payers are confronted with severe risks, such as:

■ Reputation risks and the subsequent loss of business due to security breach or unauthorized disclosure of customer data

■ Compliance risks due to absence of a liability-management structure, jurisdictional incompatibilities, or failure to meet regulatory requirements

■ Transactional risks due to fraud, disruption of service, or failure to meet service levels of reliability

5.3 Security Solutions

Security solutions can be subdivided into two categories:

1. Security procedures, which offer a variety of techniques to fight security breaches
2. Public key infrastructure (PKI), which offers a complete solution through a combination of technology and organization

5.3.1 Security Procedures

Security procedures include:

■ Entity authentication: This mechanism provides verification of the identity by comparing identification information provided by the entity to the content of a known and trusted information repository. This information may take the form of something the user knows, something the user has, or something the user is. For stronger verification, more than one of these characteristics may be required.

■ Password protection: The complexity of password protection has increased with the use of symbols, numbers, and upper- and lower-case letters being incorporated into single passport strings.

■ Access control lists and security labels: Access control lists are a form of information repository that contains data relative to the rights and permissions of access granted to each authenticated identity known to the system. Security labeling provides a mechanism to enhance or refine the levels of control imposed on a resource or entity. This is done by defining specific controls on the label tag itself.

- Encipherment/Decipherment: Cryptography is the mechanism used to provide for confidentiality service. It is also used quite frequently in complementing some other mechanisms in providing total security solutions. Encipherment and decipherment essentially deal with the transformation of data and/or information from an intelligible format to an unintelligible format and back to an intelligible format. This is a mathematical process that uses keys and algorithms to apply the key values against the data in a predetermined fashion. Data encryption standard (DES) may be used here with an encryption device that is utilizing a private secret key with 72 quadrillion possible variations. 3DES indicates triple DES, which is a three-layer version of DES. Advanced encryption standard (AES) is the next-generation DES standard in development today.

- Modification-detection codes and message-authentication codes: Data integrity is supported by the use of some sort of checking code. Three methods of calculating the checking code are in common use: cyclic redundancy check (CRC), modification-detection codes (MDC), and message-authentication codes (MAC). A CRC is relatively easy to compute and has typically been used to recognize hardware failures. It is a weak check for detecting attacks. An MDC is computed using cryptography, but no secret key is used. As a result, MDC is a much stronger check than CRC, for it is very difficult to find a second message with the same MDC as the legitimate one. However, an MDC has the same delivery requirements as a CRC, in that a CRC or an MDC is delivered with data by encrypting it using a secret key shared by the sender and recipient. The MAC is cryptographically delivered using a secret key shared by the sender and recipient, so it can be delivered with the data being protected without further trouble.

- Digital signature: In addition to data integrity, nonrepudiation services such as digital signature are becoming more important to many customers. Digital signatures provide proof of data origin and/or proof of delivery. The first provides the recipient with proof of who the data sender was. The second provides the sender with a receipt for the delivery of data to the intended party.

- Authentication by special equipment: Recently, new solutions have been introduced to identify users with their specific workstation or browsers. The use of chip cards and chip keys is based on a personalized set of information hard-coded into the chip. Loss of the card or key can still lead to unauthorized use.

- Authentication by personal attributes: In very sensitive areas, personal attributes — keystroke dynamics, signature dynamics, voice pattern, color of eyes, hand scans, fingerprints, and the like — can be used as the basis for identification, although the cost of these techniques can be very high.

- Improving data integrity: This technique deals with solutions based on a checksum computation. The results are used to expand the message that will be sent to the destination address. The techniques are expected to be sophisticated enough not to be broken easily. The original message and the checksum are encrypted together. Time stamps and message identification also have to be added to help reconstruct the message, and those additional flags can be encrypted as well.

- Prevention of traffic-flow analysis using fillers: Fillers can be used to fill time gaps between real data transmissions. If both communications can be encrypted together, an intruder listening to traffic cannot recognize any rationale or trend, or any random, periodic, or other pattern. On the other hand, the use of fillers is not unlimited. It can become very expensive, and communication facilities of intranets, extranets, and the Internet may be temporarily overloaded, resulting in performance bottlenecks.

- Secure forms of existing protocols include:
  SSL (secure socket layer) protocol for managing the security of a message transmission on the Internet
  S-HTML (secure hypertext markup language), a secure form of HTML used in Web design
  S-MIME (secure multipurpose internet mail extensions), a secure method of sending e-mail that uses the RSA (Rivest, Shamir, Adelmann) encryption system

5.3.2 Public Key Infrastructure (PKI)

The concept of a public key infrastructure is relatively simple, but actually setting up a PKI can be complex. The basic idea is to protect sensitive data through encryption. Each end-user device is equipped with encryption software and two keys: a public key for distribution to other users and a private key that is kept and protected by the owner. A user encrypts the message using the receiver's public key. When the message is received, the user decrypts it with his private key. Users may have multiple key pairs to conduct communications and data exchange with different users. With an increasing number of key pairs, it is important to implement a method of administering the keys and their usage. PKI enables the centralized creation, distribution, tracking, and revocation of keys.

The first step in setting up a PKI is establishing a system for authentication to positively identify users before receiving communication rights. Digital signature is the preferred authentication method for PKI. Figure 5.2 depicts a public key infrastructure. Each certificate contains specific identifying information about a user, including his/her name, public key, and a unique digital signature that binds the user to the certificate. To get a certificate, a user sends a request to a designated registration authority, which verifies the user's identity and tells the certification authority to issue the certificate. The certificate itself

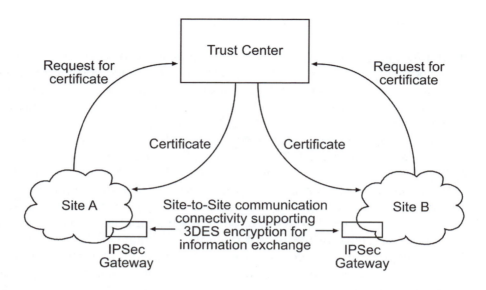

Figure 5.2   Public key infrastructure.

is a digital document that is generally stored and administered in a central directory. The certificate is transmitted automatically when needed without interrupting the ongoing work of the user. The certificate authority verifies a certificate's authenticity for the receiver. Again, for the user, this is generally transparent.

Certificates should not last forever. Each certificate is issued with an expiration date and sometimes will need to be revoked early, such as when an employee quits. A certificate authority can revoke a certificate before its expiration date by identifying it in a regularly published certificate revocation report. As with key pairs, there is a need to coordinate the issuing and revoking of certificates. That is another function of a PKI: acting as a comprehensive architecture encompassing key management, the registration authority, certificate authority, and various administrative tool sets. PKI tools are available from various vendors. Generally, a central directory is also implemented as part of a PKI as a place to store and look up certificates, along with other relevant information.

Another element of a PKI is the certificate policy, which outlines rules for the use of a PKI and certificate services. For example, if a user mistakenly shares his/her private key, it might be expected that the user notify the security staff or the certificate authority. The rules — summarized in a certificate practice statement (CPS) — are written in consultation among the IT (information technology) group, various user groups, and legal experts. The CPS provides a detailed explanation of how the certificate authority manages the certificates it issues, along with associated services such as key management. The CPS also acts as a contract between the certificate authority and users, describing the commitments and legal limitations and setting the foundation for future audits. PKI vendors can provide samples and templates for the contracting parties.

Staff is needed to set up, administer, fix, and manage a PKI. In the first step, a security officer is needed who will become responsible for setting and administering the security policy of the service provider. This person need not be part of IT but must understand the issues and will probably need a security bond. In the second step, a PKI architect is needed who will become responsible to examine requirements and design the customized PKI. This person might also support implementation as project coordinator. In the third step, a PKI security administrator is needed. This individual will use certificate-authority management tools to add, enable, and revoke users and their certificates. All of these activities are important for ongoing operations. In the last step, a directory administrator and someone to act as a registration authority are needed. However, it is possible to set up an automated registration authority to handle user requests made through their Web browsers. In that case, current staff can be used, such as database administrators, who can help to set up and maintain the automated registration authority service.

Most EBPP companies supplement these industry-standards security measures by partnering with specialist security and secure-transaction companies. The market has mirrored such developments by moving away from bundled suites of security applications to specialized best-of-breed applications. Originally, bundled suites were targeted because they offered interoperability and quick installation, which came at the expense of best-of-breed specialization. Special solutions guarantee an even higher protection of EBPP processes.

5.4 Data Privacy

The collection and use of personal data for advertising, sales, and one-to-one marketing is a critical issue of data privacy. In order to understand the importance of user confidentiality, we must first look at the state of the EBPP market and the importance that one-to-one marketing has acquired within EBPP solutions. EBPP offers opportunities for cross-sell and up-sell when customer (payer) profiles are carefully analyzed and used for one-to-one marketing. This value-added feature was considered as an addition to the basic expectation of EBPP as a way of reducing costs of producing, delivering, and collecting payment for bills. Now, in certain cases, the value-added aspects of EBPP seem more important than the original proposition. The value attached to the customer relationship enabled through EBPP, and the services attached to this relationship, have become the primary value of implementing EBPP solutions. The corresponding increase in costs is also an issue, with billers and consolidators supporting both EBPP installations and legacy bill-delivery solutions.

In order to get some payback from these investments, billers and consolidators have incorporated complex data-profiling and data-mining capabilities within their solutions. The quality of many vendor solutions are graded on the level and complexity of these services, while some solutions allow end users to analyze their own data to recognize usage patterns. However, the borderline between value-added service for customers and invasion of their privacy is murky. The restructuring of the EBPP business models has coincided with potential risks of data privacy intrusion. The issue of privacy has long been a major consideration of Internet users since the inception of cookies as a mean to track and profile customers as they use the Internet. With the explosion of Web-enabled commerce, the issue of personal data and financial details of customers has become very critical and sensitive.

In European countries, there is greater social and legal control over the issue of privacy. With EBPP set to roll out globally, the strategic importance of countries' respective privacy laws and divergent rules of social approval must be considered. In the U.S., the most accepting market for data mining, profiling, and personalized marketing, there has been an increase in aversion to privacy encroachment. Consumers are concerned about protecting their privacy online, and governments are beginning to recognize the need to investigate the issue of privacy. In most cases, even the most basic privacy standards had not been met.

Vendors of EBPP solutions provide powerful data-analysis and profiling capabilities with their tools. The vendors believe that the implementer (biller, consolidator, aggregator) should be the one to decide on the degree of implementation and usage of these tools. Participating entities are aware of the concerns of customers. They incorporate accurate details about what private information is collected, what it will be used for, and whether it is open to third-party viewing. This transparency in business practice is supported through verification by the TRUSTe group in the U.S.

TRUSTe is an approval-certification organization that awards seals for display on the Web sites of companies that agree to abide by a defined set of rules provided by the TRUSTe organization. The group awards certification after an in-depth investigation of the targeted company's Internet practices. The company's Web sites are also investigated in depth. The TRUSTe approach has migrated to the European Community as a means of combating a European law from 1998, which places significant restrictions on U.S.-based companies collecting and receiving personal data of European citizens. As a result of the collaboration between U.S. and European entities, two privacy-related services are being offered (The Phillips Group, 2001):

- Web-site privacy certification and oversight: Parallel with the U.S. TRUSTe privacy-seal program, this service includes a certification program for a Web site's data-gathering and -dissemination practices. Enforcement of privacy policies through monitoring and a watchdog body for alternative dispute management are also included.
- Online and offline dispute management: Part of safe-harbor membership is acceptance of a dispute-resolution mechanism, which is enforceable by TRUSTe.

The TRUSTe seal is likely to be more of a prerequisite in the European market because of regional privacy laws and a generally less-accepting attitude toward invasion-of-privacy issues. Such certification provides a sense of safety to customers. However, the general opinion is that there are other, more-sensitive areas concerning data privacy than data collected legally or illegally from Internet use.

5.5 Legal Issues

The legal issues surrounding EBPP are lagging behind the pace of implementing and using Internet-based applications. The Internet is a global device that transcends regional and international boundaries. Unfortunately, the laws of each country cannot be passed over so easily. There are three principal areas to be considered (The Phillips Group, 2001):

1. The liability issue in an electronic transaction and e-mail
2. The legal authority contained in electronic signatures
3. The problem of global versus national marketplaces and related country-specific laws and regulations

5.5.1 Liability Issues and e-Mail

One of the business models of EBPP is based on e-mail. Unfortunately, the legal status of e-mail is not yet clear. The question is whether e-mail constitutes a legally enforceable commitment between vendor and consumer. At this moment, e-mail does not have the same legal eligibility as a postal transaction. This causes severe problems for vendors who rely on systems that use e-mail trails — the electronic version of a paper trail — to confirm the delivery of electronic bills and the receipt of electronic payments.

The liability of billers, EBPP solution providers, and customers is a fundamental factor in the EBPP market. There is still a big question mark behind the liability for mispayments, errors involving technology, and network-related performance problems. However, there is a growing trend for many of the largest EBPP service providers to address the liability issue through insurance coverage. In much the same way as credit card companies, EBPP service providers are moving toward limited liability for illegal payments and billing-related errors.

5.5.2 Legal Authority of Digital Signatures

The legal authority of electronic transactions is held far below their counterpart paper equivalents. To address this situation, the U.S. created a new law in 2000: the Electronic Signatures in Global and National Commerce Act. This law makes any electronically signed document as legally binding as a handwritten signature. This law implements the legal framework that ratifies electronic versions of electronic contracts, signatures, notices, and records. The technology behind this law is based on public and private key encryption, and it is thus considerably more secure than handwritten signatures. Unfortunately, public acceptance has been slow, delaying full implementation for many years. A major education program and advertising campaign highlighting the benefits and the level of security contained with digital signatures would be mandatory to change the public opinion and speed up acceptance.

On the business side, there are problems with the cost of implementation. The building of public key and encryption infrastructure, including trust centers, overseers, and certification authorities, is cost prohibitive. Smaller EBPP service providers cannot afford it. In this case, smaller providers who cannot afford the implementation of digital signatures would be locked out of competing in the electronic world. The problem then becomes not the lack of security standards, as is the case in many other areas of EBPP, but the cost of implementing the standard. Customers (payers) may well be willing to use electronic signatures in their EBPP transactions, but their EBPP service provider may not be able to support it. As a result, it is likely that this technology will be implemented first in corporate environments supporting B2B solutions, where the implementation costs are justified by the high value of the transactions executed between participating entities.

In Europe, the acceptance of digital signatures has been supported by the development of Identrus, a PKI solution to improve security. Nevertheless, the laws — even within the European Community — are different. The differing states of legislation are not helpful in promoting further acceptance and rollout of the electronic-signature technology.

The same is true in Asia and the Pacific. Countries attempt to implement their own certification authorities and to develop plans for supporting legislation. Unfortunately, there is little coordination to implement a globally accepted format for e-commerce and Internet business.

The disparate developments of electronic signatures and the certification technology linked to them are a demonstration of legacy business relationships. The close market affinity between the U.S. and Europe is the result of a long-established business relationship. If e-commerce and related services such as EBPP are to be expanded, all existing business models must be reassessed. This takes time and costs a significant amount of money.

5.5.3 Global Laws for e-Commerce

Related to the need for a standards-based solution for the EBPP process, there is a specific need for a globally recognized set of laws for e-commerce. In a similar manner to international trade laws, a firm agreement is needed for legal liability and the transformation of the power of written words to electronic words. Specific regulations are needed for EBPP to deal with, e.g., legibility of online bills in relation to their paper counterparts and issues with electronic signatures in the payment process. Further regulations are needed for value-added services of EBPP to overcome present barriers and bureaucracy. Everyone involved should be aware of the complexity of EBPP business models and business processes. The process flow is simple to understand, but the underlying technologies and tools are not.

5.6 Identrus Case Study

One of the best examples of a global solution for greater security in e-commerce, particularly for B2B, is Identrus. Its mission statement is the removal of anonymity on the Internet. It is based on something stronger than just trust. The implementation of this solution is based on the following key areas:

- Authentication of customers, billers, consolidators, and Web sites
- Authorization for entities who have rights to access proprietary information and to execute privileged transactions
- Confidentiality and the assurance that information exchanged between transaction partners is private
- Integrity of the information in terms of its arrival without external interference or tampering
- Nonrepudiation of any agreement or binding covenants agreed between parties and removal of scope for attempts to dispute agreements

This security model allows its participating entities to use their financial institutions as a third-party guarantor. In essence, the financial institution resides between the entities involved in the transaction process and issues electronic passports in the form of secure digital certificates, provides transactional assurance, and offers a dispute-handling solution. In other words, the financial institute is the overseer.

The Identrus infrastructure brings business and operating rules to the security provided by digital certificates. For example, if a bid is received for goods or services and the seller does not know any details of the bidder, the seller can demand a financial warranty against the buyer's Identrus identification. This means that the buyer is liable for the cost through Identrus-sanctioned globally enforceable contracts that bind all participants to the system.

Arguments as to the origin or to the process of a transaction can be audited by an electronic paper trail, which records the whole process. The identity of parties involved is guaranteed by the Identrus warranty attached to the company at its registration. The process is shown in Figure 5.3.

The Identrus solution is accepted as a major driver in the B2B marketplace by a substantial number of EBPP vendors. This solution may occupy a similar position as open financial exchange (OFX) in the B2B EBPP field.

Identrus members and supporters include (The Phillips Group, 2001):

ABN AMRO Bank
ANZ Banking Group
Bank of America
Bank of Scotland

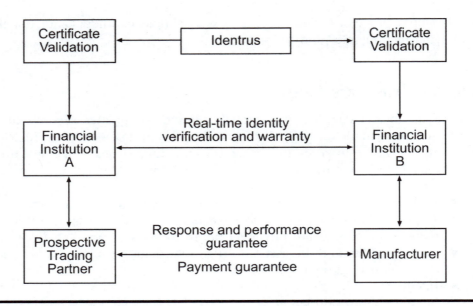

Figure 5.3   The transaction process of Identrus.

Barclays Bank
BNP Paribas
Banco Santander Central Hispano
The Chase Manhattan Bank
Citigroup
Credit Agricole France
Commerzbank Germany
Deutsche Bank
Dresden Bank
Hypo Vereinsbank
The Industrial Bank of Japan
Lloyds TSB
Royal Bank of Canada
Sanwa Bank
Scotia Bank
Societe Generale
Sumitomo Bank
Wells Fargo
Westpac

There are several issues regarding Identrus:

■ It is not completely secure; the PKI certification is resident on the computers of participating entities and hence can be attacked by intruders.
■ The use of a PIN (personal identification number) for additional protection could be violated by certain browsers that present these data when users connect to a regularly visited site.

- The regulations of various countries differ greatly from each other.
- It faces competition from other PKI-based solutions that may offer a broader scope than just supporting EBPP.

The success of the Identrus approach will promote other PKI solutions.

5.7 Open Platform for Security (OPSEC)

An integrated, secure, and manageable infrastructure can be built based on product suites that support the following security-related functions:

- Authentication and authorization: Identification management and authentication products utilizing common RADIUS, CAPI, and PKCS interfaces can plug-and-play with firewalls. The smart-card category (see Chapter 6) increases the number of options.
- Reporting: A number of reporting tools can be integrated with firewalls and certified with Check Point products.
- Securing content: Malicious code, worms, and viruses continue to be top-ranked security threats. Gateway- and server-based antivirus and content-security products, as well as the desktop-security initiative, enhance client security under one security policy.
- Intrusion detection and security (IDS) assessment: Integrated IDS products provide automated detection for networks, servers, and desktops. The new security-assessment category combines scanning tools and services for a complete detection suite of open choices.
- Use of enterprise directories: Leading directory servers work seamlessly with security products via a lightweight directory access protocol (LDAP) interface to enable the centralization of objects with granular administration rights for a distributed organization. Enterprise-management consoles provide a central high command via the log and event interfaces.
- High availability and load balancing: Both reliability and manageability are top criteria for Internet gateways and networking. The OPSEC framework allows software and hardware products to integrate and interoperate for high availability and load-balanced firewalls and gateways.
- Event monitoring and analysis: Event correlation and detection of irregular activities enhance the detection process. OPSEC-certified products collect and analyze firewall and gateway events to detect and alert billers, customers, and consolidators to adverse and abnormal activities.
- URL (universal resource locator) resource management: URL resource management offers a double benefit. Not only are questionable sites blocked based on policies, but time sinks and other unproductive sites are also managed to improve overall productivity. Performance is optimized with the new URL cache features.

- PKI compatibility and integration: Quickly becoming the hidden backbone of security infrastructures, PKI-enabled products seamlessly integrate with firewalls and gateways.
- Performance and acceleration: Acceleration cards optimized for specific OPSEC processes and complete platforms that optimize the new Secur-eXL technology can provide significant gains with performance. New capacity planning and testing tools will help with performance benchmarks.

The OPSEC initiative is supported by Check Point Software technologies, a leading company for Internet security.

5.8 Summary

Due to complex business models and the number of participating entities, EBPP is confronted with myriad security risks. A combination of tools can help to reduce these risks to a meaningful minimum. Protection mechanisms are expected to be manyfold: protecting payers' privacy, protecting business data, and protecting all resources of the value chain. Infrastructure components, such as servers, networks, and applications, are similar to other application areas, with the result that best-of-breed tools known from other areas can be successfully implemented. PKI is a promising solution for all participating entities.

Chapter 6

Documentation and Payment Standards for EBPP

Although numerous standards have been proposed for standardization in both documentation and payment areas, there is still no agreement on the right ones for EBPP. The complexity surrounding the standardization process should not be underestimated. A number of standard processes for EBPP need to be defined and implemented. Areas that EBPP touches include the banking industry, e-commerce industry, clearing business, data-processing software industry, and the financial transaction industry. The banking industry is responsible for some of the complexities. Electronic financial transactions — from automated clearinghouses (ACH) to online stock trading — are very complicated. With EBPP, this complexity is multiplied by adding a further layer of technology and interoperability problems. Cross-discipline cooperation is needed among vendors, billers, payers, and banking institutions. The banking industry must be considered as a leading player in the standardization process because of its integral position in the EBPP process. There are three main areas requiring further development:

- A single multicommunications system for financial data interchange between the banking industry, EBPP vendors, and transaction processors
- A standardized template for communication of biller data into a format recognizable and presentable by billing vendors and bill presenters
- A standardized data technology for scaling, developing, and adding to systems based on a common programming language

This chapter addresses documentation standards first, followed by payment standards. Finally, there is a discussion of potential alliances among EBPP entities that might help in implementing standard processes.

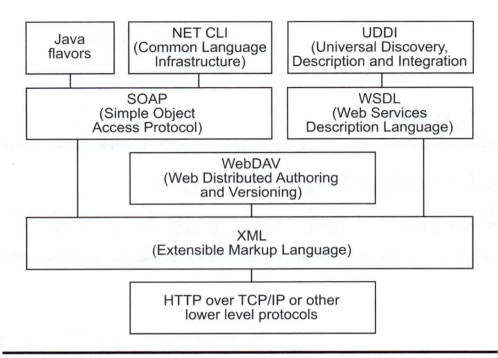

Figure 6.1   Hierarchy of Web-services standards based on HTTP and TCP/IP.

6.1   Documentation Standards

The value chain of EBPP is long. Documents such as statements, bills, and invoices are created, forwarded, exchanged, and distributed. When format changes are frequent, the process cannot be efficient. Web services have triggered revolutionary changes in the documentation industry. The various markup languages offer an excellent entry basis into the documentation standardization process. The subentries in this section summarize the present status and predict future trends for these markup languages. XML (extended markup language) receives the greatest attention, since that has become today's documentation standard.

Figure 6.1 shows a hierarchy of Web-services standards based on HTTP (hypertext transfer protocol) and TCP/IP (transmission control protocol/internet protocol) (Dorman, 2002).

6.1.1   Hypertext Markup Language (HTML)

HTML is easy to understand and can be written by hand or generated from other text formats by translators. HTML is actually a simple document type of the standardized generalized markup language (SGML).

HTML is simpler than nroff and other document languages in that it is not programmable. As a result, the descriptive capabilities of HTML are limited to low-level constructs, such as emphasis or indented lists. However, because

HTML parsers are rather forgiving of HTML coding violations, many Web pages contain coding mistakes used purposely to achieve particular layout effects on popular browsers. HTML is optimized for display rather than printing or storage. HTML has no notion of pages, making formatted printing difficult.

HTML has serious limitations. HTML does not provide the flexibility Web publishers need to create home pages. HTML pages are static, and dynamic updates are not really supported. Attributes, flexibility, and dynamics are absolutely necessary if Web technology is to be successfully implemented for network and systems management. Earlier efforts to add interactivity to pages involved the use of server-based CGI (common gateway interface) programs, Java applets, browser plug-ins, ActiveX controls, and scripting languages, all of which had little to do with HTML. With the advent of dynamic HTML, new client-side technologies, combined with scripting languages like JavaScript, can solve many of HTML's problems.

6.1.2 *Dynamic Hypertext Markup Language (DHTML)*

DHTML extends the current set of HTML elements, and a few other elements such as style-sheet properties, by allowing them to be accessed and modified by scripting languages. Dynamic features, making pages come alive with movement and interactivity, can be added by exposing tags to scripts written in a language like JavaScript or VBScript (Terplan, 2001).

The tags are accessed through the document object model (DOM), which describes each document as a collection of individual objects such as images, paragraphs, and forms down to individual characters. The DOM of DHTML can be complex, but it does not necessarily require a lot of work. Developers can use the object model to find an image on a page and replace it with another when a user rolls a cursor over it. Such rollovers, or animated buttons, are common. DHTML also can animate a page by moving objects around, build an expanding tree structure to navigate a site, or create a complex application like a database front end.

The common denominator is expected to be the DOM, which is the basis for DHTML. DOM is a platform- and language-neutral interface that will allow programs and scripts to dynamically access and update the content, structure, and style of documents. DOM has been accepted by both of the leading browser suppliers, Microsoft and Netscape. Their DOM implementation is very similar, the main differences involving other features, such as positioning, dynamic fonts, and multimedia controls.

Beyond the extras like dynamic fonts and multimedia controls, the core ideas of Netscape and Microsoft are similar. With support for CSS (cascading style sheet) and absolute positioning, advanced layout can be made to work under each browser. With DHTML and absolute positioning, it is possible to create sophisticated multimedia applications that can avoid frequent dialogs with the Web server, but building DHTML-based pages is still programming. Including dynamic elements onto a page is a major step away from a static-page paradigm and into the idea of Web pages as programs.

6.1.3 Extended Markup Language (XML)

The DOM sets out the methods by which Web developers can access elements of HTML and XML documents to manipulate page elements and create dynamic effects. It also serves as the key enabling technology for dynamic HTML. There are three principal areas of XML applications:

- High-end publishing, which views XML and SGML (standard generalized markup language) as highly structured document languages
- Use of the extensible nature of XML by Web developers to create application-specific markup tags
- Use of XML as a data-exchange format for distributed Web applications

With XML and DHTML, it is relatively easy to share the user interface and information on the Web. XML helps in eliminating the major limitations of HTML, enabling Web searches, fostering inter-industry communication, and enabling a new form of distributed Web-based applications. But XML does not solve everything, and it does not make HTML obsolete. Both HTML and XML are subsets of SGML, but XML could define HTML as a DTD (document-type definition) of its own. They meet again only with regard to dynamic HTML, in which both require the use of DOM (document object model).

While the core syntax of XML is fairly well defined, many other areas need to be addressed. XML provides no presentation services; another technology must be deployed to present XML data within a Web browser. Eventual use of a style-sheet language like CSS or the extensible style language (XSL) seems likely. Many users implement HTML as the presentation language for XML. To support presentation, Java applets can be downloaded to present even complex data forms. XML mirrors SGML in that it lacks linking capabilities. To eliminate this weakness, the extensible linking language (XLL) is being added to XML. To support scripting capabilities, there is also a need to connect XML with DOM.

Without presentation, scripting, and linking, XML is limited to just being a data format. But, there are applications — defined as vertical for supporting specific industries or horizontal for generic use — that can support these functions. Microsoft has defined CDF (channel definition format) to push content to selected targets. Open software description (OSD) has been defined in XML to support software installation procedures. Synchronized multimedia integration language (SMIL) is used to define multimedia presentations for Web delivery. Meta languages, such as resource-definition format (RDF), will be defined in the future.

XML involves a simple premise: It describes data elements and their properties in plain text, providing a hierarchical framework for representing structured data for any domain and in a language that allows for the transmission of this encoded information across any interface. XML is optimized for data exchange:

- XML enhances a communication provider's ability to expand its trading-partner Web, as XML easily transforms to the data-exchange requirements of multiple parties. By using XML, a communications provider has greater opportunities to interpret and process information with partners and across systems.

- An operations support system's (OSS) XML architecture is easy to incorporate into an overall solution architecture, since its translatable nature does not mandate a delivery method. In this way, it also addresses a fundamental business problem of what delivery vehicle to use as the landscape of downstream partner systems evolves.

- XML is tools-enabled and is easy to use, so users of XML are not required to go to great lengths to find developers schooled in XML. Additionally, XML is applicable across multiple computing platforms, laying the groundwork for a provider to develop seamless integration throughout the enterprise.

XML can provide solutions to B2B problems. As service providers fight for position and a competitive advantage in the changing communications marketplace, greater emphasis is placed on the management of customer and partner relationships. The integration of XML into the fiber of business models is helping some providers to pull away from their competitors. Still, a few areas need more work, including standardization of accompanying technologies, such as XSL and XML schemas. Even more importantly, different industries need to standardize on XML schemas for B2B transactions to better facilitate integration. Though this will involve a significant amount of work, many organizations are dedicated to seeing that it is completed because they realize that there is no future in being an island in an interconnected business world.

The challenges facing XML are significant. The specifications of associated technologies such as style sheets and linking are not yet complete. XML style sheets, which are based on DSSSL (document style and semantics specification language), will most likely compete against CSS. The linking model of XML is more advanced than HTML, but it is incomplete and overly complex. The interaction between XML and DOM needs further clarification.

Industry analysts assume that XML will be used together with HTML, which is widely used and has become more powerful with CSS and DOM. XML may add formality and extensibility. Formality allows for guaranteed structure, exchange, and machine readability, which is difficult though not impossible with HTML. Extensibility describes the opportunity to create specialized languages for specific applications. Such languages can have significant power within particular intranets or in the area of managing networks and systems.

Microsoft has rapidly implemented its XML data reduced (XDR) schema, which may be on its way to becoming a standard. There has also been a significant increase in the number of industry groups designing their own DTDs or schemas.

In order to carry out business processes, many transaction units must be assembled in real time. These units are usually maintained in directories, which are being enabled to operate across corporate boundaries and point users to services wherever they exist. To accomplish this work, directories need to be able to speak a common language. Directory services markup language (DSML) is the emerging standard that expresses directory content in XML.

Directories typically store and manage information about each user in an enterprise, including names, addresses, phone numbers, and access rights. Directories are increasingly storing metadata about available Web services, what they do, what they require for inputs, how to execute them, what the results will be, who wrote them, and how to pay for them. Combined with the power of XML, this information enables entirely new classes of individually tailored applications for e-commerce.

Applications consume DSML documents as they would XML, since DSML is a subset of XML. Applications can also transmit DSML documents to other DSML-enabled applications on the Internet. This process effectively extends the lightweight directory access protocol (LDAP) across firewalls to any Internet transport protocol, such as HTTP (hypertext transfer protocol), FTP (file transfer protocol), and SMTP (simple mail transfer protocol). This is a major benefit for B2B commercial processes, which are one of the primary targets of EBPP. Standard tags defined by DSML — object class, entry, attribute, and name — refer to well-established directory analogs. LDAP, other directories, and vendor APIs (vendor application programming interface) will remain in place, and directories will continue to operate in their traditional manner. New B2B e-commerce capabilities are also available.

XML has been considered the language of the future for the Internet. It is designed to solve many problems in existing Internet applications, most specifically the standardized description and interchange of data. It is intended to provide a single technical standard for describing documents such as bills. With the use of XML documents, a new type of data storage is needed: the XML database. Software supporting the XML database is designed to store and manage the increasing number of XML documents. XML is typically used for data exchange, but the growing number of documents, and particularly bills, justifies special repositories. The benefits are (Cox, 2002):

- Efficient storage of XML documents
- Quick search, query, and retrieval of documents
- Ease of application development
- Ease of changing to documents without changing underlying data structures
- Easy manipulation of document collections

There are also some weaknesses (Cox, 2002):

- Inefficiency in handling structured data
- Lack of query-language standards
- Need for tools and education to integrate XML with existing relational data
- Data-integrity problems

- Performance issues when converting to underlying object or relational structures
- Volume problems with large number of XML documents

There are no formal standards yet for an XML database. Database providers are beginning the process by changing or extending their product offers with an XML database capability.

6.1.4 *Wireless Application Protocol (WAP)*

Wireless application protocol (WAP), an application environment and associated set of protocols, is being developed to deliver Internet content to mobile devices. The key components of WAP are the microbrowser and the WAP gateway. In order to receive WAP content, a mobile device — be it a phone or other equipment — must be equipped with a microbrowser, which is a downscaled Web browser designed to work within the confines of small displays. The WAP gateway handles communications between the mobile device and requested Internet sites.

WAP is a global industry standard for bringing together wireless telephony with Internet content and services regardless of wireless network architecture or device types. Because WAP is designed to work with any type of underlying wireless network architecture, it frees providers and customers to concentrate on the wireless application itself, without having to worry about whether applications are portable or not. WAP provides something similar to the well-known TCP/IP (transmission control protocol/internet protocol) stack used on the Internet and in corporate intranets. The difference is that the WAP protocol stack is specifically designed to accommodate the special challenges of wireless networking.

A WAP gateway server is located between the wireless service provider's network on one side and the public Internet or corporate intranet on the other. Gateways can be located within the firewalls of service providers or corporations, or both. In addition to taking care of various housekeeping functions, the WAP server handles the interface between the two sets of network protocols: WAP and TCP/IP.

The WAP computing model is simply standard Web programming with a WAP gateway in the middle of the request/response cycle. A cell phone or other wireless terminal requests a given URL (universal resource locator); the WAP gateway server decodes and decompresses this, then sends it on to the appropriate Web server as an ordinary HTTP request. The process is then repeated, in reverse, on the response side of the cycle. The WAP gateway can be located either within the wireless network of the service provider or, for security reasons, in an enterprise environment. The HTTP server can respond with HTML- or XML-based content. However, the WAE (wireless application environment) layer of WAP specifies an alternative markup language designed for use with thin wireless clients. If standard HTML or XML are served in response to the HTTP request, it falls to the WAP gateway server, or to an additional layer of middleware, to implement some form of content translation before the request can be relayed back to the WAP client.

The WAP gateway is the mobile provider's link between the Internet and the mobile network. When a WAP device requests information using wireless session protocol (WSP), the WAP gateway uses TCP/IP to communicate with the specified Internet site, pulls down the content, converts it, and hands it over to the mobile network for transmission to the end user. Data compaction is necessary because mobile networks cannot yet handle massive data streams. WAP content is delivered using wireless datagram protocol (WDP), which is designed to send messages over any available bearer channel, including everything from short message service (SMS) to cellular digital packet data (CDPD) and a host of other mobile packet-data technologies. If a mobile network has a bearer channel for data delivery, WAP can be deployed on that network. WAP is also designed to be air-interface independent and to operate over global system for mobile communications (GSM), time-division multiple access (TDMA), code-division multiple access (CDMA), and most other digital mobile protocols supported in all parts of the world in various networks.

In summary, the WAP standard includes:

- Specification for a server-centric scripting language called WMLScript, support for which is gradually being implemented on the latest WAP-enabled cell phones
- Voice-based user interfaces written in voice-extensible markup language (VXML)
- Location-specific applications that take full advantage of the GPS (global positioning system)
- Support for mobile teleconferencing

Standards like WAP and the new XHTML specification, which lays the basis for a convergence between WML and HTML, should keep the networking site simple. In-house Web developers will have to learn some new development tools, and APIs will have to support this convergence in practical applications.

The capabilities of WML are similar to XML, but they are less developed at this early stage of wireless business application development. Given the industry acceptance of XML, it is likely that WML will follow a similar path, significantly supported by third-generation license applications.

6.1.5 Web-Distributed Authoring and Versioning (WebDAV)

Because XML is infinitely adaptable, a new version can be created to contain almost any type of data. There are already hundreds of different types, each aimed at a different industry or niche application. They are essentially replacements for old file formats, but using ordinary English phases and alphabetic characters instead of binary code. This makes them easier to support in applications and even allows people to read files manually in a text editor when the correct applications are not available. Web services — an essential part of EBPP — share data using these XML-based formats, but they go further. XML can also be used to write new high-level networking protocols, bringing them the same benefits that file formats are enjoying. The first concrete protocol of this class is Web-distributed authoring and versioning (WebDAV), a set of extensions to HTTP that turns it into a complete filing protocol with the ability to retrieve and edit data based on arbitrary fields. The creators of WebDAV hope that this will enable all Internet traffic to be run over the Web, making HTTP as useful and as popular as IP itself.

6.1.6 Simple Object Access Protocol (SOAP)

Based on XML, SOAP is a communications protocol that supports access to individual objects on the Internet. SOAP uses XML syntax to send text-based commands over the Internet, and it uses HTTP to transport these commands. SOAP is the fundamental message-passing protocol that defines how to send data, typically in XML format, among applications across networks. SOAP can be used to build connections between applications. Advanced Web services are based on SOAP.

6.1.7 Web-Services Description Language (WSDL)

The connections between applications can be described using WSDL. A developer can use the description to design an application to connect to the Web service. As these services become increasingly complex, an application will be able to use a WSDL description to automatically configure itself to connect to other Web services. These services are being located by UDDI (universal description, discovery, and integration).

6.1.8 Universal Description, Discovery, and Integration (UDDI)

There are three frequently asked questions regarding UDDI (Wilson, 2001):

- What are Web services?
- Where are they found?
- How can they be accessed?

UDDI is a recommendation for a new standard in e-commerce using XML and SOAP as underlying tools. If and when it is implemented, various alternatives will be offered to customers, similar to phone book entries. White pages contain names, mail and Web addresses, and phone numbers; yellow pages can then focus more on branch-specific attributes. But, in eCommerce, the so-called green pages take over the leading role by offering mutual direct links between businesses. These links are essential to access systems and applications of the partners. UDDI, originally developed by IBM, Microsoft, and Ariba, has enjoyed wide industry support from the very beginning.

UDDI is a combination of three elements. An electronic "white pages" that list basic contact information for parties involved. A "yellow pages" offers details about companies and descriptions of the electronic capabilities they offer to their trading partners. In addition, a data dictionary or "green pages" lists the standards and software interfaces that partners must comply with to execute those electronic functions using XML as a common language.

With UDDI, companies would enter those capabilities in a registry, essentially a listing of all the electronic functions that a company offers to its partners. Public registries, such as those currently offered by IBM and Microsoft, are likely to be accessible by any company doing business on the Internet. Most companies, however, will build private registries that can only be accessed by approved trading partners.

The UDDI specification itself is a set of rules for describing electronic capabilities via XML and a method of registering those descriptions via the Web. UDDI outlines the means of finding and connecting with suppliers, but it does not define the protocols or the exact language for data exchange. As a result, UDDI is typically used in conjunction with SOAP, which defines the protocol, and WSDL. This language provides the exact syntax that must be used for the two partner applications to interact.

6.1.9 Enterprise JavaBeans (EJB)

The Sun Company was interested in creating a hardware- and software-independent language that could support Web applications without being compiled. They were motivated by the growth of the Web and the need for programming tools that would enable browsers to create and run applications. Sun created a pseudo machine code that was available for anyone to use in building a virtual machine. In parallel, Sun introduced Java, a very advanced object-oriented programming language and development tool. Anyone who created a machine-dependent virtual machine could then run Java programs.

Each machine architecture and operating system contains services that are not specified by Java. The result is, for example, that Microsoft's ActiveX product uses Java, but it cannot run on Unix. To avoid legal problems, Sun extended Java's original standards.

Java programs are slow on machines with code interpretation. To improve performance, JavaScript was created to provide browsers with Java source code. This has helped to show visualization examples and prototypes very rapidly, because Java is friendly enough to support such services.

Similar programs — called Java servlets — have been provided for Web servers, as well. To support these servlets, a new Web-server model had to be introduced that was responsible for the server-related services.

Reusability is an important factor in design and development. JavaBeans defines a framework of software design while also supporting framework-dependent service integration. Sun is trying to control this standard very carefully. In the case of JavaBeans, networking is very well supported.

Enterprise JavaBeans (EJB) is intended for mainframe environments. They offer a solution for large software systems, such as event management, combined with excellent scalability. This model is being supported by software design tools, but the confidence in this technology has been seriously eroded by performance differences between C and Java, to the disadvantage of Java. This performance difference has recently been narrowed down to 10 to 30%. Java trades this difference against user friendliness. Java supporters include IBM, Sun-Netscape Alliance, BEA, Oracle, Inprise, Iona, Fujitsu, Sybase Gemstone, and Persistence.

The two most important EJB object types are the entity bean, a long-term object type (e.g., a customer with its data stored and maintained in a database), and a short-range session bean (e.g., executing a business process).

It is expected that EJB will incorporate the most important attributes of the common object request broker architecture (CORBA) within the next few years. Its success will depend on the power and performance of Java. EJB uses an interpreter, with all of its advantages and disadvantages. For industrial use, EJB needs a very complex fine tuning.

Java enterprise edition (J2EE) removes the complexity of usage in EBPP applications by significantly simplifying application development. J2EE provides standardized, reusable modular components that reduce programming needs and complexity. The adoption of these technical standardization technologies is likely to have positive impacts on the development of EBPP applications and will remove many of the barriers to its implementation.

6.1.10 .NET Common Language Infrastructure

The .NET common language infrastructure represents another platform for Web services. It has been written by Microsoft for several languages, but its runtimes only work under the various versions of Windows.

6.2 Payment Standards

Financial institutes have been trying to introduce and maintain various standards to exchange financial data among each other. The standardization progress is limited, however, by differences in the technical capabilities of financial institutions located in different geographical areas, and by differences in security requirements, laws, taxation rules, and the individual business interests of the institutions. In order to successfully implement EBPP solutions, financial data must be exchanged not only between financial institutions, but also between issuers of statements, bills and invoices, and payers (businesses and private customers). The following section addresses current standards and standardization trends; it can be seen that these trends are heavily influenced by the EBPP business model under consideration.

6.2.1 Open Financial Exchange (OFX)

One of the most successful standards in the financial industry thus far has been the OFX protocol. OFX was originally created for communications between personal financial managers and financial institutions. Designed to enable interoperability between the banking industry and EBPP, OFX was created by CheckFree, Intuit, and Microsoft in 1997. OFX is a unified specification for the exchange of financial data between financial institutions, businesses, and private customers in a Web-based communications environment. The specification is available free of charge. User accreditation is supported by a certification process. The primary strength of this solution is that it simplifies the exchange of financial data between billers and payers by eliminating the issue of connectivity. In essence, the various systems used by different companies are provided with an OFX front-end that allows interconnection among the OFX membership. Utilizing the Internet, OFX relies on a client-server system, which enables direct connections between the client (biller and payer) and any financial-institution server employing a request-response model. The OFX protocol sits between the legacy data, found in back-office systems, and the data and parsing technology utilized to extract the relevant information from legacy data.

The print-stream stripping and creation of messaging formats such as OFX is a bottleneck in the overall EBPP process and can cause significant delays. In the case of the biller-direct business model, this conversion into OFX is not needed. In such cases, the print stream can be read, and no additional reformatting is required. However, OFX is designed as a streamlining technology for open standards, in direct opposition to the proprietary standards of the biller-direct business model.

OFX has multiple flavors, with the result that OFX needs some standardization itself. With the latest version of OFX, the support of bill presentment includes the following transactions (Un, 1999):

- Sign On: The customer authenticates with the biller or the bill-presentment service provider.
- Enrollment: The customer enrolls with a bill-presentment service provider and is then able to receive bills.
- Activation: The customer activates bill presentment for a specified billing account. Customers can have more than one account with a biller and therefore may need to activate each account separately.
- Bill summary request: The customer requests bill summaries of activated accounts. A customer service provider can also make a request on behalf of a group of customers. The bill summaries contain the due date of the bill, the biller, the amount due, and a URL that points to the bill detail image, usually an HTML or XML page.
- Notification: A customer or customer service provider notifies the bill publisher that a bill has been viewed by the customer.

Older versions of OFX format the transaction data in SGML. Newer versions of OFX will use XML as the standard for describing data.

OFX solution providers include the following companies (The Phillips Group, 2001):

> Atris Technology
> Avolent
> Brokat Financial Services
> CheckFree Corporation
> Corillian
> Digital Insight
> Edocs
> Hamilton and Sullivan
> Intellidata Technologies
> Intuit
> Transaction Works
> WebEasy, Inc.

Typical OFX implementations are provided by the following companies, among others (The Phillips Group, 2001):

> Atris Technology
> Avolent
> Brokat Infosystems
> Business Logic Corporation
> Corillian Corporation
> Hughes Software Systems
> Intellidata Technologies Corporation
> Virtual Communications
> WebEasy, Inc.

6.2.2 GOLD

Developed in a similar environment as OFX, GOLD is the solution developed by Integrion Financial Network. GOLD was set up by 15 North American banks in 1997, including Banc One, Bank of America, First Chicago, Mellon Bank, NationsBank, and Royal Bank of Canada. IBM also participated by constructing a cross-platform messaging specification as a means of enabling EBPP, primarily using banking systems as EBPP portals. Integrion has created the GOLD standard for electronic financial service (EFS) as an alternative to OFX. Working together with Visa, Citibank, and First Union, Integrion has served a majority of U.S. households. Integrion has offered a way to automate financial processes based on EBPP, but the GOLD standard has suffered setbacks, with partners leaving the alliance.

6.2.3 *Interactive Financial Exchange (IFX)*

The National Automated Clearinghouse Association (NACHA) is working to streamline the standardization process. NACHA has created the standard automatic clearinghouse (ACH) solution that is used by many service providers. NACHA and BITS are working together to migrate OFX and GOLD onto IFX. In this way, the banking industry's and the financial community's technical standards will be incorporated to create an Internet-based client-server system. This system would connect directly between the client and the financial institution's server, enabling interoperable exchange of data among banks, service providers, billers, and customers. IFX came out as a result of the InteropraBILL, an initiative set up to promote development of Internet commerce in North America. IFX is also supported by the Data Interchange Standards Association (DISA). Closely affiliated with NACHA is the Council for Electronic Billing and Payment (CEBP). This U.S.-based council acts as a forum to facilitate, educate, and promote the use of electronic consumer-initiated billing and payment programs and services.

Benefits of IFX include (The Phillips Group, 2001):

- Support of both front-end and back-end processes
- Support of additional financial services
- Greater functionality at the transaction process stage
- More-detailed remittance data and status checking, which reduces the pressure on customer services
- Advanced administrative flow control in support of customer service representatives
- Support of CRM (customer relationship management), which is an important value-added aspect of EBPP
- XML integration capabilities that facilitate the integration between documentation and financial standards

However, there are also problems with this standard, which is not EBPP-business-model neutral. The IFX standard favors the consolidator and financial-institution business models of EBPP. The process whereby other business models are locked out somehow is clearly understood by IFX supporters:

- Use of a single password attached to a customer
- Use of a single bill list
- Use of a single point of contact for consumer enrollment
- Use of a single point of payment

This solution removes a number of problems and demystifies customer choice, but the biller is forced to accept one business model over other models. It is expected that the full adoption of this standard will take several years.

Portal channels and business models may not support the IFX standard. Certain portals are committed to OFX and now offer services similar to those provided by a fully deployed IFX-based system. One example is the Intuit portal with My Finance applications. This portal, which offers integrated EBPP and financial services, has invested into OFX and does not actually need IFX.

Many industry players consider IFX as the logical next step to migration from OFX. However, the process to complete IFX has been slower than expected. IFX represents a big architectural change from OFX, and some entities are reluctant to make the leap. In addition, there are technical issues deriving from the differences between OFX and GOLD. While IFX is getting mature for implementation, the OFX consortium will continue to release new OFX versions. Companies who are considering deploying OFX capabilities for bill presentment today will likely have their investments protected because those OFX functions will be migrated onto IFX.

All IFX specifications will be implemented in XML from the very beginning.

6.2.4 eCheck

The electronic check (eCheck) is a new payment instrument combining the security, speed, and processing efficiencies of all electronic transactions with the familiar and well-developed legal infrastructure and business processes associated with paper checks. It is the first and only electronic payment mechanism chosen by the U.S. Treasury to make high-value payments over the public Internet.

An eCheck is the electronic version or representation of a paper check. It has the following attributes:

- Contains the same information as a paper check
- Has the same rich legal framework as paper checks
- Can be linked with unlimited information and exchanged directly between parties
- Can be used in any remote transactions where paper checks are used
- Enhances the functions and features provided by bank checking accounts
- Expands on the usefulness of paper checks by providing value-added information

The electronic check leverages the check payment system, a core competency of the banking industry. It fits within current business practices, eliminating the need for expensive process reengineering. It works like a paper check, but it does so in a purely electronic form, requiring fewer manual steps. Electronic checks can be used by all bank consumers with checking accounts, including small and mid-size businesses, which currently have limited access to electronic payment systems.

There are fundamental similarities and differences between a paper check, the eCheck, and other electronic funds transfer (EFT) transactions. The payer writes the eCheck using one of many types of electronic devices and gives the eCheck to the payee electronically. The payee deposits the electronic check, receives credit, and the payee's bank clears the eCheck to the paying bank, which validates the eCheck and then charges the check to the payer's account. This new way of doing business has a number of new features, including:

- Ability to conduct bank transactions, yet safe enough to use the Internet
- Unlimited but controlled information-carrying capability
- Reduction in fraud losses for all parties
- Automatic verification of content and validity
- Traditional checking features such as stop payments and easy reconciliation
- Enhanced capabilities such as effective dating

The eCheck can be used by all account holders, large and small, even when other electronic payment solutions are too risky or inappropriate. It is considered the most secure payment instrument today, providing rapid and secure settlement of financial obligations. Furthermore, it can be used with all existing checking accounts and can be initiated from a variety of hardware and software platforms and software applications.

Electronic checks are based on the financial services markup language (FSML). They use strong digital signatures and can be combined with secure tokens such as smart cards. eChecks are secure because they support:

- Digital certificates
- Authentication
- Public-key cryptography
- Digital signatures
- Certificate authorities
- Duplicate detection
- Encryption

They further enhance banking practices with added security so that even breaking the cryptographic protections would not necessarily allow a fraudulent transaction to be paid.

Electronic checks are based on check law and have the same characteristics of paper checks but in an all-electronic form. Account agreements include provisions for eCheck transactions. Banks will keep their leadership position in this form of payment for the following reasons:

- This standard leverages and strengthens the relationship between the account holder and banking institution
- It will continue to emphasize the strengths of the check as a payment instrument
- It is based on a universal set of technologies to permit rapid and effective deployment
- It targets virtually all payment system participants

Electronic checks will lead the way to a standardized electronic commerce environment. They can streamline, unify, and simplify the payment side of EBPP.

6.2.5 NACHA

NACHA is a not-for-profit trade organization that develops operating rules and business practices for the automated clearinghouse (ACH) network and for other areas of electronic payments. NACHA activities and initiatives facilitate the adoption of electronic payments in the areas of Internet commerce, EBPP, financial electronic data exchange (EDI), international payments, electronic checks, electronic benefit transfer (EBT), and student lending. It also promotes the use of electronic-payment products and services, such as direct deposit and direct payment. NACHA represents more than 12,000 financial institutions through its network of regional ACH associations. It has over 600 members in its seven industry councils and corporate affiliate membership programs.

6.2.6 Financial Services Technology Consortium (FSTC)

FSTC is a not-for-profit organization whose goal is to enhance the competitiveness of the U.S. financial services industry. Dues-paying members include banks, financial service providers (FSP), research laboratories, universities, technology companies, and government agencies. FSTC sponsors project-oriented collaborative research and development on technical projects affecting the entire financial services industry. Particular emphasis is placed on enabling online financial services, payment systems, and services while leveraging new technologies that help banks maintain their customer relationships, boost operational efficiency, reduce risks and costs, and expand their market reach and share.

6.2.7 Bank Internet Payment System (BIPS)

BIPS is leading the way to electronic commerce. Advances in networked information technology, more computing power, and lower computing costs are driving companies toward the paperless world of electronic commerce. The Internet offers great potential in this respect by providing alternatives for communications and payments conveniently and less expensively. Both billers and payers are interested. Yet, only a few corporations are actually using the Internet in this way because there are no trusted and secure electronic payment mechanisms that are cost effective.

The financial services industry can help corporations and customers process electronic payments over the Internet by developing several components that are necessary to support secure electronic transactions. BIPS is an architecture, an open specification, a secure methodology for spontaneous instructions to be initiated over public networks, and a standard interface to existing payment systems.

BIPS is leading the way toward these goals. Sponsored by a consortium of leading technology banks, it will focus on encouraging companies to initiate a variety of payment transactions via the Internet through increased system security. BIPS supporters include Citibank, Concept Five Technologies, Fujitsu Research Institute, Glenview State Bank, GlobeSet, Mellon Bank, NCR, and Tandem Computers. BIPS demonstrates a secure, reliable, comprehensive, and widely available payment infrastructure that supports the following functions:

- Preserves existing business relationships and processes
- Utilizes existing bank back-end payment systems
- Facilitates ease of use
- Links banks' customers and business customers to bank systems
- Enables banks to provide surety, accuracy, flexibility, control, accountability, and convenience

BIPS provides a specification for a protocol and secure server for banks to offer payment transaction services over the Internet. It supports the following functions:

- Initiates payment instructions
- Allows payers and payees to agree on terms and mechanisms
- Accesses multiple payment systems, enabling customers and banks to choose the most cost-effective way to make payments
- Provides the intelligence to select the appropriate mechanisms for the payer based on the payer's requirements for cost and speed of settlement
- Provides online authentication of payers and payees and authorization for the transaction

BIPS demonstrates through working prototypes the interoperability and the infrastructure that benefits banks and their customers. The specification is modified and validated based on the prototype experiences. The prototypes also identify organizational issues, risks to the systems and participants, and potential solutions within the prototype environment.

BIPS also has additional benefits:

- Provides a secure method for Internet payments designed for corporate customers and consumers
- Provides interoperability between banks by leveraging existing settlement systems, such as ACH, Fedwire, etc.
- Provides access to multiple bank payment systems with one protocol and one interface without requiring a significant change in existing systems
- Provides the intelligence to select the appropriate payment mechanism for the payer (entity purchasing goods and services) based on the payer's requirements for cost and speed of settlement
- Provides online authentication of payers and payees (entity selling goods and services) and authorization for executing the transaction

- Builds on current standards
- Creates an environment for vendors to offer competitive assured choices for multiple banks

BIPS can be considered as an alliance between financial institutions and technology providers.

6.2.8 iKP

iKP represents a family of protocols for secure electronic payments over the Internet. The protocols implement credit card-based transactions between the customer (payer) and the biller (merchant) while using the existing financial network for clearing and authorization. The protocols can be extended to apply to other payment models, such as debit cards and electronic checks. The protocols are based on public key cryptography and can be implemented in either software or hardware. Individual protocols differ in key management complexity and degree of security. It is intended that their deployment be gradual and incremental. They are connected to the SET standard.

6.2.9 OpenSSL

The goal is to offer a robust, commercial-grade, full-featured, and open-source toolkit implementing the secure sockets layer (SSL) and transport layer security (TLS) protocols — as well as a full-strength, general-purpose cryptography library — managed by a worldwide community of volunteers. All participating entities use the Internet to communicate, plan, and develop the OpenSSL toolkit and its related documentation.

6.2.10 SET

SET (secure electronic transfer) is a European payment standard — developed by Visa, MasterCard, and Europay — based on PKI certificate technology. Started up in 1997, SET allows customers to purchase goods and services using their credit cards but without the need to send their card number through the Internet. SET has been rolled out throughout the world but suffers from some technical problems that have slowed its acceptance as a globally secure payment standard.

6.2.11 Smart Cards

The smart card is one of the latest additions to the world of information technology. Similar in size to plastic payment cards, it has an embedded microprocessor or memory chip that stores electronic data and programs protected by advanced security features. When coupled with a reader, the smart card has the processing power to serve many different applications. As an access-control device, smart cards make personal and business data available only to the appropriate users. Another application provides users with the ability to make a purchase or exchange value. Smart cards provide data portability, security, and convenience.

Smart cards come in two varieties: memory cards and microprocessor cards. Memory cards simply store data and can be viewed as a small floppy disk with optional security. A microprocessor card, on the other hand, can add, delete, and manipulate data in its memory on the card. Similar to a miniature computer, a microprocessor card has an input/output port, operating system, and hard disk with built-in security features.

Contact smart cards must be inserted into a smart-card reader. Contactless smart cards are passed near an antenna to carry out a transaction.

6.3 Alliances among EBPP Entities

6.3.1 Spectrum

The Spectrum consortium is a U.S.-based banking alliance supportive of the IFX standard. Spectrum is backed by Chase Manhattan, Wells Fargo, First Union, and their numerous partners in the banking and credit card industries. This consortium has a potential to serve millions of online users. Like Integrion, Spectrum's goal is to provide an open, interoperable mechanism for exchanging online bills, regardless of the technology employed by the individual members of the consortium.

Spectrum routes online payments, presentments, invoices, statements, and other related information through an EBPP switch. Twenty-four financial institutions belong to the Spectrum network or have signed letters of interest to participate in the network. Among them, there are 10 leading banks from the U.S. The list of founders includes JP Morgan Chase, Wachovia, and Wells Fargo. Partners include First Union Corp., First Tennessee National Corp., FleetBoston Financial Corp., Hibernia National Bank, Provident Bank, and Union Bank of California.

6.3.2 Transpoint

An alternative route to standardization is offered by Transpoint from Check-Free. Transpoint — founded by Microsoft, First Data, and Citibank — was created to offer a fully integrated end-to-end EBPP system incorporating EBPP technologies and the financial infrastructure in one place. Financial institutions could utilize all services of TransPoint while branding them as their own online banking solutions. The services were offered free of charge to the banks who showed interest in using them. TransPoint has shared the revenues made from its use and charged the biller a minimal fee, comparable with postage, for delivery of the electronic bill and remittance/payment information.

6.3.3 Credit Card Alliance (MasterCard, Amex, Visa)

Various credit card companies have also positioned themselves in the EBPP market after recognizing the market's potential. Based on their strong legacy position with credit cards, they have built strong relationships with their customers who might also be interested in EBPP. The credit card industry's strengths are based on its global coverage and international transactional and financial relationships. This industry is capable and experienced in rolling out a global standard.

The evolution of credit card-based services shows a number of similarities with the EBPP evolution. In the beginning, credit cards worked only in their issuing countries. Later on, they progressed from local to global. A similar approach will provide the necessary experience for EBPP to grow from national to international.

Leading providers are MasterCard with its remote payment and presentment system (RPPS), American Express with Electronic Wallet, and Visa with Cyber-Bills. The customer base is a very strong driver, with millions of cardholders who are already standardized under the branded credit card and hundreds of merchants who have accepted the business relationship with credit card companies. They could become key partners to banks and billers in the EBPP world.

Online payments show increasing acceptance rates due to ease of use, security, and buyer convenience. Despite the benefits of using credit cards, billers may refuse them because of the high charges imposed by the credit card company, lack of knowledge or experience, and complexity.

In summary, the credit card industry has polarized around banking and nonbanking interests.

6.4 Summary

EBPP is a chain of multiple worksteps with multiple participating entities. The complex process, as seen in Chapter 2, consists of technological steps (bill creation and presentment) and of financial steps (various payment alternatives). Powerful standards are required to collaborate among very different entities — billers, consolidators, aggregators, and payers. This chapter has addressed the documentation standards that could unify and simplify the bill creation, presentment, exchange, and distribution processes. This was followed by a discussion of evolving financial standards that regulate the secure payment process. The standardization process has not yet been completed. To enable operational EBPP solutions, alliances among participating entities might be useful, assuming the number of players is able to reach critical mass. The two leading standardization directions have been completed and extended by evolving security standards.

Chapter 7

EBPP Service Providers and Products

Chapter 3 addressed business models for billers (issuers of statements, bills, and invoices) and payers. Features of value-added solutions were outlined in Chapter 4. This chapter targets solution providers who can support one or more business models. The following groups of solution providers are of interest (Hill, 2001):

- Software vendors: Back-end technology drives all electronic systems, and EBPP is no exception. Software developers such as Avolent, Bottomline, and CheckFree (with its i-Solutions) will establish the technical direction of both B2B and B2C sectors, including settling on common standards for information transfer (open financial exchange [OFX] and interactive financial exchange [IFX] are examples). Whether or not the smaller firms will continue to pursue ventures in other areas of EBPP, such as bill consolidation and payment processing, remains to be seen. It appears likely, though, that industry giants such as CheckFree will continue to span vendor categories by offering a range of software solutions and services.
- Application service providers (ASP): They represent companies who own and host the software required to support various business models. Usually, smaller billers and consolidators start business offers with ASPs.
- Financial service providers (FSP): Because they already benefit from consumer trust and confidence, banking institutions appear to be in the best position to offer online B2C bill payment. In fact, the B2C sector will not realize its potential until banks form a workable alliance among themselves to support consumer bill consolidation. Analysts also see a significant role for service infrastructure companies as they support banks' efforts from behind the scenes. As payment processing

organizations, however, banks and credit card companies will remain central to EBPP solutions in both sectors, regardless of whether or not they band together to meet consumers' needs. Their partnerships with software vendors and consolidators will determine their futures in EBPP.

■ Billing service providers (BSP): They are large billing vendors who offer various rating, billing, and related services. These companies are interested in incorporating EBPP as part of their services.

■ Consolidators and aggregators: Acting as intermediaries and coordinators between software vendors, billers, and customers, billing consolidators, also known as aggregators, may offer the important crucial link between billers willing to offer online payment and customers willing to pay bills online. Analysts agree unanimously that the highest hurdle for the B2C sector is the fact that only one or a few of any individual consumer's bills are currently available for online payment. Consolidators can tip that scale, ensuring that most consumers can pay the majority of their bills through centralized, accessible systems. In this case, the B2C sector actually seems to be leading B2B, where demand for centralized billing services is growing more slowly.

■ Portals, distributors, and exchanges: On the consumer side, Internet portals offer a likely channel through which EBPP consolidators can offer that all-important critical mass of users. Familiar services such as Quicken and Yahoo already enjoy visibility, respect, and trust among Internet-savvy consumers. Portals stand to benefit in turn because bill presentment is a naturally "sticky" Web activity that draws visitors repeatedly to a given site and thus increases traffic — the stuff of successful Web enterprises that depend on advertising as a major revenue stream. The business sector seeks to develop similar, centralized points-of-service through Web-based trading exchanges. The most promising exchanges will be specific to particular industries. The leaders will be those exchanges that have an established base of participants and that can offer services incorporating business rules and workflows common to the companies within its target industry.

■ Document and postal service outsourcers: They are companies who originally undertook bill and document processing in paper format and have now moved to EBP and EBPP.

■ Service bureaus: They offer solutions for smaller billers who want to be connected to large consolidators. This solution enables bill-presentment aggregators to collate bills from smaller billers and to forward collated bills to consolidators.

Table 7.1 shows a matrix between business models for EBPP and the solution providers identified above. The matrix collates the EBPP products and services offered by the groups of solution providers. Of course, there are multiple overlaps, indicating that one product might support various solutions for multiple business models and that certain business models are being supported by a suite of products and services.

Table 7.1 Business Models and Solution Providers

Solution Providers	Biller Direct	E-Mail	Consolidator (thick)	Consolidator (thin)	Consumer-centric	Portals, Distributors, and Exchanges	Application Service Providers	Invited Pull	Service Bureau
Software vendors and ASPs	x	x	x	x	x	x	x	x	—
Financial service providers	—	—	x	x	x	—	—	—	—
Billing service providers	x	x	—	—	—	—	—	x	x
Consolidators and aggregators	—	—	x	x	x	—	—	—	—
Portals, distributors, and exchanges	—	—	—	—	—	x	—	—	—
Document and postal service outsourcers	x	—	x	x	x	—	x	—	x
Service bureaus	—	x	—	—	—	—	x	—	x

Important criteria for positioning and evaluating products and services include:

- Functionality of products and services
- High-level evaluation of technological capabilities
- Identification of supported business models
- Identification of value-added features
- Future expectations and directions
- Practical references

7.1 Software Vendors and Application Service Providers

Software vendors offer a broad variety of solutions. Practically all EBPP business models are supported by at least one ASP. These vendors are always partners in collaborative ventures.

7.1.1 CheckFree

CheckFree has been offering services of receiving and paying bills electronically over the last 20 years. CheckFree offers services and products for practically every aspect of the electronic presentment and payment market. With the acquisition of BlueGill Technologies and its merger with Transpoint, CheckFree became one of the largest EBPP companies in the world. The company's client base is substantial:

- More than 250 financial institutions utilize its electronic payment services.
- More than 250 money management institutions rely on its investment service products.
- More than one-third of the automated clearinghouse (ACH) transactions are processed in the U.S. through its ACH software and services.

7.1.1.1 Products and Services

7.1.1.1.1 Genesis WebPay Services

The Electronic Commerce Division offers electronic billing and payment services to consumer service providers (CSP), the sites where consumers can enroll to receive and pay bills online. CheckFree works with banks, brokerages, credit unions, and Internet portals. The company offers access to the Genesis processing engine, which handles end-to-end electronic bill presentment, pay-anyone services, customer care, and transaction tracking. CheckFree has also developed its own user interface for cases when the CSP decides to host the EBP application at CheckFree. This is the case with its new WebPay™ service. However, if a CSP wants to develop its own user interface or is working with a third-party Internet banking service provider, like Corrilian, Digital Insight, or FiServ, then CheckFree offers a tool kit that connects the external user interface to CheckFree processing services.

Genesis 2000 benefits include:

- CheckFree Web billing and payment: This product line offers a choice of front-end solutions based on experience with bank, brokerage, and credit union clients, such as First Union, Bank One, Navy Credit Union, and Charles Schwab; portals, such as Yahoo, WingspanBank, and Quicken; and personal financial management (PFM) software. The front end has complete control over customization, branding, and associated advertising.
- CheckFree e-bill: The company has been in this business since 1997; the current version of this service offers a number of dynamic billing features. There are over 100 billers from various industries. Billing contact is available to all Genesis 2000 clients.
- Pay Everyone: CheckFree clients can offer "pay everyone" capabilities to consumers, which means that they can make payments from their computers to anyone to whom they would like to send a check. This includes electronic billers and all other billers, even those who do not present electronically, such as day-care centers or lawn-maintenance providers. Pay-everyone payments can also be sent to individuals, such as children in college.
- CheckFree guarantee: CheckFree clients can display the CheckFree Guarantee symbol to minimize consumer concern about fraud or late fees. It was developed to educate consumers about the terms and conditions, including limited liability, that make electronic billing and payment through CheckFree as safe or safer than using credit cards or mailing paper checks.
- Volume-pricing opportunities: CheckFree is transitioning to contracts that offer large volume incentives to promote electronic billing and payment. As a client's electronic-commerce initiatives grow, more CheckFree Genesis capabilities can be added. This allows clients to focus on their core businesses and build relationships while outsourcing to CheckFree the transaction processing, infrastructure management, and customer service.
- Online enrollment: CheckFree Genesis 2000 enables online enrollment, including "enroll everyone" capability, in which anyone with an existing bank or brokerage checking account in good standing can sign up for electronic billing and payment. Consumers no longer have to mail in cancelled checks to get started.
- Customer care: Clients can leverage the Genesis engine that handles end-to-end processing of electronic billing and payments. Transparent to the consumer, CheckFree clients can leverage its $24 \times 7 \times 365$ customer-care capabilities and event tracking as part of one end-to-end system. Genesis 2000 also supports browser-based customer care for billers, financial institutions, and portals.

- Standards-based technology: It supports both OFX and GOLD standards, as well as support for Web, PFM software, telephone, and personal-computer dial-up interfaces.
- Integrated self-care: Customers are able to quickly access billing and payment history as well as answers to many of their frequently asked questions at their banking Web site and through online help. In addition, integrated e-mail capabilities allow consumers to conveniently contact customer service representatives around the clock.

Genesis Services can be combined with other services and with other products of the company.

7.1.1.1.2   E-Bill and E-Payments over E-Mail

Financial service providers (FSP) and portals that deploy the WebPay service can offer their customers the ability to receive and pay any e-bills via e-mail. When the bill is available, the FSP or portal simply sends an e-mail to the customer. The e-mail contains bill summary information, a link to bill details, and a "pay" button. Customers can pay based on the summary information or link to the biller site to view bill details. When the consumer clicks "pay," his or her identity is authenticated by the FSP or at the portal's secure site before the payment is validated and settled with the biller.

CheckFree has processed bill payments for Quicken Software, Microsoft Money, and the old Managing Your Money software packages for years. Bill payment (without presentment) is also offered to thousands of CSPs either directly or through value-added resale channels. CheckFree also offers electronic funds transfer (EFT), debit and credit solutions (such as balance transfer services for credit card companies), and more.

Organizations deploying the latest version of CheckFree WebPay can also offer their customers the ability to exchange money with each other electronically as a natural extension of electronic billing and payment. This service supersedes other electronic money-exchange services in several ways:

- Integration with electronic billing and payment: WebPay is the only service integrated with electronic billing and payment, which means consumers get a consolidated view of all of their electronic payment history and the same level of payment-history tracking and customer care they expect from their electronic billing and payment service. Whether they pay a bill, pay their lawn-care provider, send money to a friend or family member, or exchange money to make an auction purchase, the payment transaction is protected by the same security and customer-care services.
- Uses existing accounts at organizations consumers already trust: The service uses financial accounts consumers already have and is delivered by FSPs or portals they already trust. Consumers do not have to "prefund" an account or put their trust in an unfamiliar company to exchange money electronically with others.

- Fast online enrollment and verification of both senders and receivers: Intuitive registration and online verification using the Equifax Secure authentication engine makes enrolling in and using the service easy while maintaining stringent security standards. Both senders and receivers of money must be validated by enrolling in the service. When the system is instructed by a validated user to send money to another person, the system first checks to verify that the recipient is enrolled in the service. If the recipient is enrolled, the transaction occurs and confirmation is sent via e-mail. If the designated recipient is not already enrolled, he receives an e-mail invitation to enroll in the service to receive the money, as in "John Smith would like to send you $30." Enrolling in the service does not require the receiver to use the same financial services organization as the sender, nor does it require the receiver to accept the funds into any account other than ones she already has. The receiver can enroll in the service through any Check-Free partner offering it — enabling open, fluid money exchange without requiring consumers to change or establish any new financial accounts. Enrollment information is secured and protected by the FSP or portal offering the service.
- No need to expose account information: Users share account information only with the FSP or portal through which they enroll in the service. In the case of online auctions, the service validates to the seller that the buyer has funds to complete the transaction. The buyer never has to share account information with the seller.
- Access to multiple accounts for easy money transfers: With a single sign-on, consumers can transfer funds among accounts, whether or not they reside at the same financial institution, in the same session that they pay their bills, thus saving time and adding another layer of convenience and control.

7.1.1.1.2.1 Benefits for FSPs and Portals — FSPs and portals using Check-Free's distribution and payment network enjoy the following benefits:

- Enhanced customer retention and acquisition: By offering the services consumers want — such as billing and payment via e-mail — banks, brokerages, credit unions, and portals bolster customer satisfaction and loyalty.
- Brand exposure and increased revenue potential: FSPs and portals have the opportunity to expose their brands to consumers with every payment. FSPs can choose standard or custom branding options for Check-Free WebPay. Custom branding offers the opportunity for personalized cross-selling and targeted marketing services, strengthening the potential relationship with each existing customer.
- Integrated extension of existing services: Reception of e-bills and sending of e-payments via e-mail are extensions to existing CheckFree services already offered by FSPs and portals. These payments are covered by

the same CheckFree guarantee that protects existing electronic billing and payment transactions, and they receive the same security, privacy, and quality considerations afforded by CheckFree's Genesis, an industry-leading electronic billing and payment infrastructure.

7.1.1.1.2.2 Biller Benefits — Billers choosing to send bills through Check-Free's distribution and payment network receive the following benefits:

- Another convenient way for consumers to receive and pay bills online: The convenience of e-mail receipt and payment, combined with the control of consolidated reporting and customer care through an FSP or Internet portal, offers a new incentive for consumers to receive and pay bills electronically.
- Consistent tracking and customer care: Tracking of bill distribution and payment, along with related customer-care service, continues to be provided by the FSP or portal offering the electronic billing and payment service to consumers. Consumer convenience is enhanced without compromising consumer protections.
- Enhanced customer relationship: Consumers can access the biller's Web site directly from the e-mail to view bill detail in the biller's secure environment. There, consumers can take advantage of all of the interactive customer service and sales convenience features that billers design into their electronic bills.

7.1.1.1.2.3 Service Availability — The WebPay offering lays the foundation for a powerful suite of interoperable products that give customers excellent bill-payment access. With expanded features and enhanced interfaces, WebPay is a robust EBPP application that puts convenience and control into the hands of the customer.

Alternative payment services include:

- Wireless WebPay: This service provides customers with yet another access point into their WebPay account via wireless PDA or Internet-enabled cell phone. Incorporating many of the convenient WebPay features, this alternative provides maximum mobility to WebPay customers, who can stay connected to their accounts by receiving and paying bills remotely via a growing number of wireless devices.
- PhonePay: This service provides natural-language speech recognition technology, enabling WebPay customers to access their accounts and pay bills anywhere and anytime they have access to a telephone. Greeted by a warm, natural, human-voice recording, PhonePay customers are guided through an intuitive user interface that automatically adjusts to their speech and language patterns.
- Personal financial management (PFM): CheckFree products also support both Quicken 2001 and Microsoft Money 2002 and higher versions, giving WebPay users an additional tool to manage their personal

finances by leveraging the power of these popular PFM software packages. Likewise, with interoperability, PFM users gain enhanced bill-pay functionality and access points through WebPay, Wireless WebPay, and PhonePay.

7.1.1.1.3 i-Solutions

7.1.1.1.3.1 Products and Services — The i-Solutions division markets software, professional services, and hosted applications that enable billers to provide end-to-end B2C and B2B e-billing, payment, and e-statement delivery. These i-Solutions offer software for e-bill and e-statement creation. The software is highly customizable and is available in industry-specific versions, e.g., for insurance, utility, banking, and telecommunications companies.

7.1.1.1.3.2 Key Features — Key features of i-Series include the following:

- Business process rules support: A critical new component of the i-Series platform is the ability for billers to leverage predefined dispute codes and discount-term utilization capabilities. In addition, payers can take advantage of "roles-based" workflow support that allows personnel within multiple departments to intelligently review, dispute, and adjust charges at the line-item level.
- ERP/CRM integration: CheckFree i-Series provides for integration with leading enterprise resource planning (ERP) and customer relationship management (CRM) applications, with the ability to transfer back-office data files among other legacy systems.
- Online analytical processing support: In response to strong customer demand, CheckFree i-Solutions is providing intelligent, browser-based analytical tools under which businesses can leverage an interface between i-Series and Cognos's online analytical processing application, PowerPlay. This tool will allow users (or payers) to drill down in a multidimensional graphical "cube" environment to conduct more-detailed analysis of their bills and statements.
- Fully Java-based architecture: This product was completely reconstructed in Java so that CheckFree could leverage the Web-based development environment's portability, thus facilitating creation and deployment of Web applications in the majority of production environments.
- Payments: CheckFree offers multiple options for ACH payment by service subscribers. The CheckFree payment options range from online payments and batch transactions to completely integrated payment solutions.
- Marketing: CheckFree intends to extend its one-to-one, highly targeted messaging capabilities to the B2B environment through the Market Direct™ module. Businesses can leverage this functionality to send customer/user-specific, operational-based messages regarding business-processing collaboration.

- Additional platform support: In addition to the extensive list of operating environments certified with the i-Series engine, the new i-Series release supports the following platforms: IBM DB2 7.1 Database, SQL Server 2000 Database, and Microsoft IIS 5.0 Web/Application Server.
- Increased control and flexibility for storing objects within the i-Series engine: Primarily intended for B2B applications, this advanced feature allows for efficient handling of statements in excess of 10,000 pages while meeting Web application performance needs. Regardless of statement size, users have the flexibility to control where and how statement objects are stored within the i-Series engine for those clients with specialized needs to selectively access statement objects.
- Improved operational support: To better manage the rapid growth in the number of billers, statements, and bills being presented by clients, i-Series includes a new statement-run audit-and-tracking feature along with an enhanced log viewer. For those clients who also take advantage of CheckFree's extensive distribution network, a new module, e-Bill Connect, will seamlessly manage and control the flow of information among billers, biller service providers, CheckFree, and FSPs and portals.

7.1.1.1.4 i-Series Select

7.1.1.1.4.1 Products and Services — For those companies that want to offer B2C e-billing and e-statement services quickly and without customization, i-Solutions offers i-Series Select. This product delivers prepackaged, industry-specific software based on best practices for electronic bill creation, distribution, and payment. The i-Series Select software is for companies that want to deploy a biller-direct business model for delivery of e-bills through their own sites and/or distribute their bills through nearly 300 Web sites run by financial institutions, brokerage firms, and Internet portals served by CheckFree's distribution network.

Tailored packages for the financial services, telecommunications, insurance, and utility industries enable quick, lower-cost implementations of the most commonly required functionalities for e-bills and e-statements. Select versions are crafted for companies that do not need to integrate B2B billing functions and do not need to build highly tailored features. To meet the requirements of the four leading industries in the area of B2C bills, four packages are provided in the i-Select package:

1. i-Insurance Select
2. i-Banker Select
3. i-Utility Select
4. i-Telco Select

7.1.1.1.4.2 i-Telco Select — CheckFree's i-Telco conserves the information technology (IT) resources of the service provider. It is a solution created for telecommunications, employing feedback and the best practices of EBPP and telco industry leaders. Combining the features and functionality most requested by telcos with proven interfaces, it is a solution that can have the service provider up and running in 90 days. Table 7.2 summarizes the features of i-Telco.

7.1.1.1.4.3   Market Direct — i-Solutions sells an additional software module — Market Direct, an Internet-based marketing application enabling targeted marketing and campaign management throughout the entire EBPP process. This module is a robust software application that makes it easy to quickly create and launch Internet-based advertising campaigns. With the user-friendly graphical interface, customers can be precisely segmented, relevant online messages selected, campaigns executed, up-selling and cross-selling measured, and third-party campaigns evaluated. Only minimal IT support is required. Market Direct offers corporate marketing departments an improved graphical user interface to place advertisements and messages and construct powerful marketing campaigns. This solution can integrate message management with customer care and end-to-end event tracking to offer all aspects of EBPP customer-relationship management. Billers can deliver personalized messages to customers based on information in the monthly bill or statement as well as some external sources. In addition, marketing departments can insert multiple messages in specific locations on the same electronic bill. While this offers the potential for cross-selling and up-selling, it also can be used to deliver customer-care messages and point customers or business users to self-help tools on the Web.

Market Direct brings companies beyond electronic bills and statements into an interactive connection with their customers. Offering tailored solutions to companies in the telecommunications, banking, brokerage, insurance, credit card, and utility industries, the software builds on the powerful, scalable, XML-based (extended markup language) i-Series platform. The result is that all aspects of EBPP and customer-relations management for billers can be integrated on one platform. The Market Direct module can combine targeted message management with customer care and end-to-end event tracking from bill creation and delivery to the ultimate posting of the payment.

Moving customers to online billing presents an opportunity to handle billing questions and disputes online as well. As the majority of questions are routine and repetitive, they can be handled in a lower cost, automated manner using preprogrammed rules engines.

CheckFree i-Solutions also offers i-Processing services that include payment and distribution through more than 400 financial services sites and customer care. While this service focuses primarily on the consolidator model, the group does provide online payment service for biller-direct applications.

7.1.1.1.4.4   Hosting Services — CheckFree also offer i-Hosting services that accommodate software hosting and full-service outsourcing. Regardless of whether a customer chooses a standard or select version, CheckFree now offers software-hosting options. This enables companies that want the control

Table 7.2   Features, Functions, and Benefits of i-Telco

Feature	Function	Benefit
Data Management		
Legacy system integration	Ingests most types of currently used print streams as well as many different types of data streams	Provides new services that differentiate the service providers from each other and allow them to do more with existing legacy systems
CheckFree SmartXpress	User-friendly, point-and-click visual extraction tool used to create extraction schemes and statement definitions	Makes bill and statement changes and convergence more manageable
Enrollment functions	Batch enrollment and unsubscribe functions, including password management	Helps ensure that the information in the customer database is up to date
Web Functionality		
Telco template	Industry-specific reference tool that includes sample print stream, statement definitions, extract scheme, customer load, ASP and JSP pages, and static Web application	Helps get projects into production quicker by jump-starting extract-scheme creation and Web-application development
E-mail notification	Notification and documents are online and waiting to be viewed; embedded messages and other account-related and promotional information can be distributed	Draws customers to the Web site, increasing the opportunity for strengthening relationships and reinforcing brand awareness
Security	Secure hash standard for encryption of user passwords; compliance with external Web browser security (HTTPS and SSL); access to encryption services that implement the DES and DES3 standard algorithms	Support for standard security measures allows implementation of systems to authenticate access to statement data
Architecture		
Object architecture	Smart objects are portable, reusable, highly compressed, XML-like data structures	Allows efficient in-house development of custom applications on top of the i-Series
Scalability	Production-ready solution that can run multiple instances of software on one server or across multiple servers	Provides system flexibility, high performance, and maximum processing efficiency

(continued)

Table 7.2 (Continued)   Features, Functions, and Benefits of i-Telco

Feature	Function	Benefit
Architecture		
Industry standards	CheckFree supports industry standards such as XML, HTML, SSL, OFX, JSP, PDF, COM, Java, and C++ whenever possible	Promotes portability of data between systems and across the Web, enabling quicker project production and changes
Modular architecture	Client can add applications as needed, such as Market Direct, payment links, and statement analysis	Builds on existing core technology to add functionality as needed, such as targeted marketing for increased revenue generation
Operations		
Control center	Configure, run, and monitor the CheckFree system	Central interface provides easy command of many functions
Production management	Monitor user log-ons, password changes, statement access violations, data loading, and failed e-mail notifications	Helps to analyze site usage and traffic

Note: All acronyms are defined in the Acronyms section at the back of the book.

and flexibility derived from owning the software — but who not choose to commit their own IT resources to manage the implementation and maintain the application — to deploy a solution quickly and cost effectively. Implementations for simple deployments can be as short as 30 days.

Available hosting options include:

- Distribution: This option allows billers to outsource e-bill creation and bill-detail hosting to CheckFree. Bills can be distributed to any endpoint in CheckFree's broad distribution network, including banks, brokerages, credit unions, personal financial-management software, and Internet portals. CheckFree currently hosts bills and statements for more than 50 companies.
- Biller direct: In addition to having bills distributed through CheckFree's network, a biller can arrange for CheckFree to host the application that enables bills and statements to be viewed and paid at the biller's branded site.
- ASP software hosting: This software ownership option enables billers to purchase software and have it hosted by CheckFree with more-robust services. These include:
  Dedicated software
  Expanded biller Web-site capabilities, including Market Direct
  A simple transition path for billers who want to launch an e-billing or e-statement offering in a simple, fully outsourced model before migrating to an in-house solution

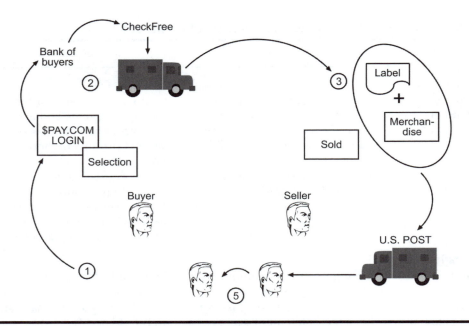

Figure 7.1   Pay@Delivery: Joint venture of the U.S. Postal Service with CheckFree.

7.1.1.1.5   Electronic Payment Options by U.S. Postal Service

Pay@Delivery™ is a feature that is similar to the existing collect-on-delivery (COD) service that has been offered by the Postal Service since 1913. Its main purpose is to facilitate access to traditional postal services by combining electronic payments with priority-mail and delivery-confirmation services. Sellers of merchandise at online auctions can, for example, print out the buyer's address label with delivery-confirmation barcodes from their PCs and drop off the package at any post office. Buyers of merchandise at online auctions can send payment to the seller online and have the money released electronically when the mail carrier delivers the package and scans the delivery confirmation barcodes. Available on the Postal Service Web site, CheckFree offers Pay@Delivery to its financial services customers as a standard feature. Individuals selling merchandise online can also place the Pay@Delivery logo and link on their Web site to offer this convenient and secure payment-on-delivery option to their customers.

Figure 7.1 shows how this service works from a consumer's perspective (buyer and seller at an online auction) and the steps that take place behind the scenes. The following legend describes the five areas of the figure:

1. Buyer and seller make a deal, agreeing on a price and the use of Pay@Delivery to close the transaction.
2. Buyer logs onto his bill-pay site and enters transaction amount and seller's e-mail address. Buyer's bank instantly authorizes payment to CheckFree. CheckFree simultaneously reserves funds, obtains U.S.

Postal Service tracking number, and sends confirmation of funds to seller by e-mail with mailing label attached.

3. Seller receives confirmation e-mail, prints out U.S. Postal Service label, and attaches it to merchandise shipping box.
4. U.S. Postal Service picks up package for delivery to buyer.
5. Upon delivery, U.S. Postal Service scans mailing label and notifies CheckFree to release payment to seller's bank account.

Other postal services include:

- Send Money: Similar to a domestic postal money order, which has been available to the American public since 1864, this feature enables anyone to send money to anyone else using the Internet. This person-to-person payment addition allows customers to send money securely to anyone with a checking-enabled account and an e-mail address. Like Pay@Delivery, individuals selling merchandise online can place the logo and link on their Web site to offer convenient and secure payment and delivery options to their customers.
- USPS Electronic Postmark (eBillPay): Combining tamper detection with a time-and-date seal applied by the Postal Service, the Electronic Postmark verification provides trusted, third-party proof of when a payment was initiated. Every payment transaction processed through USPS eBillPay, Pay@Delivery, and Send Money is postmarked when it is created and sent, when it is changed, and when it is canceled. The Postal Service has been postmarking mail since 1775.

7.1.1.2 Differentiators

CheckFree supports multiple business models and offers solutions for a wide variety of customers.

7.1.2 Avolent Corporation

Avolent (formerly Just in Time Solutions) is the industry leader in standards-based software solutions for B2B and B2C Internet billing, invoicing, and interactive customer care. The company's modular BillCast™ software suite enables relationship-centric billers to deploy secure, scalable solutions for personalized billing, statement presentment, payment, and service delivery that increase the value of each customer interaction. Avolent's data-centric BizCast™ platform is designed to deliver interactive electronic invoices between billers, biller service providers, banks, and business customers (payers). Avolent helped pioneer the OFX standard for online bill presentment and the thin consolidator model, and it continues its strong commitment to open standards. The company is also represented in IFX. With the acquisition of Solant, customer-care functions could be added into the core portfolio of products and services.

7.1.2.1   Products and Services

7.1.2.1.1   BillCast — an Internet Billing and Interactive Customer Care Solution

BillCast is an enterprise application platform for Internet billing and interactive customer care. Using BillCast, service companies can deliver billing and customer-care conveniences through the Internet, increasing customer satisfaction and reducing churn in the B2C domain.

BillCast provides all the functionality and flexibility necessary in a complete Internet billing application. The BillCast suite of application modules includes bill presentment, payment, distribution of electronic bills to consolidators (such as home-banking Web sites and portals), and integration with existing billing and enterprise systems. Right out of the box, BillCast includes a complete, brandable application with support for all the business processes needed to help billers get up and running quickly. All capabilities of BillCast are completely customizable and extensible to meet billers' exact requirements.

BillCast seamlessly integrates with Avolent's suite of Internet billing and interactive customer-care applications, providing a complete platform for managing customer relationships through the electronic channel. All BillCast applications share the capabilities of the core BillCast platform, including:

- Enterprise-class scalable application platform
- Flexible application definition via business rules
- Personalized billing and service delivery
- Modular applications that can be added as needed
- Support for direct and consolidator distribution models

BillCast is a complete solution for Internet billing and interactive customer care. It incorporates robust functionality that crosses an extensive range of applications, including vertical industry solutions. BillCast allows billers and bill publishers to start generating electronic bills quickly and easily. It provides a number of customer-support features, delivers advanced features for streamlining operations, and offers robust capabilities for translating legacy data into an electronic bill format. Their enhanced graphical user-interface tools enable end-to-end creation and deployment of e-bill-centric applications.

Customer experiences include:

- Repeat traffic: Customers want to see their bills every month.
- Interactive dialog with payers: BillCast offers customers a high level of customer service.
- Customer control: BillCast lets customers interact with their own account information for bill-related inquiries.
- Create reach: BillCast lets customers receive and pay bills through multiple channels using industry-standard protocols like OFX and IFX.
- Online relationship management: From sales inquiries through billing, all customer relationships are managed.

- Flexibility and modularity: Beyond presentment and payment, this product extends with customer needs.
- One-to-one marketing: BillCast enables cross-sell and up-sell opportunities with targeted advertising and messaging.

Solution highlights include:

- Customer self-care: Convenient options are available, such as updating user preferences, payment inquiry, and access to historical bill details. The options empower customers to self-manage their accounts, which results in fewer in calls to customer service representatives.
- Payment flexibility: Options for scheduling payments, paying via different methods, as well as visibility into the payment cycle give customers greater control and flexibility. These conveniences will help to drive higher customer adoption rates for EBPP.
- Comprehensive notification options: Biller-selectable options for required messages and customer-selectable options provide maximum flexibility. These options provide a vehicle for critical messages while allowing customers control over their online experience.
- Web-based application for online customer care: Allows customer service representatives to assist EBPP customers with billing and payment issues without integrating with CRM systems. The representatives have access to the same view as the customer, which speeds up the resolution process.
- Integrated one-to-one marketing: Creation and deployment of point-and-click rules allows marketing analysts to develop marketing campaigns as business needs change.

7.1.2.1.2 BizCast — an EIPP Solution

BizCast, the Avolent B2B electronic invoice presentment and payment (EIPP) solution, is a complete, feature-rich solution that meets the needs of B2B billers, service providers, and payers. BizCast includes the functionality required to import invoice data and then present, process, and pay invoices. BizCast is designed to provide billers with the capability to reach a wide array of payers in the B2B domain.

BizCast provides significant benefits to billers and payers:

- Billers
  Reduces day's sales outstanding
  Reduces dispute costs
  Reduces presentment costs
  Reduces processing costs
  Improves customer service

- Payers
    Reduces invoice processing costs
    Reduces dispute costs
    Improves invoice reconciliation
    Improves communication with billers
    Reduces late charges

BizCast creates an easy-to-use interactive environment for biller and payer process stakeholders. BizCast streamlines both the biller's and payer's work process and resolves typical biller and payer challenges. All creators, reviewers, processors, and approvers interact through one seamless application that keeps the process moving. Robust features, ultimate flexibility, and an appealing graphic interface make the whole process more efficient and satisfying for everyone.

For large suppliers, the traditional approaches to invoicing and customer services result in three problems:

1. High costs of sending paper invoices and manually processing payments
2. High day's sales outstanding (DSO)
3. Unnecessary resources spent in reviewing invoices and placing phone calls to dispute charges or manage accounts.

For business customers, BizCast provides:

- A complete solution: This product is more than simple invoice present-ment; this solution automates and simplifies the entire "invoice-to-pay" process of presentation, customer reconciliation, dispute handling, cash analysis, payment administration, and customer self-care.
- Internet-based application: BizCast improves service to all business customers. They simply enroll online using a secure Web browser and get access to invoice and account information anywhere, anytime.
- Electronic invoice delivery and notification: BizCast eliminates print and mail costs, and it moves invoice information to customers more rapidly, resulting in lower DSOs.
- Integration: BizCast integrates with existing enterprise systems to create a seamless "invoice-to-pay" process. Integration points include account-ing packages, ERP systems, billing systems, print streams, payment processors, and customer care. Modifications to these systems are not required.

Highlights of the BizCast solution include:

- Invoice presentment
    Open-invoice and balance-forward accounting: Configures to reflect the client's invoicing terms
    International localization of dates, languages, currency, and num-bers: Extends services to international customers

- Customer review, reconciliation, and approval

    Hierarchical account structures, including consolidated billing: Supports direct and indirect invoicing of customers and provides consolidated invoicing and reporting

    Customer-defined workflow: Improves cash cycles and customer service by streamlining customer invoice approval and payment processes

- Dispute handling

    Collaborative dispute resolution and credit request handling: Reduces costly customer service calls while increasing the level of service

- Cash analysis

    Real-time analytics and drill-down reporting: Delivers demands for reporting and analysis faster and with less effort

    A/R and A/P cash forecast reports: Provide additional visibility into cash flow and purchasing relationship for customers and payers

- Payment administration and customer self-care

    Electronic and offline payment handling: Dramatically reduces payment exceptions and improves posting accuracy

    Payer-enabled user administration: Reduces administration overhead and improves customer satisfaction

7.1.2.2 Differentiators

Avolent provides a wide variety of solutions with support for both B2C and B2B environments.

7.1.3 Edocs, Inc.

Edocs develops, markets, and supports a software platform for Internet billing and customer management. The company focuses on the presentment side, providing solutions for periphery supporting payment, marketing, and customer-relationship management. The company has experience in print application productivity tools as well.

7.1.3.1 Products and Services

7.1.3.1.1 BillDirect™

In addressing EBPP, Edocs concentrates on data extraction and bill presentment through software called BillDirect. Essentially, the application imports a biller's legacy billing data and strips away its graphical elements, presenting a clean view of the data. After BillDirect Web-enables the data, the information is then attached to cross-selling marketing messages that can be targeted against a customer's actual billing usage and spending habits. It is an enterprise-class Internet billing and customer-management platform. Highly scalable, robust, and easy to deploy and manage, it fully leverages the capabilities of current and legacy enterprise-billing and customer-management infrastructure. An account management system, AccountPost™, is also available.

BillDirect enables EBPP entities to utilize the Internet to transform the traditional paper-based bill and statement delivery process into the foundation of an online customer-account-management strategy. EBPP entities use this product to establish an interactive, online relationship with their customers, thereby improving customer care and account management. It runs on Windows NT and Solaris-based Unix servers and comprises the following components:

- A visual development environment
- The BillDirect command center
- A series of platform components
- A series of Internet interface components

The functionality of the product is layered using fully documented, open application programming interfaces (API). This approach, designed from the very beginning to use object-oriented programming techniques, enables new processes and services to be readily incorporated, thus allowing construction of an evolving, multiservice model without the need to change the underlying software foundations. Similarly, changes can be made in the object-based platform without affecting the behavior of the Internet billing and customer-management functions.

The product has been designed to be standards-compatible, scalable, reliable, and secure. Its architecture has a number of competitive advantages, including:

- Scalability and performance: It scales to handle customer growth and large numbers of customers while maintaining high levels of performance. Companies can add multiple servers as needed to any or all levels of the system, generally without incurring downtime.
- Reliability: It runs on industry-standard hardware on Windows NT and Solaris-based Unix servers to provide reliable operation. Its server-based architecture allows companies to add server capacity without incurring significant downtime.
- Security: Firewalls, proxies, and filters can be installed between every level of the BillDirect architecture to prevent unauthorized access to programs and data. Companies can determine and audit who has access to the system. Critical business functions run at the most secure business-process level, and access lists restrict the use of critical operations. Session monitoring, analysis, and control occur in real time so that problems can be identified and addressed rapidly.
- Support for open standards: This product offers fully documented open APIs at every level of the system. These interfaces give companies the ability to integrate BillDirect with legacy and external software. Bill-Direct also supports a variety of emerging standards for data exchange, including XML and OFX.

Online account information is highly "sticky," since it is personal, dynamic, and financially significant. Giving customers online access to account information, including billing and statement data, invoices, notices, policies, trade confirms, and profile information, is the key to engaging the majority of customers in a recurring online dialog. The eaSuite™ of products promotes this online relationship between billers and payers.

7.1.3.1.2   eaSuite

The eaSuite is an enterprise-class e-account solution that is scalable, feature rich, and easy to deploy and manage. Its open, modular architecture enables service providers to deploy a robust online account management solution that:

- Preserves investment in existing billing and customer-care infrastructure
- Provides payment-technology and distribution-channel flexibility
- Offers best-of-class online marketing and personalization capabilities

Giving customers anytime, anywhere access to electronic account information is the key to developing a recurring online relationship that:

- Reduces churn
- Cuts customer service costs
- Increases revenue per customer
- Improves customer acquisition

The eaSuite consists of the following modules: eaDirect™, eaPost™, eaPay™, and eaMarket™. Figure 7.2 shows the architecture of the eaSuite.

7.1.3.1.2.1   eaDirect — This module maximizes customer relationships by enabling Web-based billing, customer self-service, and targeted marketing. It is the mission-critical infrastructure required to securely manage online account information, such as bills, statements, invoices, policies, trade confirms, and other customer data, which forms the foundation for a recurring online customer relationship. It also provides customers of service providers with highly personalized online account information and self-service capabilities, improving the ability to better manage their accounts. eaDirect runs on Intel or Sun hardware and supports the NT and Solaris operating systems. The eaDirect platform also leverages relational database technologies from Oracle and Microsoft. Finally, eaDirect makes use of XML as a data-transport mechanism and offers a robust API set that facilitates integration with existing systems.

7.1.3.1.2.2   eaPost — This module handles all the complexities of distributing summary account information to any endpoint while also bringing back customers to the Web sites of service providers to securely manage and control customers' online experiences. Offering many distribution channels increases

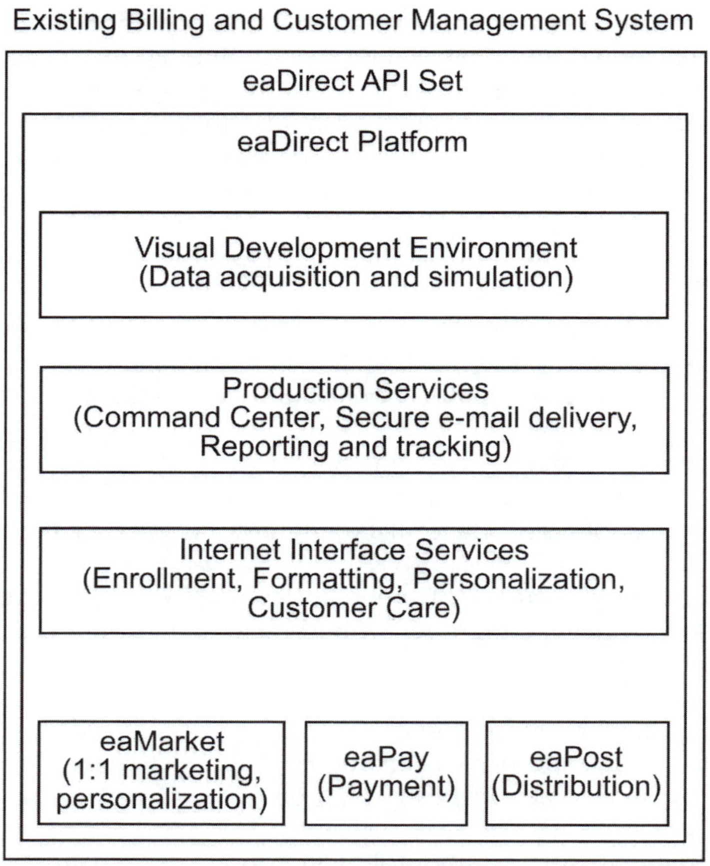

Existing Billing and Customer Management System

```
┌──────────────────────────────────────────────┐
│              eaDirect API Set                  │
│  ┌──────────────────────────────────────────┐ │
│  │           eaDirect Platform                │ │
│  │  ┌──────────────────────────────────────┐ │ │
│  │  │  Visual Development Environment       │ │ │
│  │  │  (Data acquisition and simulation)    │ │ │
│  │  └──────────────────────────────────────┘ │ │
│  │  ┌──────────────────────────────────────┐ │ │
│  │  │       Production Services             │ │ │
│  │  │ (Command Center, Secure e-mail        │ │ │
│  │  │  delivery, Reporting and tracking)    │ │ │
│  │  └──────────────────────────────────────┘ │ │
│  │  ┌──────────────────────────────────────┐ │ │
│  │  │     Internet Interface Services       │ │ │
│  │  │ (Enrollment, Formatting,              │ │ │
│  │  │  Personalization, Customer Care)      │ │ │
│  │  └──────────────────────────────────────┘ │ │
│  │  ┌──────────┐ ┌────────┐ ┌─────────────┐  │ │
│  │  │ eaMarket │ │ eaPay  │ │   eaPost    │  │ │
│  │  │(1:1 mktg,│ │(Payment)│ │(Distribution)│ │ │
│  │  │personal.)│ │        │ │             │  │ │
│  │  └──────────┘ └────────┘ └─────────────┘  │ │
│  └──────────────────────────────────────────┘ │
└──────────────────────────────────────────────┘
```

Figure 7.2   Architecture of the eaSuite from Edocs.

customer adoption. Through use of Edocs "cartridges" for each distribution channel, Edocs insulates the IT staff from rapidly changing distribution standards such as OFX and IFX.

7.1.3.1.2.3   eaPay — This module is an electronic payment and warehousing solution that provides complete payment flexibility to billers and their customers, accelerating the accounts-receivable process while reducing customer-care costs. By providing the ability to choose from a variety of payment processing technologies, including the ability to process payments using existing ACH capabilities, eaPay insulates the customer from the complexities of various payment technologies while enabling customers to choose the payment partner that is best. This module increases customer satisfaction by providing greater control over management and tracking of payments. It manages the complete payment process, including enrollment, scheduling, warehousing, notification, status checking, and integration, with all payment processors and internal bank connections.

7.1.3.1.2.4 eaMarket — This personalization management solution enables companies to increase revenue and improve customer satisfaction by weaving personalized marketing and customer-service messages throughout the online account-management experience.

7.1.3.2 Differentiators

The Edocs suite of e-commerce applications promotes strong online customer relations combined with high security, scalability, and performance.

7.1.4 iPlanet

iPlanet E-Commerce Solutions, a Sun-Netscape alliance, is a one-stop shop for Internet-enabling software that supports businesses. Built from the ground up and based on open standards designed for cross-platform integration, iPlanet solutions offer the combined strengths of usability, reliability, and efficiency. The results are seamless scalability and secure performance for e-commerce infrastructures.

7.1.4.1 Products and Services

The iPlanet BillerXpert™ application is a comprehensive Internet bill present-ment and payment (IBPP) solution. Built on the iPlanet e-commerce-ready infrastructure, iPlanet BillerXpert includes iPlanet Application Server, iPlanet Directory Server, and iPlanet Web Server. The iPlanet BillerXpert application allows an enterprise to provide customer convenience, build customer loyalty, manage customer relationships, and generate new revenue opportunities.

- Provides customer convenience
    Ability to view bills online through virtually any browser at any time
    Flexible payment options, with payment by credit card or check or ability to schedule payment for a future date
    Ability to create automatic payments for recurring bills or make partial payments against bills when appropriate
    Email notifications for new bill arrivals, past-due payments, and special offers and promotions
    Ability to view and search statements based on user preferences
- Builds customer loyalty
    Strengthened customer relationships and reduced churn by offering new conveniences to users, providing them with a higher level of service and greater control over their finances
    Ability to view bill summaries or drill down to line-item levels of detail
    Deep statement analysis and reporting for B2B billing
    Ability to track spending over time and find critical information in current or past bills with statement search and analysis capabilities

- Generates new revenue streams
    - Targeted marketing to turn billing from a cost center into a revenue opportunity
    - Base marketing on profile information and spending habits
    - Opportunities to cross-sell and sell new services to existing customers
- True multihosting capabilities
    - Maximum application availability by eliminating any single point of failure
    - Fail-safe capabilities to ensure that billing information continues to be processed in the event of a server failure
    - Failure-recovery features, including autodetection and autostart of failed servers and processes
    - Distributed state and session management to ensure that no applications or user data are lost in the event of a failure
- Provides high performance and scalability
    - High volume of concurrent users through optimized performance features, including advanced connection caching and pooling, results caching, data streaming, and a fully multithreaded, multi-process architecture
    - Scalability with dynamic load balancing and point-and-click application partitioning, enabling applications to scale dynamically to support thousands of concurrent users
- Reduces time to market
    - Integration with enterprise billing systems through data extraction and loading services
    - Integration with multiple data formats, including print streams, ASCII text, and XML
    - Prebuilt, customizable application templates designed for numerous industries, including telecommunications, cable TV, utilities, and financial services
    - iPlanet Application Builder (offered separately) to enable customization of presentation templates and business rules
    - Application designers to automatically generate application objects and templates
- Bill personalization and notification
    - Prebuilt templates to customize bill layout and branding
    - Multiple levels of information presented, from bill summaries to line-item detail
    - Ability to view past and present statements to determine spending trends
    - Ability to easily find critical information across present and past statements with parametric search capability
    - Email notification of new bills, overdue payments, or special offers
- Targeted marketing
    - Targeted advertising, promotions, and information to users based on personal profile information and behavior

Single or multiple user attributes contained in membership database used as targeting criteria

Event-based relationship management, which captures and acts on user events, including registration, bill payment, and search

Multiple launch of marketing actions, including sending targeted e-mail displaying advertising banners or presenting a personalized page via a single user event

Fine-grained analysis and reporting of user behavior by tracking user activity

- A flexible, extensible solution

Reduces time to market with prebuilt application templates for the telecommunications, financial services, cable television, and utility industries

Customizable presentation templates and business rules

Fully documented SDK (software development kit) and APIs

Remote administration from any desktop using a lightweight HTML-based interface

Modular system design, which allows application components to run on multiple systems, such as a cluster configuration, for enhanced high availability, scalability, and security

7.1.4.2   Differentiators

iPlanet provides a complete solution combined with integration capabilities with multiple platforms.

7.1.5   Metavante Corp.

With more than 3500 clients, including the largest 20 banks in the U.S., Metavante Corp. is a leading financial services enabler, delivering virtually all of the technology that an organization needs to offer financial services. Metavante offers financial technology solutions that drive customer relationship management, electronic banking, electronic funds transfer and card solutions, electronic presentment and payment, financial technology services, private label banking, and wealth management. Headquartered in Milwaukee, WI, Metavante, formerly M&I Data Services, is wholly owned by Marshall & Ilsley Corp.

7.1.5.1   Products and Services

Serving nearly 2500 clients, Metavante Electronic Presentment and Payment (EPP) offers a comprehensive, fully scalable, end-to-end solution that allows companies to prepare electronic bills and statements that their customers can receive and pay on the Internet. The Metavante EPP solution provides billers with the industry's leading technology to automate and streamline bill delivery, payment, and customer-care processes using market-leading document-composition software. It gives consumers a bill-management service that allows them to view, pay, manage, and automate all of their bills — paper or electronic — online. Metavante EPP also delivers a powerful "pay anyone" electronic bill-payment engine for businesses and consumers.

Metavante Corp. is one of the technology providers to offer solutions and services in each area of the electronic presentment and payment (EPP) delivery chain. The complete "end-to-end" Metavante EPP solution has products, services, and partnerships that deliver all biller documents to customers in the format and to the location they want. Billers realize a significant, positive impact on cash flow and profitability by using Metavante to deliver easy-to-understand customer documents, whether electronic or paper.

Metavante can offer efficiencies throughout the biller's entire document-creation and -delivery systems:

- There are solutions for billers — or organizations that regularly create and distribute customer documents — with Metavante's suite of document-composition software.
- Assistance is available to help companies to fulfill the biller service provider (BSP) role with the creation and presentation of electronic customer documents, whether for B2C, B2B, or small-business applications.
- There are established partnerships with major consolidators, the technology providers who ensure that EPP interactions between billers and their customers run smoothly.
- Consumer service providers (CSP) solutions are available, offering billers the opportunity to serve as the focal point of their customers' total online transactions in B2C and B2B situations.
- Billers receive the capacity to offer their customers "pay anyone" convenience with consumer payment-provider solutions.
- There are also portal solutions for FSPs, providing consumer and business electronic banking products and services that are easily integrated into Metavante's EPP solutions.

All Metavante EPP solutions adhere to nonproprietary, open standards, providing the widest possible distribution of customer documents. Wider distribution means greater customer access to the biller's electronic documents and increased customer adoption of the biller's EBPP solution.

7.1.5.2 Differentiators

Metavante Corp. is a proven technology provider that has strong partnerships with financial institutions.

7.2 Financial Service Providers

Financial service providers are very well positioned between the issuers of statements, bills, and invoices on one side and payers on the other side. They have a "sticky" relationship with consumers, which is the basis that supports consolidator and aggregator business models.

7.2.1 *Bottomline Technologies*

Bottomline supports over 5500 customers worldwide, including 50 of the Fortune 100 companies in the U.S. and 95 of the largest companies in the U.K. The company has formed strategic relationships with Citibank, FleetBoston, UPS, Northern Trust, United Technologies, and Royal Bank of Scotland. The customer roster of premier organizations includes State Street, Dartmouth College, Cisco Systems, General Motors, PricewaterhouseCoopers, and the House of Commons. Founded in 1989, Bottomline has grown into a global organization with over 500 employees worldwide.

7.2.1.1 *Products and Services*

Bottomline's suite of financial resource management (FRM) offerings enables businesses and financial institutions to manage their critical financial transactions, cash decisions, and trading-partner relationships by leveraging the Web. These FRM products extend and link corporate financial systems to improve communication and information within an organization. They also allow organizations to externalize their activities by enabling banks and trading partners to participate and collaborate in the information management that FRM provides. To accomplish this, the FRM modules include application, communication, information, and instruction solutions designed to streamline payables, accelerate receivables, and consolidate banking activities with single-point access to real-time information reporting. All FRM products adhere to best-practices techniques. Bottomline applications include:

- Payments and cash management
- Electronic invoice presentment and payment (EIPP)
- Electronic banking
- Information reporting

Bottomline creates solutions designed to grow with the unique business requirements of its various clients, understanding that each organization maintains its own separate payment and cash-management workflows. Bottomline offers four product suites that can be used on their own or integrated to obtain a wide range of money-movement capabilities.

Accelerating receipts provides more cash for internal and external investments and enables organizations to pay their bills. Improving cash flow means producing more goods and services faster, generating more revenue, and being paid faster to enhance shareholder value. Bottomline's electronic invoice presentment and payment (EIPP) product is a secure, interactive system for B2B transactions that allows organizations to present invoicing information, provide online dispute resolution, and accept payments over the Internet. However, moving from paper to collaboration can take time, and Bottomline understands that not all organizations are ready to transition at the same speed. To support customers that need to move in a stepwise fashion, Bottomline's EIPP solution offers the ability to print, e-mail, post-only, or post and pay invoices from a single invoice file.

Bottomline's NetTransact™ is an advanced EBPP vehicle designed to aid organizations of all sizes in online management of B2B receivables and payables. The online payment solution allows organizations to present billing information, provide online dispute resolution, accept payments over the Internet, and post the results to their accounting systems.

Bottomline's NetTransact is available in three business models: bank-hosted, corporate-hosted, and outsourced. With the addition of Bottomline's SmARt Cash™ product, customers can automate receivables matching. When it comes to accepting lockbox payments for open invoices, customers want to match the cash with open invoices as quickly as possible. Bottomline's SmARt Cash allows customers to do that by automating the receivables collection cycle, which replaces manual matching. Using sophisticated algorithms, the SmARt Cash matching engine looks to logically pair payments against open invoices according to predefined business rules of customers and payers. Without this tool, balance sheets may not accurately reflect incoming cash. Bottomline's SmARt Cash is available as an enterprise-hosted or provider-hosted application.

7.2.1.2 Differentiators

Bottomline's NetTransact has strong cash- and remittance-management features.

7.2.2 Paytru$t, Inc.

Founded in October 1998, Paytru$t™ is the flagship product of Paytru$t, Inc., a privately held company based in Lawrenceville, NJ. Through Paytru$t's acquisition of PayMyBills.com in September 2000, PayMyBills.com is a wholly owned subsidiary of Paytru$t, Inc. The company is financially backed by investors including American Express, Capital One, Citigroup, ComVentures, E*Trade, FTVentures, and Spectrum Equity Investors.

7.2.2.1   Products and Services

Paytru\$t is a Web-based service offering consumers the ultimate e-convenience — one-stop bill payment and management. Harnessing the power and efficiency of the Web, Paytru\$t can deliver 100% of consumers' bills (both electronic bills and scanned paper bills) through a single, secure Web site, where consumers can direct payments from their preexisting checking accounts. Leveraging proprietary, patent-pending technology that provides the ability to deliver bills from any biller and pay them through any bank, Paytru\$t is well positioned to be the leader in the emerging EBPP market. Unlike other EBPP providers that are focused on simplifying bill collection for billers, Paytru\$t's focus is to streamline bill payment and management to the advantage of consumers.

To make the switch to online bill management, customers need a service that is truly better than an existing mailbox. A partial solution, such as bill-pay-only or biller direct, means that customers would have to manage more parts of the bill process, not less. Unless customers are getting all of their bills online in a single location, customers have not found a better way to pay their bills!

Many banks offer what is traditionally known as "bill pay only" services to their customers. These services allow customers to go online to cut a check to their billers, so they no longer have to use checks or stamps. Nevertheless, all of the hassles of bill management still reside squarely on their shoulders. With bill-pay-only service, payers still receive paper bills in the mail, so they still have to deal with the paper clutter, missed payments, and late fees that can result from misplacing paper bills or simply not being home to receive them. Some banks may offer a limited set of electronic bills, but none of them can deliver 100% of customers' bills online. If payers are considering a bill-pay-only service, customers are encouraged to take a moment to see if that service can actually deliver all of the monthly bills online. Chances are that in today's electronic-payment environment, only 2 or 3 of their 10 to 12 regular monthly bills are available online.

With bill-pay-only, customers also have to remember exactly when to issue payments. They still have to worry about watching their mailbox, collecting their bills on the kitchen counter, remembering to find the time to go online and pay them, and stuffing them in a shoebox for future reference. Even when they do remember that they need to make a payment, they have to go online and type out payment instructions for each bill. The bank then issues either an electronic payment, as part of a batch of electronic payments to the biller, or a paper check. In either case, because there is no remittance information that ties specifically back to the customer's account, there is a chance the payment will not be accurately posted to that account. Also, bill-pay-only services typically play "float games," where the money is withdrawn from the customer's account but has not yet been paid to their biller. Customers should realize that they are losing some of the interest-earning potential of their funds during this time.

Many billers (such as credit card, telephone, and utility companies) offer what is typically referred to as "biller direct" bill payment services to their customers, enabling customers to log onto their Web sites, view their billing information online, and issue payments from their bank accounts. Still, there are inherent flaws with this model, making it extremely unappealing to customers seeking a complete bill-management solution. First of all, only the largest billers who have made the time and technology investment in online billing make their bills available online, leaving the majority of customers' bills still not available via this method. So while consumers may be able to go online to view and pay their credit card, cell phone, and electric bills, none of the rest of their bills can be paid this way, forcing them to go back to their checkbooks and continue paying bills the old-fashioned way. Secondly, even if all of their bills were to become available via the biller-direct method, who really wants to deal with the hassles and headaches of remembering which bills are due when and having to play hide-and-go-seek across the Internet looking for all of their various bills? Moreover, the consumer has to remember a unique ID and password to sign in to each of the different billers' Web sites.

In contrast, Paytru$t delivers a complete, compelling consumer experience that is truly better than the mailbox of payers. Customers can receive 100% of their bills online through Paytru$t. This service has proprietary technology that combines both electronic bills and paper bills (which are scanned and processed with patent-pending software) and delivers them to a single, secure location rapidly and accurately. With Paytru$t, customers no longer have to worry about receiving paper bills in the mail. Instead, they receive convenient e-mail notifications alerting them when a bill has arrived or when it is about to go overdue. Customers can easily pay each bill with just one click, or they can review a detailed image of the actual bill before determining how much they want to pay and when. The check is filled out for them, with their account information for that payee, the amount, the payment date, and everything else. Customers click to approve or, if necessary, they can edit any of the prefilled information fields, but this product has done most of the work for them. With Paytru$t, not only can customers set up recurring payment rules for their mortgage and other fixed monthly amounts, but they can also set up automatic payments for bills of varying amounts. They tell Paytru$t when to pay and specify the maximum amount, and the product then automatically issues the payment. (For example, customers can pre-authorize Paytru$t to automatically pay their phone bills or the minimum amount due on their credit cards five days before the due date as long as the payment is less than a customer-selected specified maximum amount.) If a bill exceeds the customer's specified maximum allowable amount, the customer receives an e-mail notification listing the amount of the bill (with a link to their secure bill center, where they can view the actual statement and all of the details) with a request that they authorize the payment before it goes out. Once authorized, the electronic payment or check goes out with a detailed remittance stub to ensure that the biller can credit the actual account promptly and accurately.

Because customers receive all their bills online with Paytru$t, all of their records are available to them online, whenever and wherever they want to view them. There are easy reporting capabilities built in to the service, and customers can download their information to Quicken® or to Microsoft® Money or Excel for more detailed analysis. At the end of the year, customers can order a CD-ROM that contains all of their bill images and transaction information for the past year. And, if they ever need assistance, Paytru$t has an excellent customer service department that is available seven days per week to customers via email or phone.

7.2.2.2 Service Features

The Paytru$t service provides consumers with a complete online bill delivery, review, and payment bill center within a single, secure Web site. Flexible account options are available, including Bill Pay Plus for basic services and Complete Bill Management to eliminate all the hassles of dealing with bills. Subscribers have 24 × 7 access to view and pay all their bills at home, at work, or on the road. The Paytru$t service further facilitates the payment process by providing consumers with detailed billing information on a monthly and month-to-month basis, ensuring that consumers have all billing information, past and present, at their disposal. Paytru$t provides e-mail notification when a bill has arrived in the Bill Center. In addition, Paytru$t can be customized to pay monthly bills automatically, further simplifying the bill payment process. The Paytru$t service also can be integrated with leading personal financial management software such as Quicken and Microsoft Money to allow consumers to easily merge their bill payment receipts with the rest of their financial records. Paytru$t offers its customers excellent client support, seven days a week, to ensure they have a continual resource for answers and assistance.

7.2.2.3 Consumer Benefits

The Paytru$t service acts like a personal financial assistant, making it easy for consumers to organize their bill receipt and payment, thereby minimizing the potential for lost bills and late payments. The time saved receiving and paying bills online with Paytru$t frees up consumers' time to enjoy other activities.

7.2.2.4 Small Business Edition

For small and home-based businesses, Paytru$t features a small business edition for $19.95 a month plus $0.75 per transaction. This version includes customized features such as integration with QuickBooks, a dedicated account manager, and the ability to include a business name on payments made to payees.

7.2.2.5   Small Business Benefits

Time spent on bill management represents lost income opportunity for business owners. For small and home-based businesses, Paytru$t is like hiring an employee to take charge of accounting and booking without having to worry about training and health-benefit costs.

7.2.2.6   Biller Benefits

U.S. billers spend approximately $150 billion annually processing consumer bills. Paytru$t has the potential to deliver significant savings for billers by automating bill-delivery systems. Paytru$t's proprietary technology allows for full integration between billers and their customers' banks, a feature that enables billers to take full advantage of the time and money-saving capabilities of electronic finance. Furthermore, the integration of Paytru$t's bill-management service provides billers with a simple and immediate means of bettering their service to customers.

7.2.2.7   Security and Dependability

Paytru$t offers the highest level of customer service and ensures that consumer information and transactions are guarded with the utmost security. All Paytru$t transactions are encrypted, all accounts are password-protected, and subscriber information is withheld from all outside parties.

Using proprietary technology, Paytru$t delivers a complete, consumer-focused bill management solution far surpassing traditional bill-pay-only or partial-bill delivery services. Paytru$t subscribers can receive, review, pay, and organize 100% of their bills online or using a wireless device. They receive bill notifications and reminders via e-mail rather than physical mail, and they can review their bill information at anytime, from anywhere they have access to the Internet. Through Paytru$t, customers can issue payments directly from any check-writing account, perform automatic checkbook balancing, access a complete history of their billing and payment information, and download data to their personal financial management software for further analysis.

The Paytru$t Bill Center is designed to seamlessly integrate with partner Web sites to extend their services with a complete consumer bill delivery, payment, and management offering, thus providing a tremendous opportunity for FSPs to drive additional traffic to their sites, encourage customer loyalty, and increase revenues with minimal impact on resources. Paytru$t has successfully deployed private-label bill centers for a number of premier financial institutions and Web innovators, such as American Express, Citibank, and E*Trade.

7.2.2.8   Differentiators

Paytru$t has very strong service capabilities with serious financial partnerships. It offers one-stop bill payment and management and is a strong force in B2C environments.

7.2.3 MasterCard

The MasterCard credit card company is well known for financial services. It participates in alliances that support EBPP solutions.

7.2.3.1 Products and Services

MasterCard's Remote Payment and Presentment Service (RPPS) acts as a connectivity hub for biller service providers (BSP) and consumer service providers (CSP). BSPs work with billers to create online bills and to present and settle transaction payments. CSPs provide an online interface — either at their own Web site or at a bank's Web site — where consumers can view, manage, and pay their bills electronically. Located at MasterCard's St. Louis processing center, the bill-presentment hub aggregates bills via BSPs and distributes them to CSPs, where they are presented for the customer. The CSPs can connect to MasterCard RPPS to send payments to BSPs, which in turn deposit the funds to the biller's account.

MasterCard RPPS supports the OFX messaging standard. Although Master-Card transmits bills and payments between CSPs and BSPs via MasterCard RPPS, it remains a neutral trusted third party in the transactional process.

7.2.3.2 Differentiators

MasterCard brings very strong financial experience combined with an exchange attribute between biller service providers and consumer service providers.

7.3 Billing Service Providers

Suppliers of billing software are interested in offering more flexible and convergent billing, in particular for biller-direct, e-mail, invited-pull, and service-bureau business models. Leading companies, like Amdocs, Convergys, and CSG, have improved their time-to-market capabilities through mergers and acquisitions. Daleen Technologies has developed its own EBPP solution.

7.3.1 Daleen Technologies, Inc.

Daleen Technologies, Inc., is a global provider of billing and customer-care software solutions that manage the revenue chain for traditional and next-generation communications service providers, retailers and distributors of digital media, and technology solutions providers. Offering proven integration with leading CRM and other legacy enterprise systems, the RevChain software and pure Internet integration architecture (IIA) leverage open Internet technologies to enable providers to increase operational efficiency while deriving maximum revenue from their product and service offerings.

7.3.1.1 Products and Services

RevChain Care™ is an intuitive solution for providing customer self-care over the Internet. This application creates a new channel for customer service that allows service providers to increase loyalty through the delivery of personalized services. RevChain Care is highly flexible and can be customized with minimal effort to represent the look and feel of the provider's organization using the latest Internet technologies and industry-standard Web authoring tools.

EBPP is included in RevChain Care to allow customers to view and pay their bills immediately, without waiting for a paper invoice. At the customer's request, RevChain Care provides a current view of charges at any point in the billing cycle, which allows them to better track usage and charges as they occur. By providing billing details to customers at the earliest point, service providers and billers can expedite the collection process and resolve potential disputes before they impact customer satisfaction or require additional treatment.

This EBPP feature of RevChain Care allows customers to:

- Make bill payments with a preapproved credit or debit card
- View billing and usage data in graphic form or export into common software packages, such as Excel, for further analysis or to be filed with personal or business records
- Initiate, resolve, or cancel billing disputes online without them ever appearing on the printed bill
- Route disputed charges immediately to a customer service representative for investigation

7.3.1.2 Differentiators

Daleen Technologies has great experience with billing software and with self- and e-care. The company has working partnerships with EBPP solution providers.

7.3.2 DST Output

DST Output is a Biller Service Provider (BSP) solution delivering proven electronic billing, invoicing, and statement solutions for B2C, B2B, and online investor communications. DST Output is one of the largest print and electronic statement processing companies, combining specific Internet development expertise with more than 30 years of billing and statement experience.

7.3.2.1 Products and Services

A comprehensive product suite, called e.bill.anywhere, comprises a standard platform and numerous exclusive extensions to meet specific B2C and B2B billing needs. The following attributes are important to implementers:

- Present electronic bills and invoices to consumers and buyers
- Enhance customer relationship management
- Increase revenue streams
- Improve customer communications
- Up-sell additional products and services
- Reduce call-center traffic
- Utilize solid data analysis and reporting tools
- Automate dispute adjudication processes
- Incorporate business rules to streamline operations

The B2C solution provides flexible end-to-end solutions that allow customers to distribute statements to corporate Web sites, single or multiple consolidator delivery channels, or whatever combination meets the needs of customers. With B2C, customers can create an online forum for product and service offerings, customer satisfaction surveys, newsletters, financial calculators, and other tools and information to offer consumers a rich and valuable electronic billing experience. By handling all conversion and routing details, B2C helps customers move to all consolidation sites by supporting key industry standards, such as OFX and IFX, and proprietary protocols offered by consolidators.

The most sophisticated, comprehensive B2B solution creates a new paradigm for electronic invoicing. B2B replaces paper invoices with practical electronic invoices featuring important tools required by businesses to fully understand and process invoicing information. B2B allows businesses to sort and analyze invoice data, register and adjudicate disputes, and segment the invoice for internal distribution.

Features and options included with this product:

- eSolution design: Conversion to full Web-site implementation is offered. This conversion can be expedited by professional services of DST Output.
- Access management: This product simplifies the consent, registration, and authentication processes to ensure smooth transitions from paper to electronic billing and invoicing. It provides Ready Access, which allows first-time customers to register and immediately view and pay the most recent bill or invoice. The Seamless Login option allows a transparent shift between corporate Web sites and hosted electronic-billing or -invoicing Web sites. It enables payers to use a single log-on to access these two different Web sites.
- Payment: It supports the complete range of flexible payment options for either corporate Web sites or consolidator sites. An integrated connection to payment gateways provides full support of EDI 820, automated clearinghouses (ACH), credit cards, and procurement cards. In addition, payers can be assigned to multiple bank accounts and banking institutions for flexible payment options.
- Targeted marketing: It includes an advertising solution that enables direct and interactive communication between service provider and

customer. Specific messages can be created and sent to individuals, and broadcast ads can be tailored to selected audiences. Performance reports are also included.

■ Bill operations support: Support features such as automated job scheduling and exception handling give access and control to improve efficiency of electronic billing operations. Direct Access, the enterprise portal of DST Output, provides access to detailed turnaround reports and progress updates on a daily basis for managing B2C relationships. eCustomerCare informs about how, when, and where customers are accessing their bills and improves communication by putting customer service teams and consumers on the same electronic page.

7.3.2.2 Differentiators

DST Output brings a strong combination of printing experience with electronic document handling.

7.4 Consolidators and Aggregators

Profiling the solution providers in this category is more difficult. Consolidator and aggregator business models are manyfold, and one EBPP solution does not fit all. High flexibility and easy customization are expected from products and services.

7.4.1 BillingZone, LLC

BillingZone, LLC, offers B2B EIPP services that provide businesses a consolidated model for presenting, receiving, and paying invoices on the Internet. The solutions are expressly designed to meet the needs of companies (billers) and their customers (payers) while providing payers the convenience of paying multiple invoices at one site. BillingZone helps companies streamline the complexity of invoicing and payment processes, realize cost savings by eliminating paper and manual processes, and speed up communications between companies and their customers or suppliers.

7.4.1.1 Products and Services

BillingZone, LLC, offers revolutionary B2B electronic invoice presentment and payment (EIPP) solutions that provide businesses with a consolidated Web site for presenting and paying invoices on the Internet. The company's cornerstone service offering is BillingZone.com™. This service provides a single Web site that brings multiple suppliers (billers) and their customers (payers) together in a convenient, one-stop transactional hub.

BillingZone.com helps streamline the complexity of B2B invoicing and payment processes. It helps companies realize significant cost savings by reducing paper-based, manual processes and speeds up the communication between companies and their trading partners.

BillingZone believes in the consolidator model. The solutions provide a single Web site through which multiple billers and multiple payers can conduct financial transactions. This consolidator model creates greater efficiency and cost benefits for payers because of their familiarity obtained by using one Web site for all electronic invoicing. It also provides a networking opportunity among buyers and sellers in one location on the Internet.

One of the major advantages of BillingZone is that it is a service offering, rather than software. Because all of BillingZone's functionality is accessed via the Internet, the user is only required to have an Internet browser for access. This eliminates a whole host of support and maintenance expenses that can be incurred with software applications. BillingZone does not require the extensive resources or equipment typically necessary with implementing a software application. This can dramatically reduce the time to market for implementing an EIPP solution. There are no licensing fees or renewal fees associated with its use.

7.4.1.2 apConnect™ and arConnect™ Services

BillingZone's apConnect and arConnect services empower buyers and their suppliers to streamline the complexity of invoicing and payment transactions, realize cost savings through the elimination of paper and manual practices, and augment trading-partner communications.

BillingZone's apConnect™ service provides progressive companies with a robust offering that incorporates the benefits of EIPP into the accounts-payable process. Using apConnect gives accounts payable the advantage of electronic receipt of invoices, online collaboration and workflow tools, flexible A/P integration options, and electronic payments. apConnect is designed to be a secure and efficient process for managing invoices and payment transactions. BillingZone offers EIPP solutions, including apConnect, through a consolidated, bank-neutral model that increases value to trading-partner networks.

arConnect™ provides companies a robust offering for the invoicing and customer-relationship processes. arConnect brings efficiency to accounts receivable with the electronic distribution of invoices, improved cash application, and visibility into the invoice-management and dispute-resolution processes for enhanced customer service. BillingZone offers EIPP solutions, including arConnect, through a consolidated, bank-neutral model that increases value to trading partner networks.

BillingZone takes a consultative approach in working with buyers and their suppliers in trading networks to effectively manage the entire invoice-to-cash process.

- Bank-neutral position allows users to retain current bank relationships: Experience has shown that businesses do not want to change their banking relationships based on e-commerce initiatives. BillingZone respects that. Unlike other EIPP services, BillingZone is not tied to any one financial institution for processing payments. The solution is designed to allow users to disburse and collect payments utilizing existing accounts through their established banking relationships.

- Payer-focused functionality manages complex B2B invoicing and payment processes: From simple-to-use yet robust online functionality to sophisticated file integration, BillingZone offers solutions for all sizes of business payers.

7.4.1.3 Features for Billers

BillingZone's solutions include features that combine ease of use, reliability, security, and privacy to bring clarity to the payment cycle for high-volume suppliers (billers). Billers' business will benefit by gaining knowledge about, and control over, their financial picture at every point in the invoicing cycle. BillingZone's focus on the needs of billers' customers (payers) is a real advantage, because payers will not use EIPP until their needs are understood and met.

BillingZone.com offers the following:

- Customizable invoice branding with the Invoice Studio feature
- Staged/direct invoicing, which allows clients to control the flow of invoices to their customers
- Multiple payment options for customers
- Configurable adjudication reason codes specific to business needs
- E-mail alerts of payer-adjusted invoices for proactive resolution
- Full, online account administration and reporting features

Additional BillingZone features include:

- Full implementation support from the BillingZone implementation team
- A comprehensive customer-adoption program for introducing EIPP to customers
- Optional biller approval on batch invoices before presentment to payers
- A wide variety of reports to track preenrolled payer status, invoice activity, payer account activity, and service requests
- Ability to track all invoice issues online
- Online help for all biller features
- Extensive customer service and support by phone, by e-mail, or by going online

7.4.1.4 Features for Payers

Most accounts-payable departments receive invoices through paper processes, enter and match those invoices in their existing accounts-payable system, perform exception processing, and finally issue a check payment. The challenge is to create a more efficient process that leverages today's technologies and is flexible enough to accommodate current and future needs of businesses. The BillingZone solution offers the following benefits:

- Introduces electronic receipt, processing, and payment of business invoices
- Routes invoices automatically to appropriate approvers
- Provides a collaborative platform with trading partners and within client's organization
- Integrates data to and from accounts-payable and ERP systems
- Remits either an ACH or credit card payment for payer's invoices, based upon payer's preference and biller's offering

7.4.1.5   Additional Features

Additional BillingZone features include:

- Invoice management tools
    - Different users within a company can manage different supplier accounts.
    - Invoices can be routed through payer-defined online approval chain.
    - Payers can search for invoices by purchase order or invoice number.
    - Payers can input issues and track responses online with their trading partner.
- Payment management tools
    - All scheduled payments are settled either through the ACH network or credit card processing (payment options may vary by biller).
    - Automatic scheduling of payments can be established within defined thresholds.
    - Payment-due reminders are available to users.
- Information-management tools
    - Payers can assign general-ledger account distributions to invoice payments.
    - Payers can export invoice and payment information in a variety of file formats.
    - Online reports summarize the transaction history for each invoice.
- Payment authorization tools
    - All of a company's BillingZone invoices can be delivered electronically in a single file.
    - Payers can integrate invoice data into their accounts-payable system for standard processing and scheduling of the payment date.
    - Invoice payment instructions are delivered back to BillingZone for automatic initiation to the payer's financial institution.
    - Exception processing can be automated or handled online using BillingZone's adjudication tools.

- Customer service

   Extensive customer service and support is available from BillingZone specialists.

The features and benefits of BillingZone are summarized in Table 7.3.

7.4.1.6 Differentiators

BillingZone's services provide several key benefits to both A/P and A/R, which include cost reductions by:

- Eliminating the sorting and data-entry processes
- Improving cash management and forecasting
- Streamlining paper-based processes
- Improving trading-partner communication
- Reducing supplier inquiries
- Eliminating the need for point-to-point solutions with suppliers

BillingZone is built on an open, scalable architecture using standards-based independent development tools and languages. The product uses a secure integrated environment as well as network, application, and commercially available products to maximize systems and data integrity.

7.4.2 NETdelivery Corp.

Founded in 1995 and headquartered in Boulder, CO, NETdelivery Corp. is the leading developer of secure online information-management and -exchange software for health, government, postal, and insurance communities. Its solution is based around an electronic postal service model utilizing the screen-scraper model, which has a close similarity with the consolidator model.

7.4.2.1 Products and Services

Open, scalable, interactive, and Web-based, NETdelivery's end-to-end solution works with any existing legacy system. Inherently secure, NETdelivery's technology assures that digital communications are auditable, authenticated, encrypted, time-stamped, tamper-proof, and confirmed.

Working with Canada Post and Cebra, Inc., NETdelivery created the world's first online post office, known as epost™. NETdelivery's customers include epost, Sweden Post, iworks/NBC5Plaza, and Kwikbill, a major U.S. telecommunications firm.

NETdelivery's software builds secure and authenticated online communities that help forge strong and lasting customer relationships and that enable private online communication between individuals and large organizations. The suite of tools enables customers to automate paper-based transactions and securely manage and exchange electronic documents of all types with

Table 7.3   Features and Benefits of BillingZone

Features	Description	Benefit
Consolidator model	—	Provides the capability to review and pay all supplier invoices at a single Web site
Direct integration	apConnect and arConnect provide direct-transmission capabilities	Direct integration with A/R and A/P systems eliminates manual processes associated with delivering, managing, and paying invoices; all trading-partner data are streamlined into consolidated electronic feeds; data entry and manual handling of invoices and payments are eliminated, resulting in significant cost reductions
Online workflow	Multitiered approval hierarchy; workflow collaboration tools	The online workflow collaboration supports the entire A/P decision process, including the routing of invoices or unmatched items for approval throughout the organization
Reduced invoice-payment effort	E-mail notification of incoming invoices; automated payment feature for recurring invoices; remittance invoice and payment data available	Customized rules can be used to automate and streamline the invoice payment tasks, resulting in additional cost savings; suppliers receive remittance data from BillingZone to streamline updating A/R systems
Online adjudication	Enables summary-level or line-item adjustments with reason codes defined by supplier; automatically calculates discounts and credit-memo balances	Adjusting invoices for discrepancies, taking advantage of discounts, and applying debit and credit memos saves time with the online management; A/R is automatically notified when an adjusted invoice is received to resolution, so research can begin quickly
Multiple payment options	Various payment options are available — ACH, credit card, purchasing card, or offline	Electronic payments enable the opportunity to reduce the cost of paying invoices for customers; suppliers can be paid easier and faster
Online collaboration	—	Supplier communication is accelerated through online capabilities to perform inquiries and to resolve discrepancies; A/R has visibility into the invoice process via online reports; both A/P and A/R can track scheduled and paid invoices, invoice payment status, adjudication reasons, and service requests

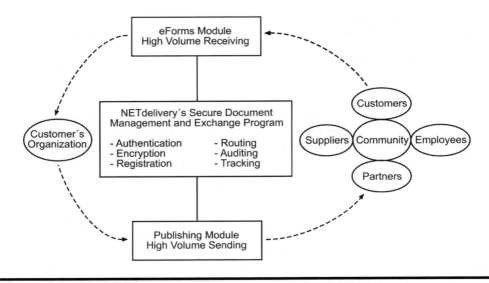

Figure 7.3   Secure online information management with NETdelivery.

their trading partners. Figure 7.3 shows the secure architecture of the NETdelivery solution. The company provides this architecture with a complete out-of-the-box solution available, including:

- Smart tools that make it easy to complete and submit documents
- A document-management and -exchange platform, along with two modules, to streamline information flow and speed response times
    - A forms module that automates how customers receive and manage documents such as applications, enrollment forms, claims, and orders from their partners
    - A publishing module that gives customers control over the documents they send to partners, including bills, statements, policies, notices, and marketing materials.
- Five layers of security protection to ensure the integrity and privacy of transactions
- Design tools that enable customers to brand the user interface and all their electronic documents

7.4.2.2   Differentiators

The NETdelivery product is extremely strong on multiple levels of security.

7.4.3 Princeton eCom

Princeton eCom offers customized turnkey solutions for complete management of the e-billing process by expediting payments, minimizing billing costs, and integrating with existing financial accounting systems. The principal focus is on midtier billers, but it also works with large companies.

7.4.3.1 Products and Services

Pay Anyone™ serves financial institutions — banks, credit unions, brokerage houses, and insurance companies — that want to offer their customers payment capability. Pay Anyone incorporates multiple payment methods:

- Electronic
- Credit card
- Paper

Both B2B and B2C billing and payment relationships are supported.

7.4.3.1.1 Business Billing

7.4.3.1.1.1 **Presentment** — Electronic bill presentment creates a central point for both customers and their trading partners to view and manage invoices. Whether customers are looking to provide a simple online invoice presentation or a more sophisticated presentment package, Princeton eCom has a scalable solution to meet the needs of customers. The billing features include:

- Web-based functionality, which facilitates accessibility
- Electronic presentment, which reduces costs of printing, postage, and personnel
- Invoice availability on the day it is posted:
    View unpaid invoices
    Review all or specific invoices
- Notification of payers via e-mail when invoices are available for review
- Access to data and account history
- Robust solutions that allow trading partners to:
    Verify invoice status
    Adjust invoices online
    View authorized pending payments
    View history of paid invoices and payment orders
    Download liability data into legacy systems without manual rekeying
- Capability of handling complex invoicing and volume detail
- Resolution of disputes online by:
    Reducing time needed to resolve disputes
    Reducing the paperwork involved in resolution
    Utilizing standard business rules
- Better cash-flow forecasting

7.4.3.1.1.2 **Payment** — When it comes to cash flow, customers want to keep it all in one place. Choosing an ASP to provide customers with an online invoicing system lets them focus on what they do best while taking advantage of the best resources and technology available. But those customers do not want to manage multiple relationships just because the company they outsourced to in turn outsourced to other companies. They need an integrated payment solution from a trusted and experienced company. The payment solution includes the following features:

- Payment is an integral part of eCom solutions.
- Premium eLockbox service — eCom's flagship product — provides the highest accuracy rate attainable: 99.6 to 100%.
- Funds post through eLockbox, ACH, or a lock box directly to the customer's bank account(s).
- Automatic posting easily integrates remittance files into the customer's legacy accounts-receivable system.
- Payers maintain control of outbound cash flow by:
    Selecting the method of payment and settlement dates
    Directing payment debits through ACH
    Specifying multiple bank accounts
- Payment options are scalable:
    Click and pay
    Create payment orders
    Authorize payment orders
    Send payment orders directly to banks
    View authorized pending payments
    Cancel payments
- Payment history is available online.
- Automatically assigned "check" numbers link back to the original invoice.
- Payables process can be automated to avoid problems, especially useful when the person who issues funds for purchases did not place the order, authorize the order, or authorize payment:
    Invoice receipt
    Reconcile with receiving records
    Identify and record discrepancies
    Approve invoice
    Initiate payment
    Authorize payment
    Schedule pending payments
    Maintain history
- A secure extranet with individual e-mail boxes is available:
    Electronic remote routing of invoices speeds the process.
    Electronic messaging alerts the next party that action is needed.
    E-mail messages remind payers that discounts are pending.
- Payers control payment initiation and settlement dates.

7.4.3.1.2 Consumer Billing

7.4.3.1.2.1 Presentment — Electronic billing is an extension of the commitment to provide customers with value-added services. E-billing gives customers the ease of online bill-paying coupled with account-management interactivity.

Providing customers with a paperless means of handling their accounts can save money in printing, postage, and manpower. The presentment features include:

- ePayBill receives a data stream to create an electronic bill:
    Data are extracted from legacy billing systems.
    Information is stored and formatted using templates or custom formats.
    The storage format easily integrates with existing Web sites.
- Customers can retain the look and feel of their paper bills.
    Reinforces brand identification.
    Makes transition to online bill payment easier and less intimidating for payers.
- E-mail notice is sent to consumer when bill is available.
    Hot-link directly to the bill
    Sort information
    Analyze usage
    Segment data
    Track history
    Use graphs, tables, and export capability

7.4.3.1.2.2 Payment — With over 16 years of experience in the payments industry, Princeton eCom facilitates fast, accurate electronic movement of money without outsourcing payment to third parties. The payment features include:

- Payment is an integral part of the ePayBill solution.
- Electronic relationships are already established with financial Institutions:
    Automated clearinghouse (ACH)
    Federal Reserve direct payment network
    MasterCard RPPS
    Visa
- Real-time data integration is available between all payment devices and the biller's site:
    Phone (IVR or VRU)
    Internet
    Personal digital assistant
    Wireless application protocol

Customers can easily switch between the auto-debit or pay-on-demand options. Customers pay using a bank account debit (checking or savings) or credit card. Premium eLockbox service provides the highest accuracy rate attainable, 99.6 to 100%.

7.4.3.1.2.3 Distribution of Bills — Princeton eCom's electronic bill distribution philosophy is simple: Consumers should be able to view and pay bills wherever and whenever they choose. The ePayBill solution is built accordingly. In addition to presenting on the site of customers, universal bill distribution uses nonproprietary open standards to distribute bills to other networks and services as well as multiple consumer endpoints:

- Aggregator Web sites (Yodlee)
- Consolidator Web sites (Paytru$t, CyberBills)
- Financial institution sites (Webster Bank, Bank of New York)
- Financial Management sites (Quicken)
- Portals (America Online, Excite)

7.4.3.1.2.4 Data Posting — Presenting an e-bill and then receiving funds is only half the battle. The final step — creating a complete end-to-end solution — is accurately posting the data into the accounts-receivable systems. ePayBill finalizes that last digital step. The product is designed to reduce the cost of human resources and virtually eliminate manual exception processing. The features of data posting include:

- Seamless integration with legacy receivable/accounting systems
- Organization, sorting, and batching of data before posting
- Automatic posting of information without personnel intervention
- No need to purchase new hardware, software, licenses, or upgrades
- Accurate daily settlement reporting via:
    - e-Mail
    - Fax
    - Internet

7.4.3.2 Differentiators

Princeton eCom brings a strong offer to both businesses and consumers with rich distribution and data-posting capabilities.

7.5 Portals, Distributors, and Exchanges

These suppliers are very well positioned with customers, and they have many partnerships with financial institutions. In this case, the solution provider matches the business model and offers the basic service platform to be utilized for bill presentment and payment.

7.5.1 Intuit

Intuit is poised as a consumer aggregator, leveraging its Quicken.com and its Quicken personal financial software package. This portal model involves presenting a summary of a biller's bill to consumers who come through the Quicken Web site to receive their bills. The company does not necessarily generate its revenues on a fee basis from billers or from fees to access by customers. Instead, Intuit generates revenue from advertising banners placed on the bill itself. The portal enables a link back to the biller's Web site, and the biller has right of first refusal to take up that advertising space on its bill. Alternatively, the biller can permit Intuit to sell the advertising space to other entities. This model seems to function well.

7.5.2 Other Portals

The use and popularity of portals is increasing. Portals are offered by many institutions, including:

- Search machines (Yahoo, Google)
- Financial institutions (community banks, state banks, global banks)
- Service providers (e-mail service provider, insurance companies, utilities, telecommunications service providers, etc.)
- Publishers (books, magazines, journals, and daily newspapers)
- Government (local, state, federal)

7.5.3 Pros and Cons

Combining portals with EBPP solutions makes sense. Consumers (payers) usually have a "sticky" relationship with one or more portals. Extending portals with consumer-centric attributes for EBPP is a reasonable step. Many issuers of statements, bills, and invoices are working toward this direction. Nevertheless, portals are not without problems. They typically overemphasize the presentation features, such as excellent graphics and colors, resulting in:

- A need for advanced browser capabilities
- Slow screen painting
- Very slow data downloads

Portal providers frequently cannot resist the marketing pressure of content providers, and payers must contend with a full-scale marketing blitz instead of personalized P2P messages from their billers.

7.6 Document and Postal Service Outsourcers

This group of suppliers has a great deal of experience with document creation and distribution. Their customer base is sound and interested in innovations with mutual benefits. Their main strength involves converting documents onto digital format, archiving documents, and supervising the entire EBPP cycle. For these suppliers, it is relatively easy to extend their services by implementing EBPP features. They either develop their own solutions, collaborate with other solution providers, or acquire EBPP products.

7.6.1 *Mobius Management Systems, Inc.*

The company's electronic document warehouse products store and integrate documents and transactions of different formats on a wide variety of computing platforms and electronic storage devices.

7.6.1.1 *Products and Services*

7.6.1.1.1 ViewDirect®

ViewDirect technology is an integrated product suite for high-volume storage, high-speed indexed access, and electronic distribution of enterprise content. It provides Internet and network-based solutions to a broad range of application and e-business requirements. This suite of products helps enterprises meet a complex challenge: the need to manage staggering volumes of diverse information and the expectation that highly customized views of this information can be delivered on demand to any customer, partner, or employee. ViewDirect stores and integrates information in virtually any format on a wide variety of computing platforms and electronic storage devices, making it instantly available through automated distribution and user access over the Internet and corporate networks. It integrates with back-office systems, including ERP applications, and Web-enables documents for use with front-office systems such as customer-relationship management and electronic bill/statement presentment.

ViewDirect serves as a unifying bridge between back-office and front-office operations by making all enterprise documents available in a secure, managed way to end users, suppliers, and customers. Documents are available for online access, can be delivered via fax or e-mail, or can be Web-enabled for use with front-office systems such as CRM, electronic statement presentment (ESP), and EBPP. Capabilities include powerful search functions, personalized views of enterprise documents, automated distribution, and tools for data analysis and export.

7.6.1.1.2 Click-n-Done®

7.6.1.1.2.1 Electronic Bill Presentment and Payment, Electronic Statement Presentment, and Electronic Invoice Presentment and Payment — Click-n-Done is the "next-generation" e-statement and e-billing solution that meets all the requirements of the companies that issue bills and statements and of the consumers who receive and pay them. Click-n-Done supports all billing models, including biller direct and third-party consolidation, and introduces the groundbreaking consumer-consolidation model. Click-n-Done provides a complete round-trip solution, taking the bill from the legacy billing system through presentment, payment, and integration with enterprise applications.

7.6.1.1.2.2 Benefits — Click-n-Done provides the following benefits:

- Supports any e-billing model
- Supports e-billing and traditional customer service with a single billing repository
- Includes a portable payment server
- Speeds and simplifies e-billing implementations
- Provides consumer access to historical data
- Provides desktop consolidation for faster consumer adoption

Click-n-Done is a fully packaged end-to-end ESP/EBPP solution that minimizes the costs and complexities of implementation and offers a uniquely robust service. It provides the ability to store, retrieve, and deliver billing data to customers and then deliver payment instructions to virtually any payment engine.

This powerful customer-care solution supports any of the e-billing models, providing an evolutionary path in this fast-changing environment. Billers can implement a biller-direct solution immediately, offer their customers the option of third-party consolidation, and ultimately provide consumer consolidation, the important innovation that will drive consumer adoption of EBPP.

Click-n-Done's dynamic registration facility eliminates preregistration preparation and manual processing, thus giving the consumer immediate access to information. A portable payment server offers billers complete flexibility, supporting in-house payment processing, outsourcing, and integration with third-party payment processors.

Unique among ESP/EBPP offerings, the Click-n-Done solution uses a single billing repository to support both e-billing and paper-based bill delivery, eliminating redundant processing, simplifying registration, and reducing the costs of hard-copy delivery while also supporting the customer service requirements of those who continue to receive printed bills. The billing repository gives consumers access to historical data as well as the current bill.

The patent-pending Click-n-Done consumer-consolidation component delivers benefits to both consumers and issuers. By consolidating bills, statements, and other financial information on the consumer's desktop, Click-n-Done resolves both convenience and privacy issues that have constrained consumer adoption of EBPP until now. It is also free to the consumer. For the issuer, Click-n-Done delivers all the cost benefits of electronic bill/statement presentment and payment while maintaining the one-to-one marketing relationship with the customer.

7.6.1.2 Differentiators

Mobius Management Systems provides solutions that support multiple business models and provide easy enrollment options for consumers.

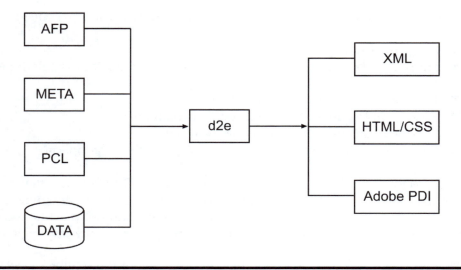

Figure 7.4   d2e conversion by Xenos.

7.6.2 *Xenos*

Xenos, the data to e-content company, provides world-leading software that transforms legacy documents and data into compelling content to drive applications such as EBPP, EIPP, and ESP. The software is also a key enabler of enterprise content management (ECM) solutions.

7.6.2.1 *Products and Services*

The Xenos d2e Platform™ is an out-of-the-box product that is fast and easy to deploy, enabling businesses to reduce the risk of e-business projects while getting them to market faster. This software transforms disparate print-stream formats — IBM AFP, Xerox Metacode, HP PCL, and database data — into industry-standard e-content formats, such as XML, HTML, and PDF. Figure 7.4 illustrates the all-in-one integrated solution.

The Xenos d2e Platform is a transformation software for e-business and collaborative commerce. It is packaged software that transforms legacy documents and data into e-content formats to drive applications, including:

- Online billing
- Online invoicing
- E-statements

The software also integrates with leading ECM solutions, such as IBM Content Manager OnDemand.

The software platform's component-based architecture allows large organizations, software vendors, systems integrators, and BSPs to select the specific technology they need to transform data from print streams and databases into e-content formats, including XML, HTML, and PDF. The Xenos d2e Platform's out-of-the-box capabilities make it easy to use and deploy, even in the most complex e-business projects. Organizations can easily and rapidly transform complex legacy data into Web-ready content formats, thus avoiding the costs associated with developing new Internet applications.

In addition to its powerful components for data and document transformation, Xenos's integrated solution also incorporates the highly sophisticated business logic that companies build up over time through intelligent document control (IDC). Xenos's latest software incorporates leading-edge technologies such as Java and XML. It runs on all major operating systems, including Microsoft Windows NT/2000, Sun Solaris, IBM OS/390 and AIX, HP-UX, and Linux.

7.6.2.2 Differentiators

Xenos provides EBPP solutions that offer great flexibility with input and output formats.

7.6.3 Pitney Bowes docSense

Pitney Bowes docSense is a wholly owned subsidiary of Pitney Bowes, Inc., that offers solutions for the creation and distribution of efficient and effective documents in paper and digital form. Pitney Bowes has been in business for over 80 years, expanding from the sale and production of mail and office equipment to the development of office management solutions. Targeting the B2B, B2C, and business-to-employee markets, docSense leverages the legacy of Pitney Bowes and has unique capabilities to understand customer requirements and provide valuable products, services, implementation processes, and aggressive ongoing support.

7.6.3.1 Products and Services

Pitney Bowes docSense's end-to-end solutions provide corporate, line-of-business, and e-commerce operations with a flexible document-output strategy to meet requirements of cost, marketing, customer service, cash flow, and compliance.

7.6.3.1.1 Digital Document Delivery

Digital document delivery (DDD) is a modular system that facilitates EBPP and ESP, including enrollment, data extraction, presentment, payment, remittance-posting, and reporting functions. The system enables EBPP through the following processes:

- Enrollment and account management: With DDD, self-service, online enrollment, and account management can be integrated into existing Web sites. When needed, DDD can automatically process bulk enrollments from biller data files.

- Data extraction and format conversion: The DDD engine accepts virtually any data source as input and converts documents for digital delivery. It interfaces between existing document creation systems and the customer's preferred document delivery channels, be they paper, digital, or both.
- Document preparation: The print-engineering software takes a biller's existing print stream, customer-preference database, and processing instructions and prepares documents for digital delivery.
- Electronic insertion: The electronic inserter separates individual documents from the print stream and attaches electronic inserts and template data to each before sending each document to a router via Web-based delivery or another method of customer's choice.
- Document routing: The document router decodes the delivery-notification preference data of each individual electronic document, executes the combined processing instructions, and sends the complete package to the appropriate output channel. Presentment of the bill to customers then takes place via a biller's own Web server, online bank, or consolidator. Hot links are provided for easy, direct access to the document site. For notification, plenty of prepackaged messages, including payment reminders and confirmations, are available.
- Bill processing: Each bill is made available to the biller's customers via the Internet and their own Internet service provider (ISP). Access can be relayed through site links from the biller's home page or through a merchant site, online bank, or service bureau.
- Remittances: Payment transaction data are then forwarded to initiate funds transfers as well as to provide payment status information to the biller's information system. ACH funds transfer and real-time credit card authorization are supported. DDD can process scheduled partial, recurring, cost-allocation, and smart-payment processing and keep track of the balance due.
- Posting: Biller's account-receivables system receives an integrated and simplified payment/posting file. Users view documents via secure browser or online interface. Complete data encryption has the highest levels of security and fraud protection. The data-exchange environment stays secure as a logged-on user navigates between document, biller, and additional e-commerce links.
- Reporting: Customers can monitor, summarize, and report on invoices and bills to analyze exact usage and bill processing status.

Billers receive the following benefits:

- Working with legacy applications to manipulate, enrich, and customize the print stream and distribute invoices, statements, and other electronic documents via the channels of a customer's choice
- Significantly lowering the per-piece cost of distributing statements and accelerating their delivery to nearly instantaneous status

- Opening a variety of messaging channels for customer communications, including Internet, e-mail, fax, and message pagers
- Increasing the value of each message by tailoring inserts — hotlinks, banner ads, or attachments — that enable cross promotions and up-sell opportunities to targeted customers
- Accommodating documents generated on several types of platforms and in a variety of print file formats, including AFP, Metacode, PostScript
- Delivering through alternative channels if the document is not viewed within a specified period of time
- Ensuring delivery regardless of the medium chosen and sending reminder notices when the document has not been acted upon
- Extracting bill information and providing it to bill consolidators and consumer service providers
- Maintaining complete security, auditability, and control
- Expediting the receipt of payments and improving cash flow
- Streamlining the accounts-receivable process by minimizing exception processing
- Consolidating payment and remittance files

In addition to the core components, docSense offers a series of optional modular components for DDD that are designed for B2B invoice processing. These components are:

- Workflow: This component supports the unique approval routing requirements of businesses to simplify accounts-payable processing. It supports bill routing into responsible departments for recipient review, approval, and payment.
- Dispute processing: This component accommodates billing disputes that can be input by the customer online and then queued for processing by a customer service representative. Provides tracking, reporting, and resolution capabilities. Permits electronic notes to be attached to disputes.
- Advanced data management: This component provides download and reporting functionality. It includes wizards that enable customers to define personalized views, reports, and downloads that can be saved and run on demand at any point in the future. Filtered billing data can be downloaded into spreadsheets and other programs for analysis. It allows for integration with ERP systems.
- Report wizard: This component helps generate standard or custom reports for more-targeted data analysis. Reports can be defined using filters, fields, and field properties. Data can be downloaded as CSV or XML.
- Advanced user management: This component enables the creation and management of users, permissions, and workflows within business customer organizations. This makes it possible, for example, to tailor workflows to each customer organization. It can be administered by customer service or by the customers themselves.

The digital statement is proving to be a powerful branding medium. It can become the key periodic contact point between the service provider and its customers. Pitney Bowes docSense is providing multiple products to build a stronger relationship with customers. They include:

- StreamWeaver™, a front-end-processing software for DDD that identifies documents designated for digital delivery, directs the print stream for digital processing, and creates electronic data files
- SiteView™, a powerful process-monitoring software that tracks the entire document production process, from inception to distribution
- EmailAngel, a forwarding system that connects old e-mail addresses to new ones, an important capability for any company relying on customer e-mail addresses for statement presentment

7.6.3.1.2 StreamWeaver

StreamWeaver is the closest to EBPP. StreamWeaver's technology provides the first step in the docSense DDD solution. Providing billers with a strong foundation for print-stream conditioning, the application performs the following core functions:

- Document analysis: determines print-stream attributes, such as page counts, data items, addresses, and barcode locations
- File extraction: creates report records for each document and produces data files for post-processing
- Document enhancement: manipulates documents and document streams to support print, mail, and marketing initiatives.
- Data and function integration: incorporates data from external files and databases for print-stream processing to enhance documents within a print-file or control-processing logic
- E-MRDF: creates an electronic mail run data file (E-MRDF) that includes a key of each mail run document to be electronically distributed, along with any instructions for customizing documents, such as adding hot links, page inserts, or special messaging

Because StreamWeaver is modular and flexible, users can select one or all of its discrete applications to build a portfolio of applications that will enhance their document production operations. Bar coding, postal automation, simple to duplex printing, document consolidation, and document reprinting are a few examples of the product's expanding range of applications. This product offers the following benefits to billers:

- Easy integration of software into existing operations, saving time and money
- No need to monopolize IT resources to reprogram business applications because the software platform conditions print streams after they leave

the business applications of the users and before they reach a user's printing and/or electronic distributions device

- Support of document integrity by automating manual processes, such as document regeneration, and by supporting file-based processing, which optimizes intelligent inserter technology
- Allows users to consolidate, add color to, enhance, and customize their documents to improve their look and content, making them more attractive and easier to use for customers

A set of tools provided by docSense helps to develop, test, implement, and operate StreamWeaver components. The Professional Workstation allows both novice and advanced users to easily reengineer print streams. A special interface brings the power of StreamWeaver to a wider base of users without the need to learn the programming language first. It simplifies the entire document reengineering process. Its tools include:

- A hierarchical tree-structured project manager provides central management of all StreamWeaver projects and a single access point for sharing projects in whole or in part, thus permitting access to projects.
- The document-view function lets users view composed images of input and output documents graphically in their current state, in their working state, and after changes are applied. It accesses the actual system resources, which means that most documents are presented on-screen as they will be printed. For most applications, new and experienced StreamWeaver users get fast feedback by seeing how their newly modified documents will appear in printed form.
- Object manipulation provides easy drag-and-drop functionality. Users can easily place and position new document components by dragging and dropping them onto the newly reengineered output document.
- Dynamic script creation lets users create StreamWeaver application scripts without knowing the syntax of the language of the script that directs StreamWeaver production processing.
- Execution lets users test newly developed applications using the actual StreamWeaver engine to speed completion and ensure production-ready results.
- Import brings existing StreamWeaver applications into the Professional Workstation's project manager, ensuring the full utilization of this tool.
- The publish application allows users to transfer or stage StreamWeaver application components to their production environment.

This product runs on all major business computer platforms and operating systems. The Professional Workstation is based on a client/server architecture that is designed for use in a networked, distributed, business-computing environment.

7.6.3.2 Differentiators

Pitney Bowes docSense supports the whole process of digital printing.

7.7 Service Bureaus

Companies that issue statements, bills, and invoices can always consider an outsourced solution in the EBPP domain. The choice of an outsource offers presentment and payment services at reasonable expenses.

7.7.1 BillServ, Inc.

With approximately 3 billion bills under contract, BillServ, Inc., is the leading EBPP outsourced service provider (OSP), delivering comprehensive, cost-effective solutions for presenting and servicing consumer bills for payment via the Internet. The company has created its portal service, Bill.com, in partnership with CheckFree. Bill.com has relaunched its service with less emphasis on financial services and more emphasis on enabling customers to view, pay, and manage their statements, bills, and invoices.

7.7.1.1 Products and Services

As part of an integrated EBPP solution, BillServ also provides market-leading interactive customer-care and direct-marketing applications. BillServ consolidates customer billing information and then securely delivers it to distribution end points and to the client's own payment site, hosted by BillServ. BillServ's impressive client list includes billers representing the financial services, insurance, utilities, oil and gas, newspaper, and telecommunications industries. BillServ's integrated customer-centric offering combines Internet direct marketing and communication, online customer service, and wide distribution channels to reach customers anywhere, anytime.

BillServ's complete integrated, outsourced billing solution provides:

- Comprehensive distribution services, including biller-direct sites
- Online real-time customer care
- Internet direct marketing and communication
- Comprehensive adoption marketing support

BillServ's eServ™ electronic billing solution provides the catalyst customers need to develop online interactive customer relationships and communication through the electronic billing process, creating a private customer communication network of participating companies.

BillServ offers two electronic billing solutions: eServ Express™ and eServ Select™. eServ Express provides all of the tools needed to connect to customers swiftly and cost effectively. eServ Select delivers an electronic billing solution that is fully customized to customers' needs.

BillServ's eConsulting™ team provides professional consulting services for electronic billing, customer care, project management, and IT support. eConsulting allows extended customization to both eServ Express and eServ Select, providing a customizable billing system to meet changing needs.

7.7.1.2 Differentiator

BillServ provides support for a completely outsourced solution. It also serves as an intermediary between billers and bill-presentment aggregators, such as CheckFree and Transpoint. Companies could outsource to BillServ to have it set up their Internet billing, then provide that information to billing aggregators. BillServ is targeting midtier companies that have been largely ignored by others.

7.8 The Selection Process

The process of selecting the right EBPP solution is extremely complex. The initiative and investments are on behalf of the biller. Payers are usually taking advantages of the options offered by billers, biller service providers, or consolidators. Some form of a generalized best-practice model is required before selecting the best-fit EBPP solution (The Phillips Group, 2001).

7.8.1 The Selection Flowchart

Figure 7.5 displays the recommended steps for selecting an EBPP provider. The evaluation team contains a flexible mix of skills and knowledge, including marketing, billing, document management, networking infrastructure, and accounting. The representation of senior management is important. The first thing to consider is to undertake a detailed study into available EBPP solution alternatives and the vendors within these models. The importance of this preliminary research cannot be emphasized enough and relates to the secondary stage of consideration, when the team identifies the best fit of tools to the biller's business.

The second stage involves choosing the right size, ability to scale, and level of experience in a partner or vendor EBPP provider, and this stage is very important. If enough time is invested at these preliminary stages, the process of implementing and using an EBPP solution is greatly simplified. Because the actual process of EBPP is also extremely complex, the selected EBPP provider needs to satisfy the biller's expectations in terms of knowledge and experience.

Figure 7.5 also indicates an "own solution" path, where the service provider (biller) develops his own solution without a vendor (in-house) or a partner (outsourced). This is a very unlikely scenario due to time-to-market criteria and high estimated implementation costs. Practically, the vendor solution competes against the partner solution. This consideration must be grounded in the biller's fit to each respective model. A decision should be possible if the initial research and business evaluation phase has been developed to a suitably advanced stage by the members of the project team. This decision has far-reaching effects for the network managers and administrators, whose roles include interfacing the legacy billing data with the new system. As a result, the experiences and knowledge of the implementation team are of primary importance.

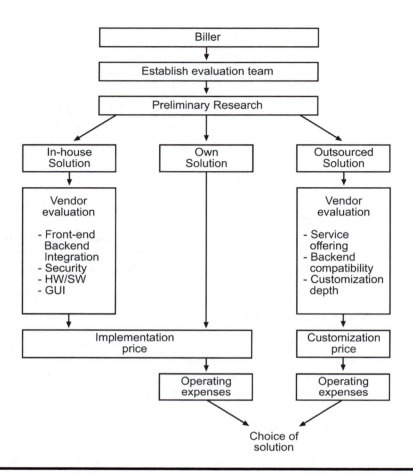

Figure 7.5   EBPP selection process.

When the vendor solution is the target, the biller should integrate the front-end and back-end processes very carefully, since this will obviate the need for redevelopment work. In addition, a fit with existing databases and graphical user interfaces (GUI) should be carefully evaluated. Security is a primary consideration with any solution. Both hardware and software needs must be considered by the biller. In-depth considerations are necessary for the firewall configuration, depth of encryption, type of digital certificates, and configuration access rights for users and maintainers. Ongoing security evaluation and audits need additional human resources.

In the outsourced model, the biller needs to determine the exact services the outsourcer would provide and what will be left to the biller to handle. Other considerations relate to the integration of the partner solution to the back-end accounting systems of the biller, the level of work that the database administrator will be required to do in enabling workflow connections, and what level of customization this solution requires.

The implementation price then competes with the customization price. The implementation price is more likely higher in both cases than the customization price. To find the optimal solution and guarantee an acceptable return on investment (ROI), operating expenses over a longer period (three to five years) should also be considered.

Both models were briefly compared in Chapter 3, with the conclusion that each model can migrate to the other. The most likely migration is from a partner model toward a vendor model.

7.8.2 Request for Information (RFI) and Request for Proposal (RFP)

When evaluating EBPP products and services supporting RFI and RFP, the following capabilities should be considered:

- Enrollment procedure
- Data extraction techniques
- Presentment alternatives
- Notification channels
- Bill payment alternatives
- B2C capabilities
- B2B capabilities
- Supported business models
- Focus on products or services or on both
- National and/or international support
- Multicurrency and multilanguage support
- Scalability of transaction volumes
- Industries supported:
    Telecommunications
    Utilities
    Insurance services
    Financial services
    Wholesale and retail
    Manufacturing
    Mortgage
    Securities/brokerage
- Support of paper bills
- Support of archiving and document management solutions
- Support of CRM
- Support of ERP

The matrix in Table 7.4 lists the major suppliers of products and services for B2C and B2B enterprises. The list of suppliers in Table 7.4 is not complete, but it offers an early entry to position and evaluate suppliers and their products and services. In-depth evaluation of potential suppliers requires further research. The following criteria are recommended for use in evaluating the short-listed suppliers:

- Focus on billers
- Focus on payers
- Focus on bills
- Focus on invoices
- Quality of the architecture
- Flexibility for customization
- Analysis and reporting capabilities

Table 7.5 lists some additional specific attributes of the products reviewed in this chapter. Again, the list of products is not complete. More details and more companies are reviewed in (Ebill, 2002). Given the industry's volatility and the likelihood of mergers and acquisitions, the list of suppliers should be revisited frequently and reevaluated. All products in this table offer support for any of the industries under consideration.

7.9 Summary

Service providers and customers should be critical in selecting their EBPP solutions. Important questions to be asked or be included into RFIs and RFPs are (Flynn, 1999):

- Where is a live EBPP site located?
- Are customers actually getting and paying their bills via this site?
- How is enrollment and registration handled?
- How are payments handled?
- Does the site support ACH and credit card transactions?
- Does the site let customers schedule automatic payments?

Table 7.4   Suppliers of EBPP Products and Services in B2B and B2C Sector

Targeted Areas	B2C	B2B
Services	CheckFree	BCE Emergis
	Spectrum	BillingZone
	Metavante	Metavante
	MasterCard	Princeton eCom
	YourAccounts.com	YourAccount.com
	Pitney Bowes	
	Princeton eCom	
	BillServ.com	
Products	Avolent	Avolent
	iPlanet	CheckFree
	Group 1	Edocs
	CheckFree	Bottomline
	Edocs	iPlanet
	Mobius	docSense
	docSense	

- Is e-mail notification supported? If yes, what trigger is used?
- How does the system interface with other systems?
- Does the site support OFX for integrating with consolidator services?
- Does the system convert existing billing streams to HTML or XML? If so, is this conversion static, or can the bill be dynamically reformatted depending on the user's profile, preferences, or some other parameters?

EBPP is an emerging area, where both service providers and their customers should be patient. EBPP is usually embedded into interactive customer care (ICC) solutions. Issuers of statements, bills, and invoices can evaluate and select from a number of products and services. They are expected to narrow down to the targeted business model first. Each EBPP business model is supported by multiple groups of solution providers. This chapter has introduced representative products and services for each provider group. While this list is not complete, it provides a good entry for preliminary research. A generic selection flowchart has been presented to help issuers of statements, bills, and invoices to decide what solution is the best for them: customized in-house software, self-developed software, or an outsourcing service. After vendor evaluation, implementation price, customization expenses, and operating costs will determine the optimal choice.

Table 7.5   Specific Attributes of EBPP Providers

Supplier	B2B	B2C	Bill Presentment	Bill Payment	Coverage	Paper Bills/Archiving
					Attributes	
Software Vendors and ASPs						
CheckFree	Yes	Yes	Yes	Yes	National/international	Archiving
Avolent	Yes	Yes	Yes	Yes	National/international	None
eDocs	Yes	Yes	Yes	Yes	National/international	None
iPlanet	Yes	Yes	Yes	Yes	National/international	None
Metavante	Yes	Yes	Yes	Yes	National/international	Both
Financial Service Providers						
Bottomline	Yes	Yes	Yes	Yes	National	None
Paytru$t	Yes	Yes	Yes	Yes	National	Both
MasterCard	No	Yes	Yes	Yes	National	None
Billing Service Providers						
Daleen	Yes	Yes	Yes	Yes	National/international	Paper bills
DST Output	Yes	Yes	Yes	Yes	National	Both

Consolidators and Aggregators						
BillingZone	Yes	No	Yes	Yes	National	Both
NetDelivery	Yes	Yes	Yes	Yes	National	None
Princeton eCom	Yes	Yes	Yes	Yes	National	Paper
Portals, Distributors, and Exchanges						
Intuit	Yes	Yes	Yes	Yes	National	Both
Document and Postal Outsourcers						
Mobius	Yes	Yes	Yes	Yes	National/international	Both
Xenos	Yes	Yes	Yes	No	National	Both
docSense	Yes	Yes	Yes	Yes	National/international	Paper
Group 1	Yes	Yes	Yes	Yes	National/international	Both
ISIS	No	Yes	Yes	No	National/international	Both
Service Bureaus						
BillServ	No	Yes	Yes	Yes	National	Both

Chapter 8

EBPP Operating Concepts

Electronic bill presentment and payment (EBPP) has the potential to fundamentally change the way that companies do business with each other and with their customers. Participating entities might select the right business model, the right tool set, and the right implementation strategies, but operational issues are equally important and must be addressed. With billions of paper bills targeted to be replaced by electronic presentment and payments, the participating entities obviously must devote sufficient attention and funding to performance, backup, recovery, data storage, quality of service, and customer support. Entities are expected to sign service-level agreements (SLA) with each other and with service providers.

When products are selected, scalability plays a big role. With each business model, large quantities of bills must be processed both periodically and on-demand. Processing and distributing bills involves bill details that are offered by billers and/or consolidators. Bill details are viewed and eventually downloaded from the Web site for further processing by the payer, requiring an adequate networking infrastructure.

Finally, complaints, questions, and inquiries by customers must be handled professionally. This support includes a hot line, help desk, escalation procedures, and (to some extent) reporting. In every case, a robust and reliable processing and networking infrastructure is expected.

The whole billing process must be supervised continuously. Each process stage requires different metrics and technology. Important subprocesses are:

- Creation of the bill: Data gathering, document composition, ensuring data quality, processing efficiency, and print-stream engineering are typical indicators for this initial stage.
- Presentment of the bill: Data and print-stream manipulation, processing efficiency, inserting one-2-one campaign management, and distribution-channel efficiency are typical indicators of this intermediate stage.

■ Payment: Payment processing, evaluation of campaign management, posting, and remittance hit ratios are the typical indicators for this final stage.

The value chain needs attention from various perspectives. These are not new, but they must be re-implemented to EBPP solutions. Particular emphasis is on SLAs, efficient fault management, escalation procedures, performance metrics, visualization of bill status, and on using best-of-breed Web-site monitoring and customer-support-desk touch-point tools.

In terms of infrastructure for supporting EBPP, the following criteria are important when selecting products and devices:

■ Estimated performance of the hardware/software architecture
■ Scalability of the hardware/software architecture
■ Reliability of infrastructure components
■ Backup and recovery capabilities
■ Support of security procedures
■ Integration with related products, such as customer-relationship management (CRM) and enterprise resource planning (ERP)
■ Ease of administration and management
■ Customer support for dispute regulations, inquiries, and payment confirmation

This chapter goes into the details of handling fault, performance, and data-management processes and tools. Particular interest is on Web-site efficiency, on SLAs, and on escalation procedures. Escalation procedures are very sensitive with thin consolidator business models due to the high number of participating entities.

8.1 Fault and Performance Management

In particular, fault, performance, and data-management applications are expected to be implemented for operations support of EBPP. Security-related issues have already been addressed in Chapters 5 and 6. All solutions relate to the servers of the billers, aggregators, and consolidators and to all communications links between participating entities.

8.1.1 Fault Management

Fault management is the process of detecting, locating, isolating, diagnosing, and correcting problems that occur in intranets. Fault management consists of the following steps, which are also illustrated in Figure 8.1:

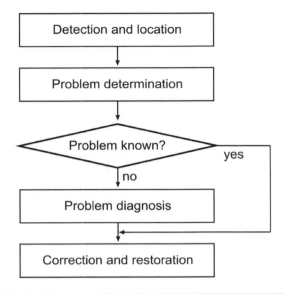

Figure 8.1   Fault-management process steps.

- Detecting and locating problems: Infrastructure components generate a number of messages, events, and alarms. Meaningful filtering, combined with user input, helps to detect abnormal operations. Management platforms and their management applications are usually able to determine the location of faults. This phase indicates that something is wrong.
- Determining the cause of the problem: Based upon information generated by element managers or correlation results provided by management platforms, the cause of the problem is being determined. This phase indicates what is wrong.
- Diagnosing root-cause of the problem: In-depth measurements, tests, and further correlating messages, events, and alarms will help to determine the root cause of problems. This phase indicates why the problem happened.
- Correcting the problem: Using various hardware and software techniques, managed objects are being repaired or replaced, and operations can return to normal. This phase indicates that the problem has been resolved.

Managing faults in EBPP support infrastructures does not introduce additional challenges to fault management.

8.1.2 Performance Management

Performance management is a very broad area to address. EBPP needs complex treatment and full-scope supervision, including Web-site activity analysis, log analysis (usage analysis), traffic measurements, server utilization, and load balancing.

8.1.2.1 Web-Site Activity Analysis

What is Web-site activity analysis and what is its purpose? Usually reporting of Web-site activity involves the analysis of:

- Basic traffic statistics (hits, page views, visits)
- Navigation patterns (referrers, next-click, entrance and exit pages)
- Content requested (top pages, directories, images, downloaded files)
- Visitor information (domains, browsers, platforms)
- Fulfillment of the Web site's objective (purchases, downloads, subscriptions)

Clearly, this last characteristic is the reason that Web-site activity analysis has become an enterprise-critical priority for organizations investing massive amounts of time and money in their Web presence. How well the Web site is performing relative to its objective is what justifies continued investment. The easiest way to quantify the return on investment (ROI) is with meaningful Web activity reports.

Reporting is also essential for making decisions about content. Web-site activity reports, by providing statistics about the most popular pages or files, give an organization quantifiable measurements as to what type of content appeals to its audience. Without reliable, comprehensive reports, a Web site's content is designed based on an educated guess by the design team or editorial staff.

Similarly, Web-site-activity analysis reports also tell an organization about their visitors. Where are they coming from; how do they get to the Web site; and what type of browser or platform are they using? When a corporation decides to deploy a Web site, it usually has an idea about who its audience will be. Does the actual audience resemble the predicted one? How does it change over time? What type of content improves visitor retention or session depth? All of these questions and many more will be answered in this chapter.

8.1.2.2 Usage Analysis

8.1.2.2.1 Log-File Analysis

Web-server monitors and management tools concentrate on how the Web server is utilized and how performance goals can be met. In addition to these tools, other tools are required that are able to continue the analysis using log files filled by special features of the server operating system. This section is devoted to log-file analyzer tools that are able to give the necessary data for in-depth usage analysis.

Usage analysis is a means of understanding what is happening on an Internet or intranet server such as a Web server. Usage analysis tools piece together data fragments to create a coherent picture of server activity. Usage analysis can answer the following questions:

- How many individual users visited the site on a particular day?
- What day of the week is the site busiest?
- How many visitors are from a certain country?
- How long do visitors remain on the site?
- How many errors do visitors encounter?
- Where do visitors enter and leave the site?
- How long did it take most visitors to view the home page?
- Which links on other sites send the most visitors to this site?
- Which search engines send the most visitors to this site?

Reports can span any length of time, making it possible to spot trends. They can also display any degree of granularity, allowing users to see both broad-ranging reports and detailed reports. Usage analysis is most frequently thought of in terms of Web servers.

8.1.2.2.2 Issues of Log File Analysis

When selecting products, several criteria must be carefully evaluated. The market is large, but it is addressed by a relatively low number of products. These criteria are also important when webmasters want to position log-file analysis within their information technology (IT) administration or when they want to deploy this functionality within their organization.

A product's architecture determines whether the product can support a distributed architecture or not. Distribution means that collecting, processing, reporting, and distributing data can be supported in various processors and at different locations. Figure 8.2 shows these functions with a distributed solution. In Figure 8.2, Web servers A, B, and C can be from very different types, such as Netscape Navigator or Microsoft Explorer. Of course, it is expected that many different Web-server types are supported. In addition, the hardware and operating system may be a differentiator for products. It is assumed that the Web-server hardware has decreasing impact on log-file analysis. The role of operating systems is more significant; the product should know exactly how log files are initiated and maintained. No problems are expected with leading Web-server solutions based on Unix and NT.

The data-capturing technique is essential with log-file analysis. The first question is where the logs are located. Figure 8.2 indicates that they are located in the Web servers, but more accurate information is required here:

- What memory area is used?
- What auxiliary storage area is used?
- What is the size of those areas?
- What types of log files are supported?

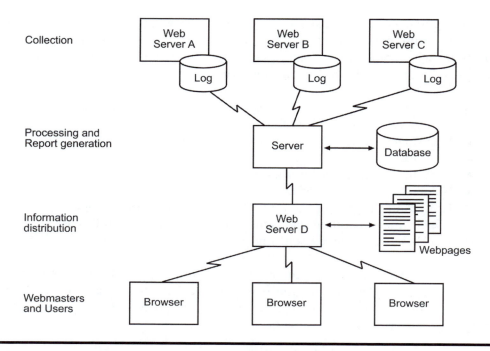

Figure 8.2   Generic product architecture for log-file analysis.

If log files are not processed in real or near-real time, it is important to know where they are stored until they are downloaded for processing. Log-file analysis deals with very large data volumes, and these volumes depend on the visitor's traffic.

Usually, log files are downloaded for processing. It is important to know how downloads are organized and how rapidly they are executed. As indicated in Figure 8.2, WANs with sometimes-limited bandwidth are involved. The bandwidth is usually shared with other applications, with the result of potential traffic congestion. Bandwidth-on-demand solutions are rare with log-file analysis. When transmission is arranged for low traffic periods, the actuality of log-file analysis results may suffer. In such cases, local storage requirements increase, and processing, report generation, and information distribution are delayed by several hours or even by days.

Two solutions may help. The first solution is to use intelligent profiling at the source of data collection. This approach removes redundant data from the logs during collection. The resultant decrease in data volumes and local storage requirements comes at the cost of a considerable increase in the processing requirements of the Web servers. A second solution involves the use of data compression or data compaction, with the same results and impacts as with the first solution.

Overhead is a very critical issue with large data volumes. Data capturing is expected to introduce little overhead when logs are stored away immediately. If local processing is taking place, overhead must be very carefully quantified; if resource demand is high, overall Web-server performance may be impacted. Data-transmission overhead can be heavy when everything is transmitted to the site where processing is taking place. WAN bandwidth is still too expensive to be dedicated just to log-file analysis. If bandwidth is shared with other applications, priorities must be set higher for business applications than for transmitting raw log-file data.

It is necessary to capture all of the data that are needed to conduct a detailed Web-site analysis of visitors or groups of visitors:

- Who is the visitor?
- What is the purpose of the visit?
- Where is the visitor coming from?
- When has the visit taken place?
- What key words have brought the visitor to the site?
- What search machines helped to access the site?
- How long was the visit?

Data losses cannot be completely avoided. Logging functions of Web servers, storage devices, or components of the transmission may fail; in such cases, there will be gaps in the sequence of events. Backup capabilities can be investigated, but IT budgets will usually not allow too much to be spent for backing up large volumes of log-file data. In the worst case, certain time windows are missing in reporting and in statistics. Those gaps can be filled with extrapolated data.

The management capabilities are also very important. One of the functions here includes automatic log cycling. Multiple logs are typically used to avoid data loss. When one of the logs is full, the other log seamlessly takes over. Another function is the translation of DNS (domain name service). Its speed is absolutely important for real-time information distribution. In order to generate more meaningful reports, the results of log-file analyzers must be correlated with other data sources maintained in other databases. In order to correlate, ad-hoc database links should be established and maintained. Management of logs of any log-file analyzer can be taken over by the operating system of the Web servers. The basic services are supported today; additional services may follow. In case of server farms or of many individual Web servers, the coordination of log transfers and processing is no trivial task. An event scheduler may help in this respect.

Cookie support is important to speed up work initiated by visitors. This is a logical connection between Web sites and browsers: A persistent identification code is assigned to a user, allowing the user to be tracked across several visits.

Given the considerable data volumes, databases should be considered as an option to maintain raw and/or processed log-file data. Database managers would then offer a number of built-in features to maintain the log files. Clustering of visitors can be deployed from various perspectives, such as geography, common applications, common interests on home pages, data, and time of visits. Automatic log cycling can also be supported here by the database managers. ODBC (open database connectivity) support helps to exchange data between different databases and to correlate data from various databases. Besides log files, other data sources can also be maintained in the same data warehouse. In addition to routine log-files analysis with concrete targeted reports, special analysis can also occasionally be conducted. This special analysis, called data mining, can discover patterns in traffic and user/visitor behavior. Both are important to sizing systems and networking resources.

One of the most important questions is the performance of log-file analysis when data volumes increase. Volume increase can be caused by offering more pages on more Web servers, by hosting more visitors, by longer visits, and by extensive use of page links. In any case, collection and processing capabilities must be estimated before specifying procedures and products.

To reduce the processing and transmission load of log files, redundant data should be filtered out as near as possible to the data-capturing locations. Filters can help to avoid storing redundant data. Filters can also be very useful in the report-generation process. Again, unnecessary data must not be processed for reports. Powerful filters help to streamline reporting.

Not everything can be automated with log-file analysis. The user interface is still one of the most important selection criteria for products. Graphical user interfaces are likely, but simple products are still working with textual interfaces. When log-file analyzers are integrated with management platforms, a request is automatically met by management platforms.

Reporting is the tool used to distribute the results of log-file analysis. Predefined reports and report elements, as well as templates, help to speed up the report design and generation process. Periodic reports can be automatically generated and distributed for both single Web servers and Web-server farms. In the case of many Web servers, report generation must be carefully synchronized and scheduled. Flexible formatting helps to customize reports to special user needs.

There are many output alternatives for reports. The most frequently used solutions include Word, Excel, HTML, XML, and ASCII. The distribution of reports also offers multiple choices:

- Reports can be stored on Web servers to be accessed by authorized users who are equipped with universal browsers.
- Reports can be uploaded into special servers or even pushed to selected users.
- Reports can be distributed as attachments to e-mail-messages.
- Reports can also be generated at remote sites; this alternative may save bandwidth when preprocessed data instead of completely formatted reports are sent to certain remote locations.

Documentation can be in various forms. For immediate answers, an integrated on-line manual would be very helpful. Paper-based manuals are still useful for detailed answers and analysis. This role, however, will be taken over by Web-based documentation systems. In critical cases, a hotline can help with operational problems.

Log-file analysis is actually another management application. If management platforms are used, this application can be integrated into the management platform. There are many ways to integrate; most likely a command-line interface (CLI) or Web services will be deployed.

8.1.2.2.3   Drawbacks of Pure Log-File Analyzers

Log-file analysis can give a good entry-level summary about the activities in and around Web servers, but this technology has some major problems.

The first major problem is traffic volumes. As traffic levels quickly reached exponential growth rates, nightly log-file downloads quickly became after-noon-and-evening and then even hourly downloads, since server disk drives would fill with log-file data so quickly. Compounding this problem was the fact that higher-traffic sites needed to load-balance across several servers and physical machines, so that log-file downloads needed to be done not only many times a day, but also across several machines each time. The quick fix to this problem was typically an automated script that would download log files on a preset schedule. However, this failed to account for unexpected spikes in traffic and clogged internal networks with huge log files being transmitted across the network several times a day.

The second major problem is data processing speed. Even in cases where there was an easy way to continuously transfer log-file data to a consolidated area, there was still the problem of how to process the gigabytes of log files into database tables in an efficient, continuous, and robust manner. Batch processing of log-file data requested a considerable amount of system time. In addition, the human-resources demand for log-file collection, processing support, and report compilation has exceeded expectations.

The third major problem involved incomplete data. Besides log files, there are significant alternative sources of site-activity data that contain more infor-mation than even the longest, most complex custom log-file format can provide. A log-file-only approach cannot guarantee a complete picture of Web activities. A good example of missing data is certain network-level data that the Web server and the server's log file never get to see. For instance, a visitor requests a page that turns out to be too slow to download and decides to terminate the request in mid-download. In this case, the network layer will log that action, but it will not notify the Web server about it. Similarly, much of the data seen by Web servers is never written to the log file. Therefore, any measurement approach based solely on log files would occasionally miss critical information about user activity on the Web site.

The fourth major problem with the log-file approach is flexibility. As sites become more sophisticated, one of the first obvious enhancements is to add dynamically generated content. Regardless of the type of content-management system used, dynamic content typically results in URLs (universal resource locator) that are very difficult, if not impossible, for a human reader to decipher. Since log files are just transaction records, dump-reporting systems simply pass the nonsensical URLs through to the end-user report as the page that was requested, resulting in an unintelligible report with meaningless page names and URLs. The ideal solution would be to interpose some intelligent classification system between the raw activity data and end-user report. In practice, however, the reality of gigabytes of raw log files often leave an in-house analysis team with few human resources to add even more complexity to an already slow log-based process. The inflexibility of log files to handle the tracking of new technologies has been observed not only with dynamic content but also with personalization applications, applet-based multimedia technologies, and a host of other new capabilities that the log-file approach was never designed to handle.

In summary, although log files were a convenient approach to measurement in the early days of using the Web, they rapidly highlighted problems of:

- Labor intensity
- Slow data-processing speeds and turnaround times measured in weeks
- Incomplete data, missing server- and network-level data
- Ineffective tracking of new feature enhancements like dynamic content, personalization, and applet-based multimedia

In response to these problems, hybrid products have been developed and deployed.

8.1.2.3   Traffic Measurements

Log files are not the only source of information for analyzing Web sites. There are other tools that are residing "on-the-wire" or on local-area networks (LAN) and collecting information on performance and traffic metrics. The information depth and the overhead are significant indicators that can differentiate between log-file analyzers and these products. In certain environments, the most effective results can only be achieved when both types of tools are deployed in combination.

8.1.2.3.1   Traffic Management on Distributed, Multitiered Infrastructures

Over the past several years, companies have adopted distributed, multitiered network infrastructures and moved business operations from traditional client/server applications to distributed Web-based applications. However, as more and more users come to depend on Web servers and transmission control protocol (TCP)-based services, IT organizations are discovering that their current infrastructures are unable to offer the performance and availability expected by users. The infrastructures also do not provide the management and monitoring capabilities required by IT organizations themselves.

Over the past several years, large corporations have begun reengineering their enterprise networks and establishing distributed, multitiered infrastructures. These multitiered infrastructures typically include three levels:

- At the WAN level, to enable communication across multiple points of presence (POP)
- At the Web level, to support server farms providing a wide range of TCP-based services, including HTTP (hypertext transfer protocol), FTP (file transfer protocol), SMTP (simple mail transfer protocol), and Telnet
- At the application level, to support farms of application servers that offload computation from Web servers to increase overall site performance

IT organizations are deploying new distributed, Web-based applications to take advantage of this new enterprise infrastructure. In place of fat software clients and centralized application servers, corporations are deploying Web browsers on every desktop, Web servers in departments and divisions, and application servers residing at multiple locations.

The new Web-centric model offers several advantages over the client/server model it replaces. IT departments can deploy Web browsers quickly and affordably to every desktop platform. Basic Web skills can be learned quickly and are popular with users. If an application requires modification to reflect changing business practices, IT departments need only modify the application itself, not the complex clients that used to work with the application. Most importantly, distributed, Web-based infrastructures move content and applications closer to users and provide greater reliability and availability. Employees can leverage this new infrastructure to improve internal business practices, communication with partners and suppliers, and services for customers.

While distributed, multitiered infrastructures offer considerable advantages over earlier network architectures, they still do not offer the performance and availability expected by end users, and they do not provide the management and monitoring capabilities expected by IT organizations. Multitiered architectures are physically well connected, but they are not logically well connected. Standard network equipment enables traffic to flow, but not necessarily to the server best suited to respond. IT departments deploying these networks need traffic-management solutions that intelligently direct TCP traffic to optimal resources at each tier of the enterprise infrastructure. An optimal traffic-management solution requires communication between tiers. For example, there is little point in a DNS server directing traffic to an overloaded or disabled local server while another server is available with processing cycles to spare. To perform its job optimally, the DNS server needs access to and load information from the servers to which it directs requests.

The multitiered model itself, when implemented with the standard software products available today, does not monitor services for system failures or spikes. The model also does not provide other capabilities that IT departments require to manage busy, distributed networks effectively. Specifically, it does not provide:

- Policies for scheduling TCP traffic based on specific events centralized
- Remote management-reporting integration with standard network management tools

IT organizations need integrated software systems that can be layered on top of the existing infrastructure to provide intelligent scheduling of requests and information.

RMON (remote monitoring) has been introduced to support standardized measurements. RMON can be defined as the extension of MIBs (management information base) supported by SNMP (simple network management protocol). There are actually two standards: RMON1 and RMON2. RMON1 is best known for monitoring media access unit (MAC)-level performance within LAN segments. Using this base, combined with product-specific extensions, valuable information can be provided for fault, throughput, utilization, and communication metrics. Using RMON2, networked LANs can also be measured. RMON2 concentrates for the networks and application layers of the communication. The result is that performance analysis can go beyond routers in internet-protocol (IP) networks.

There are two components in implementing RMON-based products. The client consists of a hardware- or software-based probe, implemented in the LAN segments, and of a server that is responsible for centrally processing data captured by the probes (or monitors). Usually, the server is implemented into management platforms. Clients and server communicate with each other using the SNMP protocol.

8.1.2.3.2 Issues of Data Collection

The targeted metrics are the same as with log-file analyzers, but the source of data is different. When selecting products, several criteria — information depth, overhead, reporting capabilities — must be carefully evaluated. The market potential for such an evaluative tool is good, but few vendors have addressed this issue. These criteria are also important when webmasters want to position traffic measurements within their IT administration or when they want to deploy this functionality within their organization.

The architecture of a product determines whether it can support a distributed architecture. The term *distribution* means that the collection, processing, reporting, and distribution of data can be supported in various processors and at different locations. Figure 8.3 shows these functions in a distributed solution. The monitors in Figure 8.3 are passively measuring the traffic in the network segments. They are actually microcomputers with ever-increasing intelligence, with operating systems that are either proprietary or based on Unix or, more likely, on NT. Usually, they are programmed to interpret many protocols, with TCP/IP, UDP (user datagram protocol)/IP, and HTTP high on the priority list of vendors.

The data-capture technique is an essential traffic-measurement tool. The measurement probes are attached to the digital interface of the communication channels. These probes can reside directly on the network (stand-alone probes) or be co-located with networking equipment, in which case, the probe is used as a plug-in. Even software probes can be used and implemented into networking components or into end-user devices. The hardware or software probes usually include event scheduling, which involves determining polling

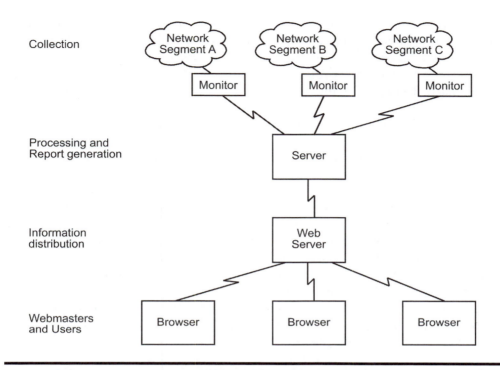

Figure 8.3   **Generic product architecture for processing traffic measurement data.**

cycles and time periods for downloading measurement data. Transmission should be scheduled for low-traffic periods. Probes are expected to deal with large data volumes that depend to a large degree on visitors' traffic in networking segments. Probes have limited storage capabilities; implementation examples show capabilities up to 24 hours. When this limit is exceeded, measurement data are overwritten by new data. Usually, measurement data are downloaded for further processing. It is important to know how downloads are organized and how rapidly they can be executed. As indicated in Figure 8.3, WANs are involved, which may have bandwidth limitations. The bandwidth is usually shared with other applications, with the result of potential traffic congestion. Bandwidth-on-demand solutions are rare with measurement probes. When transmission is arranged for low-traffic periods, the actuality of measurement results may suffer. In such cases, local storage requirements increase, and processing, report generation, and information distribution are delayed by several hours or even by days.

Two solutions may help. The first involves the use of intelligent filtering during and shortly after data collection. Removal of redundant data from captured packets during collection reduces data volumes and local storage requirements, but the processing requirements of the probes increase. The second solution uses data compression or data compaction, with the same results and impacts as for the first solution.

Overhead is a very critical issue with large data volumes. Data capturing is not expected to introduce any overhead in the case of hardware-based probes, and overhead is minimal with software-based probes. It is assumed that measurement data are stored away immediately after collection. If local processing is taking place, overhead must be critically quantified. If resource demand is high, probes must be upgraded properly. Data transmission overhead can be heavy when everything is transmitted to the site where processing takes place. Dedicated bandwidth would be too expensive for measurement and management purposes only. If bandwidth is shared with other applications, priorities must be set higher for business applications than for transmitting measurement data.

Similar to log-file analysis, it is absolutely necessary to capture all data that are needed to conduct a detailed Web-site analysis of visitors or groups of visitors. Data losses cannot be completely avoided. Probes, monitors, networking devices, user workstations, or transmission equipment may fail; in such cases, there will be gaps in the sequence of events. Backup capabilities can be investigated, but IT budgets usually do not allow for too much spending for backing up large volumes of traffic measurement data. In the worst case, certain time windows are missing in reporting and in statistics. Those gaps can be filled with extrapolated data.

In terms of database considerations — scalability with increasing data volumes, data filtering, user interfaces, and reporting — the issues are the same as with log-file analysis.

8.1.2.4   Server Performance

8.1.2.4.1   Server Management

The content of Web pages is maintained on Web servers. Usually, they are processors running under Unix or NT. They must be flexible and scalable enough to cope with significant workload fluctuations. Server management comprises several functions:

- Server monitoring: This function is the core component of server management, and it requires someone or something to keep a constant watch on the status of the managed servers. This is a tedious task for human beings, much of which, fortunately, can be automated by management platforms such as Unicenter TNG or HP OpenView. Monitoring is essential for detecting problems as soon as they occur and for gathering data for use in performance management.
- Workload management: This function consists of scheduling and tracking the jobs that run across one or more servers in a heterogeneous environment. Workload management takes into account calendar requirements like time of day, day of week, or holidays. It also considers dependencies between workloads, such as that Job A must be finished before Job B begins, as well as what to do in the case of a failure.
- Server performance management: While monitoring focuses on server availability, the purpose of server performance management is to ensure that servers are working efficiently. The keys to this function are data collection and trend analysis.

- Server capacity planning: While performance management focuses on current effectiveness, capacity planning ensures that servers will work effectively in the future. The keys to this function are historical analysis and forecasting.

8.1.2.4.2 Critical Issues with Web-Server Management

The management architecture for Web servers can be centralized, decentralized, or a combination of both. A centralized solution assumes that all Web servers can be managed from one location. When the number of Web servers to be managed exceeds a certain number, this solution could become critical in terms of networking overhead. It is assumed that with the exception of collecting raw data, all processing functions are executed in the manager module.

With a decentralized solution, domain managers take over the responsibility of managing a certain number of Web servers. Each domain is actually a centralized solution on its own. Domain managers may communicate with each other or can even be connected to an umbrella manager. Network overhead can be well controlled and kept to a minimum. Domain managers usually exchange only consolidated data with each other, which keeps the communication overhead to a minimum.

Most practical arrangements work with a combination of these two alternatives. If umbrella management is the choice, this manager can also manage other components, such as switches, routers, and other components, and can correlate data with server management.

Data-capturing techniques are critical for both overhead and performance of the management architecture. Measurement probes or agents are located inside the operating system, and they run with relatively high priority. These agents can supervise both hardware and software components of Web servers. Raw data are expected to be stored away immediately. Processing can be done here in the Web server or in the manager. The targeted metrics to be collected include:

- What is the CPU (central processor unit) utilization by applications?
- What are physical and logical I/O rates?
- Can the list of active applications be generated?
- What is the average queue length for CPU?
- What is the average queue length for I/O devices?
- How high is the CPU–I/O overlap?
- Are process wait times measured and displayed?
- How high is the disk utilization?
- How high is the memory utilization?
- Are swap-rates measured?
- What are resources that processes are blocked on?
- What reporting is used?
- Can the user be identified by application?

Raw data or preprocessed data are stored at the Web servers with the intention of being uploaded for further processing by the manager. Upload can be controlled in two different ways:

- Upload is triggered by events, such as filling a maximum percentage of storage spaces, or by time, or when critical data are captured.
- Upload is controlled by polling cycles initiated by the manager.

Both alternatives have pros and cons; the selection depends on the actual configuration, data volumes, and the communication protocols in use. Web-server management can utilize SNMP for transmitting data, assuming Web-server metrics are stored and maintained in MIBs. Another alternative is the use of DMI (desktop management interface)-like standards for storing and transmissions. The recent alternative is the use of embedded Web-based enterprise management (Wbem)-agents that support CIM (common information model) for data storage and exchange. In this case, HTTP is the protocol of choice.

Overhead is a very critical issue with large data volumes. Data capturing is expected to introduce little overhead when data are stored away immediately. If local processing is taking place, overhead must be very carefully quantified. If resource demand is high, overall Web-server performance can be impacted. Data transmission overhead can be heavy when everything is transmitted to the site where processing is taking place. WAN bandwidth is still too expensive to be dedicated just to transmittal of measurement data. If bandwidth is shared with other applications, priorities must be set higher for business applications than for transmitting raw log-file data.

Data losses cannot be completely avoided. Data-capturing functions in Web servers, storage devices, or components of the transmission may fail. In such cases, there will be gaps in the sequence of events. Backup capabilities can be investigated, but IT budgets usually do not allow for too much spending on backing up large volumes of server-related data. In the worst case, certain time windows are missing in reporting and in statistics. Those gaps can be filled with extrapolated data.

In terms of database considerations — scalability with increasing data volumes, data filtering, user interfaces, and reporting — the issues are the same as with log-file analysis.

8.1.2.5 Load Balancing

Several new vendors are offering hardware- and software-based load-balancing products to help IT managers in tracking IP performance and optimizing bandwidth usage across WANs. Load balancers typically reside at the edges of corporate networks and allocate traffic priorities by defining different traffic types and determining what happens to each. A very simple policy might call for priorities for a specific sender. Other criteria might include TCP port numbers, URLs, and DNSs. Traffic shaping can be supported by queuing or via TCP rate control. There are also products available for both categories.

Optimization is accomplished by controlling enterprise traffic flows at the boundary between the LANs and the WAN. Because these products give priority to traffic according to application type or even individual user, they will let IT managers take the first steps toward policy-based quality of service (QoS) in their networks. These products are a logical evolution from the passive probes that gave users a certain level of visibility for fault-operations monitoring but no actual control over traffic. These products go further and can manipulate traffic. IT managers expect that this new class of traffic-shaping tools will ease the contention for bandwidth without forcing them to purchase more and larger physical transmission lines.

Load balancing helps to utilize resources more effectively while stabilizing and improving the end-user response time. This is an emerging area with a number of innovative hardware- or software-based products. There are even a few that implement load-balancing functions in both hardware and software. The hardware solution is faster, but the software offers more flexibility if changes are required.

The functionality of a load balancer can be deployed in a stand-alone device or embedded into existing networking components, such as routers, switches, and firewalls. The stand-alone solution offers broad functionality without affecting any other routing, switching, or firewall functions, but it adds components into the network — and possibly another vendor — that must be managed. The embedded solution is just the opposite: easier management at the price of conflicting functions with its host.

Load balancers are only successful when policy profiles can be implemented and used. Policy profiles are most likely based on supporting various transmission priorities, which can be set by applications, by users, or by a combination of both. The technology of the solution can differ from case to case and from product to product, but most frequently, the TCP flow is intercepted.

Load balancers are expected to support a number of services, including quality control, resource management, flow control, link management, and actual load balancing. Advanced products support all these services in dependency of page content. This approach requires more work to gather the necessary information about content, but it offers better services for high-priority content.

Functions, in a narrower sense, include traffic shaping, load balancing, monitoring, and baselining. *Baselining* means to find the optimal operational conditions for a certain environment. It can be expressed by a few parameters, such as resource utilization, availability, and response time. Load balancers should monitor these few metrics and act on them. Traffic shaping and load balancing help to get back to "normal" conditions by splitting traffic, redirecting traffic to replicated servers, delaying payload transport, etc.

One of the most important questions is the performance of load balancing when data volumes increase. An increase in volume can be caused by offering more pages on more Web servers, an increase in the number of visitors, longer visits, or extensive use of page links. In any case, collection and processing capabilities must be estimated before specifying procedures and products.

Load balancing products can be managed by SNMP- or Wbem-agents. They are handled by managers, as any other kind of managed objects.

Documentation can be in various forms. For immediate answers, an integrated on-line manual would be very helpful. Paper-based manuals are still useful for detailed answers and analysis, although this role is being taken over by Web-based documentation systems. In critical cases, a hot line can help with operational problems.

Managing load balancers out of a management platform offers integration at the management-applications level. Baselining and monitoring can even be supported by other applications. In the case of using Web services, universal browsers can be used to view, extract, process, and distribute management information. The only prerequisite is that Wbem-agents have been implemented and that CIM is supported for information exchange.

8.2 Storage Management

Bills must be archived for a certain period of time, and the impact on storage requirements must not be underestimated. Most companies routinely handle storage in-house, using direct attached storage (DAS) to maintain electronic bills. In this case, the storage device is directly attached to the server through a dedicated link. The trouble is, putting the CPU and the storage on the same hardware does not scale well, is expensive, is difficult to manage, and occasionally overloads the CPU. The EBPP staff, together with IT, need a more efficient way to handle greater data complexity in a storage infrastructure with a frugal budget.

Network attached storage (NAS) solves some of these problems. NAS is based on storage appliances designed for file serving; other capabilities include backup, restore, and replication. Many of these systems are plug-and-play, fast, reliable, and have standard protocol support. Because NAS sits on the LAN of the biller, clients on the LAN can access it on a file level. However, NAS does not take LAN bandwidth limits into consideration, which can cause bottlenecks.

The next option is the use of storage-area networks (SAN). These resolve the congestion problem by linking multiple storage devices, such as RAID (redundant arrays of independent disks) arrays and libraries, over a separate, dedicated network. SANs usually run at high speeds with reliability, moving data blocks rather than files, and are well scalable. But they can become expensive, are complex to manage, and require highly trained administrators.

In both insourced and outsourced cases, there are a number of mandatory components and processes for storage systems. These include DAS, NAS, or SAN as an overall storage choice. In addition, backup, restore, disaster recovery, and remote mirroring are the most important solutions for processes. The subject-matter experts must address the complexities of storage networking and clustering requirements for storage, backup, and data replication. The overall goal is business continuity, in which the company maintains performance and availability through each processing cycle. It is important to move data rapidly from process to process and from server to server when customer service representatives are in online dialog with customers. Integration is needed across tools and databases that optimize personnel, their skill sets, and the existing infrastructure. Some of the outsourcers can handle these components and processes.

In has been estimated that, for many billers, the amount of data held in databases more than doubles every year. Storing, organizing, and retrieving this information has become a mission-critical function for billers, billing service providers, and consolidators. The effect on bottom-line profitability can be staggering if information systems go down and data are unavailable. SANs can help to guarantee availability at reasonable costs. SAN is a centrally managed, secure information infrastructure that enables any-to-any interconnection of servers and storage systems. It facilitates universal access and sharing of resources. A SAN supports unpredictable, explosive bills-related documentation growth, and it simplifies and centralizes resource management. A SAN is an investment that billing service providers cannot afford to be without.

Implementing customized SANs to meet the needs of a specific company is no easy task. There are a number of challenging questions that need to be addressed and solved: Will applications run smoothly over the SAN? Will components from different vendors interoperate, and will they work with legacy components? Is the switch backbone flexible enough to support future needs?

One key development in management of bill data is storage virtualization, which provides a single logical view of all physical storage resources, even across multiple platforms and vendors. This view is presented on the central management platform, enabling the operator to easily gauge storage use and needs. Virtualization cuts costs by allowing the administrator to manage the company's data resources from a central point.

8.3 Data Warehousing for Maintaining Data

A data warehouse is a database created specifically for the purpose of business analysis, in contrast to online transaction-processing systems, established for automating business operations. It is the logical umbrella above DAS, NAS, and SAN.

The data warehouse contains data extracted from various support, documentation, financial, marketing, and management systems of service providers. Data can be moved and altered, or transformed, to make it consistent and accessible for analysis by end users. The data can be used by service providers of all sizes with all types of hardware, software, and networking infrastructure. After proper formatting, various data sets can be partitioned. These data sets feed data to a data mart and to a common application interface to serve various end-user applications, such as:

- Consolidation of many data sources into one database
- Marketing research and marketing support

- Maintenance of product portfolios
- Consolidation of knowledge packs to support reactive fault management
- Maintenance history of trouble tickets

The data warehouse is integrated, containing data from diverse legacy applications; it is historical; and it comprises both summary and detailed data. Information in the warehouse is subject oriented, time variant, and nonvolatile. *Subject oriented* means that the data warehouse is designed and organized by the major subjects of the corporation, such as customer, vendor, and activity. In contrast, the legacy environment is organized by functional applications. The data warehouse is integrated because it contains data that have been transformed into a state of uniformity. For instance, gender can be considered as a data element. One application might encode gender as male/female, another as 1/0, and a third as x/y. As data are placed in the data warehouse, they are converted to a uniform stage; that is, gender would be encoded in only one way. As a data element passes onto the warehouse from applications where it is not encoded in this way, it is converted to create consistency.

Internal coding of data is only one aspect of integration. The representation of data should also be considered. In one application, a data element is measured in yards, while in another application it might be measured in inches or centimeters. As this data element is placed in the data warehouse, it is converted into a single uniform state of representation. A third characteristic of a data warehouse is that it is time variant. Each unit of data can be considered a snapshot of data, and each snapshot captures one moment of time at which the snapshot, like a billing cycle, was made. The values of the data are said to be time variant, that is, dependent on the time of the snapshot. Unlike time-variant warehouse data, operational data are updated as business conditions change. Operational data represent values that are updated any time the real-world objects they represent change. In the data warehouse, each time a change occurs, a new snapshot is created that marks that change. The time-variant characteristic of the data warehouse is what allows so much data to be stored there.

Finally, the data warehouse is nonvolatile; it is generally a "load-and-access" environment. After the data have been transformed and integrated, they are loaded en masse into the warehouse, from which they are accessed by end users. In contrast, data in the operational environment are updated on a record-by-record basis. This volatility requires considerable overhead to ensure the integrity and consistency of the database for such database activities as rollback, recovery, commits, and locking. The basic technology for the data warehouse does not require the underlying integrity component of the transaction-oriented database-management system.

Figure 8.4 shows a typical structure of a data warehouse. The data warehouse commonly has a four-level structure. The bulk of the data resides at the current level of detail, where it is accessed by end-user analysts. From this level, a lightly summarized level of detail is created, which serves midlevel

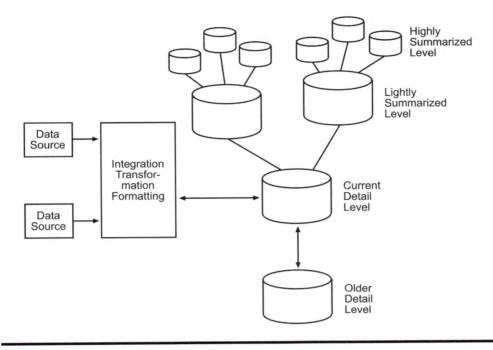

Figure 8.4   Structure of the data warehouse.

management. Next comes the highly summarized level of data for the benefit of top management. Beneath these three levels lies the older level of detail, data that are at least two or three years old.

There is a predictable flow of data into and through the data warehouse. Data enter into the current level of detail of the warehouse from the integration and transformation processes, which, in turn, have been provided with data by the legacy-type applications. The data then flow into the older level of detail as they age. As the data are summarized, they flow into the lightly summarized level of data, and from here, they flow into the highly summarized level. Finally, perhaps the most important component in the data warehouse architecture is the metadata. End users cannot efficiently access the data in the warehouse unless they have a way of knowing what data are stored there and where they are located. Metadata are data about data, a catalog of what data are in the warehouse, and pointers to the data.

Users must not only be able to locate data in the warehouse; they must also be able to manage the data. For this reason, the metadata set not only needs to describe the structure of the data in the warehouse, but it must also contain data-modeling information, including data-extraction and -transformation histories and data-summarization algorithms. This information is essential so that end users can trace the data back to operational sources. The metadata can also contain data usage statistics. The availability and increasing maturity of extraction and transformation tools, combined with powerful features for creating and managing metadata, are key drivers behind the rapidly increasing number of data-warehouse implementations.

A data warehouse can reside on a variety of platforms, depending on the data level of detail and summarization. Frequently, the data warehouse is physically distributed but logically unified. Typical solutions are:

- Highly summarized data typically reside on PC workstations.
- Lightly summarized data typically reside on client/service structures.
- Current data typically reside on mainframes or on client/server structures.
- Older detail-level data are expected to reside on bulk-storage devices.

State-of-the-art data warehouses offer Web access with the following benefits:

- Infrastructure: Using Web access shifts the burden of platform compatibility to the browser and presentation vendors.
- Access: Both internal and external users can easily have access via the Internet, eliminating the need to extend the corporate network.
- Cost: Web browsers are a fraction of the cost of OLAP (online analytical processing) and other client tools. They also have shorter learning curves.
- Leverage: The Web browser can be used in every application that provides a Web gateway.
- Control: Maintenance can be isolated to a centralized point.
- Independence: Web access allows a wide choice in hardware and operating systems.

Practically, all entities of EBPP can be responsible for operating the data warehouse.

8.4 Support Systems and Management Applications

It is very important to address all operational requirements of critical EBPP applications. There are no complete "best-of-suite" solutions available. Suppliers are expected to select "best-of-breed" products and integrate them as far as reasonable and possible.

An EBPP "suite" would be expected to have the following components: management platform and core applications; tools for content creation, deployment, and analysis; monitoring applications for fault and Web performance; management software for security and storage; and applications for testing and benchmarking.

8.4.1 Platforms and Core Applications

A basis platform provides functions that are required for all management applications. It serves as an overall coordinator for management functions and tasks. The following grouping is recommended for infrastructure: hardware

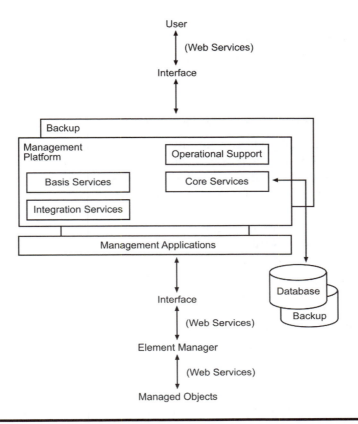

Figure 8.5 Management platform.

and software, directory services, time services, and asset management. Core applications are listed as follows:

- Basis services (internal communication, graphical user interface, Web-server functions, databank services)
- Support service for operations (installation, backup, workforce management, order management, recovery, housekeeping, software distribution)
- Integration services (eventing, monitoring and alarm management, reporting, policy management, central security functions for management systems, information management)
- Core services (trouble tracking and ticketing, SLA management, hot line)

Figure 8.5 shows the recommended architecture for the platform.

8.4.2 Management Applications

Management applications concentrate on the areas previously discussed. Best-of-breed products are briefly reviewed for each area as examples. There is no full review of products and services. The following application areas are targeted: content creation and deployment, fault monitoring, Web-performance analysis, security management, operating storage-area networks, and bench-marking and testing.

8.4.2.1 Content Creation and Deployment

Site Server™ from Microsoft offers all the necessary features to support content creation and deployment activities. The complexity and the business-critical nature of Web sites have also increased the demands on business managers, site developers, and site administrators. As a result, Web sites have become corporate assets that need to be managed, measured, and enhanced to take advantage of new business opportunities.

Companies do not want to change their existing ways of doing business to take advantage of Web technology. Rather, companies want to extend their existing business processes to the Web. Site Server is a comprehensive intranet server optimized for Microsoft Windows NT Server and Microsoft Internet Information Server (IIS). It enables users to build cost-effective Web solutions for the targeted delivery of information. Site Server can accomplish the following tasks:

- Efficiently submit, stage, and deploy the latest content while managing and troubleshooting the Web-site environment
- Provide site administrators with a tool to gather and index information and create keyword search capabilities on particular sites
- Personalize the user experience by delivering targeted information using dynamic Web pages, direct mail, and personalized push channels
- Improve access to online corporate information and provide subject-matter experts with a tool to share their expertise with colleagues
- Analyze site content and site usage to ensure an optimal return on Web-site investments

This product is a combination of content authoring and log-file analysis. It supports the publishing, searching, delivery, and analysis phases. Site Server provides an application framework for managing business information on the Web. It includes capabilities for adding content to a Web server, for organizing information in terms of end users and ad hoc categories, and for personalizing the delivery of information through various electronic mechanisms. Figure 8.6 illustrates the key components of Site Server.

The basic tasks of Site Server are:

- Publishing content on Web sites: Use the content-management feature and the content-deployment feature to manage and deploy content inside the corporate firewall or over the Internet.
- Creating search capabilities on Web sites: Use the search feature to create keyword search capabilities on Web sites.

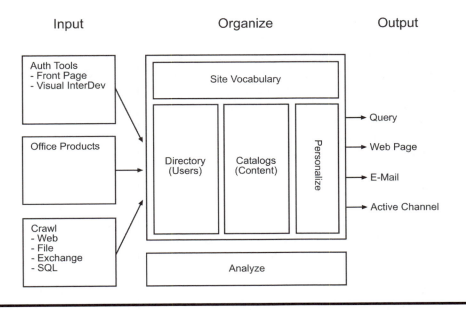

Figure 8.6   Key components of Site Server.

- Delivering targeted information over the intranet or Internet: Use personalization and membership, push, and knowledge manager to build a close relationship with site visitors and deliver targeted information.
- Analyzing Web sites: Use the content-analyzer feature to analyze the content and structure of Web sites. Users can take advantage of usage import, custom import, and report writer to analyze site usage and ensure an optimal return on Web-site investments.

Microsoft provides a set of features for building, staging, and developing Web sites and Web-based applications. Site Server contains two features that help make publishing content to Web sites reliable and secure:

- Content management: Manages the publishing process
- Content deployment: Deploys content on Web sites

Site Server supports the content developer's authoring tool of choice. Site Server includes:

- Microsoft FrontPage® Web-site creation and management tool
- Microsoft Visual InterDev™ Web-development system

These tools make it easy for authors to create Web pages and Web applications, respectively.

Site Server includes sample code that makes it easy for webmasters to develop their own custom Web pages. The Starter Sites take this sample code to the next level. Integrated with FrontPage, the Business Internet Site,

Employee Information Site, and Online Support Site are easy to deploy and customize by following the FrontPage task list. They are available for download.

Content management provides companies with a seamless environment for content sharing and management. More specifically, it is a tool that supports content authors and site administrators. Content authors can use content management to submit, tag, and edit content. Site administrators can use content management to review, manage, and publish content on a corporate intranet or the Internet.

The following tasks can be accomplished:

- Submit content for publication: For content authors, determining where on a corporate intranet to submit content is a fundamental problem. Content management provides content authors with a simple interface to submit and modify content on a server. Content can include documents, images, or Web pages. Using a Web page, content authors can drag and drop their content to a server. During content submission, content authors are asked to tag their content using predefined tags. Tagging is the process of defining the content type and the content attributes. The content type is the type of content, such as documents, spreadsheets, proposals, and so on. Content attributes are the specific properties of the content, including the author's name, the title of the document, or the date of submission. The content type and the content attributes are used by the site administrator to approve and manage the content.

- Perform common content management: Managing documents on a corporate intranet can be a time-consuming process. Site administrators are constantly overloaded with requests for content approval and site reorganization. Content management provides site administrators with an intuitive interface to view, approve, and manage content. Site administrators can manage the approval of content by defining approval settings based on the content type. For example, an administrator can specify that all proposals require approval before being posted to an intranet site. Alternatively, an administrator can specify that not all spreadsheets require approval before being posted to an intranet site. By defining approval settings, administrators can determine whether documents appear immediately on a Web site or after approval from a site administrator. When a document is tagged and submitted, it appears in a specific view of the Web site. If the Web site is in need of reorganization, it can become very expensive to retag each document and reassign the document to a new view. Content management provides administrators with the ability to apply new content attributes to multiple documents. Using this feature, administrators can apply the same content attributes to hundreds of documents and move the documents to a new view within a matter of minutes.

When content management is complete, site administrators need an efficient method to stage and deploy content across a corporate intranet or the Internet.

Security concerns, network outages, and obsolete file-transfer protocols have made large file transfers difficult. FTP is no exception.

Content deployment is used for staging and deploying content in Web-site environments. With this feature, webmasters can easily replicate file-based content, such as files, directories, metadata, and access control lists (ACL) from directory to directory, between local servers, or across the Internet or a corporate intranet. It deploys content to Windows NT and Unix destination servers. This feature can also be used to replicate and install server applications, including Microsoft ActiveX components and Java applets.

Content management is scaleable. For small production sites, content deployment features a single server with two distinct roles: content staging and content deployment. With content staging, a site administrator can test or review the content in a staging directory before deploying the content. When the content is ready for deployment, it can be replicated from the staging directory to a production directory on the same server. When the replication is complete, the content is accessible by client browsers.

For large production sites with multiple servers, each server performs a specific role. The staging server can receive files from content authors. Specifically, content deployment allows IIS to accept Web content posts from multiple sources by means of a standard HTTP connection. Before deployment, the content on the staging server can be reviewed or tested. When the testing is complete, the staging server replicates and deploys the content to multiple destination servers. Once the content is received by the destination servers, the content is placed in a production directory and is accessible by client browsers.

Other products for content authoring and deployment include PageMill from Adobe, VisualPage from Symantec, and Dreamweaver from Macromedia.

8.4.2.2 Fault Monitoring

As a representative example, the fault-management product suite from Freshwater Software is reviewed here. SiteScope™ is an example of a simple but powerful fault-monitoring and management solution. SiteScope installed on one operating system can monitor applications and servers running on other platforms, including HP-UX, AIX, FreeBSD, SGI, and other Unix flavors. The SiteScope Web server allows operations to view and configure SiteScope monitors, alerts, and reports. Important attributes include:

- Browser-based user interface: The HTML/XML-based interface runs in any browser window, allowing administrators to manage their sites over their LAN, WAN, or the Internet. Using the Web servers' own security features, Web administrators can limit access to only authorized SiteScope users. In addition, Web administrators can enable a read-only version that allows interested parties to view status and reports without being able to change the settings.
- High performance: SiteScope is implemented as a multithreaded Java server application, which enables multiple monitors to collect site data

simultaneously without significantly impacting server performance. Even active Web sites can set SiteScope monitors to run at regular intervals, typically every 5 to 10 min, with little impact on system responsiveness and performance.

- Monitoring of remote servers: Using this feature, NT and Unix administrators can monitor remote servers from a primary SiteScope installation. It can remotely monitor both NT and Unix servers from a primary SiteScope installation on NT and can remotely monitor Unix servers from a primary SiteScope installation on Unix.
- Customization of monitors: Web administrators can customize their monitoring environment in two ways: by organizing monitors into groups and by creating custom monitors. Monitors can be organized and grouped to give the administrator greater flexibility in determining how the site data are presented. By creating custom monitors, administrators can plug in existing "home-grown" scripts to create their own site-specific monitors and still benefit from SiteScope's built-in alarm and reporting capabilities.

SiteScope is implemented as a Java server application. It runs on the server as a daemon process, monitors system parameters, sends alerts, and generates summary reports. A user connects to SiteScope using a Web browser to view status information and make configuration changes. The implementation is divided into several well-defined types of objects: Web page, scheduler, monitors, alerts, and reports. Figure 8.7 displays the architecture of SiteScope. The objects are:

- Web-page objects: The Web-page objects handle requests for Web pages from a browser using the HTTP protocol. These objects display the current status information, present forms for editing the configuration, and update the configuration based on form requests. These objects also enforce any access controls, such as user name and password, that restrict who is allowed to access the SiteScope Web pages.
- Scheduler object: The scheduler object coordinates when monitors are run, alerts are created, and reports are generated. It reads the configuration to create a schedule of when these activities should occur, and it creates and starts the appropriate objects.
- Monitor objects: The monitor objects collect information about the system being monitored. There are objects for monitoring applications logs, CPU usage, disk space, processes, Web-server throughput, DNS servers, mail servers, access to Web pages, and network response. The monitor API allows custom monitor objects to be added to handle application-specific monitoring needs.
- Alert objects: These objects send alerts about exceptional events. There are objects for sending e-mail, pager, and SNMP trap messages. The script-alert object allows application of specific scripts to be run.
- Report objects: These objects generate reports summarizing monitoring activity. The objects read the history information from the log files,

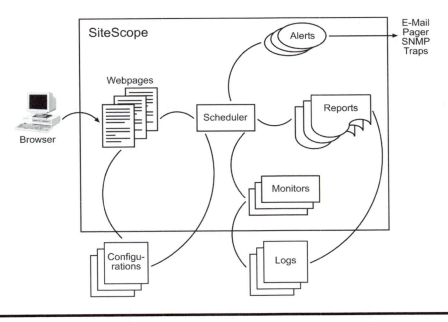

Figure 8.7   SiteScope architecture.

summarize and filter it, and generate HTML/XML reports in graph and table formats.

- Log monitor objects: This object monitors an application log and forwards events based on a rule file. Each time it runs, it checks for new entities to the log file. When it finds a new entry, it compares the entry to rules in the rule file to decide what alert to perform. A log entity can cause any of SiteScope alerts to be sent.

Freshwater Software also provides a series of SiteSeer™ monitors that measure and monitor from outside the firewall. SiteSeer reports about the availability of business applications around the clock and answers important questions:

- Are key services available from outside the firewall?
- Are Internet performance issues affecting access to particular sites?
- Are back-end databases responding?

SiteSeer users control all of the collected data. This additional product has been designed for self-service. Important features include:

- Availability of standard monitors to verify availability of key systems, polling as often as every 5 min from outside the network
- Multiple notification methods that integrate with existing technologies, including e-mail, pager, or SNMP traps
- URL monitoring from multiple global presence points to detect ISP (internet service provider) performance issues across different backbones

- Easy, self-service administration via a Web-browser interface
- Content verification features to verify that a page's contents include a specific string or ensure that specific text is not present, e.g., an error message
- Flexible monitoring reports generated daily, weekly, or monthly
- Direct integration with SiteScope to identify problems both inside and outside of the networks of customers.

Currently, the following monitors are supported: network services monitors, URL monitors, and advanced monitors.

Network services monitors test the availability of applications and services from outside the firewall. They include:

- Database monitor: verifies that SQL databases are accepting requests across the Internet.
- DNS monitor: checks a domain name server via the network. It verifies that the DNS server is accepting requests and verifies that the address for a specific domain name can be found.
- FTP monitor: connects to an FTP server and verifies that a file can be retrieved.
- Mail monitor: verifies that the mail server is accepting requests and that messages can be sent and retrieved.
- Ping monitor: verifies that specified hosts are available via the network to ensure continuous availability of critical connections.
- Port monitor: determines whether a service on a port can be connected to.
- Global ping monitor: verifies network connectivity from a number of locations across multiple Internet backbones. This lets customers see differences in Internet performance and detect ISP routing issues.

URL monitors check the availability of Web pages or sequences of Web pages from multiple locations. They include:

- Global URL monitor: verifies that Web pages can be retrieved from a number of locations across multiple Internet backbones.
- Global URL sequence monitor: verifies that a sequence can be performed from a number of locations across multiple Internet backbones.

Advanced monitors handle specific needs of complex environments and may require additional setup. They include:

- Composite monitor: monitors the status of a set of other SiteSeer monitors to allow for fault buffering.
- eBusiness chain monitor: verifies that a sequence of events is responding and fully executing. These events can be any number of network services, URL sequences, or advanced monitors.

- LDAP monitor: tests an LDAP (lightweight directory access protocol) server by sending a password authentication request.
- News monitor: connects to a new network news transfer protocol (NNTP) server and verifies that groups can be retrieved.
- RADIUS monitor: sends an authentication request to a RADIUS server.

Other tools for fault management include product suites from Agilent, in particular NetExpert™, and Netcool™ from Micromuse.

8.4.2.3 Web-Performance Monitoring

There are a number of choices for monitoring Web performance. AppManager™ from NetIQ is a very popular software solution that measures and monitors everything — hardware and software components — for Web servers. Using these basic data, administrators can correct bugs and tune their systems to match the daily ebb and flow of demand for the site, keeping everything running optimally for visitors. It does an excellent job in terms of log and workload analysis, which look at server activity as well as user sessions. The presentation capabilities could be improved. This product is limited to Windows-only environments. Competitive products from BMC, Hewlett-Packard, and IBM address multiple operating systems. Topaz™ from Mercury Interactive Corp. is application oriented. Besides supervising the availability of servers, it is able to correlate health data of servers with impacted business processes.

Determining how users/visitors spend their time allows webmasters to customize sites for an optimal return on the organization's investment. Site Server from Microsoft can be utilized to accomplish the following:

- Site usage analysis: Understand how site visitors interact with Web sites.
- Site user analysis: Target particular messages to increase the likelihood that site visitors will be interested in the information that sites provide.
- Site content analysis: Analyze the content and structure of Web sites.

8.4.2.3.1 Site Usage Analysis

Site Server visualizes the structures of the sites and how they are being used to quickly identify patterns and trends. It identifies high-traffic reports for advertisers and can import non-Web data to compare usage patterns with other business information. With Site Server, users have the ability to analyze data from advanced Web features such as search queries and results.

Understanding how users interact with particular sites is critical to the success of the site. For business managers or site administrators, it can be time consuming and costly to translate network log files into usable information. The analysis feature provides users with the tools they need to determine how visitors are spending their time on particular sites. More importantly, this information can be used to optimize the return on investment for a Web site.

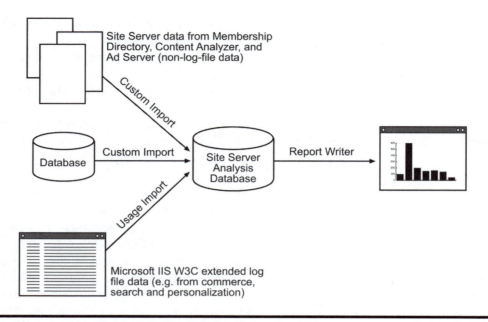

Figure 8.8 Reporting features with Site Server.

The analysis features include: usage import, custom import, and report writer. These features help to analyze Web-site usage, produce comprehensive reports, and elicit valuable insights for making informed decisions about Web sites. Every aspect of a site can be analyzed by means of approximately 45 preconfigured reports.

Figure 8.8 illustrates how Site Server processes complex server log files. In this picture, Usage Import imports server log files and employs several algorithms to reconstruct the actual visits, users, and organizations that interact with Web sites. The information is stored in a database. Then, Report Writer queries the database and generates a detailed report based on site activity. Usage Report, Custom Report, Report Writer, and Scheduler can be used in combination to accomplish the following tasks:

■ Manage servers and build a usage database: Usage Import provides an organizational structure for easily managing log-file content. Users can utilize Usage Report to import and filter log files. For example, each time a user interacts with a particular site, information about the interaction is recorded. The information is imported and filters into a relational database. Usage Import examines the data and employs several algorithms to reconstruct the actual visits, users, and organizations that interact with a particular site.

■ Design complex analysis: Report Writer can be used to view log-file data for a single site or multiple sites. By generating reports using the log-file data that are imported into the database from Usage Import or Custom Report, every aspect of Web sites can be analyzed. For example, it can be analyzed how visitors navigate sites, determine which page is viewed most often, and understand the geographic distribution of site visitors. Both canned and custom reports can be generated.

■ Integrate data from other Site Server features: The Custom Import can be used to cross-reference data from multiple Web sites or integrate data from other Microsoft BackOffice servers and Site Server features, including Search and Personalization and Membership. Once the data are imported, users can launch Report Writer to generate reports that integrate and analyze the usage data. Custom Import can also be utilized to categorize and classify Web-site usage data for enhanced analysis. For example, users can create, view, and edit data properties in the database. Users can also modify the structure of the database.

■ Automate analysis: The Scheduler feature can be used to automate the task of analyzing and importing log-file data. The Scheduler feature is ideal for unattended tasks, such as importing log files, resolving IP addresses, and running reports.

8.4.2.3.2   Site User Analysis

A set of standard reports helps users understand how the site is being used. Customized reports can also be created. Reports are presented in familiar formats, including HTML, Microsoft Word, or Excel format, and can be generated from over 25 different Web servers, including IIS, Netscape, Apache, and O'Reilly. Site Server helps to build stronger relationships with customers by targeting messages to match their interests. Whether users are selling goods on the Web or providing high-value content, they can use targeted e-mail campaigns to keep customers informed when new versions, new products, special offers, or new content become available that may interest them. The messages will be well received and appreciated, and personalization of content may enhance the customer's online experience. Depending on the event, information can be sent in a particular metropolitan area or distributed nationally. The ability to target communications to customers can be considered as a differentiator among sites. The following features can be supported:

■ Create user lists for targeted e-mail campaigns: Customers should be associated with target audiences to deliver targeted messages that produce strong responses to actions. Using business rules developed in the Rule Builder, Analysis creates a customer list based on their online behavior. For example, the Rule Builder could request Analysis to identify all customers who visited a specific content three times during a week.

■ Correlate user interests and contents: Users should drive their content-creation process with a strong insight into the interest of their customers. Reports identify top customer interests and correlate those interests with content topics and types.

■ Identify user locations: Users can better serve their customers when their geographic location is known. This information can be used to

locate mirrored sites in heavily trafficked locations for improved customer experience.

■ Measure effectiveness of targeting rules: Users are expected to identify
which rules in the Rule Builder are most often used to determine
content displayed along with the content that is typically displayed for
each rule. This feedback mechanism should be used to fine-tune rules
to deliver even better targeted content to customers.

8.4.2.3.3   Content Analysis

Monitoring complex Web sites can be a time-consuming task. Links, site
content, and site resources can be difficult to track down in a timely manner.
Using the task-oriented approach provided by Content Analyzer, users can
analyze the content of sites quickly and efficiently.

Content Analyzer, a feature of Site Server, lets users execute Web-site
management tasks from a central location. Content Analyzer is designed to
show the content of particular sites at a glance. Using a map as a starting
point, site structures can be analyzed, contents can be tracked, local and
remote sites can be maintained, and access to key content can be improved.
Content Analyzer provides more than 20 analysis reports. The following tasks
can be performed by Content Analyzer:

■ Visualize the site: Content Analyzer provides site visualization capabilities. Using the Outline pane or the Hyperbolic pane, users can display
the structure and content of particular sites. The Outline pane displays
pages and resources in a hierarchical tree. Users can expand or collapse
the tree to display dependencies or interrelated site resources. The
Hyperbolic pane displays a site map, a visual representation of the site.
Site maps reveal the structure, content, and resources, such as images,
audio files, and video files, that are linked. Maps can also be used to
see what has changed on a particular site. Changes, like adding or
deleting pages, changing links, etc., can be identified by comparing an
old map with a new map of the site. By comparing maps, users can
see what is new, what has happened, what has changed, and what no
longer exists.

■ Analyze site content: In order to streamline Web-site management,
Content Analyzer can provide detailed information based on site reports
or custom searches. This information can be used to monitor site content
and maintain site quality. Searches can be broad or narrow, can be for
outdated content, focus on a single resource type, or focus on multiple
resource types. All site views, reports, and search results can be printed
and distributed to help webmasters to solve problems and enhance the
usability of particular Web sites.

■ Improve access to key content: Content Analyzer can verify the status
of off-site links, and ensure that site visitors are provided with the most
direct route to key content. Routes can be identified based on usage
data. Most sites have multiple routes or links to specific content. Content

Analyzer can examine all the routes that point to a specific resource and identify the most frequently traveled route. If the most frequently traveled route is not a direct route, Content Analyzer can show how to reorganize the site to improve access to popular content.

8.4.2.3.4   WebSniffer from Network Associates

WebSniffer™ combines expert-sniffer-network-analyzer technology with Web-performance management tools to create an early warning system of Web-performance degradations. WebSniffer differentiates between problems rooted on the network and those occurring on the server.

WebSniffer is a performance management system that analyzes network protocol packets and host operations to quickly identify problems related to end users. It assesses Web-site availability, response time, and user abort rates to isolate whether problems are rooted on the Web-server host or are network- and client-based. For host-based problems, WebSniffer correlates availability, response time, and end-user abort rates with host-resource constraints to pinpoint Web-site problems originating at the host CPU, memory, or disk drives.

WebSniffer monitors, analyzes, and automatically identifies problems with Web-site end-user experience, all in real time. Trouble conditions trigger alarms in both WebSniffer's browser-based user interface and externally. For Web-site managers, that translates into powerful benefits:

- Faster problem resolution: WebSniffer reduces the time spent trouble-shooting and solving problems by automatically identifying problems, suggesting solutions, and providing the data underlying its decision making.
- Early warning of problems: Analysis and alarming occurs in real time, and alarms can be sent outside WebSniffer in an e-mail message, to a pager, via an SNMP trap, or through user-written scripts. This provides immediate notification of problems, even if you are away from the site.
- Remote accessibility: It finds out what is happening wherever the user is. Its user interface can be brought up rapidly in a Java-enabled browser.

WebSniffer has three principal components — agents, repository, and information center — that gather, analyze, and then display information:

- WebSniffer agents are lightweight processes that reside on each Web-server host and gather Web-site performance data by watching network traffic and host resources.
- The WebSniffer repository analyzes the raw data gathered by the agents and delivers information vital for troubleshooting and managing the Web site. The repository resides on a dedicated host machine.
- The WebSniffer information center displays the information produced by the repository and is the primary point of interaction with the product. It is accessible from Web browsers that support Java.

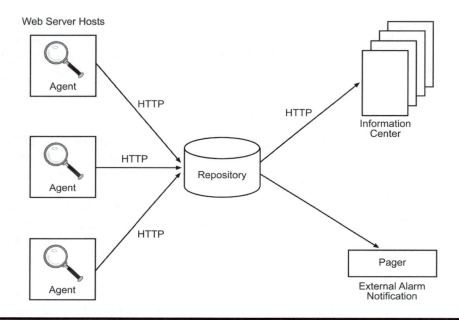

Figure 8.9   Architecture of WebSniffer.

Figure 8.9 shows the architecture of WebSniffer. The agents gather the pertinent network and host data, and the repository periodically polls the agents for their latest data. The repository then analyzes the data and stores the resulting information. The WebSniffer repository is also responsible for generating external notification of alarms. The information center retrieves the information from the repository and displays it for the user.

Having an agent on each Web-server host enables WebSniffer to gather data critical to understanding how a Web site is behaving. WebSniffer is able to measure important network and server timing information and to characterize host operations.

Web servers and Web browsers communicate via HTTP, which is part of the TCP/IP protocol family. WebSniffer agents observe the TCP/IP protocol stack on each Web server to get a view into the client-server communication process. Collecting detailed timing data for HTTP communications is how WebSniffer derives its end-to-end response-time measurements for URLs. When a client wants to exchange information with a Web server, it issues an HTTP command such as GET or POST to the server. This process has three phases:

- The client establishes a connection to the server and issues a command.
- The server works to fulfill the command.
- The connection is closed.

During each phase, WebSniffer gathers a unique set of data that is used by the WebSniffer repository to analyze Web-site availability, response time, and user abort rates.

WebSniffer agents gather host-performance data directly from the operating-system API, available from commands such as vmstat and netstat on Unix, or the permon utility on Windows NT. Additionally, WebSniffer accesses data that operating-system commands do not consider or display, and WebSniffer is more efficient than these command in many cases. Regardless of the host data origins, it is what WebSniffer does with the data that makes the information it produces valuable. It feeds the raw network and host data to the repository, where they are analyzed and expert rules applied to extract useful information. WebSniffer then displays this information in graphs and tables for easy visualization of patterns and anomalies.

WebSniffer Internet agent enables a Web-site manager to see how the site is performing from the perspective of users at various spots throughout the Internet and compares that result with the responsiveness of other major Web sites. WebSniffer accesses a database of measurements taken by Keynote Systems every 15 min from 10 major U.S., Asian, and European cities. The repository polls the Keynote server and downloads response-time information for a specified URL and compares those data with 40 Internet performance indices. This index averages the response time for accessing and downloading the home pages of 40 Web sites deemed most important to business users. These measurements are a natural complement to the data WebSniffer produces on its own and provide another way of assessing whether problems are based in the network or on the Web-server host.

The four functions of the WebSniffer repository are:

■ Collecting, correlating, and analyzing WebSniffer agent data
■ Generating alarms based on problems identified during data analysis
■ Storing collected WebSniffer agent data and configuration data
■ Acting as a Web server for the Java-based user interface

To identify problems with Web sites, the Repository applies internal rules to the data WebSniffer agents collect. Once a problem is identified, the repository includes the problem on a list of active alarms so that a user can see what has occurred. The WebSniffer repository can also generate external alarm notifications such as sending a message via e-mail, sending a message to a pager, or sending an SNMP trap. Additionally, a scripting capability allows users to specify their own external alarm notification actions. All alarming capabilities are accessible from the information center. Alarm conditions, product configuration, and data retrieved from the agents are stored in the repository for viewing by the user interface. Data are accessible for 24 hours. However, alarms are stored longer, so that even when data can no longer be viewed, a record of the problem exists. Because the user interface is browser-based, the repository also acts as the Web server that serves the user interface.

The final component is the information center, the graphical user interface (GUI). The information center's GUI is written in Java that runs in a browser. The GUI uses a tab metaphor for quick switching between functional areas and to allow data to be grouped and sorted hierarchically. Its three main areas of functionality are:

- Alarm screen
- Data drill-down areas
- Expert solutions guide

Network Associates is offering a combination of Web-site analysis tools that go far beyond the capabilities of just monitoring communication links.

8.4.2.3.5 PacketShaper from Packeteer

Packeteer was formed to address the crowd-control problems caused by the growth of the Internet and its adjunct, the World Wide Web. This growth has created dissatisfaction among end users frustrated by poor quality of service (i.e., slow response time and unpredictable Internet access), corporations unable to exercise precise control over their own networked resources, and Internet service providers unable to deliver differentiated levels of service to their customers. PacketShaper™ optimizes and controls Internet traffic over wide-area links, letting network managers set and enforce policies with regard to bandwidth allocation and prioritization.

Given a population of a few high-speed users and many low-speed users contending for a server with an access link, a reasonable goal would be to give every user a certain minimum committed rate at which information would be transferred, and to allow for an even division of excess bandwidth on demand. Also critical is providing the network manager with visibility into how often users find their Web servers stuck — due to congested links, poor server performance, ISP infrastructure problems, etc. — and abort their transactions in disgust.

8.4.2.3.5.1 TCP Rate-Based Flow Control — The aim of the product is to enable network managers and ISPs to manage their piece of the Internet, i.e., the specific access links under their control. Fundamentally different from queuing-based QoS approaches, Packeteer explicitly controls the rate of individual TCP connections by managing end-to-end TCP flow control from the middle of the connection. This direct feedback to end systems smoothes out the normal burstiness of the TCP traffic, avoiding retransmissions and packet loss and delivering a quality of service perceived as consistent by the user. The benefits of this approach are realized by both enterprise network managers and ISPs. Network managers can establish policies for explicit allocation of committed and excess bandwidth, maximizing the number of users accommodated on a given access link and improving each user's quality of service. Packeteer has devised a method of detecting the access speed and network latency of remote users in real time, allowing resource-allocation decisions to be made with information about the potential data rate of individual connections. In contrast to routers, which cannot manage incoming bandwidth, the

Packeteer solution controls both inbound traffic (e.g., Web-site access) and outbound traffic (e.g., Web browsing from corporate intranet users).

With the ability to control of the mix of different traffic types that characterize every enterprise network, network managers can cope with the new generation of "push" applications that have contributed significantly to network congestion and slowdown. They can "push back" at these applications, assigning them a low priority. Thus mission-critical data such as e-mail, electronic commerce, or Web-site inquiries are guaranteed to get through, while a push application, for example, is transmitted at a slower rate using excess bandwidth.

ISPs hosting Web sites for many customers can now set access policies ensuring that "bandwidth hogs" — bandwidth-intensive sites that typically use extensive graphics or animation and frequently download large files — share the available bandwidth. Furthermore, Packeteer technology lets ISPs establish different tiers of service, based on bandwidth guarantees, for which they can charge different rates. They can also match a user's request for content to the Web-based service most appropriate for his connection speed. For example, low-speed users might be directed to text or concise graphics, while high-speed users can access rich, data-intensive images.

8.4.2.3.5.2   PacketShaper IP Manager — The PacketShaper family of products consists of IP bandwidth-management devices, typically placed on the network between an access router or access concentrator and a LAN. These transparently manage bandwidth, report on the user's experience, and match content delivery to connection speed. PacketShaper is a passive network element that operates system-independent and requires no changes to, or reconfiguration of, the TCP/IP network or end stations. Figure 8.10 shows PacketShaper in operation. It resides behind WAN devices, enabling network managers to control bandwidth for inbound and outbound traffic flows.

Two scenarios in which the benefits of PacketShaper are readily apparent are corporate WANs and ISP Web-hosting services. In a typical geographically dispersed corporate environment, access to the headquarters-based central data bank from a remote regional office can be guaranteed a minimum required rate, while casual Internet access and Web surfing is allocated only to the excess bandwidth. In an ISP Web-hosting scenario, different bandwidth levels can be explicitly allocated to co-located servers. Thus, one excessively used site will not dominate available bandwidth and negatively impact service at the other sites. PacketShaper provides bidirectional TCP rate control, permitting users to set priorities by user and/or applications and to allocate bandwidth according to those priorities. Bandwidth allocation can be fixed or dynamic, based on the network load. PacketShaper also reports on the metrics of the user experience. Problems are isolated by server, access link, and service provider, allowing the network manager to pinpoint a problem and speedily resolve it. Reports are delivered via the browser to any station on the network.

PacketShaper's technology differs from RSVP (resource reservation protocol). RSVP was designed to reserve bandwidth for inelastic, real-time network

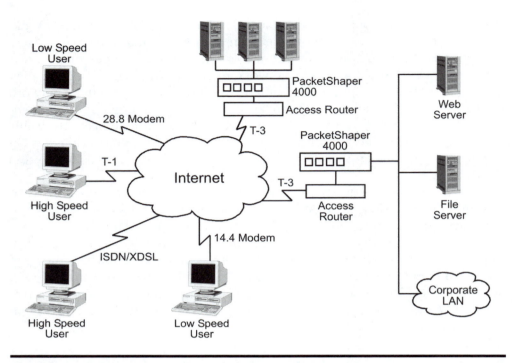

Figure 8.10   PacketShaper from Packeteer in operation.

traffic. Inelastic traffic does not tolerate delay conditions, i.e., certain applications require a minimum amount of bandwidth within a specific time frame. RSVP is intended to solve problems with multicast sessions, i.e., audio and video streams on backbones. This protocol requires end-to-end RSVP deployment, which means that end systems and routers require updates so that they can communicate reservation requests. Even if the whole network is RSVP-aware, there is no policy server or arbiter to apply network-wide rules for priorities and resource allocation. RSVP effectively supports applications like video-conferencing, but in its current form, it will not have any impact on Web experience. It is designed for a small number of persistent flows, whereas Web traffic is characterized by a large number of transient flows.

PacketShaper enables control of both inelastic traffic, which requires a constant rate, and Web traffic, which tends to be bursty. Packeteer addresses Internet QoS for interactive services, such as Web browsing. Most Web traffic does not require a constant bit rate. To accommodate the very different data types, such as text versus 24-bit graphics, it is very important to smooth the bursty nature of the Web. PacketShaper can be managed by SNMP, and the product can incorporate SNMP agents.

Other tools for Web performance management include:

- Log analyzers: Aria from Andromedia, NetTracker from Sane, WebTrends products, net.Analysis from WebManage, and Hitlist from Marketware

- Traffic monitors: IntelliFlow from Resonate, Telemate.Net from Telemate, and NetScope from Apogee Networks
- Load balancers: AC200 and AC300 from Allot Communications, WiseWan product suite from NetReality, FloodGate from Check Point Software, and Bandwidth Allocator from Sun Microsystems

8.4.2.4 Security Management

VeriSign is mentioned in many bill presentment and payment scenarios. The PKI (public key infrastructure) services authenticate the identity of users conducting business across the Internet and protect the integrity of information and data transmitted. As a managed service, VeriSign PKI is a fully outsourced solution that provides easy integration with popular desktop applications and systems, allowing enterprises to immediately take advantage of a secure, highly scalable, and highly available infrastructure while lowering the total cost of deployment, training, and support.

The VeriSign Authentication Service Bureau allows enterprises, net marketplaces, financial institutions, and portals with large numbers of disparate users to outsource authentication of partners, suppliers, and customers to VeriSign, avoiding the time and expense of managing it themselves. VeriSign capitalizes on its scalable infrastructure and processes to verify identities of users according to required criteria, such as organizational affiliation. VeriSign issues authenticated users the digital credentials necessary to conduct business.

8.4.2.5 Storage-Area Networks

EMC is one of the most widely used solutions for deploying and operating storage-area networks (SAN). The Control Center™ suite of products enables operations managers to simplify and automate the management of multivendor storage infrastructures through a single, consistent information-centric strategy. It displays status; it informs about performance; and it recommends actions to ensure high service levels. Figure 8.11 shows the architecture of EMC Control Center.

The attributes of this product are:

- Discover: Maps and displays all elements and relationships of a multivendor storage topology
- Monitor: Views status and performance of those elements in real time; integrates with leading framework applications
- Automate: Provides policy-based storage management
- Provision: Configures and reconfigures resources to meet changing business demands
- Report: Obtains real-time and historical information on performance, utilization, and allocation

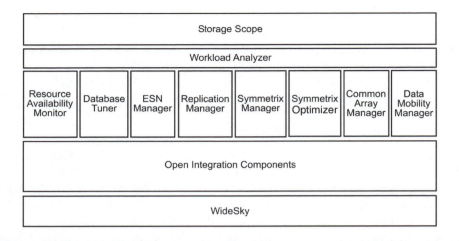

Figure 8.11   Architecture of EMC control center.

The following management applications are included in this product suite:

- Common Array Manager masks the complexity of the information infrastructure by enabling the consolidated management of multivendor storage arrays.
- Database Tuner helps operators monitor, automate, and report on Oracle or IBM DB2 databases for optimal performance. Correlates host, database, and storage performance for fast and easy detection and resolution.
- ESN Manager centralizes, simplifies, and automates IT operations across SANs.
- EMC Navisphere manages all functions of the CLARiiON storage environment, including discovery, monitoring, provisioning, and performance reporting as well as administering enterprise storage functionality such as point-to-point copies and remote data mirroring.
- Replication Manager operates in combination with replication technologies, like EMC TimeFinder, to dramatically simplify and accelerate the management and use of local disk-based replications.
- Resource Availability Manager simplifies and automates host storage resource management across the whole enterprise.
- Symmetrix Remote Data Facility/TimeFinder Manager and Symmetrix Data Mobility Manager monitor, provision, and automate the usage of SRDF and TimeFinder in the given environment of customers.
- StorageScope provides reporting capabilities that enable operators to answer important questions about existing storage, location of storage, and utilization of storage, which is helpful in capacity planning.
- Symmetrix Manager monitors, automates operations, and provisions storage for the Symmetrix platform from a single console.

- Symmetrix Optimizer automatically tunes Symmetrix storage for optimal performance based on performance requirements.
- Workload Analyzer collects host and Symmetrix performance metrics and enables users to configure how they are displayed, making it easy to determine the relationship between host and Symmetrix storage objects. Web-based reports can be generated daily or by exceptions when issues arise.

Other tools for storage-area network management include products from McData, Network Appliance, and Brocade.

8.4.2.6 Benchmarking and Testing

The market offers a number of new Web services and applications that can help businesses to optimize Web sites. One of these is a service-based option. Under this model, vendors such as Keynote Systems, Inc., install probes at points in the Internet and use them to continually access customers' Web sites or even run through entire artificial transactions, creating a model of how the site functions. This product can measure how quickly a site processes a transaction or how long it takes to download information from various sites. It tracks what is causing a site to perform slowly: Internet backbone lines, local access lines, or the Web server itself. This product offers an excellent overview on performance, but it provides little information about the internal processes. Operations managers need additional tools to do that.

The benchmarking solution includes:

- Web-site perspective: Diagnoses performance problems at Web sites across dial-up, xDSL, or T3 connections
- Transaction perspective: Assures the end-to-end quality of business transactions
- Streaming perspective: Measures the quality of multimedia broadcast over the Internet, including Internet radio, live sports and news events, movie trailers, music videos, and educational videos
- Wireless perspective: Measures the performance of wireless applications from the end-user perspective

The testing solutions include:

- LoadPro: This solution helps with predeployment capacity planning. It enables users to dynamically test applications, avoid over- or under-provisioning, and determine the optimal configuration for high availability.
- Test perspective: This represents a self-service solution. It allows users to run diagnostic and load tests on demand and receive immediate feedback on modifications to the Web sites and to the infrastructure.

8.4.3 Service-Level Management

Service-level agreements (SLA) determine the service and its security requirements in a legal sense. Using legal contracts such as an SLA, disagreements
between contracting parties can be avoided. Disagreements can include the
type of the service, limits of a service, quality of a service, and compensation
for a service. In order to inform the customer about the actual quality of
services, support interfaces are recommended between the service provider
and the customer.

SLAs can be signed between service providers and customers, and this
represents a usual legal contract between businesses. SLAs must be signed
with all relevant suppliers of services and equipment, and they must be
provided in written form. SLAs must describe and quantify the available service
level, and all responsible persons must be identified. Service-level agreements
and service-level management can be defined as follows:

- Service-level agreements: Written agreements about the service and its
  QoS metrics between contracting parties.
- Service-level management: Process of determining QoS metrics, preparation and maintenance of SLAs, continuous collection and distribution
  of information about QoS metrics, and supervising whether conditions
  of SLAs are met.

The SLA is more than just a list of service metrics; it lays out the ongoing
monitoring, reporting, and response process. The SLA should clearly define
the responsibilities of both parties. For each function that is defined, the person
responsible for controlling that function performed needs to be identified by
position.

An SLA is a formal, negotiated agreement between two parties. It is a
contract that exists between the service provider and the customer, or between
multiple service providers, or between service providers and network operators. It is designed to create a common understanding about services, priorities,
and responsibilities.

An SLA should also cover corrective actions, i.e., the steps to be taken in
the event that a service-level objective is not met. This section should define
who resolves the problem of each service deficiency as well as consequences
for not resolving the problem. Consequences can appear in the form of penalty
clauses or, alternatively, as a bonus clause for meeting the objectives. The
end result is the same.

SLAs can cover many aspects of the relationship between the customer
and the service provider, such as quality and performance of services, customer
care, billing, and provisioning. Performance reporting uses the SLA as a
reference and does not address the other parameters that are part of SLAs.

SLAs are an excellent tool for customer and service-provider management.
A well-crafted SLA sets and manages expectations for all elements of the
service to which it refers. It assists the service provider by forcing it to undergo
operational change, improve internal measurement and reporting, assess

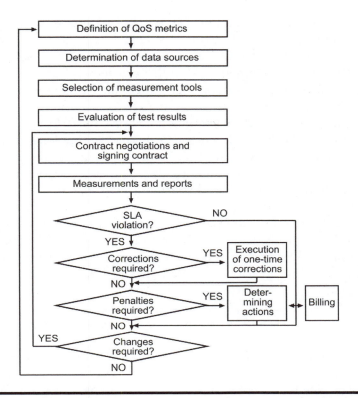

Figure 8.12   The service-level management process.

trends, improve customer relationships, and provide a vehicle for potential differentiation from their natural competitors.

8.4.3.1   Preparation of Service-Level Agreements

Figure 8.12 shows an overview of the most important activities within the service-level management process. Figure 8.12 identifies the following functional blocks:

- Definition of QoS metrics
- Determination of data sources to compute metrics
- Selection of measurement tools that are acceptable to both parties
- Evaluation of test results with the measurement tool

8.4.3.2   Contract Negotiation and Signing the Contract

Contract negotiation involves the following steps:

- Draft of the agreement: A subject-matter expert collects information about the functionality, application goals, and security requirements of the service. Based on this information, alternatives for service levels and their goals are defined. Depending on the specific requirements of the customer, the SLA can be specific, as well.

- Definition of metrics: In the phase of defining and selecting service metrics, only those metrics should be selected that can be met, that can be measured and controlled, and that cannot be interpreted differently.
- Definition of security requirements: For this definition, the internal security standards of the customer should be implemented.
- Agreement on the textual draft: Prior to displaying the contract to the contracting parties for signing, the text of the contract should be coordinated with the legal department, with the purchase department, and with top management.
- Signing the contract and handling changes: After the contract is signed, it becomes legally valid. Given the rapid changes of communications technology, changes in the service contract cannot be avoided. How those changes are to be handled should be included in the original contract.

A typical contract should cover most of the following items:

- Parties for the agreement: All parties to the agreement should be listed, especially when there are multiple service providers and/or client groups. Each party defined as a contracting party should sign the contract. All parties must be documented, particularly when multiple service providers, operators, and customers are signing the contract.
- Terms of the agreement: The period of time that the agreement will be in place should be specified carefully. A typical length is between 1 and 3 years.
- Service included: Each service should be identified and described in detail in the agreement. For each service, service-level metrics should be defined individually. The SLA should describe how the indicator is measured and who is responsible for performing the measurement. Further regulations should be included for emergencies, reaction time in case of outages, and escalation procedures to mutually inform relevant contracting parties.
- Optional services: All optional services should be listed that the service provider is willing to supply on request, in addition to those listed in the current agreement.
- Priorities of customers: sites, applications, users, and user groups.
- Service offer (e.g., $7 \times 24 \times 365$, 5×24, or 5×8).
- Metrics for services:
  - Number of outages by service
  - Availability by service
  - Network delay in both directions
  - Utilization of network and systems components
  - MTBF, MTTI, MTTR, MTTE
  - Maximal duration of outages

Recovery speed after system crashes

Volume of lost data

Ratio: proactive and reactive problem detection

Ratio: referred problem and total number of problems

- Definition of outage: Exact definition of outages that do not affect the fulfillment of SLAs.
- Responsibilities of customers: Written confirmation that customers will ensure physical access to managed objects and will assist in outage detection and problem resolution.
- Reporting and reviews: Reports should be defined and created so they are supported by the monitoring tools. In addition, the frequency of reporting, access to reports, and availability of real-time reporting as well as periodic reports should be defined. In many cases, Web access to these reports is required by customers.
- Modifications: The process for changing the SLA, if necessary, should be defined along with identification of persons who are authorized to initiate changes.
- Refinements: Technology may require refinement of the SLA and a redefinition of the commitment. For example, new equipment might be added, and the client might therefore have increased expectations of performance.
- Tracking changes: Changes in the client organization — e.g., increase in size or acquisitions — can place unexpected traffic on the network, resulting in poorer response time. Introduction of new applications can also change QoS and the cost of delivering it. Changes must be documented, and parties must take into account the impact of these changes.
- Authorization: Authorization for signatures, representative persons, and changes.
- Nonperformance: An SLA also defines nonperformance, or what is to be done when the indicators do not meet the levels specified. However, some consideration has to be given to the amount of deviation. For example, instead of requesting a 2-s response time, it is more realistic to request a response time of 2 s for 90% of transactions, and 5 s for 99% of transactions.
- Agreement on tools: Determining what measurement techniques and tools are going to be used by contracting parties.
- Help-desk services:

    What services are supported

    Availability of these services

- Escalation procedures: Contracting parties are expected to agree on the tasks, persons, priorities, and time frames of the escalation.
- Communication between contracting parties: Selection of phone, fax, letter, e-mail, or a combination of these.
- Billing for services:

    Price for services

    Discounts if objectives not met

- Payment regulations: Collection alternatives are specified here. Basically, there are two: flat rates for each month or usage-based payments.

Closing comments:

- Services of the agreements must be realistic, i.e., the service provider can meet them.
- Measures for QoS should be accepted by both negotiating parties.
- The expected service level must be measurable. If a service metric cannot be measured, it should not be in the SLA.

8.4.3.3 Measurements and Reporting

The detailed process description includes the measurement data sources, the periodicity of measurements, data processing combining different databases, and finally reporting. Feedback from this activity decides whether SLAs have been met or violated.

8.4.3.3.1 Corrections in SLAs

If corrections and rectification are required, they should be executed in quasi real time. Measures include:

- Completing missing measurement data
- Data correction
- Correlation with manually collected data for some metrics

These corrections do not change the contract, but they do help to solve single and sporadic deviations. They represent a response for customer complaints over short periods of time.

8.4.3.3.2 Reimbursement for Noncompliance with SLAs

If noncompliance happens, measures will be agreed upon periodically. Review periods should correspond to billing periods. This process step is heavily correlated with accounting.

8.4.3.3.3 Changes in SLAs

When the number of corrections and noncompliance cases exceeds a given threshold, SLAs are expected to be reviewed and, if necessary, changed.

8.4.3.4 Maintaining and Supervising SLAs

Service-level management (SLM) requires that multiple QoS metrics be continuously supervised and measured. Depending on the agreement between client and service provider, reports may be generated and distributed, or information may be presented on Web servers. Data sources for SLM include:

- Trouble tickets generated automatically or prepared manually
- Events generated by network elements (managed objects) — filtered, modified, and classified
- Alarms (SNMP traps or alarms from other sources), which represent a specific class of events
- Logs of systems and network components
- Performance metrics, provided by various tools
- Manual logs based on observations

The middle part of Figure 8.12 can be further detailed. The collected data are unified and converted into a common denominator, as seen in Figure 8.13. No complex processing is expected here. The output is a special table (Table 8.1) with a number of different events that are utilized to supervise SLAs. In the first step, separate tables are generated for each service provider.

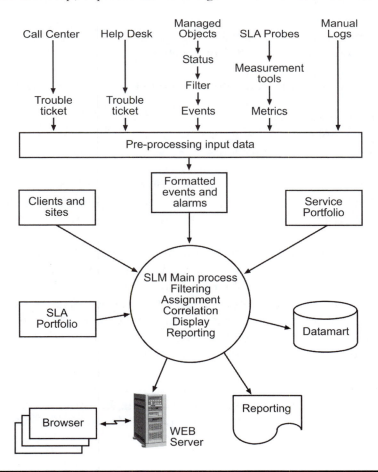

Figure 8.13 Supervising SLAs as part of the SLM process.

Table 8.1   Events Used to Supervise SLAs

Events	*Example 1*	*Example 2*	*Example 3*
Type	Outage	Lost data	Outage
Severity	High	High	Middle
ID	Router CE	Server 07	Load balancer
Importance	Middle	High	Middle
Time stamp	10/11/2002	10/11/2002	10/11/2002
Class	Principal problem	Critical event	Noncritical
Comments	Customer edge	Daily billing lost	Three sites impacted

Table 8.1 is the basis for triggering escalation steps. Alarms are derived from events. The following hierarchy is generally valid:

- Managed objects
- Status notification
- Filtering processes
- Generation of alarms
- Generation of notifications
- Distribution of alarms and notifications

But first, the problems must be classified. There are three classes:

- Critical problems
- Major problems
- Minor (noncritical) problems

Table 8.2 shows the classification of problems.

Escalation steps must be clearly defined for each problem class in advance. The preparation may look like the following:

- Definition of emergencies: Emergency is when critical problems occur or when multiple problems occur with a certain combination. In the second case, not all problems are necessarily critical.
- Determining the escalation layer: The number of layers depends on the organization of the participating service providers and operators. Usually, two layers are defined for the customers and one for each service provider and operator, respectively.
- Identification of persons: For each layer, subject-matter experts are named, and site and reach numbers are identified.
- Description of processes: Each problem triggers specific escalation steps that may contain both automatic and manual steps. The time windows for each step are also determined.

Table 8.2 Classification of Problems

Problem	Severity of Problem	Comments
Outage of nodes without backup	Critical problem	—
Outage of nodes with backup	Major problem	—
Generic node problems	Minor problem	—
Node isolated	Critical problem	—
Site isolated	Critical problem	Escalation step 2
Region isolated	Critical problem	Escalation step 2
Country isolated	Critical problem	—
Change of circuit's media	Major problem	—
Network operations center outage	Critical problem	Escalation step 2
Line problem without backup	Major problem	—
Line problem with backup, but with performance problem	Minor problem	—
Line problem without backup	Critical problem	—
Performance degradation in the whole network	Critical problem	Escalation step 2
Performance degradation in network segments	Major problem	—
Performance degradation for a limited number of sites	Minor problem	—
Outage of the management system	Critical problem	Escalation step 2
Outage of network management applications	Major problem	—
Routing problem in whole network	Critical problem	Escalation step 2
Routing problem in networking segments	Major problem	—
Virus in the whole network	Critical problem	Escalation step 2

Table 8.3 shows examples for escalation procedures.

Another table (Table 8.4) is constructed for each customer (biller, consolidators, or payer) detailing the services for each site. Table 8.4 shows an example for three sites. Considering all the sites, each service must have at least one source and one destination site.

The list of all offered services are summarized in another table (Table 8.5). The service ID describes the specific ID used by service providers. The relevant metrics can also be added to this table.

This service-portfolio table is generic, and all service providers customize it to their own needs. This is the first step. In the second step, metrics are defined and offered for each of the services. The actual SLAs — standardized as far as possible — are maintained in a separate database. In the best interest of clients and service providers, the total number of SLAs should be kept to a minimum. When reports are requested, this SLA database is used to produce periodic and *ad hoc* reports.

Table 8.3   Escalation Procedure for Service-Level Agreements: Critical, Major, and Minor Problems

| | *Escalation Steps* | | | |
	0	*1*	*2*	*3*
Critical problems				
Duration of escalation step	0.5 h	1.5 h	2 h	24 h
Party responsible for solving problem	Help desk	Operator	Service provider	Crisis manager
Information sent to	Customer Operator Network operations	Customer Operator Network planning	Customer Operator Service provider Network planning	Customer Operator Service provider Network planning
Major problems				
Duration of escalation step	2 h	3 h	4 h	—
Party responsible for solving problem	Help desk	Operator	Service provider	—
Information sent to	Customer	Customer Operator	Customer Service provider	—
Minor problems				
Duration of escalation step	4 h	8 h	18 h	—
Party responsible for solving problem	Help desk	Operator	Service provider	—
Information sent to	Customer	Customer Operator	Customer Service provider	—

Table 8.4   Customer File with SLA Entries for Three Sites

Customer	*Site A*	*Site B*	*Site C*
Service ID	SID1: FR2MEG	SID1: VOIP	SID1: FR2MEG
	SID2: ATM64MEG	SID2: Managed E1 Line	SID2: Managed E1 Line
	SID3: IP-VPN	SID3: IP-VPN	SID3: IP-VPN

Table 8.5 Portfolio of Services

Portfolio of Services	Service Identification
Hosting applications	H01A
Billing service	BS01
Bill consolidation service	BC01
Bill aggregation service	BA01
Credit checking service	CC01
Payment collection service	PC01
Settlement service	SS01
Networking infrastructure service	NI01

8.4.3.5 Service-Level Alternatives

There are two alternatives for SLAs from the perspective of service providers and network operators: individual SLAs and standardized SLAs.

8.4.3.5.1 Individual Service-Level Agreements

Customers (particularly large and important ones) may negotiate individually tailored SLAs with their providers. This is because they, in turn, have SLAs with their own customers (the end users), and there is a desire to make these SLAs line up. While this is certainly understandable, it is extremely difficult for service providers and network operators to keep track of the many SLA variants that might be developed or to respond effectively to problems when the terms of a service might vary widely from one customer to the next. Contract management and access to contracts in real time are extremely important in maintaining tailored SLAs.

8.4.3.5.2 Standardized Service-Level Agreements

Customers who are not large enough to demand tailored SLAs are subjected to multiple SLAs from multiple service providers and network operators. They may see some measures, such as availability, that sound the same but represent very different metrics. They also may see multiple terms for the same metric. With no standard terms or definitions, they are left having to translate these terms in order to produce some coherent measure of overall performance. Contract management and access to contracts in real time are extremely important. It is very beneficial when both parties are using the same tools to supervise SLAs.

In summary, SLAs can be either:

- Generic, robust, and simple
- Specific, flexible, and complex

In every case, simplification, unification, and standardization of SLAs is the main goal.

8.4.4 Help-Desk and Self-Care Tools

8.4.4.1 Key Components

Help desks, hot lines, and support centers are usually part of customer-relationship management (CRM). At a technical level, CRM Web-based self-service requires the following key components (Verma, 2002):

- Portal interface: The portal extends the capabilities of service representatives to customers. This product should provide a browser interface that lets customers modify their profiles. It should also provide case-management capabilities to let users view, create, or edit trouble tickets or service requests. In addition, it should let them run reports, such as summaries of all outstanding trouble tickets, and provide search engines for customer use.
- Collaboration tools: These features let customers interact in real time with service representatives or with other customers to share information such as simple fixes for problems via Web chat or e-mail discussions. Many products allow these group discussions to be posted in a threaded manner and let representatives moderate the discussion groups. Access control is a critical capability, because CRM products must automatically authenticate and control discussion-group access and limit it to authorized users.
- Comprehensive knowledge base: This component provides an extensive repository of content and includes a search engine that lets users locate all documents and information related to their queries or requests for service. Customers can use the knowledge base to manage product or company information and invoices, bills, transaction records, and histories of service inquiries. Different types of search techniques should be supported. Case-base reasoning may be included as well. This system might also be able to automatically learn from a previous knowledge-base session and then use this information when determining the relevance of information the customer is looking for.

The uCI from Altitude is shown as an example of touch-point solutions.

8.4.4.2 Product Suite from Altitude

The Altitude uCI™ suite for unified customer interaction allows customers to manage not only the various touch points into a service provider's organization — for both self-service and assisted interactions across voice, email, and Web channels — but also enables service providers to optimize the long-term value of each customer relationship. Using the unified customer interaction (uCI)

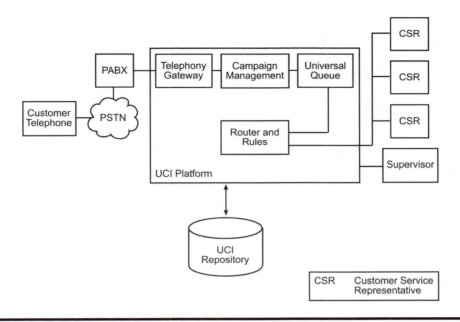

Figure 8.14   Architecture of Altitude Voice.

architecture, a true 360° view of customers is obtained by capturing and then consolidating customer-driven business transactions in a single data repository.

The Altitude uCI suite has different touch-point managers to enable interaction with customers through telephony, e-mail, and Web collaboration or through traditional interactions such as the point of sale and fax. Furthermore, uCI suite provides an IVR (interactive voice response) solution for a self-service option that is completely integrated with the assisted channels. Because all touch-point managers leverage the uCI architecture, the context of interaction maintains consistency as customers move seamlessly from one channel to another. Regardless of whether the customer requires self- or assisted-service via voice, e-mail, or Web channels, the Altitude uCI suite has a response engine to meet customer needs.

8.4.4.2.1   Altitude Voice

Altitude Voice is a robust voice-management application that provides intelligent handling of inbound and outbound calls, seamlessly synchronizing relevant data with every call received or generated. Altitude Voice ensures that pertinent customer information, from customer contact history to buying patterns, is available from customer-based and enterprise applications to support service representatives during a customer call. This coherent context enables personalized and effective handling of interactions, which in turn nurtures customer loyalty. Figure 8.14 shows the components of the product.

Altitude Voice maximizes the productivity of the contact center by offering comprehensive blended call management and utilizing full-function CTI (computer telephony integrated) capabilities. With Altitude Voice, service providers

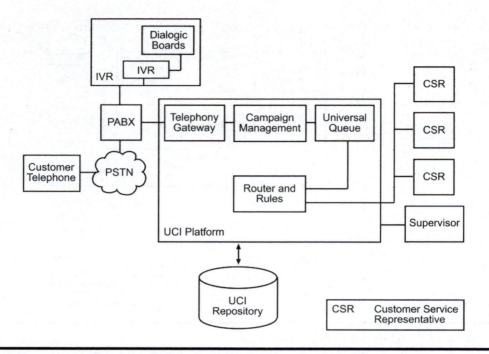

Figure 8.15   Architecture of Altitude Interactive Voice Response.

can leverage customer and business information across multiple applications and systems together with information from Altitude's centralized uCI repository.

8.4.4.2.2   Altitude IVR (Interactive Voice Response)

Altitude IVR is an interactive voice-response solution that maximizes staff productivity by enabling customers to serve themselves using voice menus and touch-tone phone controls instead of relying on personal service from a customer representative. It is fully integrated with Altitude Voice, a call-management application that provides intelligent handling of inbound and outbound calls so that customers can seamlessly move from self-service to assisted service on the phone. Figure 8.15 shows the product's architecture.

The Altitude IVR system acts as a front door to service providers, since it is often the first point of contact a customer has with an organization and should, therefore, always be designed with customers in mind. When used in this way, it delivers distinct advantages to both the customer and the contact center operation.

8.4.4.2.3   Altitude E-Mail

Altitude E-Mail allows organizations to deliver high service levels for e-mail inquiries. With its automatic processes for message filtering, intelligent routing, and message answering, it enables companies to manage e-mail service levels

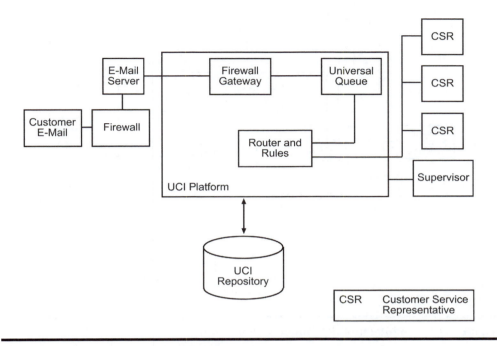

Figure 8.16   Architecture of Altitude E-Mail.

within the context of their overall customer-contact strategy. Figure 8.16 displays the components of this product.

Altitude E-Mail is fully integrated with other interaction channels in the contact-center environment, so service providers can implement the same routing conditions and interaction support as are usually implemented for voice-based interactions, thus achieving service consistency across all channels.

8.4.4.2.4   Altitude Collaborator

Altitude Collaborator provides a bridge between virtual self-service and the real world by offering human collaborative assistance on the Web. With Altitude Collaborator, service providers can integrate contact centers with the Internet, providing customers the convenience of the Internet as a self-service channel while delivering more personalized assistance when customers require it. Figure 8.17 shows the architecture of this product.

Altitude Collaborator can improve the profitability and reduce the abandonment rates of Web sites. Customers request collaborative assistance while browsing the Internet simply by clicking on a button on the Web site. Providing this type of help-on-demand service reduces Web-site abandonment by closing the sales or service loop to maximize a sales opportunity and maintain high customer service levels.

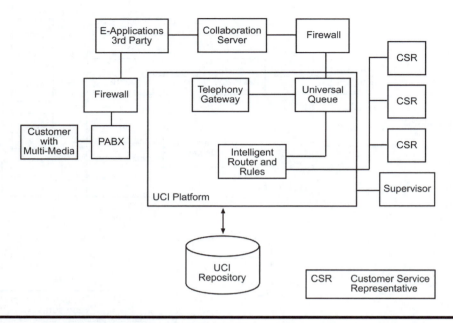

Figure 8.17   Architecture of Altitude Collaborator.

8.4.4.3   Other Products

There are a number of additional tools supporting these or similar activities, including:

- Interaction Center (Avaya)
- EService Enterprise (eGain)
- E.5 (E.piphany)
- Kana iCare (Kana)
- PeopleSoft 8 (PeopleSoft)
- RightNow Web (RightNow Technologies)
- Siebel 7 (Siebel Systems)
- Talisma Service (Talisma)

8.5   Integration of Core and Management Applications

This is the first time that a common method of describing management information has been agreed to and followed through with implementation. Previous efforts failed because of the lack of industry support. Because this common information model (CIM) is implementation independent, it does not provide sufficient information for product development. It is the specific product areas — applications, system, network, database, and devices — and their product-specific extensions that have produced workable solutions.

The CIM will take advantage of emerging object-based management technologies and ensure that the new model can be populated by DMI (desktop management interface) and other data-management suppliers, including SNMP and CMIP (common management information protocol). The CIM is being designed to enable implementations in multiple object-based execution models, such as CORBA (common object request broker architecture) and COM (common object model), and object-based management technologies such as JMAPI (Java management API).

With CIM data encoded in XML, it is possible to access the data using simple HTTP, allowing management solutions to be platform independent and distributed across the enterprise.

The Desktop Management Task Force (DMTF) has recently announced that it is incorporating the directory-enabled networking (DEN) initiative into CIM. With CIM extended to support directory information, there will be a consistent and interoperable way of modeling network elements and services in heterogeneous networks that is consistent in directories and management databases.

The beauty of this approach to tool integration is that it allows each vendor to use its own agents and information-collection infrastructures as demanded by its own particular functional and device-coverage needs. The dependencies among different management software vendors are reduced while still allowing particular pairs of vendors the freedom to exploit each other's services and infrastructure as part of strategic partnerships. For independent software vendors, this strategy for tool integration will significantly reduce the resources spent on compatibility testing and porting. Only one user interface needs to be supported — the browser — and the basic points of integration with other tools and frameworks are potentially limited to standards defined by Wbem/DMTF. This means that more resources can be spent on enhancing functionality and exploring ways to use advanced Web technologies such as Java, XML, and multicasting, or to take advantage of advanced Internet standards and services such as the lightweight directory access protocol (LDAP) standard.

Figure 8.18 shows the basics of Web-based support-systems integration. For users, this means a quick, simple, task-level integration that allows network operators to shift rapidly from tool to tool, e.g., troubleshooting a network problem highlighted in the alarm manager of the management platform. Solving the system- and service-management challenges of the Web era demands a new generation of network management systems featuring tighter linkage between network, system, and application-level management information. Effective allocation of network resources requires that network elements understand the different performance and business-criticality profiles of the applications and users riding the network. Management information for computing and network elements and resources — whether for purposes of configuration, troubleshooting, or performance management — resides in enterprise-management applications that will be able to share this information using CIM and XML. However, information describing users, binding them to applications services and computing resources, is more often the province of enterprise directory systems. Directories already hold some of this kind of data because of the role that they play in locating systems, mailboxes, Web pages, and application processes.

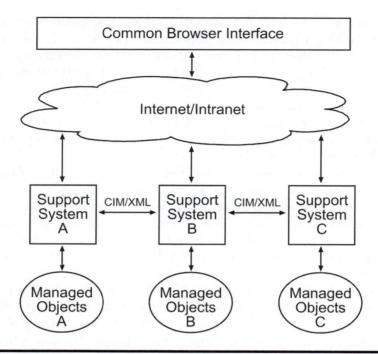

Figure 8.18   Web-based support of systems integration.

8.6 Summary

EBPP is one of many applications in a networked environment, and it is competing with these applications for network systems resources. Resource allocation is key. In an effort to optimize and assure service, billers, BSPs, and consolidators are expected to select and implement "best of breed" tools for content creation and deployment, fault monitoring of Web performance, security management, storage optimization, benchmarking and testing, and installation of touch-point tools in help-desk environments.

The whole process should be supervised, rectified, and controlled using SLAs between service providers and their clients. Specific EBPP-related SLA metrics include systems and network outages and crashes, lost data, and lost statements/bills/invoices. The CRM solutions that provide a direct interface with customers (who could also be billers and payers) are supported by many tools that are running continuously or on-demand in the background.

In the value chain of EBPP, fair payment distribution is key. Using online mediation solutions, settlements between contributing entities are well supported.

Critical success factors for EBPP include:

- Management and maintenance of data
- Integration of tools
- End-to-end process control
- Excellent Web-site performance
- Fair financial settlements between participating entities of the value chain

Chapter 9

Case Studies of Successful EBPP Implementations

Issuers of statements, bills, and invoices are taking different approaches in their implementation of EBPP (electronic bill presentment and payment) solutions. The solution-selection process was reviewed in Chapter 7. The current chapter presents two case studies that take completely opposite approaches to EBPP implementation. These are followed by a third case study with a clear financial analysis of the return on investment (ROI) for a successful implementation of EBPP. In the first case study, an incumbent service provider wants to open the billing module of a legacy operations support system (OSS) for electronic bill presentment. In the second case study, a competitive service provider demonstrates how start-up service providers can enter the market without any paper bills. The third case study presents financial data illustrating the potential profitability of deploying EBPP.

9.1 Case Study 1 — HTC with WebOSS to Implement EBPP

The Hungarian Telecommunication Company (HTC, Matáv), the leading Hungarian wire-line telecommunications company with more than 2.5 million subscribers, has developed a unique, free-of-charge biller-direct EBPP solution. The present version is for HTC's domestic market only, and support is provided for the native language only. The business goal was to retain existing customers by deploying a value-added EBPP service while reducing operating costs.

Their EBPP system has detailed bill-presentation functionality and a number of expansion capabilities using special state-of-the-art technologies. The functionality covers the common bill-presentment tasks, display of call details, and some interactive functions. Further extensions with payment options and other value-added functions are in progress.

Call-detail records (CDR) and billing data are copied directly from the billing module of the current OSS. The bill-presentment system creates the bill using the data received from OSS, generates the bill image, and presents it in HTML format through the Internet. Despite this success, extensive system integration and security issues have caused some difficulties for the system development team.

9.1.1 Background of the Service Provider

HTC is the leading Hungarian wire-line service provider with more than 2 million residential clients, high-value corporate clients, and a countrywide backbone infrastructure. The service portfolio covers common fixed-line services like ISDN (integrated services digital network), ADSL (asymmetrical digital subscriber line), and data-transfer services like flexcom (leased line), managed lines, automated teller machines (ATM), and X.400. Most of these services are postpaid billing solutions. IP (Internet protocol)-based services are being planned and deployed. One example is the use of MPLS(multi-protocol label switching)-based IP-VPNs (virtual private networks) for business customers.

After the political changes in 1989, HTC was separated from the Hungarian Post, became privatized, and inherited a monopoly on the wire-line market. Ever since, HTC has rationalized its organization, enhanced the network quality, and fallen into line with other European telecommunications service providers. Its monopoly ended in 2001. With the end of the monopoly, HTC was forced to focus on new values: increasing customer satisfaction, retaining existing customers, and reviewing and expanding the service portfolio. The new bill-presentment system that they have developed will support HTC's new business initiatives.

HTC is a subsidiary of Deutsche Telecom and the owner of market-leading mobile and IP service subsidiaries in the Hungarian and Macedonian markets.

9.1.2 Bill-Payment Culture Changes

More than 10 years ago, in 1990, bill presentment and payment represented a very cumbersome process in Hungary. People were receiving their salaries in cash. Phone bills and other invoices were printed on paper and distributed through postal services. Attached to this mail came a typical "yellow check and the stub" filled in with provider and billing data. Consumers had to go to the post office to pay the invoice amount with the yellow check in cash. This method was very slow, cumbersome, and the transaction costs were unreasonably high.

In the 1990s, everything changed but the distributed paper invoice. Employees were receiving their salaries by banking fund transfer, credited directly to their banking accounts. Many consumers were paying their bills through their banking accounts using direct debit. In this case, the consumer of the service received a printed-paper invoice, and the service provider debited the amount of the bill from the consumer's banking account on the due date of the payment. Before the first transaction, the consumer had to authorize the bank to handle direct-debit transactions with the given service provider. Consumers could determine a limit for each service provider, and amounts over the limit were not to be paid automatically.

A cultural change led to the more widespread use of direct debit. Consumers had to trust both the service provider and the bank. They had to trust that the provider would charge the due amount to the banking account and that the bank would pay the right amount at the right time. The consumer could check the transaction using the bank's monthly account-transaction report and compare that with the paper-based provider invoice. In 2001, 38% of the residential invoices were paid using direct debit in Hungary.

The payment ethic is relatively good, similar to other West- and Mid-European countries. The most common causes of problems with direct debit are overdrawn accounts, insufficient funds, or customers moving their banking accounts to another bank.

9.1.3 Legal Situation

The Act of Electronic Document Management Law is expected to pass through Hungary's Parliament in 2003. At the moment, only paper-based documents, including invoices, are valid. In most European countries, detailed call lists (detailed data for each call) are accessible in printed or electronic form. According to the legal directive from the European Union, the detailed call lists are not for reviewing the numbers dialed but, rather, to enable checking whether the invoice is correct or not. Therefore, the last four digits of the numbers dialed must be truncated on each document. With the system implemented by HTC, the client has to sign (by means of an electronic signature) an additional agreement at each log-in to view the whole number dialed.

The system uses a PIN code as a password for user authentication, which creates a problem for corporate consumers: The PIN code is personal, but a personal code is not bound to a corporation. Therefore, every corporation needs an individual agreement that empowers given employees to use the PIN code representing corporate consumers.

9.1.4 Details about the Case Study

The project scope covered business planning, technical planning and implementation, testing, and the final launching phase. Stratis (a META Group company) was in charge of overall project management and provided technical consulting from the end of the technical planning phase until the completion of the project.

The main business goals of this project can be described as follows:

- Retain existing customers
- Gain competitive advantages

- Provide a value-added service for residential customers at a reasonable price
- Reduce printing and postage costs after ratification of the Electronic Document Management Law.

Reducing costs is a very important advantage; a significant amount of money can be saved by not printing and sending 2 million invoices monthly.

9.1.5 Limitations and Restrictions

There were several limitations to consider in implementing the EBPP system:

- The load of the OSS running on the Tandem machine could not increase significantly.
- System and data security had to be extremely high to protect the OSS and sensitive data from becoming accessible through the Internet.
- In certain cases, the whole telephone number could not be displayed (see Section 9.1.3, Legal Situation).
- The design of the user interface had to match the standards of HTC.
- The electronic bill had to look exactly the same as the paper-based printout.

Given these requirements, it was clear that no off-the-shelf product could be used.

9.1.6 System Architecture

The EBPP system, originally called WebOSS™, has implemented functions very similar to those used by the billing module of the paper-based OSS. Customers who use the electronic system can only use these existing functions, but they enjoy the benefit of a significantly improved user-friendly interface. The WebOSS has several customer-accessible functions, including:

- Balance details: The customer can view relevant information such as the billing period, the amount due, the due date, and billing status. The customer can choose different views (payment, bill, invoices, balance, bill details) or access the electronic bill by clicking on the billing period. (The payment module can be integrated into this screen.)
- Electronic bill: After choosing the billing period, the customer can view an electronic bill that looks the same as the printed one. The bill is prepared online in less than 5 s. The customer can group billing data by phone numbers or services and truncate or display each service detail.
- Call details: Detailed information about each billed call can be displayed for a given billing period. The displayed information includes phone number, date, time, the number called, duration, service, discounts,

and call cost. Information can be grouped based on all data types, displayed by services, and filtered by called numbers, costs, and dates.

- Nonbilled call details: Customers can view detailed information about nonbilled calls, i.e., calls placed since the end of the last billing period. Displayed information, grouping of data, and filter options are the same as with billed calls.

- Nonbilled call amounts: Customers can view the time and amount (decreased by discounts) of all calls since the end of the last billing period. (Corporate client can use this function to forecast communications costs before receiving the bill.)

- Call search: Customers can search calls between billed and nonbilled calls by called number, date, duration, and cost. The result is a list of calls according to search options and the sum of the calls. The results list can be grouped and filtered.

- Data download: Customers can download electronic bills, lists of billed calls according to billing periods, and nonbilled calls in zipped CSV (comma-separated variables) format, directly importable to Excel. The downloadable file is prepared online. Files are valid only for 24 hours; older files are deleted.

- Friends and family (F&F) statistics: Customers can generate F&F statistics consistent with different service packages. The goal of this function is to help the customer calculate how much he/she would save by ordering different F&F-based tariff packages. Customers choose the billing period, phone numbers, and F&F package options, and the system estimates net savings, showing a detailed calculation of costs.

- Customer information: Customer data (name, billing address, identification, subscriber code) are displayed, and the customer can change e-mail addresses or opt to change the number-display status (see Section 9.1.3, Legal Situation). A service-ordering function is also planned for this screen.

- Log search: The system logs all successful and unsuccessful log-ins, utilization of system functions, and failures. Based on the created logs, the EBPP service can be charged according to customer data access. Customers can view the logs containing the event, date, time, and status, sorted by date. There is a separate log to display the "whole-number display status" changes (see Section 9.1.3, Legal Situation).

- Log out: The system safely logs the customer out. (Customers can simply close the browser window, but in this case, they cannot log in again for a specified period, usually a few minutes.)

If the customer has more than one phone number or has access to different services, he/she can switch between numbers and services while using each function. All of these functions are free of charge at this moment.

The billing system is running on a Tandem platform (provided by HP/Compaq) under the Guardian operation system and the nonstop SQL (structured query language) database manager. The Tandem machine and this configuration is an extremely fault-tolerant solution that can survive various disasters and handle a large number of parallel transactions. The architecture is very specialized, with the result that development, operations, and maintenance require specialized knowledge. The OSS in use is a modification of MARS (mobile administration system), which Tele Denmark had designed originally for its own operations. The OSS used by HTC is written in Cobol, running on 16 processors, each with 2 GB main memory.

The WebOSS server and all other platforms in use are based on Sun Trusted Solaris running on different Sun models. The database manager is Trusted Oracle 8, so the main system is written in PL/SQL, and some smaller software components are CGIs (common gateway interfaces) and UNIX shell scripts.

This trusted architecture was the best choice meeting the high-security requirements. The security standard is very strict, with access to each data record controlled by multiple underlying security levels. The administration of the operating system uses one serial port of a dedicated workstation.

Figure 9.1 shows an overview of the WebOSS system architecture. The huge gap between the Tandem Non-Stop SQL and Sun-Oracle platforms can be bridged using complex integration technologies and tools. There is a difference between data formats, the methods of system and data access, security models, and the performance of hardware elements. The integration tools needed for bridging this gap between the Tandem and Oracle sides are:

- IBM MQSeries for registration purposes
- Extractor/Replicator (E/R) product of Golden Gate Software (GGS) for mass data synchronization of call details and billing data

Working with these tools requires special expertise, knowledge of both architectures, and programming experience. The Web server (Oracle IAS) and the session-layer protocol (SQLnet or Net8) are Oracle products. The default communication with the client is supported over HTTP, and the secure communication runs over HTTPS (secure hypertext transfer protocol using secure socket layer [SSL]). Of course, firewalls are also used to control access to sensitive data.

9.1.7 Operational Details

The WebOSS presents the billing and call-detail data using raw data downloaded from the legacy OSS. At the end of the registration process, generic customer data and the CDRs of the last three months are downloaded to WebOSS. After changes (new CDRs, new bills) with registered customers, data are synchronized from WebOSS back to the OSS. The WebOSS displays the call details and generates the electronic bill image online using the same logic as OSS, but it is implemented on the WebOSS Oracle side.

9.1.7.1 Initial Load

Before starting this service, generic data (service parameters, basic customer data, etc.) are transferred to WebOSS using an MQ channel. All data are held in synchronization with GGS E/R software.

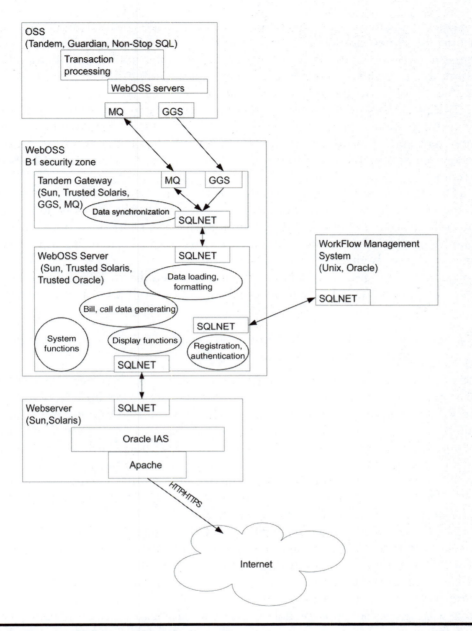

Figure 9.1 HTC-WebOSS architecture.

9.1.7.2 Registration and Authentication

The customer registers on the WebOSS website using the client identification code printed on each bill and his/her PIN code. The PIN code can be set up by calling the call center from the customer's phone. After successful registration, the customer generates his/her secret key pair by clicking on appropriate icons. This online registration process takes less than 1 min.

Due to legal reasons, customers receive a paper-printed agreement that has to be signed and sent back by the customer. After accepting the signed agreement by HTC, the customer receives an e-mail notification that contains a link to the generated secret keys. After downloading the key, the customer is able to log in to the system and use the services.

During the online registration process, WebOSS is in contact through WFMS (workforce and fault management system) with the PIN system, which manages the client and PIN codes. The WFMS system handles the registration process, so an online connection is necessary between WebOSS and the WFMS/PIN system.

The WebOSS sends registration data to OSS, and OSS sells the EBPP service to the customer, sets up the needed flags, and sends the client's general, CDR, and billing data to WebOSS. This communication is running through two MQ channels (one for each direction) as a batch job. The batch job runs several times a day in both directions.

Changes in registration data (modifying or deleting) are managed the same way. These data are also held in synchronization with GGS E/R software.

9.1.7.3 Data Synchronization between Tandem and Oracle — Role of the Extractor and Replicator

"Static" data (initial data load, registration data) and "dynamic" data (CDRs, bills, payments) must be synchronized between the OSS and WebOSS. The easiest solution to synchronize these databases would be to copy the required tables of the database onto the WebOSS machine or to implement some more-advanced logic on the Tandem side. This was not feasible because the development team was limited in its use of resources on the Tandem machine, so the development team had to minimize the WebOSS load on the OSS. Given this situation, the Extractor/Replicator (E/R) technology from Golden Gate Software seemed to be the best choice.

The OSS on the Tandem platform (with Guardian and Non-Stop SQL) writes a log to the audit trail after each transaction, database access, and other events (TM/MP — transaction monitoring and massive parallel processing). The logs in the trail files are used to recover failed transactions if necessary. The extractor of the E/R processes the whole audit trail, approximately 150 GB/day, with a few seconds of delay. The extractor can scan each data record and decide whether it belongs to the data of registered customers.

The replicator, which runs on the WebOSS Tandem Gateway, receives the data sent by the extractor and enters them into the Oracle database. This gateway uses data buffering to smooth out the capacity difference between the Tandem and Sun platforms. All changes in the registered customer's data are synchronized this way. Figure 9.2 shows the principal role of the extractor and replicator.

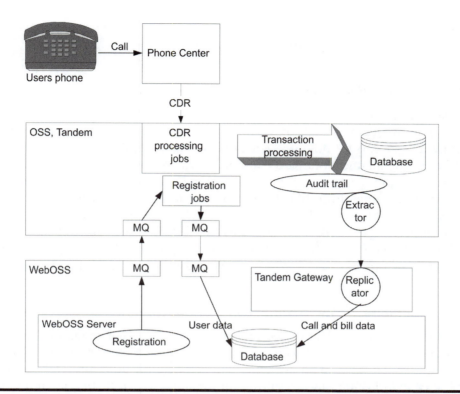

Figure 9.2 HTC WebOSS replication process overview.

9.1.7.4 Data Loading and Formatting

There are scheduled jobs on the WebOSS Server for formatting and managing received data. The data loaded by the Tandem gateway is handled as follows:

- If it is a CDR, it is added to nonbilled calls.
- If it is billing data, a new bill is created, with the appropriate nonbilled calls assigned to the bill.
- If it is a change in customer data or service data, the changes are processed and the necessary updates executed.

There are also some system jobs operating in the background, including deleting old bills or canceled customers, managing secure key generation, and supervising overall security.

9.1.7.5 System Log-In

If a registered customer is logging in with customer and PIN codes, the system verifies his/her downloaded secure key (certificate), contacts the PIN system, and checks the PIN code. If everything is okay, the WebOSS establishes a secure connection (HTTPS) for the session with the customer. The customer can use the service as a common Web page.

9.1.7.6 Online Bill Generation and Data Displays

The system creates all displayed screens online. After collecting, calculating, and arranging necessary information, the WebOSS produces a standard HTML document that can be downloaded only by clients' universal browsers.

The call-detail and nonbilled call-detail lists are displayed directly from the database. A job generates principal billing data (see Section 9.1.7.4, Data Loading and Formatting); bill details and bill images are prepared online.

Friends-and-family savings and call searches are processed online using Oracle PL/SQL programs. The data download is the most difficult part of this process: Internal PL/SQL jobs collect data and prepare the file for download, and a system process packs (zip format) and forwards it to the customer.

9.1.7.7 Setting Display to Show Entire Phone Number

By default, customers cannot see and review the last four digits of the called numbers (see Section 9.1.3, Legal Situation). However, the customer can sign electronically an agreement with his/her certification authority (CA) to view the full called phone numbers during the online session. If such an agreement is not signed, certain functions must be limited:

- The last four digits of call details are hidden in each display.
- F&F statistics and call search are not supported, because this would allow indirect identification of numbers.
- Downloading of call details and nonbilled calls is not allowed.

9.1.7.8 Service Usage Logs

WebOSS writes a log detailing each log-in, data display, and data download. The customer can view the logs to track his/her activity, successful and unsuccessful log-ins, and data accesses. Logs are stored for 20 days. The log is useful for future charge-back — a feature that is under consideration — for the EBPP service to customers.

9.1.7.9 Security Considerations

Common security measures (firewall, access control, physical separation, etc.) are implemented to protect hardware, operating systems, databases, connections, and applications. Customer authentication is based on certificates, customer IDs, and passwords. The registration is also password-protected using a PIN code generated from the customer's phone number.

During registration, the customer's browser generates a private key and sends the public key pair to the WebOSS server. After registration, customers can download a digital certificate using the key pairs generated previously. This process ensures that nobody else can obtain the generated certificate. The customer logs in with his/her ID and PIN code using his/her certificate. The certificate must be changed at least once annually. A single customer can use only one session at the same time. A session that has been inactive for 10 min expires and is terminated by the system.

9.1.8 Operational Issues

The WebOSS system has a complex architecture, with the result that operations and maintenance are not trivial. The main problems are load balancing, holding the whole system in synchronization, and supervising the high security level.

As seen before, the extractors must handle a very demanding workload: reading every record (each phone call can generate multiple records) and comparing it with the database of registered customers. To balance this enormous load, the extractors are divided into four parts: one for static data and three for dynamic data. The three dynamic extractors read the different parts of the database. If one of the extractors stops (except for the static one), the system does not lose any data, and the extractor can be restarted. If the static extractor stops, the system must be restarted, perhaps with a request to reload all customer data, a process that can take two weeks. Fortunately, this is not a likely event.

If the MQ connections are in use, registration data flow between system modules, and the E/R synchronization needs to be suspended. Otherwise, the data of recently registered customers might be duplicated or lost. MQ and E/R are synchronized using a semaphore solution:

- MQ sets a flag showing it wants to start.
- Each extractor suspends itself and sets the flag.
- After all extractors are suspended, MQ starts the data transfer.
- At the end of the data transfer, E/R updates its database with newly registered or modified customers.
- E/R starts and picks up the backlog in the audit trail.

Monitoring of the system and security is centralized in Tandem's Prognosis monitoring and alerting software. There is a test environment to test changes and verify their impacts before bringing the system online, but the capacity of the test environment is much lower than that of the online systems. There is also a reporting service used by management for quality assurance and monitoring of service and usage data. The reporting service sends an e-mail every day about the previous day's traffic. The WebOSS-related customer-care functions are managed through the standard customer-care channels, such as call centers and Internet-based inquiries. If necessary, back-office experts are available to provide additional help.

9.1.9 Direction of Future Developments

The rollout of the pilot project is currently in progress. The trusted Oracle technology, presently in use, is not supported any further, so the application will be migrated to the LBAC platform (label-based access control), which is a supported, advanced technology from Oracle.

There is a possibility of directly interfacing the EBPP system with an ERP (enterprise resource planning) system, with the WebOSS collaborating with SAP R3. The client benefits from this solution. It is not necessary to reenter billing data manually, since they are directly accessible in the SAP system.

Simple solutions are available today. Table 9.1 shows the result of downloading call details directly into an Excel spreadsheet. Each cell in this spreadsheet can be processed or embedded into other cells.

The usage of WebOSS is currently free of charge. In the future, there may be a charge for this service by using the data-access logs or imposing a monthly fixed price. After ratification of the Electronic Document Management Law, the majority of customers will receive only an electronic bill.

The following additional functions can be developed:

- Payment by direct debit or through the Web
- Number inquiry by clicking on displayed numbers
- Package selector based on consumer's monthly call data

The WebOSS system can be used as an EBPP platform for other services within the HTC Group, including mobile, network service-level agreement (SLA), or IP. The system can also be connected to customer-relationship management (CRM) systems, which would provide better management of certain customer-care issues.

9.1.10 Screenshots

Screen layout is identical on all WebOSS screens. The attributes are:

- At the top, there is a navigation bar on HTC's Web site.
- Under the navigation bar, there is the name of the current screen and icons for help and feedback.
- On the left bar, there are icons representing the WebOSS functions.
- Data are displayed on the main screen.
- Ads are located on the top and on the left bar.

The final part of this case study presents screenshots that were generated during a practical walk-through of solution features.

Screenshot 9.0 is the entry screen showing customer information. This same screen is being used for parameter setups and for processing changes. The electronic bill is displayed in Screenshot 9.1, detailing the wire-line phone

Table 9.1   Downloaded Detail Data into a Spreadsheet

Inv.Nr	Phone	Date	Time	Called Number	Duration	Type	Discount	Cost
51	(34) 372-701	20020626	18525400	3431****	20	Helyközi I.	0	5
51	(34) 372-701	20020626	19084600	3437****	57	Helyi	0	7.22
51	(34) 372-701	20020627	18182900	3433****	85	Helyközi I.	0	8.9
51	(34) 372-701	20020627	18400700	630916****	16	Westel	0	14.47
51	(34) 372-701	20020627	18553700	3437****	30	Helyi	0	5.6
51	(34) 372-701	20020628	16063900	3451****	65	Helyközi I.	0	11.6
51	(34) 372-701	20020628	16245400	630902****	32	Westel	0	35.8
51	(34) 372-701	20020630	9220200	630902****	29	Westel	0	23.13
51	(34) 372-701	20020702	18300800	630916****	12	Westel	0	11.8
51	(34) 372-701	20020702	21231100	67226****	814	Belföldi táv.	0	166.6
51	(34) 372-701	20020703	20480500	63340****	38	LTO III-as díjz.	0	11.4
51	(34) 372-701	20020703	21425200	63340****	37	LTO III-as díjz.	0	11.2
51	(34) 372-701	20020703	22502000	64036****	50	Belf. kék szám	0	6.8
51	(34) 372-701	20020705	19503700	67226****	28	Belföldi táv.	0	9.4
51	(34) 372-701	20020705	20174300	630287****	147	Westel	0	101.8
51	(34) 372-701	20020707	9402500	620919****	212	Pannon GSM	0	138.07
51	(34) 372-701	20020708	19125400	630916****	51	Westel	0	37.8
51	(34) 372-701	20020708	20525100	620207****	12	Pannon GSM	0	11.4
51	(34) 372-701	20020708	21121400	620207****	467	Pannon GSM	0	299.57
51	(34) 372-701	20020709	20085200	3447****	841	Helyközi I.	0	54.26
51	(34) 372-701	20020710	12151600	3437****	46	Helyi	0	9.32
51	(34) 372-701	20020711	9425500	620534****	7	Pannon GSM	0	11.15
51	(34) 372-701	20020711	9434700	630916****	20	Westel	0	23.8
51	(34) 372-701	20020711	21051800	620919****	123	Pannon GSM	0	81.7
51	(34) 372-701	20020712	13015600	630916****	160	Westel	0	163.8

(continued)

Table 9.1 (Continued)   Downloaded Detail Data into a Spreadsheet

Inv.Nr	Phone	Date	Time	Called Number	Duration	Type	Discount	Cost
51	(34) 372-701	20020712	13120200	63751*****	105	Belföldi táv.	0	45.8
51	(34) 372-701	20020713	12472700	620534*****	71	Pannon GSM	0	48.77
51	(34) 372-701	20020716	20065400	620919*****	167	Pannon GSM	0	109.57
51	(34) 372-701	20020716	20100800	67226*****	254	Belföldi táv.	0	54.6
51	(34) 372-701	20020716	21085100	3437*****	40	Helyi	0	6.2
51	(34) 372-701	20020717	19493900	630309*****	304	Westel	0	206.47
51	(34) 372-701	20020717	20070300	630318*****	575	Westel	0	387.13
51	(34) 372-701	20020718	22001300	630309*****	64	Westel	0	46.47
51	(34) 372-701	20020719	18473700	670211*****	5	Vodafone	0	7.55
51	(34) 372-701	20020719	20071300	67226*****	1160	Belföldi táv.	0	235.8
51	(34) 372-701	20020719	21141900	63340*****	174	LTO III-as díjz.	0	38.6
51	(34) 372-701	20020720	21400700	67226*****	23	Belföldi táv.	0	8.4
51	(34) 372-701	20020721	8413300	67226*****	582	Belföldi táv.	0	120.2
51	(34) 372-701	20020721	9424400	3437*****	54	Helyi	0	7.04
51	(34) 372-701	20020721	11190800	620919*****	30	Pannon GSM	0	22.8
51	(34) 372-701	20020722	18425800	620919*****	195	Pannon GSM	0	127.3
51	(34) 372-701	20020722	18582000	630318*****	1049	Westel	0	703.13
51	(34) 372-701	20020722	19161200	63340*****	179	LTO III-as díjz.	0	39.6
51	(34) 372-701	20020723	8563200	620355*****	194	Pannon GSM	0	207.5
51	(34) 372-701	20020723	9010900	61210*****	142	Belföldi táv.	0	60.6
Sum:								**3745.12**

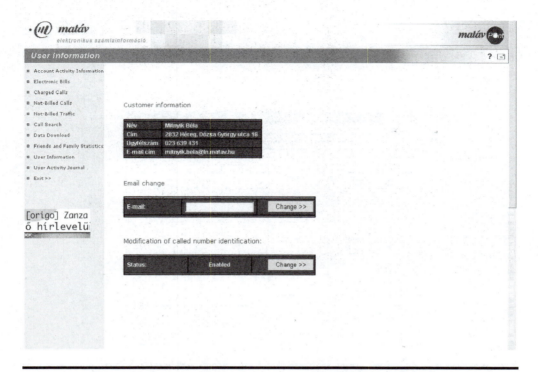

Screenshot 9.0   Customer information: principal customer information and setup options.

number, the services utilized, the call volumes, prices, and the amount for each line item. Local, long-distance, domestic, and international calls are differentiated. The total amount to be paid is shown for each wire-line phone number. With separate agreements, other items might also be charged to the same phone number. Screenshot 9.2a helps to select the wire-line phone number, where call details are requested. These call details are shown in Screenshot 9.2b, listing all calls made from the targeted caller number. All call details are shown for the selected billing period.

Consumers can obtain information about traffic and amount-due details for the ongoing billing period, as seen in Screenshots 9.3 and 9.4, respectively. In certain circumstances, a consumer might want to further analyze specific calls from a specific calling number. Screenshot 9.5 shows the filter menu for searching. The results look like call details, discussed previously.

HTC is using Friends & Family, as a marketing tool to promote certain services. Screenshot 9.6a presents the selection menu, e.g., preferred targeted country of calls. Screenshot 9.6b displays the country and the impacts of the 10% discount rate. Finally, Screenshot 9.6c can be used by customers to evaluate several options and decide whether the volume discounts outweigh the subscription fees.

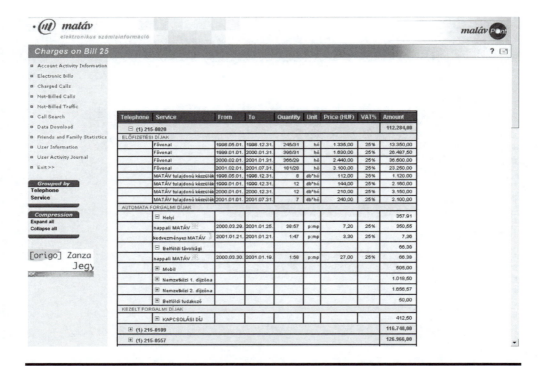

Screenshot 9.1   E-bill: electronic bill generated online.

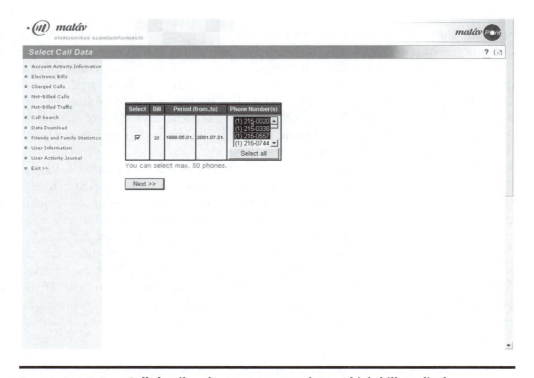

Screenshot 9.2a   Call details select: customer selects which bill to display.

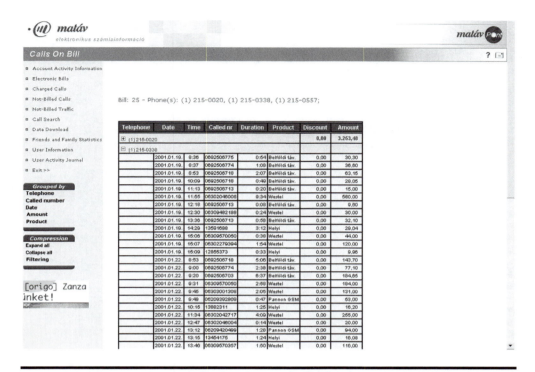

Screenshot 9.2b   Call details: details of each call in the selected billing period.

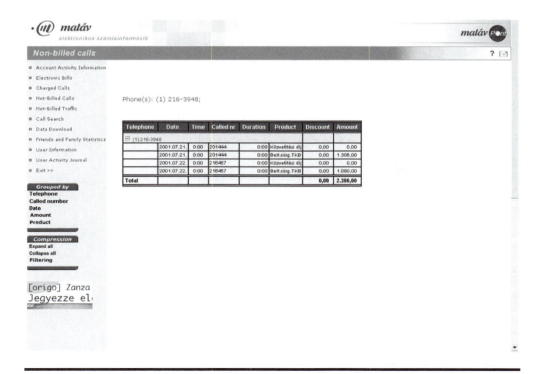

Screenshot 9.3   Nonbilled calls: details of each call since the last billing period.

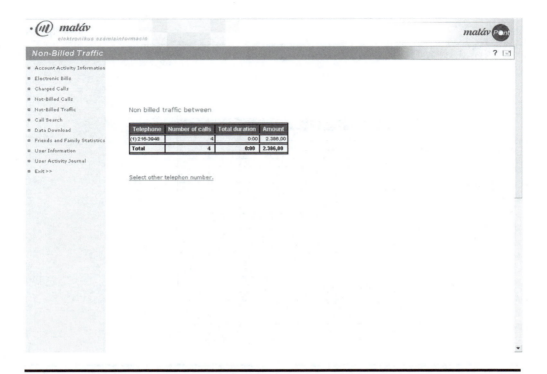

Screenshot 9.4   Nonbilled amount: the amounts of charged calls since the last billing period.

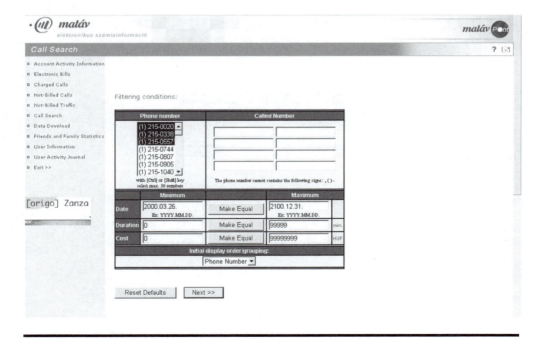

Screenshot 9.5   Call search: set up search options (results look like call details).

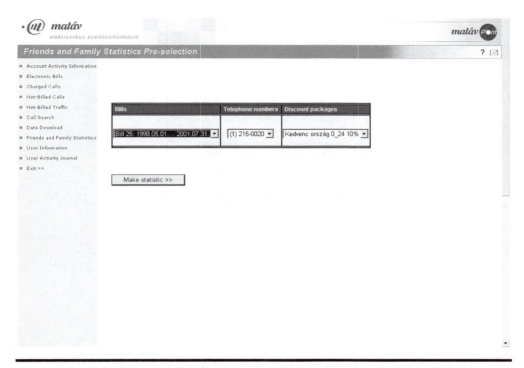

Screenshot 9.6a   F&F select: choose source bill, phone number, and F&F package for F&F statistics.

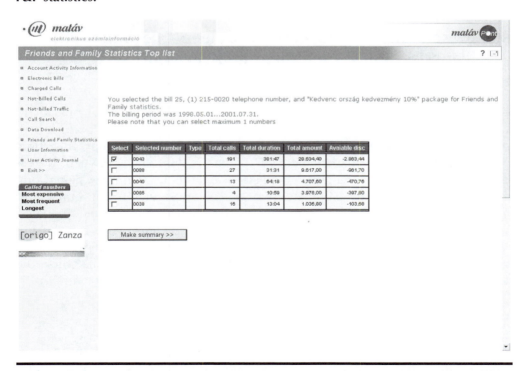

Screenshot 9.6b   F&F top list: most frequently called numbers according to selected bill and F&F package.

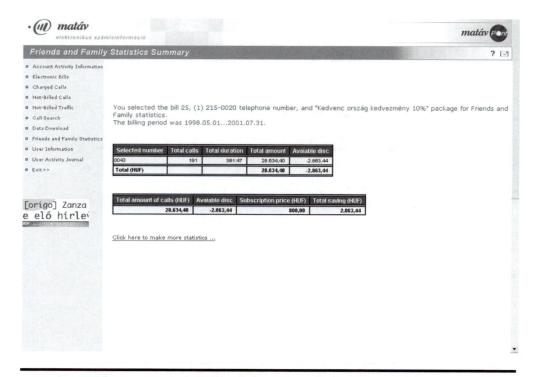

Screenshot 9.6c   F&F sum: F&F results, the available discount, and savings.

9.2   Case Study 2 — CheckFree/Daleen/Cbeyond with Paperless Bill Presentment and Payment

9.2.1   Background

Cbeyond is a new, privately held service provider targeting small businesses with state-of-the-art communications solutions. Service providers place a high priority on efficient operations and keeping costs to a minimum. In a tight economy, effective cost management can mean the difference between success and failure. Cbeyond Communications is using the Daleen RevChain Commerce billing system to eliminate two of the most significant hurdles to profitability: redundant data entry and the costs of issuing paper invoices. Tight integration and seamless automation between customer relationship management (CRM) from Siebel and EBPP on the basis of CheckFree's i-Telco solution has enabled Cbeyond to eradicate these obstacles and maximize the return on investment (ROI) of their IP-based communications network.

9.2.1.1   The Company

Cbeyond Communications is a leader in the emerging local voice and broadband services market and the first service provider to build from the ground up an integrated, purely IP-based network for local telephony. The company provides small-business customers with an integrated package of high-quality local and long-distance phone service, broadband Internet access, and Internet-based applications for significantly less than what they would pay elsewhere for voice alone.

9.2.1.2 Challenges

Cbeyond faced the challenge of providing excellent customer service at the right price by minimizing costs through integrating mission-critical billing and CRM back-office systems and operating a completely paperless billing environment.

9.2.1.3 Solution

Daleen's RevChain billing system and Siebel's eCommunication suite, directly linked with CheckFree's EBPP solution, allowed Cbeyond to streamline and automate mission-critical business processes.

9.2.1.4 Benefits of the Solution

Through the elimination of error-prone human intervention and paper invoices, and by successfully integrating its systems, Cbeyond is continuing to meet its goals of excellence in customer service and extended service offerings, all at prices set to help its customers to succeed.

Redundant manual data entry, separate systems, and paper invoices are avoidable costs that continue to erode the profits of service providers. By implementing a truly convergent billing system that enables tight integration with CRM and 100% paperless invoicing, the hard costs associated with billing can be reduced by as much as 75 to 90%. The key to success is to meet the challenge to the OSS solution: end-to-end cost management from order entry to billing.

The drive for cost management is pressuring forward-thinking providers like Cbeyond to come out of the starting gate operating at peak efficiency. Cbeyond identified and implemented several initiatives that allowed the company to surpass its aggressive cost-management objectives:

- Automation of CRM, billing, and flow-through provisioning
- Single solution for convergent billing
- Sound, repeatable operations processes
- 100% paperless invoicing

9.2.2 Automation of CRM, Billing, and Flow-through Provisioning

Cbeyond has effectively linked its billing and CRM systems using industry-standard solutions from Daleen, Vitria, BEA, and Siebel Systems. These systems

Integrated OSS

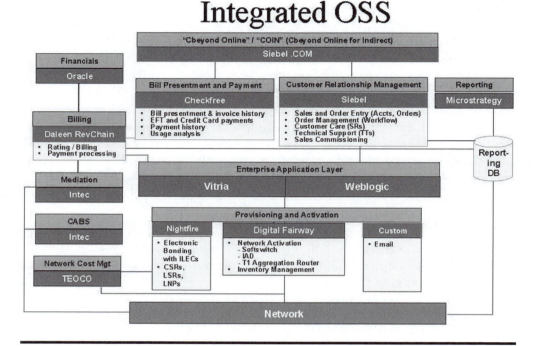

Figure 9.3   Integrated operations support system.

were joined through direct Enterprise JavaBeans and API integration within BEA's WebLogic middleware, using Vitria to manage the business workflow.

The integration of CRM and billing offers numerous benefits:

- Consistency of customer data across the environment
- One tool to manage multiple customer interactions
- The assurance that what is ordered is what is then provisioned, delivered, and billed

The integrated OSS architecture is shown in Figure 9.3, which identifies all of the implemented products and their principal tasks. Process flows are subject to further unification and simplification. Figure 9.4 displays future plans of connecting existing and planned products with each other.

Establishing a single point of data entry has the most immediate and greatest impact on operating efficiency. This efficiency is further enhanced by the workflow automation derived through the WebLogic and Vitria integration layer.

Another important efficiency of Cbeyond's integrated OSS environment is that customers are consistently billed in the current month in which they initially consume their services.

9.2.3 Single Solution for Convergent Billing

A true convergent provider, Cbeyond offers integrated services, including high-quality local and long distance, broadband Internet-based applications, calling

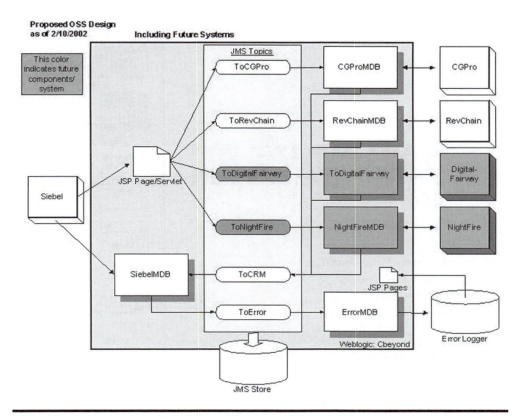

Figure 9.4   Future integration architecture.

cards, toll-free calling, and conference calling. Many of the legacy providers they compete with are still using multiple convergent systems to manage disparate functionalities, resulting in redundant operations and multiple invoices for subscribers. Because the RevChain system is able to process call records from various sources and handle billing for every service that Cbeyond offers, the company is able to deliver a single consolidated invoice to each subscriber.

9.2.4 Sound, Repeatable Operations Processes

Even with the best tools, efficient cost management remains dependent on sound, repeatable processes. Cbeyond has defined and documented an end-to-end methodology that covers the entire life cycle of sales, service-order provisioning, billing operations, and CRM. Figure 9.5 displays a high-level process flow. Each process can be broken down into highly detailed levels.

For billing operations, Cbeyond has established a fixed schedule in which certain activities from prebill review to postproduction reporting occur in the same sequence and timing each month. Bill validation includes a review of static and newly developed items and is performed by various groups within the organization. Consistent execution of the production bill trip each month is accomplished by following a well-defined procedural checklist. This results

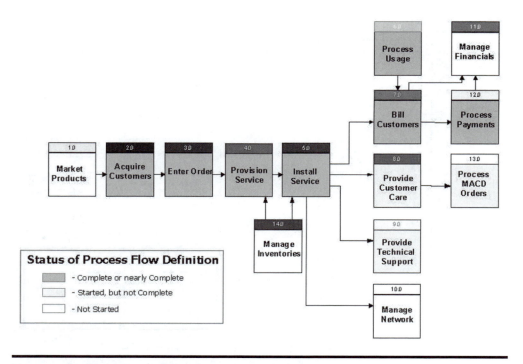

Figure 9.5   High-level process flow with level-one functions.

in the consistent and measurable posting of invoices online four days after the close of every billing period.

Best-in-class tools, established and documented business processes, and a dedicated, seasoned staff of service-provider professionals close the loop on a formula for success. This formula's sound, repeatable processes afford Cbeyond the ability to regularly evaluate monthly billing performance and identify areas of improvement.

9.2.5   100% Paperless Invoicing

Service providers have underestimated the value of a paperless environment for decades. For Cbeyond, this was a fundamental requirement for their business. To support this initiative, Cbeyond integrated the billing software with the EBPP support software.

The online billing process begins with an XML output from RevChain, which is distributed to and processed by the CheckFree application. An e-mail notification is sent to the customers when the invoices are available online. Customers are taken directly from their notification e-mail to Cbeyond's online account management center, where they can easily view, print, analyze, and pay their bills. The invoices' encrypted URLs are also posted to the Siebel application for easy access to the invoice by Cbeyond's customer care organization. Figure 9.6 shows this EBPP solution in greater detail. Customers can make payments online via automated clearinghouse (ACH) using CheckFree

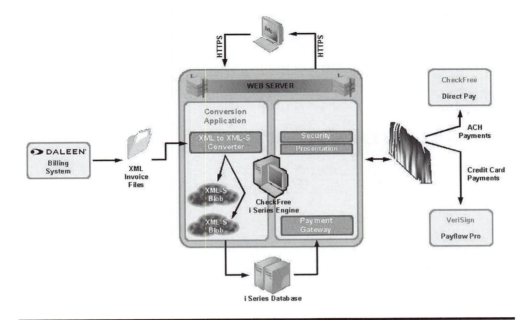

Figure 9.6   Electronic bill presentment and payment.

services, via credit card based on Payflow Pro from VeriSign, or by printing a remittance coupon and mailing a traditional paper check.

Screenshot 9.7 shows the e-mail notification to the payer. The payer selects an option: view bills or pay bills. If the "pay" option is selected, the payer receives payment options and up-to-date information on the Cbeyond bulletin board. This offers the opportunity of up-selling or cross-selling the customer (Screenshot 9.8). If the "view" option is selected, invoice and payment history (Screenshot 9.9), invoice summary (Screenshot 9.10), and call details (Screenshot 9.11) can be selected. If necessary, a printable version of the invoice can also be selected (Screenshot 9.12).

The principal benefits are:

- Fast and on-time delivery of invoices
- An increase in the number of customers who use online payment options
- A decrease in the number of billing- and payment-related service center calls

There were a few lessons learned during the design and implementation process. Implementation of EBPP involves a paradigm shift. Payers must be educated before implementation of the system. Cbeyond is a new service provider without legacy billing systems, and management fully supports the aggressive goal of 100% adoption rate by subscribers. On behalf of the payers, very few disconnects could be observed due to paperless billing operations. Management should invest in reporting tools and techniques, including Website monitoring, data archiving, log analysis, performance, and data mining.

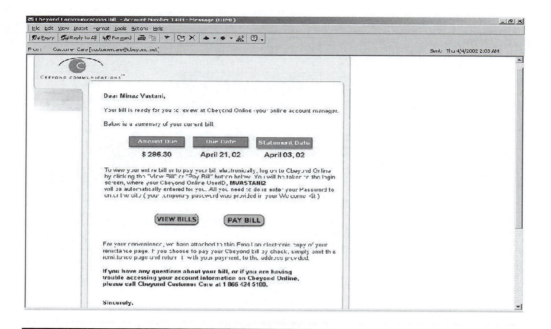

Screenshot 9.7

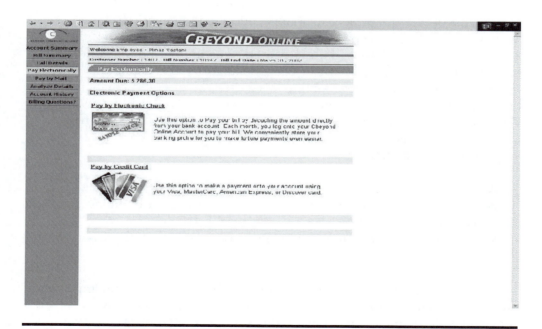

Screenshot 9.8

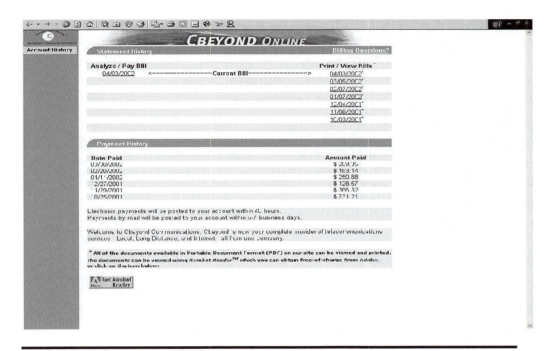

Screenshot 9.9

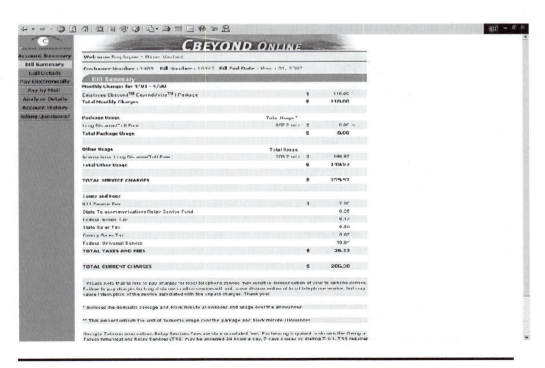

Screenshot 9.10

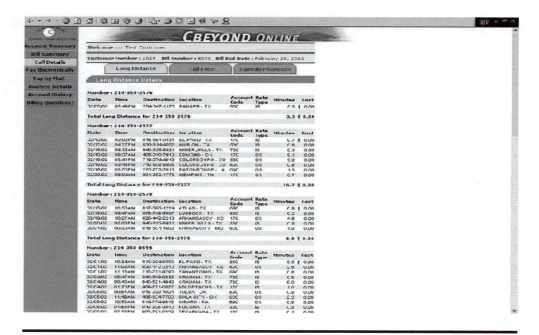

Screenshot 9.11

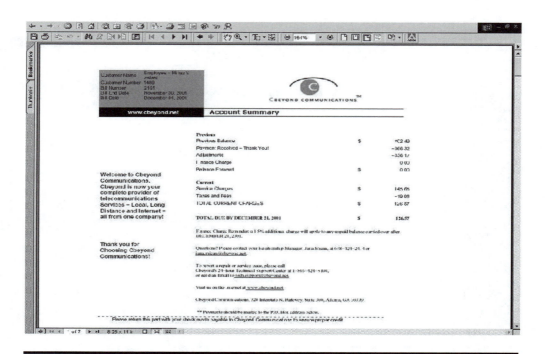

Screenshot 9.12

Freeware solutions have been gradually replaced by COTS (component off the shelf) for maintenance reasons. Web security is always a critical issue; by using the right infrastructure design, Web servers can be well protected by firewalls in demilitarized zones (DMZ). In addition, separating the billing and the EBPP systems proved to be a very sound decision.

Cbeyond's future EBPP plans include leveraging additional CheckFree i-Solutions products and services to help customers better understand their telecommunications spending, provide customers with additional electronic payment options to simplify Internet payment, and give Cbeyond the ability to conduct highly targeted marketing campaigns to promote products that meet their customers' needs.

9.3 Case Study 3 — The Pitney Bowes Story

9.3.1 Integrating the Messaging Process

There is a tremendous benefit in treating the billing process strategically, regardless of whether the output medium is electronic or paper. Companies today are looking to integrate the various components of the messaging process to form a closed-loop, continuous dialogue with their customers, helped by Web presentment, call centers, and other technologies.

EBPP offers the customer more choice in viewing and payment options and can give sales and marketing organizations improved account information for CRM initiatives. But EBPP technology that does not consider the hard copy and digital document as one holistic process creates channel conflicts, causes service issues, and needlessly duplicates processes.

For instance, one of the most important justifications for EBPP — savings on postage and paper costs — requires the ability to selectively suppress print for the EBPP customer downstream in a manner that allows back-end reconciliation. If issuers of statements and bills are interested in seeing a return on their investment, they may want to think twice about implementing technology from pure Internet companies who are not grounded in the hard-copy world and have little or no ability to create and manipulate print streams. Print suppression is not a trivial matter. There may be dozens of different print streams created by legacy systems. Each one of these needs to be decomposed and recomposed for digital delivery while only printing the documents that still must be delivered on hard copy. Technology vendors have largely put the emphasis for separating those streams designated for digital delivery, with no plan for print regeneration. A base requirement for EBPP is a robust print-stream engineering software to offer options for print suppression.

Legacy systems drove documents through the mail for many years. Those well-entrenched back-end systems — general ledger, name-and-address files, shipping and transaction databases, accounts receivable — are highly valuable and largely impervious to change. Companies are learning the value of extracting and formatting data from these back-end systems and connecting that data to the enterprise front-end initiatives like CRM and ERP. Likewise, the data should be fed back into those legacy databases from the customer-facing initiatives to create a closed-loop system. Having highly interoperable EBPP technology that fully leverages de facto e-business standards, such as the Java2 Enterprise Edition (J2EE) specification from Sun, can be used to interface with Siebel, SAP, and PeopleSoft systems more efficiently and effectively.

9.3.2 The e-Consolidation Site of Pitney Bowes

In the current economy, the emphasis for IT (information technology) projects has shifted away from "business transforming" initiatives to projects that emphasize a significant return on investment (ROI). However, while customer adoption of EBPP has been steadily growing, it has not yet reached 10%, which is the threshold percentage estimated by noted industry analysts for an acceptable return on investment on behalf of issuers of statements, bills, and invoices.

The good news is that there is no reason to wait for the customer adoption numbers to increase. With the right technology and the right strategy, issuers of statements, bills, and invoices can achieve considerable savings and break even from their investment within two years at the current consumer adoption rate. In order to be successful, however, EBPP has to be tied to hard-copy documentation strategies. The EBPP solution must have the ability to turn off paper flows and adjust the scope of projects, with the goal of reducing the overall interaction costs with customers, with partners, with suppliers, and with their own employees.

Pitney Bowes is committed to using its own technology to improve business processes and enhance its interaction with customers. The company has used its EBPP technology for a number of internal projects that have yielded impressive cost reductions. These include the digital delivery of bills and invoices for Postagebyphone.com and Pitney Bowes Credit Corp. More recently, Pitney Bowes began to electronically deliver direct-deposit pay stubs for its employees on behalf of Pitney Bowes Accounting Services. Each project was analyzed for results, and all proved to be winners.

These results led to another, more aggressive initiative — an online e-consolidation site that gives Pitney Bowes's customers access to bills, statements, and invoices across all the many lines of businesses within Pitney Bowes via a single log-in and password. From a CRM perspective, the e-consolidation site will improve customer satisfaction by providing a more coherent, singular view of Pitney Bowes while giving customers better access to their own account information.

The e-consolidation site will also allow Pitney Bowes to target marketing messages and to cross-sell by offering relevant services and products to its customers. But, like every other company, Pitney Bowes wants to see a hard return on its investment. By tying the EBPP project to its document strategy, Pitney Bowes will see a reduction in interaction costs in terms of paper, postage, and telephone time for call-center representatives. A Pitney Bowes enterprise value analyst, Kevin Jonsson, developed a return-on-investment analysis that considers savings in transaction costs, float benefits, and reduced call-center resources.

9.3.3 *Analyzing the Return on Investment (ROI)*

The analysis posited an average savings of $0.63 in paper and postage per transaction. In addition, the remittance processing fees were estimated to save Pitney Bowes $100,000 within the first year. The reduction in cycle time created a float benefit of 20 days, although a more conservative estimate of 10 days was used in this analysis. Through carefully written FAQs, online self-help, and e-mail inquiries, billing inquiries can be reduced by 30% at a cost of $2.50 per call.

Customer adoption rates were assumed to be 5% in the first year, increasing steadily to 25% by year five. This assumption is much less aggressive than the adoption rates predicted by many industry analysts and less aggressive than actual results experienced by Pitney Bowes Credit Corp. and Postageby-phone.com, two other Pitney Bowes billing entities that have been Web-enabled with the company's own Digital Document Delivery (D3) software products.

Based on these conservative assumptions and the volume of bills involved, the savings for just one Pitney division, Global Mailing, is estimated as follows: $70,000 in float benefit, $100,000 in check processing fees, and $31,000 in call-center savings in the first year, ramping up in years two and three as the adoption rates steadily increase. The call-center savings for Pitney Bowes Credit Corp. alone were calculated to be $24,000 the first year, increasing to $180,000 in year five. Table 9.2 shows detailed ROI numbers for years one through five.

Table 9.2   ROI Analysis — Part I

Benefits	Year 1	Year 2	Year 3	Year 4	Year 5
Float benefit (GMS)	70,685	141,370	212,055	282,740	353,425
Check-processing savings (GMS)	100,832	201,663	302,495	403,327	504,158
Call-center savings (GMS)	31,985	95,956	143,934	191,913	239,891
Call-center savings (PBCC)	24,064	72,192	108,289	144,385	180,481
Call-center savings (PbP)	7,146	21,439	32,159	42,879	53,598
Total quantifiable benefits	234,713	532,621	798,932	1,065,242	1,331,553

Table 9.3   ROI Analysis — Part II

Summary of Results	Year 1	Year 2	Year 3	Year 4	Year 5
Pretax cash benefits	234,713	532,621	798,032	1,065,242	1,331,553
Depreciation expense	(206,880)	(206,880)	(206,880)	(206,880)	(206,880)
Up-front expenses (noncapital)	(42,207)	0	0	0	0
Ongoing maintenance and support	(95,665)	(95,665)	(95,665)	(95,665)	(95,665)
Impact on pretax operating income	(110,029)	230,086	496,397	762,707	1,029,018
Taxes	(44,012)	92,034	198,559	305,083	411,607
Impact on net income	(66,018)	138,052	297,639	457,624	617,411
Depreciation expense	206,880	206,880	206,880	206,880	206,880
Capital expenditure	(1,076,607)	0	0	0	0
Free cash flow	(935,745)	344,932	504,718	654,504	824,291

Note: IRR (internal rate of return) = 42%; NPV (net present value) = $688,769 (at 12% discount rate).

The analyst for the consolidation project has estimated a 42% return on investment based on after-tax cash-flow impacts. An accounting scenario (which depreciated much of the upfront investment costs over the period of five years) was also run that resulted in an 18-month break-even period, as seen in Table 9.3.

A white paper written by Killen and Associates several years ago predicted virtually instant ROI when EBPP technology is used to reduce interaction costs within large companies. The Pitney Bowes case study illustrates that digitizing the messaging process can dramatically impact cash flow and return significant value to businesses. EBPP technology can:

- Reduce cycle time and enhance float benefits
- Significantly reduce customer transaction costs in terms of paper and postage
- Connect enterprise projects in CRM and ERP to back-end legacy systems for greater value
- Significantly reduce costs in the customer service call centers

Industry analysts say that consumers are beginning to come online in greater numbers. Rather than wait for those numbers to hit critical mass, issuers of statements, bills, and invoices can use the right EBPP technology to achieve cost reductions in the messaging processes — and be ready for them when they arrive.

9.4 Summary

The three case studies presented in this chapter illustrate the practical benefits of EBPP implementations. While they emphasize the success stories, they also focus on lessons learned during design, deployment, and operations. All three cases present a number of tangible and intangible metrics to justify the cost of implementing EBPP solutions.

Chapter 10

Summary and Trends of Designing, Implementing, and Operating EBPP Solutions

Electronic bill presentment and payment (EBPP) has a great potential to reduce costs and generate revenue. To achieve this potential, two major obstacles must be overcome: Bill payers will have to change their behavior, and issuers of statements, bills, and invoices will have to make the investment required to bring EBPP services to market. Organizations contemplating an EBPP implementation should be aware of the potential benefits.

10.1 Benefits of Offering and Using EBPP

10.1.1 EBPP Benefits for Service Providers

The most significant benefits include:

10.1.1.1 Savings on Paper and Postage

Billers can save as much as $1 per bill by converting a paper-based transaction to electronic. For companies with customer bases that range in the hundreds of thousands or even millions, the potential savings are significant. Unfortunately, these savings are not likely to offset the initial investments until a substantial level of customers accepts this method of presentment and payment.

10.1.1.2 Improved Customer Care

Studies indicate that Internet users tend to have higher education levels, higher incomes, and higher levels of discretionary spending. Consequently, people likely to use EBPP services are profitable customers. With consumers increasingly able to choose providers as a result of deregulation in the utility and telecommunications industries, companies have been looking for ways to improve customer service, find other revenue-generating activities, and reduce customer churn. EBPP is very helpful in these areas. For business customers, EBPP can add a great deal of value by providing online analysis results. Bills can be segmented by department for bill-back purposes, an important option for business-to-business (B2B) applications. An EBPP site can also enhance customer services by providing related functionality such as fraud detection and analysis, provisioning, and dispute resolution. The importance of the recurring bill as a means of cementing the relationship with customers cannot be reemphasized too strongly. In the customer-focused world of deregulated markets and the Internet, it is considerably easier for dissatisfied customers to change their provider of services or goods. Such behavior is prevalent in the telecom and utility environment, which both have very high churn rates.

10.1.1.3 Self-Care Options

Enhanced self-care capabilities are the processes that will allow the CRM (customer relationship management) environment to move forward into e-care. Customer self-care will ensure large-scale saving for the biller and enhance its competitive position in the marketplace. Most EBPP vendors, as well as the companies that are implementing an EBPP solution, now recognize that EBPP is part of a whole suite of services rather than a stand-alone solution. It is the primary driver in customer care as part of a Web-enabled CRM suite.

10.1.1.4 Saving Time for Customer Service Representatives

Self-service incorporated into the bill allows the provider to save a great deal of time and CSR (customer service representatives) resources. Frequently asked questions (FAQ) help to deal with routine problems, freeing CSRs to concentrate on more complex questions. Self-care is popular with customers for the following reasons:

- The perception that self-care saves time
- The sense of confidence that consumers feel when they control the problem-resolution process
- The "ego" syndrome, which leads consumers to believe that they can solve their own problems more quickly and efficiently when they are empowered to do so
- The self-service revolution that now pervades many other areas of life

10.1.1.5 Better Cash Management

Many companies believe that EBPP will negatively impact cash flow because it enables bill payers to hold onto a payment until the very last minute. Actual experience contradicts this point of view, indicating that e-bill payers release their funds, on average, a few days sooner than with paper-based bills. Online billers can also offer customers the option to automatically schedule payments for a recurring bill. An e-mail can notify the customer that a billed amount will be automatically debited to their checking account or credit card on a specific date, which is similar to a direct debit. To make this more acceptable to the customer, the e-mail notification can contain a hyperlink to a Web site where the customer could view bill details, reschedule the payment, or cancel it altogether. Because the customer is never more than a click away from full control over the payment process, it is much more acceptable to the customer than a direct debit. For the biller, cash flow is improved because scheduled payments are almost never changed.

10.1.1.6 Faster and Cleaner Remittances

Electronic payments replace the error-prone process of inputting, processing, and reconciling paper-based payment transactions. Electronic payment transactions can be aggregated by an EBPP server and processed by the biller's bank at low cost. Many EBPP systems can also generate credit card payments via third-party service providers. It is important to note, however, that third parties charge for initial deployment and for the transactions executed. And billers can still expect charges from their own bank when credits arrive at their account. EBPP is easy to implement, but transaction fees can be as high as 3% of the transaction's value.

10.1.1.7 Reduced Costs for Customer Care

The cost of customer care can be substantial. It is not unusual for customer transactions to cost up to $20. In the case of a well-equipped customer help desk, the cost of an average call might drop to $2. But with self-care, this cost goes down to $0.05. Services linked to online customer care, e.g., one-to-one marketing, also profit by it. Analysts have calculated that much of a company's direct-marketing budget can be absorbed by addressing errors, duplications, changed addresses, and other mailing-related problems. Online handling can reduce these errors and the costs involved.

10.1.1.8 Cross-Selling and Up-Selling Revenue

EBPP can be a revenue-generating opportunity. EBPP can enable the kind of interactive one-to-one marketing that is not possible with paper bills. The bill itself contains information that can be used for targeted promotions. The bill amount and the customer profile can be matched, and a special advertisement can be included into the attachment of the bill. Marketing is always targeted: the consumer (payer) is known and can be contacted more effectively through profile data available at the EBPP site. Unlike other forms of advertising, such as television, the audience is completely identifiable to the marketer, while the effect of the advertisement can be measured by click-through rates or sales of the advertised product or service. The real opportunity of one-to-one marketing for billers lies in the information embedded in a consumer's bill. Using this information as a basis of analysis, a biller can produce targeted, personalized messages that position the biller as a concerned partner interested in helping and empowering individual consumers to make smart decisions.

10.1.2 EBPP Benefits for Consumers

Billers motivated to implement EBPP systems can cite the usual list of benefits: reduced costs related to printing, processing, and mailing paper; improved cash flow and receivables management; opportunities for cross-marketing and information distribution; customer retention; market leadership; reduced call-center requirements; and more. At the same time, billers need to target customers who might be interested in using the EBPP service and provide them with a satisfactory experience so that word-of-mouth propaganda can spread.

Customers (payers) want features like easy enrollment; easy implementation; flexible payment alternatives; more delivery options (e.g., biller direct, e-mail delivery, consolidator, or aggregator); savings on checks, envelopes, and postage; the ability to check statements, bills, and invoices on a 24×7 basis; the ability to control the timing and amount of payments; good customer service; incentives; privacy; and most importantly, a guaranteed process that never breaks down.

10.2 Positioning EBPP

EBPP is always part of an integrated OSS/BSS/MSS (operations support system/business support system/marketing support system) environment. In particular, it is glued to the billing systems, to CRM, and to enterprise resource planning (ERP). Figure 10.1 shows this positioning for telecommunications service providers. Note that a number of bidirectional interfaces must be maintained. A powerful workflow tool can play the role of an internal broker and connect applications to each other while controlling the information exchange and flow. EBPP will help to streamline Web services and their underlying interfaces and services. Web services represent the business logic; WSDL (Web-services description language) describes the functions; and the UDDI (universal description, discovery, and integration) directory maintains them. All of these services can be called using SOAP (simple object access protocol).

EBPP is a driver for value-based billing models in the realm of content economy. EBPP can contribute to the value apportioned by being a tool for collecting information on the payer's interests, behavior, aspirations, etc. By

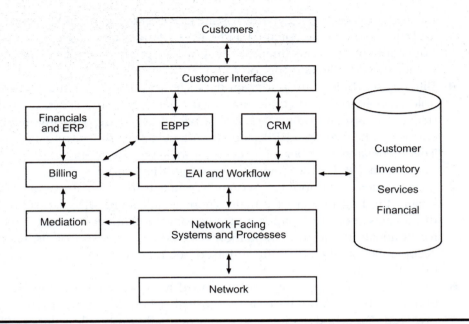

Figure 10.1   Positioning EBPP.

doing so, EBPP plays the role of enabling next-generation service billing. The use of EBPP allows the speed of billing cycles to be rapidly increased. In the case of Internet protocol (IP) networks, this option is extremely important, as it allows near-real-time billing for provisioned services. In an IP environment, there will be a massive potential for services that consumers will wish to switch on and off at their leisure. Billing data must be delivered rapidly and in a user-friendly way to consumers. This is where EBPP fits into the picture, with its rapid delivery capabilities and potential to deliver bills in near real time. The speed depends on the billing system used as well as its various components, such as the rating component. With developments in XML technology, real-time billing, rating, and delivery to EBPP systems is becoming a viable service. The result is that EBPP is a possible solution to overcome some of the issues surrounding billing within the IP services.

10.3 Key Issues to Be Solved for Successful EBPP Applications

EBPP solutions are not yet mature. All participating entities must address key challenges in order to be successful. These issues include:

- Lack of standardization: There are conflicting and divergent developments in business processes, law, taxation, and technologies pertaining to EBPP. All level of standards should be addressed and supported.
- Customer (payer) fears over privacy of personal and banking information: Consumer anxiety — real and perceived — regarding privacy

intrusion, cybercrime, cyberterrorism, advertising, marketing intrusion, and the misuse of personal data are all challenges to solution providers. Education of the consumer combined with guarantees of secure payments should alleviate this problem.

- Biller costs: Billers are understandably reluctant to incur the considerable costs involved in converting legacy delivery channels to electronic delivery channels. Billers are also anxious about the risk involved in choosing the wrong EBPP standard or selecting the wrong vendors. The increasing number of success stories with acceptable return on investment (ROI) is helping to overcome this hurdle.

- Legal issues surrounding e-commerce electronic signatures and the legally binding power of e-mail: There is still some distance between the legal standing of paper and electronic documents. E-mail is used for notification and in combination with other business models. Global acceptance of digital-certificate-based security has been an important breakthrough.

- The degree of complexity and the need for collaboration between all entities: The collaboration is not trivial when so many parties are involved. Everybody is interested in a mutually profitable solution. The financial industry is ready to take responsibility for a number of roles in the EBPP process.

10.4 Successful Business Models — Impact of Demographics

It is difficult to predict what business model will dominate the EBPP market during the next three to five years. Biller-direct models are driven by the cost-saving potentials for billers and biller-service providers. Despite the apparent inconvenience inherent in this model — the user must log-in at each payment site using a different user ID and password and, perhaps, deal with different payment methods — billers in the credit card and telecommunications businesses seem to be successful using this approach. Savings potentials of $0.50 per bill and $0.16 per payment have been reported (Gardner Group, 2000).

In particular, forward-thinking organizations, anxious to capitalize on the potential savings of automating their billing processes, aggressively courted consumers early on by offering EBPP as a free service coupled with some sort of incentive, like cash, services, and prizes. This is a small price for billers to pay for realizing significant savings by shutting off paper and by leveraging EBPP's proven power of improving customer retention. As a result, many billers have started by distributing bills to their own sites.

The success of the biller-direct business model depends also on the type of consumers and the number of monthly recurring bills for a given consumer. Women prefer biller-direct models; men tend to go for aggregated business models. Billers and financial services organizations, in conjunction with some technology providers, have identified the significance of catering to women, who are critical to driving overall EBPP adoption. As a result, they have already begun to launch targeted marketing campaigns aimed at women, touting the convenience and time savings associated with viewing and paying their bills online. Another important finding is that biller-direct users tend to receive and pay only three or fewer bills online on a monthly basis (CheckFree, 2001).

This situation is changing toward the aggregation model, with financial institutions taking on the role of consolidator. For many consumers who are not yet viewing or paying their bills online, the trigger for participating in EBPP is to have an average of five or more of their bills delivered to them electronically (CheckFree, 2001). Some EBPP providers have the ability, via their bill-distribution networks, to deliver six to eight bills electronically in a typical market. This is particularly true for consolidators who deploy "screen scraping" technology that, with the customer's consent, pulls a consumer's bill content off biller-direct sites and delivers it to an aggregated site, where consumers can get a holistic view of their bill-payment history.

To capture these mainstream online consumers, many organizations are already participating with financial services organizations and portals in this bill-distribution approach. In fact, leading billers in the telecommunications, wireless, utilities, oil and gas, and lending and financial services industries are operating both biller-direct sites as well as partnering with financial services organizations to provide full electronic billing and payment services at an aggregated site.

Many billers have been successful in getting consumers to enroll and actively view and pay their bills directly at their sites. However, research indicates that full bill distribution to centralized sites has had even greater success in drawing EBPP subscribers at aggregated sites hosted by bankers, brokerages, portals, and personal financial management providers.

Table 10.1 contrasts the profiles of typical biller-direct and bill-consolidator customers. The profiles of biller-direct and bill-distribution consumers reveals some key findings: biller-direct users, who have significantly less online-bill-payment tenure than their bill-distribution counterparts, tend to hit a ceiling of receiving and paying three or fewer bills per month directly at a biller's site. As users become more EBPP savvy and become aware of more-robust services, coupled with the greater availability of compelling bill content, they tend to gravitate toward the most convenient, cost effective, and easy-to-use solutions.

Table 10.1   Consumer Profiles for Two Dominant EBPP Business Models

Profile of a Biller-Direct Consumer	*Profile of a Bill-Distribution Consumer*
Female (54%)	Male (54%)
Male (46%)	Female (46%)
Average age 42 years	Average age 42 years
72% began using PCs to pay bills in 2000 or later	53% began using PCs to pay bills in 1999 or earlier
Average annual income of $60,000	Average annual income of $75,000
Pays about three or less bills online	Pays about nine recurring bills online
Typically pays credit card, long distance, and local phone bills online	Typically pays credit card, local telephone, and cell phone bills online

Suppliers of EBPP solutions will come from different backgrounds, such as independent vendors, billing software vendors, document management vendors, financial service providers, and industry-specific vendors. In terms of suppliers, it is the quality of the solution that counts, and not the origin of the supplier. Some suppliers offer only products, others only services, and some offer a combination of both. A company considering implementing an EBPP solution might decide to go with a fully outsourced or an application service provider (ASP) model at first, and then migrate to a product solution later. There are specific suppliers for these cases, as well.

10.5 Regional Expectations

The acceptance and penetration levels of EBPP are very different in the various geographical regions of the world.

10.5.1 North America

The U.S. has the most developed market for EBPP in terms of full presentation and payment facilities, the proliferation of vendors offering an EBPP solution, and billers willing to make use of these solutions. Unfortunately, consumer acceptance of the technology has not yet grown to satisfactory levels. Nevertheless, as billers begin to recognize the inherent value of EBPP, they are moving from a passive strategy of waiting for an online customer base to develop to an active strategy of implementing EBPP and driving consumers to utilize the service by offering it with other applications. Customer education is key in this process. Incentives can be helpful as well.

10.5.2 Europe

Europe is the second market in development after the U.S. The European market is more diverse, with numerous languages, currencies, and social, regulatory, and legal issues. Given this diversity, a unified EBPP rollout is very unlikely. Fine-tuning for regions or even countries is absolutely necessary. This market offers opportunities for the smaller EBPP companies with specialized solutions that can be adopted to national needs.

Electronic bill presentment has great potential. The payment side is different from the U.S., since European consumers are generally much more comfortable with using direct debit as a payment vehicle, although this does differ from country to country. The European banking sphere is also quite different from the U.S., which has placed emphasis on retail electronic banking. Europe has focused more on corporate electronic banking. Given the current developments within the EBPP market, and with B2B as the primary target for EBPP, corporate Europe is well positioned to leverage the core strengths of the banking industry and dominate the EBPP marketplace.

The consolidator model of EBPP is likely to dominate the European market for a number of reasons. The proliferation of presentment rather than payment in Europe provides a strong argument for consolidation. People generally only check the top-level details of their bills. The thin consolidator business model allows just the top-level details of the bill to be viewed. Obvious errors can be detected and disputed at this top view. Direct debit was designed as a means to streamline payment and save time, and it has been very successful in Europe for that reason. Consolidation is another means to streamline transactions and save time, and it can be successfully combined with direct debit. Consolidation is also more conducive to presentment on wireless devices — because of screen-size limitations — which play a special role in Europe and proliferate in that market. With a huge consumer base — including some customers without wire-line access — consolidation is a very popular option.

10.5.3 Asia/Pacific

The Asian market is highly accepting of useful new technologies such as EBPP, and the significant increase in the Internet penetration rate is increasing the demand for EBPP services. But the typically narrow bandwidth in the Asian market slows down site log-in and page updates. Under these circumstances, the biller-direct business model might suffer.

Most Asian countries have direct debit, as in Europe, and transactions are simple, without the usual layers typical in the U.S. Most national payment systems in Asia are directly owned or managed by government-related agencies. As a result, they are more likely to be organized and controlled in a constant manner. EBPP approval by the government may penetrate vertical industries.

This region is significantly larger than the U.S. and Europe. There are ethnic, language, and many other differences that must be considered when offering EBPP solutions. Australia, Japan, and South Korea will be very responsive to implementing the technology; China and India are not yet sufficiently explored for their likely acceptance.

Local EBPP suppliers are important and should not be overlooked. Local providers may offer their products and services alone or in combination with global vendors.

10.6 Summary

Given current trends, the following predictions about the future development of EBPP seem reasonable:

- There will be slow but steady penetration of the business-to-consumer (B2C) market, combined with excellent personalization and one-to-one services.
- There will be increasingly significant successes with small and medium-size enterprises (SME).

- There will be serious inroads with B2B, challenging even well-established EDI (electronic data interchange) business relations.
- Consolidator, aggregator, and portal business models are receiving more attention and popularity; the proprietors of these services will share customer ownership in some collaborative forms with billers.
- Financial institutions are waking up and will want their share of the EBPP business.
- Utilities and telecommunications service providers will be the biggest early adopters.
- Industry analysts predict that ROI in the majority of EBPP implementation cases will be between three and six months and, in the worst case, not greater than two years.

Acronyms

ACH	automated clearinghouse
ACL	access control list
ADSL	asymmetrical digital subscriber line
AES	advanced encryption standard
AFP	appletalk filing protocol
AMA	automated message accounting
A/P	accounts payable
API	application programming interface
A/R	accounts receivable
ASP	active server pages
ATM	automated teller machine
B2B	business to business
B2C	business to consumer
BIPS	bank Internet payment system
	bill and invoice presentment and settlement
BSP	billing service provider
BSS	business support system
CA	certification authority
CDF	channel definition format
CDMA	code-division multiple access
CDPD	cellular digital packet data
CDR	call-detail record
CEBP	Council for Electronic Billing and Payment
CGI	common gateway interface
CIM	common information model
CLI	command-line interface
CMIP	common management information protocol
COD	collect on delivery
COM	common object model
CORBA	common object request broker architecture
COTS	component off the shelf
CPS	certificate practice statement

CPU	central processing unit
CRC	cyclic redundancy check
CRM	customer relationship management
CSP	consumer service provider
	customer service provider
CSR	customer service representative
CSS	cascading style sheet
CSV	comma-separated variables
CTI	computer telephony integrated
DAS	direct attached storage
DCN	data communication network
DDD	digital document delivery
DEN	directory-enabled networking
DES	data encryption standard
DHCP	dynamic host configuration protocol
DHTML	dynamic hypertext markup language
DISA	Data Interchange Standards Association
DMI	desktop management interface
DMTF	Desktop Management Task Force
DMZ	demilitarized zone
DNS	domain name server
DOM	document object model
DSML	directory service markup language
DSO	days of sales outstanding
DSSSL	document style and semantics specification language
DTD	document-type definition
EBP	electronic bill presentment
EBPP	electronic bill presentment and payment
EBT	electronic benefit transfer
ECM	enterprise content management
ED&EP	electronic delivery and electronic payment
EDI	electronic data interchange
EFS	electronic financial service
EFT	electronic funds transfer
EIA	enterprise integration architecture
EIPP	electronic invoice presentment and payment
EJB	enterprise JavaBeans
E-MRDF	electronic-mail run data file
EPP	electronic presentment and payment
EPPS	electronic payment and presentment service
ERP	enterprise resource planning
ESP	energy service provider
FRM	financial resource management
FSML	financial services markup language
FSP	financial service provider
FSTC	Financial Services Technology Consortium
FTP	file transfer protocol
GIF	graphical interface format
GPS	global positioning system

GSM	global system for mobile communications
GUI	graphical user interface
HTML	hypertext markup language
HTTP	hypertext transfer protocol
HTTPS	HTTP secure
IBPP	Internet bill presentment and payment
ICC	interactive customer care
IDC	intelligent document control
IDS	intrusion detection and security
IFX	interactive financial exchange
IIA	Internet integration architecture
IIS	Internet information server
IN	intelligent network
I/O	input/output
IOS	internetwork operating system
IP	Internet protocol
IPDR	Internet protocol detail record
ISDN	integrated services digital network
ISP	Internet service provider
ISV	independent software vendor
IBPP	Internet bill presentment and payment
IT	information technology
IVR	interactive voice response
JMAPI	Java management application program interface
JPEG	Joint Photographic Experts Group
JSP	Java server pages
LAN	local-area network
LBAC	label-based access control
LDAP	lightweight directory access protocol
MAC	message authentication code
	media access unit
MARS	mobile administration system
MDC	modification detection code
MIB	management information base
MPLS	multi-protocol label switching
MSP	management service provider
MSS	marketing support system
NACHA	National Automated Clearinghouse Association
NAS	network attached storage
NNTP	network news transfer protocol
NOC	network operations center
NSP	network service provider
OBPP	online bill presentment and payment
ODBC	open database connectivity
OFX	open financial exchange
OLAP	online analytical processing
OMR	optical mark recognition
OPSEC	open platform for security
OSD	open software description

OSI	open system interconnection
OSP	outsourced service provider
OSS	operations support system
P2P	person to person
PCS	personal communication service
PDA	personal digital assistant
PDF	portable document format
PFM	personal financial management
PIN	personal identification number
PKI	public key infrastructure
POP	point of presence
PSTN	public switched telephone network
QoS	quality of service
RAID	redundant arrays of independent disks
RAM	random access memory
RDF	resource definition format
RFI	request for information
RFP	request for proposal
RMON	remote monitoring
ROI	return on investment
RPPS	remote payment and presentment service
RSA	Rivest, Shamir, Adelmann
RSVP	resource reservation protocol
SAN	storage-area network
SDK	software development kit
SET	secure electronic transfer
SGML	standard generalized markup language
S-HTML	secure hypertext markup language
SLA	service-level agreement
SLM	service-level management
SME	small and medium enterprises
SMIL	synchronized multimedia integration language
S-MIME	secure multipurpose Internet mail extensions
SMS	short message service
SMTP	simple mail transfer protocol
SNMP	simple network management protocol
SOAP	simple object access protocol
SOHO	small office/home office
SQL	structured query language
SRM	supplier relationship management
SSL	secure socket layer
TCP	transmission control protocol
TDMA	time-division multiple access
TLS	transport layer security
TNG	the next generation
UDDI	universal description, discovery, and integration
UDP	user datagram protocol
UMTS	universal mobile telecommunications system
URI	universal resource indicator

URL	universal resource locator
USPS	U.S. Postal Service
VoD	video on demand
VoIP	voice-over IP
VPN	virtual private network
VRU	voice response unit
VXML	voice extensible markup language
WAE	wireless application environment
WAN	wide-area network
WAP	wireless application protocol
WBEM	Web-based enterprise management
WDP	wireless datagram protocol
WebDAV	Web-distributed authoring and versioning
WFMS	workforce and fault management system
WML	wireless markup language
WSDL	Web-services description language
WSP	wireless session protocol
WWW	World Wide Web
XDR	XML data reduced
xDSL	extended digital subscriber line
XHTML	extensible hypertext markup language
XLL	extensible linking language
XML	extended markup language
XSL	extensible style language

Bibliography

Bassa, P., Billing for Content — Evolutionary Billing, paper presented at European Communications, Summer Edition, 2002, pp. 46–49.

Brown, D., Precision Cost Management, paper presented at Billing World 2002, Baltimore, June 19, 2002.

CheckFree Corp., Biller-Direct versus Bill-Distribution, white paper, Atlanta, GA, July 2001.

Cox, J., Working out the bugs in XML databases, *Network World*, January 7, 2002, p. 24.

Dorman, A., The Next Wave in Distributed Processing? *Network Mag.*, Apr. 2002, pp. 38–42.

Ebill, 2002, Who is who in e.billing? e.bill — source for electronic delivery and payment, June/July 2002, pp. 28–29

Finegold, E., The Role of Mediation Systems in Changing Networks, *Billing World*, Sep. 1998, pp. 32–36.

Flynn, J., The business case for E-Billing, *INFORM Magazine*, Association for Information and Image Management International, September/October 1999, pp. 14–18

Gardner Group, E-Billing Shake-Out: The Dust Starts to Settle, Oct. 2000.

Gooding, E., B2B — What Do We See?, *e.Bill*, Mar. 2001, pp. 7–9

Hill, K., The Directions of the Industry, Part I: What You Need to Lead, *e.Bill*, June 2001, pp. 8–11.

Hurley, H., E-bills Gain Outsourcing Contingent, *Billing World*, Mar. 2000, pp. 67–72.

Karvé, A., Strategies for Managing IP Data, *Billing World*, Dec. 1999, pp. 60–66.

Kumar, R., *Electronic Bill Presentment and Payment, Data Base Management*, Auerbach Publications, CRC Press, Boca Raton, FL, 2001.

Lewitt, J., Developing with Web services, *Information Week*, October 1, 2001, pp. 39–42.

Lucas, M. and Cohen, O., Usage Collection and Analysis in an IP OSS, *Billing World*, Mar. 1999, pp. 52–56.

McCalpin, W., Migrating from Print to Online, *e.Bill,* Oct. 2001, pp. 24–27.

Meta Group Research, Customer Focused Architecture: CRM and Innovative Bill Presentation, Teleconference 038, Aug. 1998.

Patel, J. and Greenfield, A., Online Invoicing Ready for Business to Business Users, *Information Week*, Nov. 12, 2001, pp. 80–84.

Patel, J., The State of Bill and Invoice Presentment and Settlement (EBPP), paper D5, presented at Billing World 2002, Baltimore, June 19, 2002.

Pfeiffer, P., EBPP in the Insurance Industry, Insurance Information Strategies, Meta Group Research Report, Delta 057 and Delta 072, Jan. and Mar. 2001.

The Phillips Group, *EBPP — The Market Opportunity, Development Patterns, Current/ Future Drivers and Global Expansion*, London, 2001.

Schumacher, K., Tracking eBilling Data Online, paper presented at Billing World 2002, Baltimore, June 19, 2002.

Schwartz, S., Premediation May Pave the Road to Mobile IP, *Billing World*, July 2002, pp. 15–19.

Terplan, K., *Web-Based Systems and Network Management*, CRC Press, Boca Raton, FL, 1999a.

Terplan, K., *Intranet Performance Management*, CRC Press, Boca Raton, FL, 1999b.

Terplan, K., *OSS Essentials — Support System Solutions for Service Providers*, John Wiley & Sons, New York, 2001.

Un, E., XML's Impact on Billing Standards, *Billing World*, Feb. 1999, pp. 72–75.

Verma, G., CRM Makes Strides in Self-Service, *Information Week*, Feb. 18, 2002, pp. 67–70.

Wainscott, J., Driving E.Billing Adoption, *e.Bill*, Mar. 2001, pp. 14–16.

Wilson, T., UDDI Promises Link to Web Services, *InternetWeek*, Nov. 26, 2001, p. 26.

Wood, J., EBP Success Criteria and Lessons Learned, paper presented at Billing World 2002, Baltimore, June 19, 2002.

Index

D

E